Smart Money Moves for the '90s

By the Editors of **MONEY** Magazine

Oxmoor House®

Library of Congress Catalog Number: 89-064138
Hardcover ISBN: 0-8487-0798-2
Softcover ISBN: 0-8487-1008-8
ISSN: 0891-172X

Manufactured in the United States of America
First Printing 1990

Published by arrangement with Oxmoor House, Inc.
Book Division of Southern Progress Corporation
P. O. Box 2463, Birmingham, AL 35201

Vice President, Editorial Director: Candace N. Conard
Production Manager: Jerry Higdon
Associate Production Manager: Rick Litton
Art Director: Bob Nance

Smart Money Moves for the '90s
Compiled and Edited by Junius Ellis

Editor: Clark Scott
Editorial Assistant: L. Amanda Owens
Designer: Nancy Johnson
Photographer: Colleen Duffley
Stylist: Connie Formby

To order *Money* magazine, write to: *Money*,
P. O. Box 54429, Boulder, CO 80322-4429

Money Staff
Managing Editor: Frank Lalli
Assistant Managing Editors: Richard A. Burgheim, Frank B. Merrick
Senior Editors: Joseph S. Coyle, Caroline Donnelly, Richard Eisenberg, Eric Gelman, Diane Harris, Tyler Mathisen, Kevin S. McKean, Michael Sivy, Robert Wool
Picture Editor: Deborah Pierce
Editor, Money Scorecard: Pauline Tai
Senior Writers: Jerry Edgerton, Joanna Krotz, Eric Schurenberg, Walter L. Updegrave, Jack Willoughby
Staff Writers: Charles E. Cohen, Beth Kobliner, Lani Luciano, Marsha Meyer, Suzanne Seixas, Marguerite T. Smith, Leslie N. Vreeland, Penelope Wang, Clint Willis
Chief of Reporters: Katharine B. Drake
Senior Reporters: Debra Wishik Englander, Jersey Gilbert, Jordan E. Goodman, Holly Wheelwright
Reporters: Sian Ballen (deputy chief), Veronica Byrd, Carla A. Fried, Beth M. Gilbert, Mary Granfield, Bruce Hager, Miriam A. Leuchter, Deborah Lohse, Elizabeth M. MacDonald, Prashanta Misra, Daphne D. Mosher (letters), D. Jacqueline Smith, Teresa Tritch
Design Department: Traci Churchill (associate art director), Stephanie Phelan, Joseph E. Baron (designers), Warren Isensee, Maria Taffera
Picture Department: Miriam Hsia (deputy picture editor), Leslie Yoo (assistant picture editor)
Director of Editorial Operations: Anne R. Davis
Copy Desk: Patricia A. Feimster (deputy), Andrew Schwartz (editorial systems manager), Sukey Rosenbaum (senior coordinator), Kathleen Beakley, Mark Hudson Giles, Bill O'Connor, Sarah Plant, Suzanne Justin Riggio, Jane Rigney, Judith Ryan, Eve Sennett, Margaret J. Stefanowicz
Editorial Production Manager: Karen Harper Diaz
Editorial Production: Sally Boggan, Gary S. Costello

Editor's Note

Welcome to *Smart Money Moves for the '90s*. By picking up this book, you have made an important decision to take charge of your personal finances, to protect your hard-earned money, and to make it grow in the decade ahead.

This volume, the fourth in the series the Editors of *Money* have prepared with Oxmoor House, summarizes in one convenient place the most valuable insights we have gathered over the past twelve months. Here you will learn useful tips, for example, on cutting your tax bill, building your assets while trimming your debts, financing a secure retirement, and putting your estate in order. You also will find risk-reducing strategies for investing in today's increasingly manic markets, plus our comprehensive rankings of the top performers among 900 mutual funds.

This handy sourcebook is set up to enable you to do for yourself what you might hire a financial planner to perform. Professional planners customarily begin by interviewing you and asking you to fill out forms concerning your net worth, what you earn and spend, your long-range goals, and your tolerance of risk. Then planners develop strategies for achieving specific goals such as buying your first house, sending your kids to college, and retiring comfortably.

The following chapters—and the many do-it-yourself worksheets that accompany them—will take you through all those steps, and more. The planning shouldn't stop here. The rules of the financial game change too much and too often for you to stick with a single playbook. There have been six major federal tax overhauls since 1982, and more are sure to come. You must also constantly adjust to unexpected changes in the economy, the financial markets, and your own personal circumstances.

The purpose of *Smart Money Moves for the '90s* is to aid you in determining what measures to take—now and in the future—to make the most of your family's growing wealth. We trust this book will be invaluable in attaining that goal.

Frank Lalli

Frank Lalli
Managing Editor, *Money*

Contents

Where to Put Your Money Now

When the stock market fell 508 points on Black Monday, October 19, 1987, small investors braced for further financial disaster. Instead, stocks skipped to record highs over the next two years. Then, investors were stunned again when stocks went into a 190-point free-fall on Friday, October 13, 1989.

There's no question about it: Market volatility has become an unsettling fact of life for investors large and small. Many economists also see another threat ahead—a recession. Among their forecasts:

● The long-lived economic expansion that began in 1982 will stall by mid-1991.

● Interest rates will decline, with long-term Treasury yields, recently around 8%, falling to 7% before the end of 1991.

● Inflation could surge in the year ahead but will probably stay around 5% after the economy slumps.

If all this leaves you a little unsure about where to put your money, take heart. By following the advice in this chapter, you should be able to reduce your risk significantly and still earn an average of 8% to 9% annually in the face of an erratic stock market, fluctuating interest rates, and the threat of a possible recession. Your best course is a traditional value-oriented strategy. The cornerstones of this old-fashioned approach to investing are:

Stick to classic tests for value. For stocks, this means prices that are cheap relative to a company's earnings, assets, and dividend yield. With Treasury bonds, look for a yield at least four percentage points above the inflation rate. Since most economists expect inflation to average around 5% over the next five years, Treasuries would be an excellent buy if their yields went above 9%.

Buy and hold. Stock market volatility has almost no effect on where stocks go over the course of a year. But it does provide opportunities for disciplined investors to increase their holdings at lower prices.

Diversify broadly. Spread your money—and risk—among different types of assets: stocks, high-quality bonds, and cash investments such as money-market funds and certificates of deposit. The diversified portfolio of *Money*'s Small Investor Index, which tracks the monthly performance of the average investor's holdings, fluctuates only a third as much as the stock market. In late 1989, the average investor had 32% of his or her money in stocks, 25% in bonds, and nearly all of the remaining 42% in money funds or CDs.

Prospering in Today's Manic Markets

Rather than feeling victimized by the stock market's volatility, look for ways to make it work for you.

Small investors are understandably wary of the stock market's ineffectual regulators, greedy professional traders and heartless institutions. In a poll conducted in the week following October 1989's Friday the 13th panic selling, 23% of *Money* subscribers said their confidence in stocks had been shaken. The plunge prompted 16% of the magazine's subscribers to make immediate changes in their portfolios, and another 22% were thinking about doing so. Fully 55% of those who made changes sold stocks or stock fund shares, and 50% put money into certificates of deposit, money-market funds, and savings accounts.

Fleeing to money funds, however, is not the long-term answer to the question of where to put your investment dollars. Historically, money funds outpace inflation by only one or two percentage points annually—probably not enough for you to reach future investment goals such as sending your children to college or retiring in style. Nor can you escape volatility by simply shunning stocks. For example, holders of seemingly secure long-term bonds were stunned in the spring of 1987, when a sharp rise in interest rates reduced their principal as much as 10% in just six weeks (bond prices fall when interest rates rise and vice versa).

Instead, your portfolio mix should be determined by your current economic outlook, your appetite for risk and your future financial requirements. With many economists predicting recession in 1990, small investors should consider maintaining a fairly large cash cushion—from 30% to 50% of your portfolio. "If you need your money within a year, put zero percent of it at risk in stocks," counsels Paul

Merriman, president of Merriman Mutual Funds in Seattle. Otherwise, he explains, you might be forced to sell when share prices are depressed.

To see how a diversified portfolio protects you, consider what would happen to each type of asset as a recession approaches. Stock prices would fall, perhaps as much as 30%, as the deteriorating economy squashed corporate profits. But long-term Treasury bond prices could rally by as much as 15%—offsetting some of the stock losses—because a stalled economy usually sends interest rates downward. (For further information on evaluating stocks, bonds, or other securities, see the next chapter, "Investing Like a Pro.")

Stocks: Go Back to Basics

While the recent manic-depressive mood of the stock market can be unsettling for shareholders, these price swings can also improve the pickings for disciplined bargain hunters. "Institutions have focused on takeovers, index futures, and other short-term games that have little to do with investing," says George Yeager of Yeager Wood & Marshall, an investment counseling firm in New York City. "They have left some of the best values to individuals."

Unlike professional money managers, you don't have to beat or match the market averages every quarter to keep clients happy. You can avoid the hottest market sectors and buy unglamorous stocks, which carry lower risk. And there will be ample opportunity in the new decade to buy stocks at discount prices. The institutional traders who are quick to sell into a falling stock market don't care that they are letting shares go at absurdly low prices— they just want to dump their stocks.

To spot bargains, you should rely on such fundamental yardsticks of value as company earnings, dividends, and assets. Much of the data you need is in publications such as the *Value Line Investment Survey*, available at many libraries. Or you can enlist a full-service broker to answer questions about the most attractive companies in the following four major categories:

Growth stocks. Many companies' annual earnings soared 25% or more during the two years that ended in mid-1989. As a result, investors were underwhelmed by the track records of firms that had delivered steady but unspectacular annual earnings gains of 10% to 15%, in good times and bad. But investors are increasingly likely to rediscover the charms of such firms. Profit gains of 25% or so are now behind us; in the third quarter of 1989, earnings of the industrial firms in Standard & Poor's 400-stock index declined on average 7%.

Most companies are expected to post mediocre profits increases in 1990 as well. If there is a recession, quite a number of firms could lose money. Stocks of companies that buck that trend will command premium prices—but for now, they are bargains. "Many traditional growth stocks are trading at their cheapest levels since I entered this business in 1961," says Robert Chesek, manager of the Phoenix Growth mutual fund in Hartford.

Lots of companies can point to a golden past in terms of growth; the challenge is to identify those that can sustain it. One earmark is a high reinvestment rate, which indicates that the firm is very profitable and that it plows most of its earnings back into its business. When a company's reinvestment rate, which is a proxy for its future growth rate, is equal to or higher than its price/earnings ratio, the shares may be a buy. To determine a company's reinvestment rate, start with a readily available figure called return on equity (ROE). Then calculate the payout ratio of the stock—its dividend divided by annual earnings. Now plug those numbers into this equation: ROE x (1 - payout ratio) = reinvestment rate.

Thanks to investors' neglect of proven growth stocks, there are many such companies with dominant market positions whose P/Es are roughly at or below their growth rates. Among them are three classic growth stocks listed on the New York Stock Exchange: McDonald's (recently traded around $32), Merck (recently around $76), and Wal-Mart (recently around $43).

High-yield stocks. Shares of banks, insurers, utilities, and some industrial companies often pay above-average yields that can help to cushion losses in a slumping stock market. Dividend income offsets modest price declines, and the promise of future payouts can prevent steep drops. But don't buy a stock for its current yield alone. Many troubled companies offer sky-high yields that could disappear if their problems get worse.

When a high yield beckons, first check the debt level of the company to make sure the firm is financially sound, notes James Burnett, editor of the *Value Income Investor* newsletter in Winter Park, Florida. He shuns companies with debt amounting to more than 40% of their total capital. For extra comfort, he favors firms that have paid uninterrupted dividends for at least two decades. One well-known example is Bristol-Myers Squibb (recently around $55, NYSE), which hasn't missed a dividend since 1933.

You can gauge future dividend prospects by calculating a stock's payout ratio—dividend divided by earnings per share—for each of the past five years. If the ratio is shrinking, that means the firm has a growing store of profits to cover its dividend. Similarly, a payout ratio of less than 50% suggests that the company can maintain its dividend even if profits decline in a recession. To estimate a yield stock's fair price, divide its dividend by its average yield over the past five years. If, for example, you divide USF&G's $2.80 dividend by the insurer's five-year average yield of 7.1%, you get a price of $39.50. That suggests the NYSE-listed stock is a buy at its recent price of around $30, where it yielded 9.3%.

Asset plays. Patient investors with a keen eye for value can profit from stocks of firms with overlooked assets—real estate, oil reserves, cash, or other properties—coveted by corporate acquirers. Absent a takeover bid, managements of such firms can redeploy or sell off valuable assets, buy back shares of their stock, or distribute excess cash to shareholders. To unearth asset plays, compare a stock's book value (or net worth per share) with its price. The average stock recently sold for about 2.5 times book value; if that ratio is considerably lower—say, 1 to 1.5 times book—the stock is

definitely worth a second look. The most dependable assets a company can own, and the easiest for a lay investor to value, are cash and marketable securities. Divide the liquid assets on the company's balance sheet by the number of shares outstanding. If the result is more than 25% of the company's stock price, investigate further. Consider, for example, Petrie Stores (recently around $23, NYSE). It operates nearly 1,600 department stores and holds cash and securities recently worth about $20 a share, or 93% of the stock's price.

Out-of-favor stocks. It's a Wall Street cliche that the best time to buy a stock is when nobody wants it. The old advice is especially timely these days. The less speculative froth a stock generates, the greater the likelihood that it will hold up in a market sell-off.

Tom Broadus, co-manager of the T. Rowe Price Equity Income fund in Baltimore, calculates a stock's relative P/E—its ordinary P/E divided by the average P/E for an index such as the S&P 500—for each of the past five years. If the stock is out of favor now, its relative P/E will be lower than usual. Similarly, the stock's relative dividend yield—its current yield divided by the average yield for an index—will be higher than usual.

Broadus' holdings that meet those criteria recently included General Electric (around $60, NYSE) and K-Mart (around $34, NYSE). Of course, a stock may fall from favor for the excellent reason that the company is sliding toward the financial brink. To avoid such disasters in the making, advises Broadus, bypass shares of firms with debt that exceeds 40% of capital.

Bonds: Watch Out for the Old Squeezeroo

Predictions of an economic slump are generally good news for bonds. A recession-triggered drop in interest rates could produce capital gains of 10% to 15% for issues with maturities of 10 years or more. While bonds are fairly conservative investments and an ideal hedge against the risks of stocks, they do present two hazards of their own. One is volatility; bond prices fall when rates rise and vice versa. The other is credit risk—the danger that any issuer short of the U.S. Treasury may default on payments of interest or principal.

Even if most economists are correct in predicting lower interest rates over the next two years, rates probably won't move in a straight line. "You have to watch out for the old squeezeroo," says Richard Young, who heads his own Newport, Rhode Island research firm. You may have to ride out a six- to nine-month drop in bond prices at the same time stocks are falling, he explains, because "interest rates usually go up right before a recession and peak after the recession has already started."

Some investment strategists believe that rates on long-term Treasuries, recently yielding about 8%, could spike to 9% in 1990 and knock 10% or more off bond values. To guard against this possibility, you might want to buy now only half or two-thirds of the bonds you would eventually like to own. Buy the rest if yields rise to 9%.

James Stack, editor of the newsletter, *Investech Market Analyst*, expects inflation to slow to 2% or 3% by 1991 and then heat up again later in the 1990s. So he would sell bonds if rates go as low as 7%. "The profit opportunity may last for only two years," he says. Most economists are more optimistic than Stack; they expect annual inflation to remain below 5% in the 1990s. They believe, therefore, that you buy bonds with terms of five to 10 years and hold them until maturity. As a general rule, the longer the maturity of a bond is, the more volatile its price. Most bond strategists say issues that mature in five to 10 years offer the best combination of high capital-gains potential and moderate risk.

Credit quality is the second most important consideration for bond investors. The greatest risks lie with junk bonds—those issues graded BB or lower by Standard & Poor's or Moody's. Junk bond fund yields as high as 16% may look awfully tempting. But experts maintain that for many individual investors, junk bonds may be a disaster waiting to happen (see "The Coming Crisis in Junk Bonds" below). Says Erich Heinemann, chief economist at

The Coming Crisis in Junk-Bond Funds

Many small investors who grabbed on to high-yield junk bonds may soon find themselves hoisted atop extremely greasy poles. The funds sponsored by leading independent mutual fund companies, such as T. Rowe Price and Vanguard, roughly broke even in the first 10 months of 1989, compared with 10% to 15% gains for top Treasury-bond funds. Worse still, other junk funds have actually had negative returns even after their double-digit yields are taken into account. Dean Witter High Yield, for instance, lost 10% over the 10-month period. Moreover, says Gerald Perritt, editor of the *Mutual Fund Letter* in Chicago: "The real danger is ahead of us."

The problem: Since July 1989, jittery investors have yanked billions of dollars out of junk-bond funds. "At some big funds, redemptions are running as much as $30 million a day," says

Erich Heinemann, chief economist at Ladenburg Thalmann in New York City. As a result, fund managers are being forced to raise cash by selling what's readily salable—their best-quality issues. Eventually, many funds will be reduced to an unmeltable core of low-quality bonds that rarely trade, if at all ("the dregs," says Heinemann).

Small investors should avoid making new investments in junk funds. And those who already own shares in some of the weakest performers—many of them brokerage house offerings—might be wise to cash out.

Because there is no market for the junk bonds at the bottom of some of these funds' portfolios, "a lot of fictitious pricing is going on," says Perritt. Thus, the net asset values being used to redeem shares may actually be inflated—at least for now.

Ladenburg Thalmann, a New York City brokerage: "When investors finally realize what's been going on with junk bond funds, Wall Street is going to have a new credibility problem much worse than the one caused by program trading."

Your wisest choice among federally taxable issues is Treasuries. Their yields are modest compared with those of riskier alternatives, but their interest is exempt from state and local taxes. If you are in the top bracket and live in a high-tax state—with state and local taxes of, say, 8%—a Treasury paying 8% offers you the equivalent of 8.7% on a nongovernment issue.

The one alternative to Treasuries that income investors should consider is high-quality municipals—those rated AA or better. The interest munis pay is exempt from federal taxes and is usually also free from state and local taxes if the issuer is in the state in which you reside. A muni yielding 6.8% can offer the taxable equivalent of 10% to a buyer in the 33% federal bracket. Keep in mind, however, munis' several disadvantages. Tax-exempts don't always trade actively, which means that if you try to sell, you will probably have to accept a price 1% to 2% below what your bonds are really worth. If you don't plan to hold a muni to maturity, you should consider a muni-bond fund so you can redeem your shares anytime at their true value.

Even the highest-rated munis aren't free from default risk, and you need at least $25,000 for a diversified portfolio of five bonds. A bond fund would alleviate this problem, or you could turn to so-called pre-refunded munis, which are backed by Treasuries that yield enough to meet all future interest and principal payments. Among such bonds are the New York Triborough Bridge & Tunnel Authority 9⅝% maturing in 1995, recently yielding 6.7%, and Sweetwater Wyoming (for Pacific Power) 6.5% of 2001, yielding 6.9%.

Cash: Aim for Yields above 9%

Most individuals think of cash investments—money-market funds, money-market deposit bank accounts, and certificates of deposit—as savings. And while it's always true that you should have an emergency fund handy, in today's markets cash is an increasingly important part of your total investment portfolio.

A high cash position of, say, 40% to 50% of your portfolio serves two crucial functions. First, it reduces volatility; changes in the prices of your stocks and bonds will have a proportionally smaller influence on the value of your overall holdings if your cash balance is large. Second, cash gives you buying power when a wild market pushes the stocks you like down to bargain prices.

You probably can get the highest yield on your cash in a top money-market fund. The average bank money-market account recently yielded 6.4%, while the average money fund yielded 8.5%. By keeping expenses low, some top funds pay as much as 9.4%. The money fund advantage could shrink in 1990, however. "Much of the rate gap would be erased if interest rates decline as expected," says Robert Heady, publisher of the newsletter *Bank Rate Monitor*. Money fund yields would follow rates down, he explains, while bank rates would fall only slightly.

Money funds that invest only in U.S. government or municipal securities are attractive choices, despite their lower yields, because of the tax advantages they offer. Funds containing U.S. government issues recently yielded an average of 8.2%. Interest from Treasuries is exempt from state and local taxes, which is equivalent to adding half a percentage point or more to your after-tax return in high-tax states such as New York and California. Be sure to ask whether a government fund holds a lot of federal agency securities; in many states, interest on agency issues is not tax-exempt. Muni-fund interest is exempt from federal taxes and is usually also exempt from state and local taxes if all the securities in the fund were issued in the state where you live. Triple-tax exemption can give a fund that recently yielded 5.8% the equivalent of a 9.7% taxable yield for some investors.

Choosing the money fund that's best for you, though, depends on more than just yield. "The fund you choose should have assets of

$200 million or more," says William Donoghue, publisher of *Donoghue's MoneyLetter* in Holliston, Massachusetts. "Although no small investor has ever lost money in a money fund, in the unlikely event that a fund does have a problem, it's better if there's a big management company behind it."

Among the taxable funds that Donoghue recommends are Dreyfus Worldwide Dollar ($2,500 minimum investment, recently yielding 9.3%); Fidelity Spartan ($20,000 minimum, 9.2% yield); and Vanguard Money Market Reserves Prime ($3,000 minimum, 9.0% yield). Kemper Money Market Fund ($1,000 minimum, 8.7% yield) may also be appealing, despite its slightly lower yield, because it offers unlimited check writing for $65 a year. Most funds permit only checks of $200 or more.

Among the government funds that hold chiefly Treasuries is the top-yielding Vanguard Money Market Reserves—U.S. Treasury ($3,000 minimum, 8.4% yield). The municipal funds that lately have offered the best yields include Evergreen Tax-Exempt ($2,000 minimum, 6.4% yield) and Calvert Tax Free Reserves ($2,000 minimum, 6.3% yield).

Strictly speaking, certificates of deposit are not cash investments because your money isn't available on demand. But CDs with maturities of six months or a year can serve almost the same function in a portfolio, since your cash is available each time these short-term certificates are rolled over. For the best buys, check rates at banks around the country rather than settling for whatever your local institution offers. (The top rates are listed each month in *Money*'s Scorecard section.) You often can get a CD yield at least one percentage point higher by going to an out-of-state bank.

Precious Metals: Gold Loses its Glitter

A few latter-day alchemists still think you can turn gold into a glittering investment. But to most portfolio scientists, gold looks leaden in 1990. Investors no longer hoard it in a crisis; dollars are now their haven of choice. With

consumer prices climbing less than 5% a year, there is little clamor for gold as an inflation hedge. And during the 1980s, new technology has led to increased mine output, helping to hold down prices despite strong demand from jewelers and other manufacturers.

Forecasts for silver and platinum are equally lackluster. The one bright spot for precious metals has been North American mining stocks. The latest technology has helped many companies step up production and maintain their profits in the face of weak bullion prices.

Should you hold gold at all? Perhaps not, unless you disagree with the majority view among economists that inflation is not likely to pick up soon. In that case, you may want to allocate 5% to 10% of your portfolio to gold.

Are You a Smart Investor?

When the Securities and Exchange Commission proposed that new closed-end mutual funds affix warning labels on prospectuses noting that such funds often drop in value right after their initial public offering (IPO), SEC Commissioner Joseph Grundfest wrote a statement exploring why investors would ever buy the IPOs. He concluded that there are two types of investors: "smart enough" and "not smart enough." Here are examples of actions that separate the two:

What "smart enough" investors do:
● Buy closed-end funds after their initial offerings
● Consider investing in one of last year's worst-performing sector mutual funds
● Buy a stock right after it lowers its dividend
● Avoid most limited partnerships
● Hang up on brokers making cold calls

What "not smart enough" investors do:
● Buy closed-end funds during their initial public offerings
● Invest a bundle in one of last year's best-performing sector mutual funds
● Sell a stock right after it lowers its dividend
● Buy any limited partnership
● Send money to a broker after getting a telephone tip

The Best Funds for the 1990s

These 10 up-and-comers have the traits you should look for, whether you are seeking conservative or aggressive plays.

Peter Lynch, manager of the renowned Fidelity Magellan fund, says that the secret to building a world-beating portfolio is to hit a few 10-baggers—stocks that pay you back tenfold over time. The challenge is much the same for mutual fund investors: Find the one fund (or maybe several) that over the long haul can reward you with returns that justify your research and worry. The tricky part, of course, is finding the 10-bagger before it has rounded nine of them.

To help hasten your search, *Money*'s researchers identified 10 funds that have the potential to become the 10-baggers of the 1990s—or, if you prefer, the next Magellans. What's more, by one or more important measures, all are relatively early in their quest for possible stardom. Eight began trading no earlier than 1984. The oldest fund, SoGen International, founded in 1969, has been available throughout the U.S. only since 1986. Indeed, six of the funds are decidedly diminutive up-and-comers: Babson Value, Baron Asset, Gabelli Growth, GIT Equity-Special Growth, Pasadena Growth, and Strong Discovery. These are so small that they do not meet the $25 million in assets threshold for inclusion in *Money*'s fund rankings, which begin on page 185.

All 10 standouts are stock funds, since history suggests that this fund group alone can produce superlative long-term returns (see the table on page 18). But aside from the similarities of size, age, and investment objective, these promising portfolios are by no means clones of one another. They range from audacious growth funds, like Baron Asset and Columbia Special, to more conservative dividend-payers such as Vanguard Equity Income and Babson Value.

Most of *Money*'s funds for the 1990s do have a value orientation, meaning that their managers seek to pay a risk-dampening maximum of 60¢ to 70¢ for a dollar's worth of value. Then, too, all are low- or no-load funds, and all are positioned to capitalize on the economic climate that the consensus of investment authorities projects for the 1990s. Hallmarks of that environment, say the seers, will be:

● Moderate inflation averaging 4% a year for the decade.

● A drop in interest rates to an average of 8% to 8.5%, compared with 10.8% in the 1980s.

● An increasingly favorable prospect for small-company and growth stocks, which can take advantage of those lower interest rates to finance expansion.

The list's bias toward funds that are small themselves—most have less than $50 million in assets—reflects the conviction among many investment theorists that such entities are nimbler than mammoths like Magellan ($10.8 billion at last count). Because it's easier to find buyers or sellers for 100,000 shares of a stock than it is for a million-share block, smaller funds can move quickly to take advantage of attractive situations or just as rapidly back out of issues that don't pan out. Moreover, the smaller the fund, the greater the impact of individual picks on performance.

The combined effect of these advantages can be considerable. During its first seven years under Lynch, for example, Magellan averaged $330 million in assets and trounced the Standard & Poor's 500-stock index by 26 percentage points a year. In a recent five-year period, however, assets averaged $6 billion and the fund has beaten the S&P 500 by only about three points a year. But small is not necessarily all beautiful. Small funds are less diversified and, typically, more volatile and risky than their billion-dollar counterparts. Further, operating fees take a bigger bite per share in such funds because the expenses are spread across a smaller asset base. Most funds on *Money*'s 1990s list manage to keep expenses relatively low for their size.

Investors moving into these funds should build their positions slowly. Ante only the minimum initial investment at first. Then, add to your holdings by putting in an equal amount at regular intervals—a technique called dollar-cost averaging that lowers your average price per share. Moreover, regard these candidates for what they are: funds for the whole decade. They are long-term, buy-and-hold investments, period. Herewith the list, beginning with the most conservative category and proceeding alphabetically within categories to the most aggressive:

Vanguard Equity Income. For 26 years, institutional investors knew Roger Newell as one of America's top bank fund managers. From 1975 to 1986, for example, his Bank of California Income Equity Fund piled up 19.4% compound annual gains—three percentage points better than the S&P 500. Then, in March 1988, after more than two years of running his own Palo Alto investment management service for institutional clients, Newell signed on with the Vanguard Group to pilot an income-oriented stock fund for small investors. He soon filled the $150 million portfolio of the low-expense no-load with dividend-paying companies whose shares have been

battered by, say, earnings disappointments to the point that their yields are at least 25% higher than that of S&P industrial stocks (lately 2.9%). Conversely, once a stock returns to favor and its yield drops below that benchmark, Newell sells. His investing style often leads him to names like Chevron and Xerox that have total market capitalizations of $1 billion or more, distinguishing Vanguard Equity Income from most other funds on the 1990s list.

Babson Value. This $11.2 million growth and income fund, founded in 1984, recently yielded 4.4%, versus 3.5% for the S&P 500. Befitting Babson's value-minded focus, its price/earnings ratio was 8.8, compared with the S&P's 12.3. Cambridge, Massachusetts-based manager Nick Whitridge keeps the fund fully invested, primarily in small to medium-size growth issues like SmithKline Beckman and Weyerhaeuser, giving roughly equal weightings to some 40 stocks.

Gabelli Growth. Mario Gabelli, ace manager of the Gabelli Asset Fund (with a steep $25,000 minimum investment), is the kind of hands-on entrepreneur who doesn't delegate authority lightly. So the fact that he gave Elizabeth Bramwell a fund to run with his name on it suggests that she's good, and the record confirms it. Bramwell's fund, the $43 million Gabelli Growth Fund of New York City, posted a 39.2% gain in 1988, its first year of operation, placing it in the top 1% of stock funds followed by Lipper Analytical Services. Bramwell does much of her own research, drawing on her 20 years of experience as a top Wall Street analyst.

Pasadena Growth. After rewarding private and institutional clients with 20% compound annual returns from 1971 to 1986, Roger Engemann founded a fund for the rest of us named after his California headquarters town. He has long gone for the roses with companies whose earnings are growing at least 15% a year but whose P/Es are roughly in line with the market's. Though he was prescient enough to be 30% in cash before the October 1987 crash, over half his portfolio was in hard-hit small-company shares, causing a loss of 11% for a year in which the average stock fund broke even. The strong rebound in small-cap stocks in 1988, however, helped propel Pasadena to a 36% annual gain. Lately, though, Engemann has cut his small-cap exposure to about half the fund, replacing the flighty shares with steadier issues—like Cap Cities/ABC and Merck—that are unlikely to get clobbered in a recession.

SoGen International. Despite its name, this fund, originally sold to French investors, recently had 70% of its assets invested in the U.S. That, says its New York City-based manager Jean-Marie Eveillard, is only because the U.S. lately has offered the most attractive investment opportunities. Although the $133 billion fund can invest anywhere on the globe, its first priority is not to lose money. Consequently, Eveillard had 15% of his assets in gold securities and foreign currency to help offset

the fund's risk of rising inflation; 15% in U.S. bonds to shelter it from recession; and 20% in cash. That defensive stance made it the stodgiest performer on the list for the 12 months to June 22, 1989, gaining just 7.2%. Over the past 10 years, though, the fund's compound annual return was a superb 20.2%.

Baron Asset. Manager Ron Baron, who runs the $31 million fund from New York City, seeks out companies that sell at big discounts to their asset value, have the potential to grow at least 50%, and are possible candidates for a takeover or restructuring. Baron does not bide his time; he expects results within a two-year period. Too much to ask? Not if you can find it, which Baron evidently has. The fund's 12-month gain to June 22, 1989 landed the high-priced ($10,000 minimum) entry in the top 3% of funds ranked by Lipper Analytical Services. Longer term, its manager has returned 20% annually to institutional and private clients of Baron Capital Management since 1982.

Mutual Funds That Could Be Winners

RANKED BY 1989 RETURN	Type	% gain (or loss) to June 22, 1989			% yield	% maximum initial sales charge	Five-year expense projection
		1989	One year	Three years			
1. Pasadena Growth	Gro	28.7	38.2	—	0.0	3.0	$135
2. Baron Asset	SCG	26.7	36.0	—	4.1	None†	138
3. Gabelli Growth	Gro	26.4	33.7	—	0.3	None†	123
4. Strong Discovery	Max	25.7	26.6	—	7.8	2.0	126
5. Columbia Special	Max	23.3	38.5	55.9	0.0	None†	76
6. GIT Equity-Special Growth	SCG	16.3	20.3	27.7	1.9	None	82
7. Vanguard Equity Income	EqI	16.2	22.4	—	3.9	None	35
8. Babson Value	G&I	14.1	14.2	46.5	4.4	None	61
9. Nicholas Limited Edition	SCG	11.3	18.1	—	0.8	None	72
10. SoGen International	Gro	7.2	9.9	45.2	4.4	3.75	109

Types: EqI—Equity income; Gro—Growth; G&I—Growth and income; Max—Maximum capital gains; SCG—Small-company growth   †2% exit fee on Baron Asset shares redeemed within three years of purchase, on Gabelli Growth shares within one year and on Columbia shares within two months.   **Source: Lipper Analytical Services**

GIT Equity-Special Growth. You can't tell by the record of manager Richard Carney that small-company growth stocks have been out of favor during the blue-chip bull market that's prevailed during most of the 1980s. He artfully managed Special Growth to a 20.2% compound annual return over the recent five-year period, and he did it while exposing shareholders to 16% less volatility than the S&P 500. Carney, who since 1974 has run a Los Angeles money-management firm, attributes much of his investment success to a mastery of pain avoidance. He shuns higher-risk start-ups and turnarounds for small, fast-growing, low-debt firms that are already doing well. Such traits make some of Carney's holdings prime take-over candidates. In 1988, for example, 11 firms in his $20 million portfolio were bought out, helping place the fund in the top 11% of stock funds that year.

Nicholas Limited Edition. This is an open-end fund with a twist. Once it sells 10 million shares—at last count there were 3.8 million shares outstanding—the $45 million small-company growth fund will close to new investors. The idea is to keep the fund at a size that will allow Milwaukee manager Albert Nicholas to try to duplicate his top-performing Nicholas II strategy: Buy carefully and then h-o-l-d. That keeps turnover to a low 20% to 35% a year. Indeed, International Dairy Queen, a favored midwestern discovery of his original Nicholas Fund in 1982, represents 4% of the assets of Limited Edition, launched in 1987.

Columbia Special. Portland, Oregon money manager Alan Folkman is another buy-and-hold growth stock investor. Yet he's not averse to playing a well-thought-out hunch or two. Accordingly, he divides Special's $62 million portfolio into three parts: 50% for small and medium-size growth issues; 30% for stocks that anticipate market or business trends; and 20% for special situations like turnarounds or companies that are restructuring or are takeover candidates. Although Special was founded in 1985, Folkman is no neophyte. Under his management from 1979 through 1984, another of Columbia's funds—Columbia Growth—scored a 21% average annual return, six percentage points better than the S&P 500.

Strong Discovery. This 1988 addition to Milwaukee's 11-fund Strong family gives free rein to the short-term trading skills of its two stars, Richard Strong and William Corneliuson. And trade they do: Portfolio turnover rate in 1988 was a dizzying 442%, in part juiced by a defensive 40% move to cash in midsummer of that year. (That maneuver helps explain the fund's high 12-month yield.) When in the market, the managers generally keep half the portfolio in small-company growth stocks. The other 50% is reserved for special situations and larger outfits with market capitalizations of $500 million or more. Yet, as their 1988 switch to cash indicates, Strong and Corneliuson have no qualms about taking cover when the stock market seems iffy, and cash recently stood at 17% of the portfolio. Some call that market timing. Manager Dick Strong calls it risk control.

Minimum initial investment	Telephone Toll-free (800)	In state
$ 1,000	882-2855	818-351-4276 (Calif.)
10,000	992-2766	212-759-7700 (N.Y.)
1,000	422-3554	212-490-3670 (N.Y.)
1,000	368-3863	—
2,000	—	800-452-4512
1,000	368-3195	703-528-6500 (Va.)
3,000	662-7447	—
1,000	422-2766	816-471-5200 (Mo.)
2,000	—	414-272-6133
1,000	334-2143	—

Investing Like a Pro

Entries from a stock watcher's 1989 diary:

Wednesday, October 11: In a report to clients, Greg Smith, chief investment strategist at Prudential-Bache, takes note of "the general unease everyone feels about October markets." But he reasons that "the existence of this uneasy feeling is probably the greatest argument that nothing very bad will occur." The same day, Standard & Poor's *Outlook*, a weekly stock market newsletter popular with individual investors, leads off with an article titled "Peak Not Yet in Sight."

Friday, October 13: In the final hour of trading, the Dow tumbles 190 points—the second largest one-day point decline in history.

When even Wall Street's professionals can be so badly blindsided, what chance do individual investors stand? A much better chance than you might think. Turmoil in the markets and the threat of recession don't mean that you should give up on investing. Shareholders who build well-diversified portfolios should be able to weather the market's sudden squalls and to take advantage of the lower prices they bring.

The crucial issue is how much risk you can afford to take in pursuit of long-term gains. The answer depends on the coolness of your nerve, the security of your current economic circumstances, and your age. In general, you can afford to emphasize chancier growth investments when you are young and have ample time to recover from periodic market downturns. But you should gradually switch to a less aggressive combination of investments as you near retirement and rely more heavily on income-producing assets after you stop working. At every stage, however, you should invest part of your money for growth to help ensure that your portfolio's gains outpace inflation.

Of course, there is no single recipe for success that encompasses the financial movable feast covered in "Reading the Economic Trends" below. As conditions change, you may have to add a dash of certain assets and dollops of others. If inflation were unexpectedly to accelerate, for example, you should lighten up on bonds to protect your purchasing power. This is because bonds, which are detailed on page 38, promise to pay only fixed dollar amounts in interest and principal—not what those dollars will buy in the future. Instead, you might favor the high yields and appreciation potential of real estate investment trusts—publicly traded companies that pool investors' cash to buy properties, as described on page 46.

If you do not have the time or skills to take charge of your portfolio, you probably should concentrate on mutual funds, which offer professional management and broad diversification at a low cost. This chapter covers most types of funds, with advice on how to select the ones that best match your financial objectives with your appetite for risk. Also, don't overlook "Organizing an Investment Club," beginning on page 44, as a means of making timely investment decisions with a little help from your friends.

Reading the Economic Trends

When you understand changes in the business cycle, you gain an investing edge.

Economic statistics often seem intimidating or irrelevant to everyday life, but ignoring them could be lethal to your financial health. By learning how to interpret such data, you gain advance warning of the economic trends that determine the returns you earn on your money and can take action to keep your portfolio profitable. Consider, for example, these unsettling reports on rising inflation and interest rates in April 1989: Many forecasters warned that inflation, which stayed below 4.3% from 1983 to 1988, had moved above 5% and could surpass 6% in the next few years. Resurgent inflation usually fuels higher interest rates, which generally depress prices of stocks and bonds and sometimes presage recession.

At the same time, interest rates on supersecure three-month Treasury bills climbed as high as 9.2%—or 2.7 times the dividend yield on the bellwether Standard & Poor's 500-stock index. That ratio has exceeded 2.5 only four times in the past two decades. In each instance, the stock market fell within eight months, dropping on average a total of 30%.

To make sense of such economic statistics, you must first understand the framework that gives them shape, known as the business cycle. This wavelike pattern of economic activity has undulated from boom to bust for more than a century. The cycle, which normally takes three to four years from start to finish, begins when interest rates and inflation are low or falling. This reduces the price of borrowing, making it easier for consumers to buy homes, cars, and other expensive items. Faced with surging demand for their products and services, businesses also take advantage of the favorable borrowing costs and begin expanding.

Pumped-up consumer and business spending leads to higher revenues and profits for businesses and thus nationwide economic growth. When investors expect higher corporate profits, stock prices shoot up.

As demand for credit increases, interest rates rise because more borrowers are competing to get loans. Similarly, when consumers and businesses buy more goods, the inflation rate goes up. Ultimately, inflation and interest rates climb high enough to send stock prices down, stifle business and consumer borrowing, and choke off the expansion. This results in flat economic growth or even a recession—two or more quarters of declining gross national product (the value of all goods and services produced in the country). As this happens, the demand for credit ebbs, interest rates fall, and the cycle starts anew.

As you flip through the newspaper, look for these signs of change in the cycle:

Inflation. You can get a reading on this with the consumer price index (CPI). A high rate for this measure of the cost of goods and services is public enemy No. 1 for financial assets such as stocks, bonds, annuities, and certificates of deposit. For example, if you buy a $1,000 five-year U.S. Treasury note or CD that pays 9% annually, you will receive $90 a year in interest. But if consumer prices are bounding ahead by 5%, the real purchasing power of your $90 will be declining by 5% a year. And when you get your principal back in five years, it will have lost 25% of its original value. Inflation usually hurts stock prices as well because higher consumer prices lessen the value of future corporate earnings, which makes shares of those companies less appealing.

You can keep tabs on the pace of inflation during the fourth week of every month, when the Department of Labor announces the consumer price index. An annual inflation rate below 2% is low; 2% to 4% is moderate; above 4% is high. Check to see, too, whether the inflation rate has been rising—a negative, or bearish, sign for stock and bond investors—or whether it has been falling, which is bullish.

Interest rates. These give you an idea of what rates you will earn on cash investments such as bank CDs and money-market accounts. Rising interest rates also depress bond prices, and they can send stocks down for two reasons. First, higher rates mean bigger borrowing expenses for companies, which erode corporate profits and, in turn, cut stock prices. Second, share values fall because high rates lure investors away from stocks and into interest-paying bonds and money-market funds.

You can discern broad trends by focusing on two key rates. One is the prime rate, which is what banks charge their best business customers for loans. When the prime rate is climbing, it means companies are borrowing heavily and the economy is still on an upward swing. Since consumer loan rates are also pegged to the prime, you can use this barometer to tell whether your own borrowing costs are likely to rise or fall. During the 12 months that ended April 1, 1989, the prime rate rose steadily from 8.5% to 11.5%. The second rate you should follow is the yield on three-month Treasury bills. When their yield rises sharply—as they did from 5.8% to 8.9% for the year that ended April 1, 1989—this may signal a resurgence of inflation. Subsequently, the economy could slow down.

Key government economic figures. At the very least, you should track three statistics: the nation's gross national product (GNP), the balance of payments, and the index of leading economic indicators. GNP is the nation's broadest gauge of economic health. About three weeks after the close of each quarter, the government announces the annual rate at which GNP has grown in the previous three months. Less than 2% is viewed as low growth, 2% to 5% is respectable, and anything above that is generally considered an unsustainable boom.

The balance of payments figure—reported quarterly as a surplus or a deficit—will help you monitor trends in international trade. It measures the flow of goods, services, and investments between the U.S. and the rest of the world. When deficits persist, this generally reduces the value of the dollar abroad and can boost inflation. Reason: A weak dollar makes foreign goods relatively expensive, often allowing American makers of similar goods to raise prices as well.

For a glimpse at how the U.S. economy could perform in the near future, look to the index of leading economic indicators, which is usually reported during the first week of the month. The indicators represent an average of 11 components of economic growth ranging from stock prices to housing permits. If the index is consistently rising, the economy is still chugging along and a setback is unlikely. But if the indicators fall for three or more consecutive months, look for an economic slowdown or even a recession in the next year or so.

The stock market. Its behavior sometimes gives advance warning of an economic upswing or downturn because investors buy or sell shares based on their expectations of the future. For example, stock prices typically explode midway through a recession, usually a good six to 12 months before the economy itself recovers. Similarly, sharply declining stock prices—a drop of 10% or more over one to three months—may warn of an impending slowdown or recession. The stock market is no guarantee of the economic outlook, though. As Nobel laureate economist Paul Samuelson quipped, "The stock market has predicted nine of the past five recessions."

Monitor basic stock market trends each weekend by reading about the previous week's movement of the Dow Jones industrial average, which averages the stock prices of 30 large industrial companies ranging from IBM to McDonald's. Should you become interested in investing in stocks of small and medium-size companies—or mutual funds that buy such shares—keep tabs weekly on the Nasdaq composite of stocks that trade over the counter.

Industry and company news. If you own shares in a particular company or have a stock mutual fund that is invested heavily in one type of business, be sure to read any news stories on the company or that industry. These articles can alert you to the possible rise or fall in the fortunes of the business. No matter how woeful or wonderful the news, though, never buy or sell an investment solely on the basis of a newspaper story. What may seem like good news to you may be disappointing to professional investors who follow the company.

Most important, by the time you read about a company in the newspaper, many professional investors have already acted on the information and bought or sold the stock. As a result, the news is already discounted in the price—you're more likely to get burned than make a killing by investing on the story.

The Mutual Funds Advantage

You can pool your money with thousands of other investors and leave the day-to-day work to a professional.

There comes a point in every saver's life when it is time to venture beyond the bank. Federally-insured certificates of deposit and savings accounts are secure, but their modest yields take you on a slow voyage to long-term

goals. Stocks and bonds may get you there faster, but investing in them directly takes more time, money, and expertise than most people have. The solution for more and more armchair investors is mutual funds, which can be as rewarding in practice as they are sensible in theory.

A fund is a company whose business is generally to buy stocks, bonds, or money-market securities (short-term debt obligations such as Treasury bills) to earn its investors the best possible return. You invest in a mutual fund by buying shares, making you a part owner and entitling you to a portion of the fund's earnings. In addition, you get full-time management by professionals who select securities, monitor them daily, and decide when to replace them—sparing you the work and research.

A mutual fund also delivers diversification; your money is spread among the scores of securities the fund owns. For a tyro investor, this benefit is especially desirable. If you own shares in a mutual fund and one of its stocks plummets in value, the rest of the fund's holdings will cushion your investment. But if, for example, you own stock only in IBM and the price drops sharply, you could really suffer.

Picking a fund may require a few hours of research, but you needn't spend more than two hours in the course of a month keeping records and tracking its performance. You can buy into most funds for a minimum initial investment of $1,000; some have no minimum ante at all. Thus, for as little as $5,000, you can invest in five types of funds—maybe two stock, two bond, and a money-market—and be as broadly diversified as a multimillion-dollar pension fund.

Even diversification is no guarantee of investment success, however. Remember: When you buy shares in a stock or bond fund, you are subjecting yourself to the risks inherent in those markets. In the October 1987 stock market crash, the average stock fund fell 21%, nearly as much as the market as a whole.

There are nearly 3,000 funds to choose from, so you should have no trouble finding one that matches your tolerance for risk and your investment goals. Funds range from the supersafe to the chiefly chancy. For more information, refer to *Money*'s comprehensive rankings and alphabetical listings of the 900 biggest stock and bond funds, beginning on page 185.

How Mutual Funds Work

Fund management companies range in size from basement entrepreneurs to giants such as Merrill Lynch and Fidelity. As compensation, the managers take annual investment advisory fees of typically 0.5% to 1% of a fund's assets.

A fund can make money for shareholders in three ways: by receiving dividends or interest on the securities it owns; by selling securities at a profit; or by owning securities that appreciate in value, thereby pushing up the price of the fund's own shares. A fund pays shareholders most of its income and profits in the form of dividends and capital-gains distributions. You can take the money in cash or automatically reinvest it in the fund. Funds that emphasize income tend to pay dividends monthly, while those that go for growth usually pay theirs once or twice a year. You can claim appreciation in the price of your fund shares anytime by redeeming them.

Depending on the fund, you buy shares either directly from the management company (generally by mail) or through a stockbroker or financial planner. The price of the shares, called the net asset value (NAV), is calculated daily by the fund manager. If the fund is sold exclusively by brokers and financial planners, you will have to pay a sales commission, known as a load. Many funds with loads levy sales charges of 4.5% to 8.5% whenever you put money in. Others charge no initial commission but assess what's known as a back-end load when you sell shares—typically 1% to 5% of the amount you're taking out. Still others skim off an annual charge, known as a 12b-1 fee, equal to between 0.5% and 1.25% of the fund's assets. Some funds charge a combination of these fees.

If you choose a mutual fund that sells its shares directly to investors, you may pay no sales charge. This type of fund is called a no-load. An offshoot of these funds, known as a low-load, charges a sales fee of 1% to 3% of your investment. (Discount brokers sell no-loads, too, but they charge fees of 0.6% to 2.5%.) Studies have shown that no-loads, low-loads, and load funds all perform about the same on average. If you have the interest and

The Choices in Mutual Funds

Most mutual funds fall into one of the 15 investment categories explained below. The average annual returns and best-performer figures are calculated over the past 10 years.

Type of Fund and Investment Objective	Risk level	Over the past 10 years		
		Category's average annual return	Category's worst year/ best year	Category's best performer (sales charge; phone)
SMALL-COMPANY GROWTH. Share-price appreciation from stocks of up-and-coming companies	Very High	15.5%	−8.5%/38%	**Quasar Associates** (5.5%; 800-222-4615)
MAXIMUM CAPITAL GAINS. Price appreciation but negligible dividends from fast-growing companies	Very high	17.8	−8.2/42.2	**Phoenix Stock** (8.5%; 800-243-4361)
GROWTH. Appreciation and possibly dividends from established firms with rising earnings	High	16.5	−2.7/37.2	**Fidelity Magellan** (3%; 800-544-6666)
GROWTH AND INCOME. Similar to growth funds but with more emphasis on dividends	Moderate to high	15.9	−0.2/27.7	**Mutual Shares** (no load; 800-448-3863)
BALANCED. Price appreciation, dividends and interest from blue-chip stocks and corporate bonds	Moderate	14.7	+0.7/28.5	**Phoenix Balanced** (8.5%; 800-243-4361)
EQUITY INCOME. Primarily dividends from shares of utilities, banks, and other high-yield stocks; share-price gains are a secondary goal	Moderate	16.8	−1.5/25.1	**Lindner Dividend** (no load; 314-727-5305)
HIGH-YIELD CORPORATE. Lofty yields from interest on corporate bonds with low credit ratings	Moderate to high	11.2	+1.9/29.1	**Kemper High Yield** (4.5%; 800-261-1048)
HIGH-GRADE CORPORATE. Income from corporate bonds with high credit ratings	Low	10.4	+1.1/31.6	**Axe-Houghton Income** (no load; 800-366-0444)
HIGH-YIELD MUNICIPAL. Lofty tax-free yields from municipal bonds with low credit ratings	Moderate to high	12.2	−9.2/34.2	**Colonial Tax-Exempt High Yield** (4.75%; 800-426-3750)
HIGH-GRADE MUNICIPAL. Tax-free yields from municipal bonds with high credit ratings	Low	11.6	−11.3/35.7	**MFS Managed Municipal** (4.75%; 800-343-2829)
U.S. GOVERNMENT. Income from bonds issued by the Treasury and other federal agencies	Low	10.4	−0.9/23.9	**Lord Abbett U.S. Gov.** (4.75%; 800-223-4224
MONEY MARKET. Income from a variety of safe, short-term securities such as U.S. Treasury bills and corporate IOUs	Very low	9.9	+6.1/17.1	**Kemper Money Market** (no load; 800-537-6001)
TAX-FREE MONEY MARKET. Tax-free income provided by short-term municipal issues	Very low	4.2	+4.1/7.5	**Calvert Tax-Free Reserves** (no load; 800-368-2748)
INTERNATIONAL. Appreciation and dividends from stocks of foreign firms	High to very high	17.4	−4.0/50.3	**Merrill Lynch Pacific A** (6.5%; 800-637-3863)
GLOBAL. Appreciation, dividends, and interest from stocks and bonds that may be issued anywhere in the world, including the U.S.	Moderate to very high	18.5	−3.6/37.7	**Oppenheimer Global** (8.5%; 800-525-7048)

SOURCES: LIPPER ANALYTICAL SERVICES AND MORNINGSTAR INC.

self-confidence to go it alone, buy directly from the fund's management company. That way the money you would otherwise pay in sales charges will go into your mutual fund account.

Choosing a Fund

The first direction to look when seeking a fund is inward. Could you sleep nights owning shares in a fund that might lose a year's gains in a week? If not, you should stay away from the chanciest fund categories. Keep in mind, though, that in the long run the riskier funds tend to have the higher returns. The trade-off is that such funds also have intervals of miserable performance. One question to ponder before buying a fund is: How soon might you need to sell your shares? If you can leave the money untouched for five years or more—about the average length of one up-and-down cycle in the stock and bond markets—there is a good chance your fund will have time to rebound from downturns. If you might need the money sooner, consider only low-risk funds. The basic fund groups are:

Growth funds. These are the riskiest funds, but they also have the best long-term performances. Growth funds invest in the stocks of companies that the fund managers think will grow in value. They are suitable for investors who can hold the shares for at least five years and won't sell in a panic during scary periods when the value of their investment shrinks.

Total-return funds. This group includes growth and income, equity income, and balanced funds, which invest in a mix of growth stocks, stodgy high-dividend stocks, and bonds. As their names suggest, the funds aim to provide steady returns from a combination of capital gains and interest or dividends. This strategy keeps their share prices steadier than those of growth funds but also can dampen their long-term performance. Total-return funds are suitable for people who are investing for a goal five years or more in the future but who lack the nerve needed for growth funds.

Income funds. These funds seek to give investors dependable streams of income from bonds and sometimes from high-dividend stocks such as utilities. The strategy keeps the share prices of most income funds fairly stable. Because the funds offer little prospect for big capital gains, they are best suited to people who want dividend income now—for example, to supplement a pension.

Two types of income funds invest exclusively in bonds: taxable bond funds and tax-exempt bond funds. The first group buys corporate and U.S. Government bonds; the second, municipal bonds, which pay income that is free of federal taxes. Tax-exempt funds tend to pay shareholders 20% to 35% less than comparable taxable funds. On an after-tax basis, however, people in the 28% to 33% federal tax brackets usually come out ahead with tax-exempt funds.

Whether tax-free or taxable, a bond fund's share price will fluctuate with bond prices. In recent years, that fact has come as an unpleasant surprise to some investors misled by unscrupulous brokers or vaguely worded ads into thinking that bond funds can never lose value. Only money-market fund share prices remain constant, typically at $1.

Some bond funds are riskier than others. As a rule, the higher the yield, the riskier the bond fund. That's because there are basically two ways for a bond fund to increase its payout:

● A fund can buy the bonds of companies or municipalities with low credit ratings. The risk here is that those issuers are the likeliest to run into financial trouble and stop paying investors interest—that is, default—on their bonds. The most credit-conscious funds buy U.S. Government bonds. Next down the safety ladder are bond funds that stick to the high-quality securities of rock-solid corporations or municipalities. Last are high-yield funds that invest in so-called junk bonds issued by financially shaky companies or municipalities.

● A fund can also boost its yield by holding mostly bonds that will mature in 10 years or longer. Here, understanding the risk requires knowing the neo-Newtonian law of the bond market: When interest rates rise, bond prices fall, and the longer the bonds' maturity, the farther prices fall. The converse is also true: When rates drop, bond prices rise.

Never choose a bond fund solely because of its yield; look instead at its total return. Yield measures only the fund's income payments to investors. Total return includes fluctuations in the fund's share price as well. The distinction matters because a bond fund could lose more in value than it is paying in yield. For instance, if a fund yields 10% over the course of a year but its price drops by 15%, its total return to investors is a 5% loss.

International and global funds. These may aim for growth, income, or total return, depending on their investment approach. International funds invest all of their money in foreign securities. Global funds can invest both in the U.S. and abroad. Investors in international and global funds run a risk not encountered by other funds: currency fluctuations. Because the funds' investments are denominated in foreign currencies, the value of the holdings to U.S. shareholders depends on the relative strength of the dollar. A weakening dollar boosts the returns of these funds, while a strengthening dollar reduces them. International funds, for example, reaped a windfall gain of nearly 30% a year from 1985 through 1988, largely because of the dollar's sharp decline. When the dollar rose during the early 1980s, however, the funds returned an average of 7.2% a year.

Once you've chosen a fund category, you can select a specific fund. Don't buy one purely because it boasts the best return in the past month or year. No investment strategy excels all the time. As often as not, the top performer one year winds up on the rocks the next. A better starting point is a fund's performance over at least five years. Funds with long-term performances that beat the averages in their categories have proved they can sail in both headwinds and tailwinds. You can tell whether a fund whipped its category average by checking the fund listings at the back of this book.

When zeroing in on a fund, select several solid long-term performers in a category and get their prospectuses from either the funds or your broker or financial planner. In each prospectus, study the statement on investment objectives to learn the manager's investment approach. If it is a stock fund, for example, you will want to know whether the manager concentrates on undervalued stocks—those out of favor with the market—or searches for companies that seem to have the best prospects for earnings growth. Mutual funds that take the value approach tend to hold up well in shaky markets; ones following a growth strategy often shine when the economic outlook is bright.

If the fund buys bonds, check the prospectus for the credit quality and the average maturity of the issues in its portfolio. The lower the ratings on the bonds—anything graded below BBB by Standard & Poor's is iffy—the more vulnerable the fund will be to an economic downturn. The longer the portfolio's average maturity, the more sensitive the fund's share price will be to interest-rate swings.

In addition, you should compare the costs of investing in the funds you're considering. Each prospectus has a table that gives the fund's total annual operating expenses. As a rule, avoid funds whose expenses exceed 1.5% of their assets. Compare the convenience and service of funds, too. Does the management company offer a variety of funds and let you switch among them? Are the phone representatives helpful and knowledgeable? Service should not be your main criteria, but if two or more funds seem equally promising, choose the more convenient and helpful one.

Buying and Selling Shares

You don't have to worry much about whether the market is high or low when you invest in a mutual fund, if you use a technique known as dollar-cost averaging. It requires you to commit equal amounts of money to a fund at regular intervals. Each installment buys more shares when the fund's price drops and fewer when it rises. So unless your fund's price goes straight up—dream on—you will end up acquiring shares at a lower average cost than if you had invested all of your money at once.

Suppose you decided in late August 1987 to invest $5,000 in the popular Fidelity Magellan fund. Had you done so at one time, you would have been clobbered in the crash and would have had only $4,305 in your account at the end of 1988—14 months after the crash. Had you instead invested five $1,000 monthly installments from August through December 1987, your stake would have grown to $5,463 by the end of 1988.

When should you sell your fund shares? Get out gleefully when you've reached your financial goal. Also sell if your fund consistently lags behind its peers. If it has trailed its category's average performance for four consecutive quarters, you should probably give up on it. But don't let intermittent rough patches goad you into a hasty sale. Leave worrying about the short term to the fund manager while you keep your eye on the real prize—attaining your long-term investment goals.

Go for Cash Flow

This yardstick may be an investor's best guide to a stock's true worth.

When investors go bargain hunting, they look for stocks that appear cheap in comparison with standard benchmarks. The two most common measures of value are share price relative to earnings and book value (net worth per share). But both have shortcomings and, as a result, top stock pickers are increasingly turning to a less well-known vital sign: cash flow. In simplest terms, this is the amount of cash per share a company actually generates from its operations.

The ratio of price to cash flow has also been growing in popularity because it can tip off investors to stocks that are potential takeover targets. Dealmakers seek out companies with high cash flow because the money is available to pay interest on any debt used to finance an acquisition. In fact, cash flow is now considered so significant that in November 1987 the Financial Accounting Standards Board, the accounting industry's rule-making body, began requiring that all annual reports for fiscal years ending after July 15, 1988 include a statement of cash receipts and payments—all of the information you need to calculate the cash-flow measures that analysts rely on.

To understand the importance of cash flow for stock pickers, it's helpful to look first at the advantages and drawbacks of ratios based on earnings or book value. Both have long been popular because they are simple and readily available.

Generally, a stock's book value—the company's assets per share minus its liabilities per share—moderately understates what the firm is worth. The reason is that assets are carried on a company's books at their purchase price minus depreciation (the estimated cost of wear and tear) without any adjustment for inflation. With Standard & Poor's 500-stock index recently trading at 2.1 times book value, stocks selling for less than 1.5 times book value look cheap. The weakness of book value is that the historical prices of assets can be an unreliable guide. A company can carry a major asset on the books for years at its original cost—even though that may be only a tiny fraction of its current worth.

Price/earning ratios suffer from a different problem. A stock is considered undervalued if it trades at a price less than 10 times annual earnings per share. But this can be misleading because what a company reports as earnings can be greatly influenced by the imagination of its accountants. Businesses that require accountants to make a lot of estimates are especially vulnerable to such earnings distortion. Two frequent offenders are technology and financial services companies. These industries are most likely to accelerate revenues, defer expenses, and use other accounting techniques to make earnings look rosy.

Cash flow is free from such problems. In essence, you start with a company's earnings and then add back all expenses that did not actually require an immediate outlay of cash. Here is the basic method:

Using a company's annual report, turn to the statements of income and cash flows. Start with pretax income, the company's earnings after it has paid interest on its outstanding bonds but before taxes and nonrecurring gains and losses. Add the company's noncash expenses, such as depreciation for aging manufacturing equipment and facilities. Other noncash expenses include amortization, the gradual reduction of the accounting value of intangible assets such as goodwill.

The result is cash flow from operations. But companies cannot spend their cash just as they please—some is committed to important uses, most notably reinvestments to maintain operations. To find so-called free cash flow, subtract capital expenditures from operating cash flow. Some analysts also subtract the cash required to pay dividends on preferred stock and the tax payments that a company makes each year, as well as other cash outlays. Others use a shorthand method to arrive at approximate cash flow. They simply add depreciation per share to net income per share. As long as you use the same method for all of the companies that you are comparing, you can draw the line where you like.

Once you have a figure for a company's cash flow, divide it by the number of shares the firm has outstanding to get cash flow per share. What you are looking for is a ratio of price to cash flow that is below the market average. Investment adviser Robert L. Renck Jr. of New York City calculates that the S&P 500 recently traded at about 11 times its free cash flow. Stocks selling for less than 7.5 times Renck's measure of free cash flow are bargains. Also, check to see that the company's cash flow doesn't vary a lot from year to year. Firms that consistently generate high cash flow not only shine when the economy booms but have the financial stamina to survive lean times.

When to Sell Your Stock

Look for these exit cues to take profits or cut losses.

Financial gurus are positively prolix when spinning theories on how to pick winning stocks. But sage advice is scarce on the flip side of the equation—when to sell. Of course, there is no proven system for buying at market troughs and selling at peaks. By observing a few warning signals, however, prudent investors can judge better when to sell to lock in profits from stocks that have gained in value and, equally important, when to jettison the weak ones. There are two good reasons to consider selling your stocks. One is that you believe the market is headed for a significant setback that will carry down most shares. Not all issues are equally vulnerable to broad market declines.

To see how much your stock tends to fluctuate with the market, check its beta (a standard measure of volatility) in the *Value Line Investment Survey*, which is available in most public libraries. The higher the beta (Standard & Poor's 500-stock index, a proxy for the market, has a beta of 1), the more the stock moves up or down in response to market moves—and the quicker you should sell if stocks seem ready to tumble. The second reason to sell is that you think a company's prospects have peaked or, worse yet, begun to decline.

To make sure that you don't bail out of your stock too early or too late, watch the following indicators. Except as noted, you will find them reported in the *Wall Street Journal* and the financial pages of major newspapers:

A rise in interest rates. Climbing rates hurt stocks by diverting money to competing investments such as certificates of deposit and bonds. Two key rates to watch are the ones on three-month Treasury bills and the Federal Reserve discount rate (what the Fed charges member banks for loans). Both are reported daily. If the three-month T-bill rate rises to more than twice the S&P 500 dividend yield, stocks may soon slide. The market also has a history of falling when the Fed raises the discount rate three consecutive times.

A recession appears imminent. Since the market usually declines six to nine months before an economic slump, investors focus on indicators that provide early warning of recession. One is the Department of Commerce's index of leading economic indicators, which is reported monthly. If the leading indicators are down three months in a row, a downturn is likely.

Stock market breadth is narrowing. Sometimes gains in a handful of high-priced stocks can push an indicator such as the Dow Jones industrial average higher, even though most stocks decline. When that happens, analysts say the market's breadth is narrowing. The easiest way for individual investors to spot this is to follow the advance/decline line—a running tally of the difference between the number of gainers and losers each day (it appears in *Investor's Daily* and *Barron's*). If the market is moving up but the advance/decline line is down, there is a strong likelihood that the rally will fizzle. A second trouble sign: When one broad index, such as the S&P 500, rises while another, such as the Dow, declines. Market technicians call this divergence; you should call it a sell sign.

Stock prices overall are inflated. One telltale signal that investor ebullience has boosted prices to an unsustainable level is when the dividend yield on the S&P 500 index, normally about 4.5%, drops below 3% (as happened in February 1987, for example). Price/earnings ratios provide another benchmark: if the S&P 500's P/E is at or near its peak in prior bull markets (it went to 23 in August 1987), chances are good for a setback.

Your stock has become overvalued. Even if stock values in general are not bloated, your stock's price might be. For example, if an issue's P/E normally hovers around the average P/E of the S&P 500 but suddenly rises 30% higher, the stock may be overvalued and due for a fall. Make sure, however, that the P/E hasn't soared because of such welcome events as a new product line or better cost controls.

There is a sudden sharp price change. If the price of a stock spikes up 20% or more over a month or so, run with your profit for the exit. Reason: Stocks often stall or even drop back after such a leap. If the price suddenly dives 20%, you have a more complicated decision. Find out the cause of the drop, and reevaluate the investment.

Quarterly earnings fall 10% or more below expectations. Since analysts base their projections on information from the company, earnings that fall below those estimates should cause concern. Management often resorts to every accounting trick possible to avoid a disappointing earnings report, so be wary of the company's prospects when there's a shortfall. Your suspicions should rise even further if shortfalls happen two or more quarters in a row.

Finally, if you don't have the discipline to sell your winners and cut your losers, consider a stop-loss order that instructs your broker to sell if the stock dips below a specified level—at 10% to 20% below the current price. If the price rises, periodically raise the stop-loss point, too. Remember, though, your stock will be sold if the price dips below that level even temporarily. But don't despair if you sell an appreciated stock and it later zooms ahead to new highs. As the old saying goes, no one ever went bankrupt taking a profit.

Avoiding Hidden Investing Costs

The surest way to enhance your return is to elude these submerged fees.

You would naturally be suspicious if a broker tried to convince you that there was a risk-free way to boost your returns on stocks, bonds, or mutual funds. In fact, such a path to higher returns does exist, though you are not likely to hear of it from a broker or any other salesperson. The secret is learning how to reduce your investing costs.

The effect these costs have on your profits can be immense. If, for example, you had paid an 8.5% commission to invest $10,000 in Delaware Decatur I Fund, which earned a compound annual return of 15.2% over the five years through 1988, you would have ended up with $1,636 less than you would have gotten in Loomis-Sayles Mutual, a no-load with comparable performance.

In general, there are three types of investing costs. The first is sales commissions, which you pay when you buy stocks, bonds, and some mutual funds. The second consists of management expenses for money-market or other mutual funds. The third is called the spread: the difference between the retail, or ask, price at which dealers sell a security to you and the

lower wholesale, or bid, price at which they buy it back. Spreads can exact a particularly heavy toll if you are purchasing zero-coupon or municipal bonds as well as over-the-counter stocks.

You can cut sales commissions dramatically by buying through discount brokerages, although you will have to forgo the research and personal attention a full-service firm offers. Discounters spare you another expense now becoming common at full-service brokerages: annual fees for customers who do not trade actively. Merrill Lynch, a leader of this galling trend, charges $30 annually for accounts that generate less than $100 in commissions a year.

Here is a guide to costs you may encounter for various investments, along with tips for minimizing them:

Stocks. The spread you pay grows wider the lower the trading volume of a stock. For an actively traded stock such as General Motors, the spread is likely to be narrow—typically 12.5¢ a share. With GM recently at $85, that spread works out to less than 0.2%. On the other hand, a thinly traded over-the-counter stock could have an ask (to buy) price of $3 and a bid price of only $2.50—a 20% spread. If you buy an OTC stock from a market maker—a broker/dealer firm that has agreed to keep the stock in its inventory and buy or sell whenever an investor wants to place an order—you pay only the spread. But if you buy through a broker who must first get the shares from a market maker, you pay the spread plus the broker's commission. Furthermore, if you buy fewer than 100 shares of any stock, you pay an odd-lot charge of 12.5¢ a share. Under National Association of Securities Dealers guidelines, the spread and all other sales charges combined for actively traded stocks and bonds should not exceed 5% of the amount invested.

Advice: If you are buying an over-the-counter stock that is not listed in the newspaper tables for the National Market System, which include most actively traded issues, buy from one of the market makers listed for that stock in a directory known as the pink sheets and available from most brokers.

U.S. Treasuries. You pay sales commissions when you buy or sell Treasury securities through a bank or brokerage firm. These run $25 to $40 for $10,000 purchases of bills, notes, or bonds.

Advice: Avoid commission charges entirely by buying securities direct from the Treasury. This technique—called Treasury Direct—requires some annoying paperwork, but you can't beat the price. To obtain a free brochure, call any Federal Reserve Bank or write to the Bureau of Public Debt, Department F, Washington, D.C. 20239-1200.

Municipal bonds. Your yield is reduced by the amount of the spread, which is built into the bond's price. Spreads are higher for odd-lot purchases—those under $25,000. If you buy a previously issued bond from a broker that does not have it in inventory, your yield will be further reduced by an eighth of a percentage point or so to compensate your broker for his costs in obtaining the bonds from another dealer.

Advice: Favor actively traded bonds—especially new issues. Their spreads are usually no more than 0.75% versus as much as 5% for odd lots of existing bonds. Otherwise, select from the bonds your broker has in inventory.

Zero-coupon bonds. Rather than paying cash interest every year, zeros are sold at a fraction of their face value; they provide their interest by rising to that value at maturity. Because the pricing of zeros can be confusing, some brokers get away with sizable spreads—5% is not uncommon.

Advice: Comparison shop among several brokers, asking how much you must invest per $1,000 of face value for the precise zero you want and what the effective yield to maturity is. Choose the broker with the lowest price, which should also mean the highest yield.

Mutual funds. Many funds, including all sold by brokers, charge front-end loads of as much as 8.5%. Some funds sock you with back-end loads of as much as 1.5% when you sell, and with 12b-1 fees, annual levies of up to 1.25% taken against fund assets to cover marketing costs to attract new shareholders. Any 12b-1 fees are applied on top of annual management fees, which range from 0.3% for the most economically run bond funds to 1.5% for the generally costlier small-company or international stock funds. An SEC rule requires that all sales charges and fees be listed prominently in a fund's prospectus, along with a table showing their dollar impact on a $1,000 investment after one-, three-, five-, and 10-year holding periods.

Transaction costs. These are the commissions and spreads the fund pays to trade securities. The average portfolio turnover rate for stock funds is about 80%, which puts annual transaction costs at more than 3% of assets. A fund with 200% turnover is paying 8%, which represents a real handicap.

Advice: Favor no-loads, and comparison shop among top performers, checking the turnover rates and the fee tables in their prospectuses. A fund with expenses totaling less than $75 at the five-year line is a good buy.

Money-market funds. Money funds are sold without sales charges, but their management expenses eat into your yield.

Advice: Compare prospectuses to find funds with expense ratios below 0.67%. If you select a fund with extremely low expenses, though, be aware that the managers may be eating some costs to boost the fund's yield and lure in new money. But once such a fund has enticed enough unwary investors, the sponsor will probably raise expense charges, thus nibbling away at your returns.

Watch Out for "Guaranteed" Investments

Pursuing investors' cravings for safety, sales of these investments are booming. Be wary: Most guarantees are more hype than help.

Desperate to recoup flagging commissions, brokerage firms and sponsors of investment products are resorting to a new gimmick that uses the word "insured" or "guaranteed" in a product's title or its marketing brochure. The objective is to entice buyers into high-risk investments that look more like certificates of deposit or similar products covered by the federal insurance that guarantees bank accounts.

Even some potentially volatile mutual funds are trying to pass as ultraconservative investments. In just two months, Shearson Lehman Hutton sold $190 million worth of a new fund that invests in stocks and zero-coupon bonds. Although actually named the SLH Principal Return Fund, brokers referred to it as the SAFE fund—the Secured Asset Fund for Equity Investing. The fund's come-on: assurance that it will return investors' original principal after seven years. But that implied promise isn't as impressive as it sounds. Because the fund invests less than half your money in stocks, your potential for capital gains is reduced. And in the extremely unlikely event that after seven years you get back only your original investment, inflation and taxes on the interest from the zero-coupon bonds may have wiped out a third of your purchasing power.

In practice, the guarantees in supposedly low-risk investments are more hype than help. Sometimes the guarantee or the ostensible insurance contains so many loopholes that it is difficult to invoke. And even when the insurance is legitimate, it may last for only a limited term or cover a narrow range of risks. In real estate limited partnerships, for example, investors are protected against minor dangers, such as a tenant defaulting on a lease, and left unprotected against such serious perils as a general decline in property values.

To avoid being bamboozled by a guarantee, make sure you understand exactly what is covered, what the limitations of the promises are, and who stands behind them. To help you spot the catches and escape clauses, here's a critical look at some of the guaranteed investments that lately were being sold:

Federally insured CDs. Despite the highly publicized financial problems of some banks and savings and loans, the federal insurance on certificates of deposit is the closest you can get to an unequivocal guarantee. Even if thrift or bank losses should sink the Federal Savings and Loan Insurance Corporation or the Federal Deposit Insurance Corporation, the U.S. government ultimately guarantees payment of principal and interest up to $100,000.

Ginnie Mae mutual funds. The words "government guaranteed" emblazoned on ads have helped attract billions into Ginnie Mae and other mortgage-backed securities funds. What many investors still don't realize, though, is that while the interest and principal payments on the securities held by the funds are guaranteed, the prices of the mutual fund shares are not guaranteed at all. The securities that Ginnie Mae funds invest in are guaranteed against default by a federal agency such as the Government National Mortgage Association, or a federally chartered corporation such as the Federal National Mortgage Association (Fannie Mae). But just like any other fixed-income investment, the value of Ginnie Mae fund shares will fall whenever interest rates rise.

When rates ticked up more than half a percentage point in April 1987, for example, some funds dipped 5% to 6%. Unlike bond fund investors, however, Ginnie Mae shareholders don't enjoy big capital gains if interest rates fall. The reason: When rates drop, homeowners often refinance their home mortgages, which shortens the overall life of high-yielding Ginnie Maes and limits their gains.

Insured mortgage partnerships. Like Ginnie Mae mutual funds, limited partnerships that invest in government-insured mortgages also lose market value when rates rise—and can miss out on capital gains when rates fall. In addition, insured mortgage partnerships often have other shortcomings. Sales commissions, loan-origination fees, and administrative charges can eat up 10% or more of your investment—meaning that only 90¢ or so of each dollar you invest actually goes into mortgages. And since these partnerships may not be traded actively, they can be difficult to unload.

Insured municipal bond funds and unit trusts. By limiting their portfolios to municipal bonds whose interest and principal payments are backed by an insurance company that has received the highest (triple A) rating from Standard & Poor's or Moody's, insured muni-bond funds and unit trusts greatly reduce the risk of losses resulting from a bond default. As with any insurance, there is a premium cost, which is why investors often receive a yield one-quarter of a percentage point or so lower than that of uninsured funds.

The most important question with insured muni funds and trusts is whether the insurance protection is worth the cost. Muni-bond defaults are rare—less than 1% of all bonds issued. An uninsured muni-fund portfolio consisting of a hundred or more issues could easily sustain a single default. And there are major risks that bond insurance does not protect against. If interest rates rise, the value of insured bond funds and unit trusts will fall right along with the value of uninsured funds and trusts. Investors would also suffer if the rating of a bond's insurer is downgraded from AAA to AA, for example, since the ratings of bonds insured by the company would also drop. Such downgradings are rare, but they have occurred. In 1985, for example, Industrial Indemnity was downgraded to AA. The result: The bonds it insured dropped 5% in value.

Insurance makes a bit more sense for unit trusts because they contain fewer bond issues, generally 20 or so. But you will pay an up-front sales fee of 4% to 5%. If you have more than $25,000 to invest, you can just as easily buy insured bonds directly and forgo making this cash contribution.

Real estate limited partnerships. The new crop of insured real estate limited partnerships is perhaps the most egregious example of how sleight of hand is being used to disguise an investment's true risks. With guarantees and insurance, many people lose sight of the more important questions about real estate investments—namely, what are the fees; what income is being generated; how much are you paying for the properties; what is the likelihood of appreciation?

To woo income investors away from CDs,

some partnerships offer limited guarantees of minimum cash distributions, typically 6% to 8% a year. But the general partners usually commit themselves to making this distribution for only a limited time—perhaps two to eight years. Further, a guarantee of distributions does not assure that the partnership will actually earn enough to make those payouts. The guaranteed distributions may have to be financed by loans from the general partner. For example, Paine Webber Equity Partners Three can borrow up to $1 million from the general partners to make its distributions. Obviously, those loans would eventually have to be repaid. Therefore, you could be sacrificing return in the later years of a partnership for the illusion of a healthy rate of return in the early years.

Another partnership ploy is the use of rental guarantee insurance, which supposedly assures a steady stream of income. For example, TMI Income Plus leases fast-food facilities to Taco Bell franchises and takes out insurance that will pay up to 80% of the rent for any that fail. The catch is that the insurance company will make those payments for only 12 months. After that, unless TMI can find another franchise willing to pay the same rent—which may be unlikely after the first franchise goes belly up—the value of that property could turn more sour than a five-day-old burrito.

Other real estate partnerships purport to guarantee your principal by buying insurance policies that, in effect, promise to make up the shortfall if the value of properties when the partnership dissolves is not as high as was originally estimated. One problem is the difficulty of actually enforcing the insurance policy, which is filled with escape clauses. For example, the insurer may not have to pay if a property loses value because of a lawsuit or a change in environmental regulations. In

How Safe Are "Guaranteed" Investments?

INVESTMENT	WHAT IS GUARANTEED
Federally insured certificates of deposit	Principal and interest, up to $100,000 per person at each institution; joint accounts of up to $100,000 may be covered, too
Ginnie Mae and other mortgage-backed funds	Timely payment of interest and principal on mortgage-backed securities that the fund holds
Insured mortgage limited partnerships	Principal value and interest payments on most mortgages in a partnership, which are insured by U.S. government agencies
Insured muni bond funds and unit trusts	Timely payment of interest and principal on bonds that are held by the fund or trust
Real estate limited partnerships	Minimum cash distributions or full return of principal by the time the partnership liquidates, usually within 10 years
Commodity futures partnerships	Return of original investment, usually after five or seven years

addition, the guarantee is usually made to the partnership and not directly to the investors. Thus, if a property drops in value because of litigation, insurance proceeds could easily be eaten up by legal costs.

Commodity futures partnerships. These partnerships—which trade contracts for the future delivery of everything from pork bellies to foreign currencies—are blatant speculations. Although their sponsors trumpet money-back guarantees, partnerships such as Shearson's F-1000 Guarantee Futures Fund and Dean Witter's Principal Guaranteed Fund do not really protect investors from the loss of purchasing power.

Shearson's program shows how some guaranteed partnerships work: The commodity fund uses 70% of your capital to buy zero-coupon bonds and the rest for daredevil commodities trading. The theory is that even

if the commodities portion of the fund gets wiped out, the zeros will appreciate enough to return your original capital on a redemption date, five to seven years in the future.

In the meantime, though, the value of your fund can fluctuate wildly because zeros themselves are highly volatile. Thus, if you need to sell before the fund's redemption date, you could easily suffer a substantial loss. And even if you recover your original capital seven years from now when the zeros mature, its purchasing power will have been eroded by inflation and taxes.

The only guaranteed winners in this kind of fund are the sponsors, such as Shearson and Dean Witter. By charging brokerage fees as high as 8% a year and taking as much as 20% of any trading profits the fund earns—while sharing in none of the losses—they make scads of money no matter how their funds perform.

WHO BACKS IT UP	THE CATCH: RISKS THAT ARE NOT COVERED
Federal Deposit Insurance Corporation or Federal Savings and Loan Insurance Corporation; ultimately, the U.S. government	There are virtually none, although it is possible for a CD's high yield to be lowered if the institution fails.
Federal agencies such as Ginnie Mae or quasi-government agencies such as the Federal National Mortgage Association	The prices of fund shares are not guaranteed at all. Prices will decline if interest rates rise, while capital gains may be limited if rates fall.
Same as above; a portion of some mortgages may be insured by a private company affiliated with the partnership sponsor	Market value will fall if interest rates rise. In addition, the fees may be quite high, partnership units may be hard to sell, and some mortgages may not be insured up to their full value.
A bond insurance company, normally rated AAA by services such as Standard & Poor's and Moody's	Prices will decline if interest rates rise. Prices will also fall if the rating of an insurer is downgraded, causing bonds to be downgraded as well.
An insurance policy, bank letter of credit, or guarantee from a company affiliated with the sponsor	The money for payouts may come from loans that will have to be repaid. Principal guarantees may be hard to invoke or proceeds may never be distributed because of prior claims.
A letter of credit issued by a major bank or a portfolio of zero-coupon bonds	By the time you get back your original investment, inflation and taxes may have eaten away its purchasing power by as much as a third.

Looking for Value in Bonds

Taking a buy-and-hold approach is often best for investors interested in safety.

Prudent investors should move at least some of their savings into bonds. The most tempting—and difficult—strategy is to buy long-term bonds as rates peak, though most investors fare poorly at such precision timing. Thus, you probably should take a buy-and-hold approach to bonds. If you do, you won't be too disappointed should interest rates rise and bond prices fall; you'll receive the interest payments that led you to bonds in the first place, and you'll get your money back in the end. To play it safest, you probably want to emphasize high-quality, intermediate-term (five- to 15-year maturity) bonds, thereby reducing the time you might be stuck with a bond whose yield is no longer attractive.

While buying and holding is best as a rule, it doesn't insulate you entirely from interest-rate storms, for a couple of reasons. First, rising rates are usually accompanied by higher inflation—and inflation is a bondholder's biggest worry. While stocks can keep up with moderate inflation through rising earnings, bonds can't because they are fixed-dollar investments. If inflation consistently runs higher than the rate you lock in, the interest and principal you receive will be worth less in purchasing power than what you paid for the bond.

The other reason that buy-and-holders aren't immune to rate fluctuations is that most corporate and municipal bonds are sold with call provisions. These allow issuers to buy back the debt before it is due if interest rates fall. The bondholder receives a premium, usually equal to a year's interest or less. The effect is to cap the amount you can earn from your bond, by both limiting your potential price gain and depriving you of high interest income. Why would issuers do such a thing? Because they want to be free to refinance their debt at a lower rate. U.S. Treasury securities are not callable, except for 30-year Treasury bonds, which can be called after 25 years.

Most investors are better off catching the wave of high yields by buying shares of bond funds rather than individual issues. One advantage that funds offer is diversification. By spreading their portfolios over 50 or more separate issues, corporate and municipal funds protect investors' capital from being ravaged by one or two defaults. And as long as you avoid load funds—those that levy a front-end sales charge—as well as those with expense ratios greater than 1%, investing in funds is usually cheaper than buying individual bonds. You sidestep a broker's commission, typically 2%, and also avoid the undisclosed dealer markup that can add 1% to 4% to the bond's price.

Investors, however, must understand a crucial difference in the way rising interest rates affect bond funds versus bonds. If rates go up one percentage point, the net asset value of a fund with an average weighted maturity of 10 years drops about the same as the price of a 10-year bond. The similarity ends there. With a bond, no matter what interest rates do, you know that you will receive full face value at maturity, assuming there is not a default. But a bond fund never matures; it continually buys and sells bonds. Thus, there is no date when you are certain to recoup your original investment.

The following overview of bonds and bond funds available can help you to put together a portfolio that provides the highest returns without undue risk:

U.S. Treasury bonds. Whether you are interested primarily in high yields or capital gains, funds that invest solely in bonds backed by the U.S. government or federal agencies can help you reach your goal with the greatest degree of safety. The government guarantee, of course, protects you only against loss through default. You still run the risk that your Treasury bonds will drop in value if interest rates rise. As a result, you must find a fund whose sensitivity to interest-rate movements matches your tolerance for risk.

First, check the fund's average weighted maturity with the fund's telephone representative. Conservative investors interested in earning high yields but avoiding hits to principal should stick to no-load funds that usually keep their average maturity between five and seven years. If you want a better shot at capital gains, and are willing to take slightly more risk, opt for funds that have average maturities of 10 or so years.

Investors hunting for big capital-gains, however, are better off to bypass funds and buy long-term Treasury bonds through their brokers or directly from the Federal Reserve, which charges no commission. The problem is that many long-term government funds invest up to 85% of their portfolios in mortgage-backed securities issued by the Government National Mortgage Association (nicknamed Ginnie Mae) and other agencies. These issues add to the fund's current yield but limit potential capital gains. Reason: When rates drop, homeowners often refinance their mortgages. This results in early repayment of mortgage-backed securities, which robs investors of capital gains. There is one drawback to buying individual Treasuries: While a bond fund lets you reinvest your interest, however small, in additional fund shares, Treasury bonds are sold in $1,000 minimums. At yields of between 8.1% and 8.8%, then, it would take roughly $11,000 in Treasury bonds to throw off enough interest to buy another $1,000 bond each year.

Municipals. Individuals' voracious appetite for tax-free income has inflated prices of muni bonds, which are usually sold in $5,000 denominations, and kept their yields from rising in tandem with those of Treasury bonds (see "Investing in Municipal Bonds," page 42). Even though munis' rate advantage over taxables has slipped, investors can still get an edge by going to funds that invest in tax-exempt bonds with maturities of 15 years or longer. High-quality, 10-year munis recently yielded around 6.6%, equivalent to a 9.2% taxable yield for a married couple in the 28% tax bracket—joint 1989 taxable income of $30,950 to $74,850. That is about one percentage point higher than taxable issues with comparable maturities.

For investors looking for top tax-equivalent yields, some advisers suggest long-term, high-yield muni funds, which recently paid at least a half a percentage point more than their high-grade counterparts. Unlike high-yield corporate bonds (a.k.a. junk bonds), the credit quality of many high-yield muni funds is quite high because managers often keep 85% or more of their portfolio in investment-grade bonds. A spike in interest rates, of course, would zap the value of long-term funds. If you are inclined to bail out during such a free-fall, opt instead for the lower yields and greater security of intermediate-term funds.

If you live in a high-tax state, such as New York or California, you can grab an effective half-percentage point of extra yield by investing in a fund that buys only bonds of your state. One caveat: Restricting your portfolio to one state increases your credit risk. In addition, if you live in a state with a puny supply of munis—Ohio or Minnesota, for example—high demand can depress yields.

High-grade corporates. Investment grade corporate bonds, typically sold in $1,000 denominations, are those issued by companies sound enough to earn a BBB rating or higher from

High-Gimmick Yields

In today's fierce competition for investors' dollars, many financial institutions are using misleading ads and gimmicks to puff up the yields they claim and disguise the true risks involved. To avoid a wipeout when riding for awesome income, watch out for these common ploys:

Teaser CDs. Some banks and savings and loans promote certificates of deposit paying teaser rates—initial yields as high as 20% that expire within a few weeks. For example, in 1989, Am-South Bank of Alabama offered a three-year CD with a 19.89% teaser rate; after 30 days it declined to 8.35%. The combined rates return only $260.12 on a $1,000 investment, compared with $304.09 that an investor could earn on a three-year CD paying a fixed rate of 9.25%. Other teaser CDs switch to variable rates after a short time, making it impossible to predict their actual return. But it is likely to be lower than the initial rate—and also lower than that of fixed-rate CDs of similar maturity. A better buy is six-month, fixed-rate CDs, which recently yielded as much as 9.2%. When the CDs mature, investors can reinvest the money in new six-month certificates—or switch to longer-term certificates if yields seem likely to fall.

Phantom yields. A number of institutions quote annual yields on three- and six-month CDs without disclosing that the yields are strictly hypothetical. Reason: There is no guarantee you will be able to reinvest at an equally attractive rate for the rest of the year when the CD matures.

In 1989, Massachusetts state regulators cited six savings institutions in the Boston area for an even worse variant of this practice—showing compound annual yields for CDs that pay simple interest. The culprits included Bank of New England, which advertised a 9.58% compound yield on a three-month CD along with its actual 9.25% simple interest rate.

Tiered rates. Many institutions advertise high yields on savings accounts and other investments, but you have to deposit big bucks to earn them. For example, First Federal Savings & Loan of Rochester, New York advertised an 8.5% yield on a savings account, compared with an average yield of 6.42% for similar accounts at other banks, but paid that high rate only on deposits of $25,000 or more. Small savers who deposited less than $10,000 earned a piddling interest rate of 5.25%.

Pseudo-CDs. Consumer lending companies, banks, and S&Ls sell certificates yielding up to 13% that resemble bank CDs but actually are nothing more than IOUs. While the government guarantees deposits of up to $100,000 at federally insured banks and thrifts, pseudo-CDs have no federal protection.

Waived fund fees. About 20% of the 540 or so money-market funds available to investors waive all or part of their annual management fees to boost yields. But, typically, when such a fund's high yield has lured enough investors, management increases fees and the yield may decline by as much as three-quarters of a percentage point.

Excessive distribution rates. The SEC issued regulations in 1988 that prevent income funds from advertising yields inflated by options trading and other speculative activities. But some government bond funds—which often carry names like "Government Plus" or "Government High-Income"—still quote unusually high "distribution rates" in sales literature. Some of these funds sell call options on the bonds in their portfolio and pay out the profits to shareholders. But that options strategy reduces the funds' potential for capital appreciation. Worse, high distributions may eat up gains that a fund could use to offset losses in its portfolio. Result: Over time, the fund's share value may fall as such losses accumulate.

Standard & Poor's. But in an era of merger-mania, the term high-grade corporates is rapidly becoming an oxymoron. The mountain of debt heaped onto a company to finance a takeover can turn investment-grade bonds into junk faster than you can say leveraged buyout. Standard & Poor's lowered its ratings on 284 issues in 1987 and a record 386 in 1988, representing $356 billion in debt for the two years. Then, too, corporate bonds lately were yielding only from one-half to one percentage point more than lower-risk Treasury bonds. As a result, analysts recommend that most investors shun high-grade corporates and opt instead for the safer returns found in U.S. Treasuries.

Junk bonds. In 1988, daredevils who seized the ultra-high yields in corporate bonds rated below BBB by Standard & Poor's came away winners. Funds that invest in such junk bonds topped all other fixed-income funds with a 12.4% total return, compared with 11.3% for second-place, high-yield munis. But the craze for leveraged buy-outs financed by a more default-prone strain of high-yield debt ended in September 1989, when junk bond prices plunged on news that some bigger issuers were on the verge of bankruptcy. In a recession, according to estimates from Standard & Poor's, $15 billion of the roughly $186 billion in junk bonds outstanding could default—more than three times the volume of defaults in 1988. So, many strategists suggest that investors avoid junk altogether until after the next recession hits.

Closed-end bond funds. Hybrid closed-end funds hold securities like conventional mutual funds do, but trade on an exchange like stocks. Shares are issued to the public through brokers at the fund's initial public offering, or IPO. After that, you buy shares at the current market price—which, depending on investor demand, may be higher or lower than the fund's underlying net asset value.

Be wary if a broker calls touting the IPO of a new closed-end bond fund. For each $1,000 you invest, $70 is usually siphoned off in underwriting fees—which means you are, in effect, paying $1,000 for $930 worth of bonds. Instead, look for a closed-end fund that already trades on an exchange and is currently selling at a discount to its net asset value. As with an open-end fund, turn to the fund's prospectus and annual report to assess the overall riskiness of the fund by examining the credit quality and average weighted maturity of its portfolio. And steer clear of *leveraged* closed-end bond funds that tout tantalizing yields by borrowing at short-term rates and investing the proceeds in long-term bonds. This strategy can backfire when short-term rates rise above those on long-term bonds, as they did in 1989. Rising rates can also trigger defaults in leveraged corporate-bond funds, which will magnify losses of principal.

Zero-coupon bonds. These issues sell at a deep discount to face value rather than pay interest regularly and are redeemed for face value at maturity. As a result, zeros make sense for two opposite types of investors: risk-takers seeking hefty gains and conservative savers hoping to lock in a given rate of return.

If you are convinced that interest rates are at or near a peak and are poised to slide, then 10- to 30-year, zero-coupon Treasuries are your best bet for spectacular capital appreciation. The price of a zero is more volatile than that of a conventional bond because all interest is paid in a lump sum at maturity. For instance, if interest rates drop two percentage points, the price of a 30-year zero yielding 9.1% will jump 78%. On the other hand, if interest rates rise two percentage points, you will get mauled with a 45% loss.

If you must be sure your investments will grow to a specific sum at some future date, like retirement, zeros are tailormade for you. The only drawback: Even though you receive no income until your zero matures, you are taxed as if you were paid interest each year. Thus, unless you plan to sell your zeros as soon as possible for capital gains, invest in taxable zeros only in a tax-exempt account, such as an Individual Retirement Account or Keogh. Or you can avoid the tax complications altogether by investing in tax-exempt, municipal zeros. There are no zero muni funds, so you must buy the actual bonds.

At last count, only two investment companies offered taxable, zero-coupon bond funds: Scudder Stevens & Clark and Benham Management. But if you intend to hold the zeros more than a few years, buy individual bonds instead of the funds. Reason: The longer you hold, the better off you will be because you won't get hit with the fund's expense ratio year after year.

Investing in Municipal Bonds

Skill is required to lock in the superior returns of tax-exempt issues.

When interest rates seemed to peak in spring 1989, many conservative investors began a headlong rush toward accepted highest, safest yields. The most daring were hoping for capital gains because the prices of all bonds rise when rates fall. Less aggressive investors simply wanted to lock in high income for years to come. For income investors in the 28% federal tax bracket or higher—1989 income of $30,950 or more for couples filing jointly, $18,550 for singles—one solution was municipal bonds. They frequently offer such investors the most generous after-tax yields of any reasonably safe, fixed-income investment. In midyear 1989, for example, a 10-year top-grade municipal yielded 6.6%, the equivalent of a 9.2% taxable yield to someone in the 28% tax bracket and 9.9% in the 33% bracket. By contrast, 10-year Treasury bonds yielded only 8.7%.

State and local governments issue munis to finance such public projects as highways, airports, and hospitals. The interest from most munis is exempt from federal tax. Better yet, if a bond was issued in the state in which you live, its income is usually free of state and local taxes as well. But investors entering the muni market for the first time may find it full of obstacles and pitfalls. For starters, you usually need at least $5,000 to buy individual munis at face value. If you have less, you will have to invest in a municipal bond fund or a unit trust—a fixed portfolio of bonds whose units are sold by brokers for as little as $1,000.

Moreover, you cannot always sell a bond quickly and at the price you want. Reasons: There's no exchange where munis are instantaneously bought and sold; each transaction must be negotiated by brokers over the telephone; and trading costs are hefty, ranging from 0.5% to 5% of your investment, depending on the size of the transaction, maturity of the bond, and greed of the broker.

As a result of these drawbacks, individual investors are usually advised to invest in munis with the idea of holding them until maturity. This is not always possible, however. Muni issuers commonly reserve the right to call in the bonds for early redemption if interest rates drop. Bonds usually become callable 10 years after the issue date, but some issues carry extraordinary call provisions, allowing issuers to redeem them at any time if rates fall far enough. If your bond is called, you may have to reinvest your money at a lower rate. To avoid unpleasant surprises, don't buy a bond unless you know when it might be called.

Like all bonds, munis are rated for safety against default by Moody's and Standard & Poor's. Because of a relative scarcity of munis in recent years, the yield advantage of an A-rated bond over a top-quality triple A was recently the lowest in nearly 20 years. What follows are the main categories of munis, ranked in descending order of security of principal, and their midyear 1989 yields on 10-year issues:

Pre-refunded bonds. The issuers of these bonds back them with escrow accounts of U.S. Treasuries, which are the most secure of all bonds. Yield: 7% for Aaa.

General-obligation bonds. They are very safe because the bonds are repaid from taxes. Yields: 6.7% for Aaa, 6.8% for Aa.

Revenue bonds. These issues are repaid with income from the highways or other facilities built with the bond proceeds. Yield: 6.9% for Aa.

Bonds secured by third parties. These munis finance facilities or equipment—pollution controls, for example—to be leased to a company. The bonds are backed only by the company's credit. Yield: 7.1% for Aa.

Once you have identified the type of bond you want, you will have to ask a broker to suggest specific issues and to quote yields. Even if you already have a trustworthy stockbroker, he or she may not be qualified to handle your muni trades. To find one who is, call the office managers of three or four full-service brokerage firms—discounters don't have muni research departments—and request the names of brokers experienced in munis. Or call a firm specializing in tax-exempts. Next, interview each broker, asking the following questions:

Do you regularly buy and sell blocks of fewer than 100 bonds? Some brokers aren't interested in selling so-called odd lots.

How many new issues did your firm underwrite last year? You will pay lower transaction costs on new issues than on bonds traded in the secondary market. So you want to know whether new issues are often available. Also ask about the firm's inventory of previously issued bonds—the larger it is, the greater your choices.

What spread will I pay on trades of the size that I'll be making? Brokers don't charge commissions on bond trades as they do with stocks. Rather, their profit—known as the spread—is built into the price of the bond. Spreads are quoted in basis points, which are hundredths of a percentage point. Each point of the spread increases the cost of a bond by 0.01% and shaves 0.01% from your yield. The longer the maturity and the smaller the trade, the wider the spread. On a $5,000 trade of five-year bonds, look for a spread of about 2.5 points, or $125.

All other things being equal, you should choose the broker charging the lowest spread for the bonds you want and figure on using him or her for subsequent trades. Shopping around among brokers each time you want to buy or sell isn't really practical. You aren't going to get the service you need if you call to get quotations from brokers who never know whether they're going to get your business.

Should You Seek Tax-Free Yields?

Here's how to calculate the yield you would need on a taxable bond, money fund, or other investment to match available tax-free returns.

1. Tax-free yield		_____ %
2. Your tax bracket		_____ %
3. 1 minus your tax rate (for example, in the 28% bracket, subtract 0.28 from 1 to get 0.72)		_____
4. Equivalent taxable yield (divide line 1 by line 3)		_____ %

Organizing an Investment Club

A team approach can make serious investing less tedious and more rewarding.

The premise of an investment club is disarmingly simple. A group of investors pool their money—usually starting with stakes as little as $30 each month—then meet regularly to decide how to invest it. The financial rewards also can be impressive, judging by the long-term record of clubs that belong to the National Association of Investors Corporation, a nonprofit organization that represents nearly 7,000 clubs nationwide. In almost every year since the mid-1960s, 50% or more of these clubs have beaten or equaled the annual return of Standard & Poor's 500-stock index.

But the benefits of belonging to an investment club go beyond the potential appreciation of the group's collective holdings. For novices, the clubs are an ideal way to gain valuable investing experience without risking a lot of money. For the more sophisticated, the club's group discussions often generate profitable leads for their personal portfolios. And since most clubs leaven their number-crunching analysis with group dinners and other recreational outings, members can broaden their network of business and social contacts.

Consider the BHILL investment club in Milwaukee (named after a *Forbes* magazine article on investing titled "Bargain Hunting in Loaded Laggards"). The club has used profits from its $175,000 portfolio to fund group outings to Scottsdale, Arizona, Palm Springs, Mexico, and Jamaica. Says club founder Don Stockhausen, a professional money manager: "We think of the trips as one of the dividends on our investments."

Similarly, the 30 women professionals of the Washington Fringe Benefit club hold a slightly tongue-in-chic annual fete, the Hats & Gloves Luncheon, where white gloves and fancy chapeaux are de rigueur. Though club members look more like socialites than seasoned investors at this affair, their strategy of investing in local companies has produced an average annual return of roughly 16% since 1981, beating the S&P by two percentage points a year over this period. Still, says Candice Hooper, the club's founder and a vice president at Enserch, a large energy and engineering firm, "The friendship and the personal support we've given each other mean more to us than any money we've made."

Before you start planning festivities for your club, however, you must get properly organized. Here's a rundown on what you need to know:

Setting up the club. Your first move should be to get in touch with the National Association of Investors (1515 East 11 Mile Road, Royal Oak, MI 48067; $30 a year plus $8 for each member). NAIC can help you with mundane but pivotal organizational details, such as filing for the federal tax identification number needed to open a brokerage account, structuring a legal partnership, and setting up a record-keeping system that is flexible enough to handle contributions and withdrawals of varying sizes. You will find a step-by-step guide to setting up a club in NAIC's *Investors Manual*, which costs members $5 and is available to nonmembers for $14.

Though all partnerships are technically required to file a tax return each year, NAIC can explain how to get an exemption so that your club can avoid the annual drudgery. Of course, you must still report on your individual return your share of the club's dividend and interest payments, as well as any capital gains or losses from the sale of securities. You may also be able to deduct a portion of club expenses, such as payments for subscriptions to investment publications and rent for meeting rooms—but only to the extent that your share of the costs plus other miscellaneous business expenses exceed 2% of your adjusted gross income.

Aim to keep the size of your club to 15 to 20 members, advises the NAIC. Smaller groups have trouble generating enough capital to build a diversified portfolio, while larger groups often don't last long. Indeed, as many as half of all clubs fold within 18 months of being formed.

Choosing a broker. If members do their own research and the club invests in 100-share lots, it usually pays to go with a discount broker. But since some full-service firms' maximum commission on small transactions is less expensive than a discounter's fee, a club that buys in small amounts of $200 to $400 a month may actually save money by dealing with a full-service broker. For example, to buy 10 shares of a $20 stock, Charles Schwab charges its minimum commission of $39. Dean Witter's maximum charge for such a small transaction, however, is 10% of the amount of the trade, or $20. Full-service brokers may also discount their fees for investment clubs. The motivation is not altruism but the broker's desire to sign up individual club members as clients. The take on such so-called radiation business can be substantial. The average NAIC member's personal investment holdings are worth some $119,000—compared with just $57,000 for the average club's portfolio.

Full-service brokers can genuinely help clubs by providing their firms' recommended stock list and analyst reports on stocks. But members should be wary of relying too heavily on professional advice. After all, the main purpose of the club is for members to learn how to pick profitable stocks themselves. Moreover, a close relationship with a broker may invite scrutiny from state securities regulators. If it appears that the broker, rather than club members, is making the investment decisions, the group could forfeit its exemption from securities laws that govern mutual funds and other professionally managed investment pools. For example, the Tampa Bay Investment Club, a 110-member group for singles, was investigated in 1989 by the Florida Division of Securities, at least in part because of its dealings with stockbroker John Miller. The authorities are concerned that Miller, who helped found the club and serves as its financial adviser, improperly used his relationship with the group to drum up business. Miller says he has collected 300 or more clients from his association with the club and sold them an estimated $1.5 million in annuities.

Remember, too, that the broker's interest in generating commissions could undermine the club's goal of making gains with the lowest possible transaction costs. Since the commissions involved in frequent trading can easily wipe out profits, clubs should be especially wary of brokers who are happiest when the club is constantly buying and selling.

Your club may be able to dispense with some brokerage commissions altogether if it plans to invest in any of the 40 or so major companies enrolled in NAIC's Low-Cost Investment Plan. Under this program, clubs can buy as little as one share directly from a corporation, such as McDonald's, Colgate-Palmolive, and Quaker Oats, for a one-time charge of $5 per firm. Most of these companies do not charge a commission for buying or selling, although a few impose a nominal fee of roughly $3 for each transaction to cover administrative costs. The majority of firms also allow dividends to be reinvested in additional shares at no charge.

Devising an investment strategy. For most clubs, the quirky names and occasional partying belie a deadly sober attitude toward investing. According to NAIC, the most successful groups adhere to four basic principles: they invest regularly without trying to guess where the market is headed; stay fully invested and reinvest all dividends and interest; diversify across industries and in at least 12 issues; and focus on companies whose earnings and sales are growing faster than the overall economy.

In practice, clubs' strategies are as diverse as the groups themselves. BHILL seeks out undervalued stocks that are shunned by other investors. Other clubs home in on local companies that members can follow firsthand every day. Fringe Benefit bought the stock of Woodward & Lothrop, a local retailer, because club members learned that a new subway stop was planned beneath one of its department stores. Members' work experience can lead to winning picks, too. On the endorsement of a member who sells Disney products, a 14-woman club in Honolulu named LIPS (ladies investing and perhaps speculating) bought Walt Disney at $50 a share in November 1987. In October 1989, the stock was about $134.

Are REITs Right for You?

Real estate investment trusts offer enticing yields and plenty of potential for long-term gains.

While the once-sizzling market for single-family houses may be cooling, real estate experts say there is still plenty of profit potential in commercial properties. But how can anyone who doesn't have a big bankroll invest in office buildings and shopping malls? One answer is to form a partnership with friends and relatives. Another is to invest in real estate investment trusts. These companies, whose shares trade on stock exchanges, pool investor cash to buy properties or make real estate loans.

The opportunities in commercial real estate have as a foundation the tax law changes of 1986. Before then, tax breaks attracted a flood of investor cash to real estate. When those tax breaks dried up, so did new construction in many areas. With supply shrinking, most analysts expect both rents and values for existing properties to rise. As a result, carefully selected REITs could produce compound total returns of 15% to 20% annually over the next five to seven years. (Total return takes into account both income and capital appreciation.)

While increasing property values will eventually translate into higher REIT prices, holders of these securities receive a substantial portion of their return in the form of high current yield. Equity REITs, which own property, yielded an average of 8.3% in midyear 1989. Mortgage REITs, which make loans, yielded 11.8%. By comparison, 10-year Treasuries yielded 9%, and Standard & Poor's 500-stock index had a payout of 3.6%.

Yield is an important component of the total return from REITs because they are required by law to pass through 95% of the income they generate to shareholders in dividends. Often, a portion of the yield is a return of the investor's capital. This portion reflects what the REITs accountants have written off as depreciation—the wear and tear on the assets that the REIT owns—and is free of current income tax. When you sell your REIT, however, the total of such payouts of your principal must be subtracted from your original purchase price, increasing your taxable capital gain.

There are three types of REITs, and the

source of the cash a REIT distributes to shareholders depends on which type it is. Equity REIT dividends include rental income and capital gains from the sale of properties, while a mortgage REIT's income comes from interest payments. A hybrid REIT combines income from mortgages and equity holdings. Yields can fluctuate considerably as profits change with economic conditions. Thus, REITs are not suitable for investors seeking steady income.

Equity REITs are clearly the superior performers over the long term, according to one recent study. A $1,000 investment in the average equity REIT in 1972 would have grown to $7,946 in 1988 if dividends were reinvested, compared with only $1,094 for a mortgage REIT and $2,717 for a hybrid. If, however, you believe that interest rates will move down, you might consider mortgage REITs as a speculative investment. All REITs, like bonds, rise in value when interest rates fall, as investors flock to high-yielding securities. But because they are highly leveraged, mortgage REITs react much more dramatically to interest-rate movements than do equity REITs.

For example, as interest rates declined from 15.8% in 1981 to 11.5% in 1982, mortgage REITs climbed on average 44.6%, compared with equity REITs' 20.4% gain. But mortgage REITs can suffer especially sharp losses when interest rates rise. In 1974, rates rose two points before recession hit, forcing some loans held by mortgage REITs into default. Such REITs lost on average 67% in value, while equity REITs lost 22%.

Many REITs focus on properties in specific geographic areas. As a result, REITs in booming regions can vastly outperform those in depressed areas and even those whose holdings are scattered across the country. To avoid putting all your cash to work in the next Houston, diversify by buying several REITs whose properties are concentrated in different regions. Parts of the country that real estate analysts say have the best outlook include Southern California, the gateway to the expanding economies of the Pacific Basin, and the area within 200 miles of Washington, D.C., where government-related employment keeps the economy strong.

The information you need to assess a REIT can be found in its current and past annual reports. *Value Line Investment Survey* and Standard & Poor's stock report, available in most large libraries, also provide key data. In evaluating equity REITs, consider the following:

Track record. Avoid any REIT that is not at least three years old. Past performance is your best tool for assessing management's ability to select and profitably lease properties.

Dividend growth. Since dividends constitute the bulk of your return, a pattern of increases is vital. Look for dividend growth of at least 10% annually.

Cash flow. To sustain dividend growth, a REIT needs consistently growing cash flow. Calculate the REIT's cash flow per share for the past three years by adding depreciation to net income before capital gains. Divide this sum by the number of shares outstanding. Beware if the REIT's annual dividend per share is higher than its cash flow per share. The dividend may be coming out of borrowings or one-time gains on property sales.

Leverage. The less debt a REIT carries, the safer it is and the greater its ability to take advantage of falling rates by borrowing to expand its portfolio. Favor REITs with total debt that is less than 50% of market value (the share price multiplied by the number of shares outstanding).

Fees. Total management fees and other charges should not exceed 1% of gross assets a year. To minimize fees, choose REITs that are identified in the annual report as self-administered, meaning their property managers are employed by the trust. Outside advisers, who add another layer of costs, are typically used in finite REITs—those designed to sell all of their properties at a specified future date. Finite REITs should generally be avoided; they tend to underperform other REITs because they cannot achieve growth by expanding their portfolios.

Tax-Saving Strategies

The tax battle that begins every January only *seems* hopeless. You fighting the dreaded Internal Revenue Service. You standing up to that nemesis known as the 1040. You trying to keep up with hundreds of pieces of information. Do not despair. What follows are three key steps that should help you win the battle and cut your taxes in April more intelligently than ever before:

Overcome your fear of filing. The IRS has carefully cultivated this anxiety. The service reasons that if it can scare you deeply enough, you will be a more forthcoming taxpayer. It is no coincidence that as April approaches each year, there are more and more press stories about famous people being caught cheating on their taxes. In addition, the tax law can be numbingly complicated. If you have any special situations in your tax profile—a rental property, passive losses or gains, even the sale of mutual fund shares—you stand a great chance of making a costly mistake either for or against yourself. What you don't know can hurt you.

Decide whether to do your return or hire a preparer. The complexity of your return—not the amount you earn—determines whether you should do your own taxes. You could be a Wall Street broker making $300,000 a year, but it's all accounted for on your W-2. All your business expenses are reimbursed by your company. You give $5,000 to charity and have an interest deduction on a mortgage. Even if you do make all that money, you may not need a preparer. On the other hand, your brother-in-law could be earning $50,000 a year but be self-employed in the consulting business—lots of Schedule C deductions—deriving income from a rental property, and using his car for business purposes. Although he has only a sixth of your income, he probably needs to consult a tax professional.

Take control of your tax life. If you decide to do your return yourself, you will get valuable help from "Developing a Year-Round Tax Plan" below. If you decide that the task is beyond you, don't just toss all your bankbooks, receipts, 1099s, and other records into a box and hand it to a pro. Instead, first read "Getting Professional Help" on page 52 and "Working With Your Tax Preparer" on page 54. Then, push your professional to be aggressive, to interpret the law on your behalf, and give you the benefit of any doubt. Seizing command of your tax campaign demands adherence to the first law of using a tax preparer: Yours is only as good as you force him or her to be. You don't need a graduate degree in taxation. But you do need to ask the right questions, many of which are discussed in this chapter.

Developing a Year-Round Plan

Get in the habit of trimming taxes from January through December.

After tax day (April 16 in 1990), the temptation is overpowering to rid your mind of all thoughts of taxes. Don't do it. The only way to ensure happiness at the next tax-filing deadline is to take action throughout the year to fend off the Internal Revenue Service. That means learning to distinguish tax preparation from tax planning.

Tax preparation is the distasteful task of filling out your federal and state income tax returns. By the time you or your tax preparer start doing it, there is very little you can do to reduce your tax liability. By contrast, tax planning is a year-round effort to lower your tax bill, which may well be your biggest regular expense. The process consists of keeping tax records (see "Tax Information You Need to Collect" on page 61); staying abreast of ever-changing rules and terminology; remembering to consider how investing, borrowing, and other financial moves will affect your IRS bill; and looking for shrewd ways to lower your tax liability. All that self-defense work from January through December can shave as much as $1,000 off a typical family's tax bill.

In operating as your own tax planner extraordinaire, it will help to divide the calendar into three periods:

January through April

These are the months to plot your overall strategy for the year. If you anticipate earning much more than usual, start looking for new, tax-deductible expenses that can help cut your tax bill. For example, if you have a home office, buy any needed equipment or supplies.

You can also open and contribute to an Individual Retirement Account for the previous year, assuming you had employment income that year. The maximum contribution is $2,000 ($4,000 for working married couples and $2,250 for married couples with one breadwinner). Your earnings on the investment will grow tax deferred until they are withdrawn. The deductibility of your IRA contribution depends on your income and whether you are covered by a pension at work. If you are self-employed and opened a Keogh retirement account before December 31, you have until tax-filing time to contribute money to this account, too. (For the precise rules about IRAs and Keoghs, see page 164.)

May through July

After filing your tax return, you'll know whether a big refund is due. If so, your next step should be to adjust your W-4 withholding form at work so that less money is taken out of your pay for taxes during the year. This way, you—not the IRS—will write the check next year. In the meantime, you can earn interest on money that otherwise would be an interest-free loan to the IRS.

Slashing your withholding by too much, however, could leave you vulnerable to penalties and fines. You can avoid these charges by having your employer withhold at least as much as your previous year's tax liability. Keep in mind that every additional allowance you claim on your W-4 form will increase your take-home pay. Self-employed people not subject to withholding should initially determine their quarterly estimated payments by dividing last year's tax bill by four. If you expect your income to drop substantially, reduce your withholding accordingly. Just be sure to pay in at least 90% of your total liability for the year so you won't owe a penalty.

In June or July, give your taxes a mid-year review. By then, your income forecast for the year should be based on more than a hunch. Pull out your previous year's tax return and plug in what you think will be the figures for the current year. This will provide a rough idea of your next tax bill and remind you of tax breaks that you may still be able to use.

October through December

As the year comes to a close, take one last shot at finding tax-deductible expenses. For example, this is the time to determine whether you have spent enough on miscellaneous and medical expenses to exceed the thresholds for writing them off. Deductible miscellaneous expenses are those that exceed 2% of your adjusted gross income; deductible medical expenses are those above 7.5%. If you're not even close to those cutoffs, try to postpone paying more money for those expenses until next year, when you might be able to deduct them. But if you're just a bit shy of the thresholds, hunt for additional expenses that will help you jump the hurdles.

The final days of the year also offer opportunities to buy or sell investments to lower your present and future tax bills. For instance, employees of companies that offer tax-deferred savings plans should be sure to sign up for the accounts when their benefits department sends around application forms in November or December. If you are ready to give up hope on a mutual fund that has fallen in value, sell the shares for a tax-deductible loss. If you anticipate child-care or medical expenses in the following year, see if your company offers flexible spending accounts. These let you finance the expenses with pretax earnings.

Other smart tax-planning tactics should be taken all year round:

Become a pack rat. In a tax audit, if you cannot document an expense you deducted, you may lose the write-off. So get in the habit of holding on to relevant receipts, statements, and canceled checks. Medical expenses that may qualify for deductibility include health insurance premiums, prescriptions, and fees to doctors and psychotherapists. Among the canceled checks and statements you should save to document miscellaneous deductions are fees to financial planners and tax advisers, any subscriptions to trade and professional journals, costs related to looking for another job in your current profession, and safe-deposit-box rental fees.

Give to charity. You can write off charitable contributions if you itemize deductions on Schedule A of your tax return. Besides cash donations, you can deduct the fair market value of investments, clothing, furniture, and artwork that you give to charities. Keep a log of trips you make to perform volunteer work. You can deduct those travel expenses at the rate of 12¢ a mile.

Trade investments shrewdly. Before unloading part of your holdings in a particular stock, bond, or mutual fund, check the prices you originally paid for the securities. Then, tell your stockbroker or the mutual fund transfer agent to sell the block or blocks that cost you the most. This way, you will owe taxes on the smallest possible capital gain or you'll be able to claim the largest possible tax-deductible loss.

Ask for a sales receipt identifying the securities that were sold by their purchase date.

Reorganize your debts. Paying off your plastic should be an urgent priority now that you can deduct only 20% of the interest on credit cards and personal loans in tax year 1989 (10% in 1990 and zero after that). If you own your residence and must borrow for a major expense such as college or home improvements, consider taking out a home-equity loan rather than a personal loan. All of the interest is deductible on home loans of up to $100,000. In contrast to the limits on the deductibility of consumer interest, all business-loan interest can be written off. Loans taken out for investments are deductible up to your annual investment earnings plus $2,000.

Those varying interest rules make it crucial to maintain in separate accounts loans intended for different purposes. Otherwise, if you commingle business, investment, and consumer loans, you could easily miss out on a deduction.

Getting Professional Help

High prices don't always mean you're getting the best service.

It is fairly easy to find someone to fill out your tax return. Your Yellow Pages probably lists dozens of tax practitioners. But picking a preparer who will do your taxes properly at a price you can afford can be a major project. The best tax professionals tend to be the busiest, so you should start looking now. There are three sources worth considering:

Tax preparation chains. You may find good value in H&R Block's Executive Tax Service,

which is designed for people with incomes of $40,000 or more. This by-appointment-only service is not available at Block's 7,462 storefront outlets. Rather, Executive Tax Services has its own offices in more than a hundred cities nationwide. It also charges double what you'd pay at a regular Block office—about $160 for a typical return for a family with $60,000 in salary, a modest portfolio of securities and some rental income. Unlike Block's storefront customers, Executive Tax Service clients are interviewed in private by a preparer to whom they are assigned year after year. Although planning is not offered, clients receive a quarterly newsletter on tax rule changes. As with any Block preparer, those employed by the Executive Tax Service will accompany you, free of charge, in the event of an audit. While technically preparers are not allowed to speak for clients, in fact, they often know the auditors and may be permitted to make your case.

The quality of return preparation is the same or better at Executive Tax Service as at Block's regular outlets; in both cases, employees are well-trained, according to a *Money* study. Thus, if you are unwilling to pay a premium for hand-holding and a continuing relationship with your preparer, a regular Block storefront or an outlet of one of the lesser-known chains modeled on Block might be the answer. Block's nearest competitor is Jackson Hewitt, which has some 300 offices across the country.

Enrolled agents. To qualify as one of these government-approved tax experts, a person either has to have worked for the IRS as an auditor (or in a job with equivalent responsibility for at least five continuous years) or to have passed the agency's strenuous two-day test on federal taxation. To maintain accreditation, the nation's 25,000 enrolled agents usually must spend 24 hours a year in college-level, continuing-education courses.

Generally less expensive than C.P.A.s, enrolled agents charge hourly rates of $40 to $150. That would translate into $200 to $380 for the typical return of a $60,000-a-year family with stocks, bonds, and rental income. In addition to preparing returns, enrolled agents will provide tax advice and are authorized to represent clients at IRS audits. Names of practitioners near you can be had by calling the National Association of Enrolled Agents' 24-hour referral service (800-424-4339).

Certified public accountants. These professionals—there are roughly 373,000 nationwide—must have college degrees, pass a four-part national exam in accounting

practices, and take annual college-level refresher courses. Certification requirements vary from state to state, however.

Make sure that the C.P.A. you're considering is enrolled in continuing-education programs that deal with individual tax returns and not corporate taxes. Reason: At large accounting firms whose main business is corporate clients, your return is likely to get bumped down to a junior employee for processing. As a rule, the bigger the C.P.A.'s firm, the more you pay.

An accountant at a small firm or in private practice is likely to charge $250 to $500 for the hypothetical $60,000-a-year family's return. Or for $800 to $1,000 a year, that same client might also be entitled to a face-to-face strategy session as well as twice-annual phone consultations. At one of the so-called Big Eight national firms, fees could be as much as 50% higher. Another important service C.P.A.s offer is that they can represent you at an IRS tax audit.

What about financial planners or tax attorneys? Though some planners may do returns for clients, tax preparation usually is not their strength. And most tax lawyers are expensive and don't routinely prepare returns. They are best used to resolve questions about divorce settlements, estate matters, or other complicated tax-planning issues.

Whatever type of preparer you target, make sure the one you choose has been in business at least four years. Most practitioners will agree to an initial free consultation, which should give you a chance to size them up and inquire about fees.

If a practitioner quotes a flat fee, find out what, if anything, is included beyond return preparation. If he or she charges by the hour, get an estimate of the total bill.

Also, be sure to ask how many 1040s the practitioner prepares annually. For how many clients did he or she seek an extension last year? Few preparers can expertly handle more than 300 returns a year unassisted. And any preparer in a strong practice should not file extensions for more than 10% to 15% of clients. Practitioners who file for more may be stretching themselves too thin.

Working with Your Tax Preparer

Here's how to get the services—and savings—that you deserve.

Once you hire a tax preparer, do not succumb to the temptation to put your tax life in his or her capable hands and relax. Seasoned tax experts contend that top-notch preparers should be able to save you at least 1½ times their fees over two or three years. But to get that result you have to become involved in the process. That means working with your tax professional and, in a sense, taking charge of the relationship.

Such a strategy calls for a modicum of work and a soupçon of gutsiness. Do not embark upon it if you are one of those taxpayers with no patience for the unruly discipline of tax preparation or if you lose sleep over the idea of being even a little aggressive in claiming write-offs. Nor is it appropriate if your returns are so uncomplicated that you know you can get excellent results paying $50 to a large storefront tax service. But if you are paying several hundred dollars or more to a preparer, your situation is complicated enough to warrant some effort on your part.

You start with a phone call. Whether you are dealing with a new tax preparer or someone who has been doing your returns for years, schedule an exploratory meeting as early in January as possible. Prepare for this crucial session by going over your past two or three tax returns to remind yourself which deductions you have been taking and by putting together whatever current records you have. At the meeting, you can follow up by asking the pro what additional deductions he or she thinks you can take. Thumb through

tax articles in *Money* or sections of a tax manual such as *The Arthur Young Tax Guide* (Ballantine, $12.95) to find possible write-offs or other tactics to suggest. When dealing with a busy tax pro, even a modest show of knowledge in what he or she may see as a sea of client apathy and ignorance could inspire special attention.

Tell the preparer that you expect to take an active role in getting the best tax deal you can. If the preparer seems uncomfortable with that idea, it may be a signal that you have chosen the wrong person. But chances are you should hang on until you have been through the filing of one year's return. Only then will you have a clear idea of how the relationship is working.

Your next revelation is critical. Tell your tax pro that while you do not want to be reckless, you do want all the deductions you have coming even if the IRS may argue about them later. The rationale: Accountants may assume that clients whose returns prompt IRS audits will be so angry and upset that they will start looking for a new preparer. As a result, many will simply pass over a deduction when they feel the IRS might question it.

Your preparer obviously knows more tax law than you ever will. But if you suspect that he or she is being unduly cautious, confront this wimp factor head-on. If you believe you are entitled to a write-off, however risky, arm yourself with a tax manual and other supporting documents and challenge your preparer. The key dialogue with your tax preparer will be about gray areas in which IRS or tax court

What You and Your Tax Preparer Owe Each Other

In dealing with a tax preparer, you have a right to expect certain things, including:

Straight talk about fees. In your initial interview, an accountant or enrolled agent should spell out how his or her charges are calculated.

Ready access. Calls should be answered promptly in or out of tax season. At a large firm, you ought to be able to confer with a partner who supervises preparation of your returns if the work is done by subordinates.

Clear explanations. Your preparer should make clear everything that he or she is doing on your return and fully explain all deductions and other items. If your preparer enters a gray area that may trigger an audit—for example, taking a deduction that might be challenged—he or she should make sure you are in agreement.

Education. After you have spent a few years with a tax preparer, he or she should have given you a much better understanding of how tax law affects you. You should be more sensitive to changes in your finances that might cause tax complications, and be fully aware of all the records you need to keep to save time and reduce fees.

Year-end tax tips. By November, your accountant should call or write to alert you to last-minute moves that might cut your current tax bill, such as prepaying deductible state and local taxes that are coming due early in the next year.

Long-range tax planning advice. From fresh angles on investments to decisions about your corporate benefits, a good adviser should be giving you tips that go well beyond your tax return for this year.

Audit aid. A C.P.A. or enrolled agent should be willing not only to advise you and fill out your returns but also to accompany you to an IRS audit, if necessary.

In return, your preparer will expect the following from you:

Honesty. You can disagree over deductions, but failing to report income is a crime. Preparers have every right to demand your full financial details.

Complete and organized records. Even the most accommodating tax preparer can't file a proper return if you do not supply the necessary records. By not organizing them into such categories as business expenses and stocks bought and sold, you are forcing him or her to guess about matters that only you are expert in. And you'll do a much better job of record keeping if you know which tax rules and deductions apply to you.

Clear policy statement on aggressiveness. It is best to spell out from the beginning how aggressive you want to be to prevent painful misunderstandings later on. If you fail to make your intentions clear, the preparer will have to guess, particularly on gray-area write-offs, and may err on the side of caution and a heftier tax bill.

Careful reading of your return. Since your preparer is working with information that you have provided, you must check to make sure his or her interpretation of your records is accurate. Any errors could raise your tax bill.

A phone call before you make a major decision. If you buy or sell a house, make a large charitable contribution, or set up accounts for the children's college tuition, your tax adviser can serve you best only if you consult him or her before you act. How and when you make a transaction may not only save you taxes but also determine how such an event should be reported to the IRS.

rulings on deductions have been ambiguous. Taking a write-off in such cases may still make sense. Or you may have a situation in which the size of your medical or business expenses goes beyond the informal IRS guideline amounts, but you feel that yours are legitimate and well documented. Your tax pro may automatically take a much more conservative stance unless you push him or her to adopt a more aggressive position.

Whether your return contains such gray areas will depend on your investments and your business life. If you own rental property, for example, you must determine whether work done on it is a repair, fully deductible in the current year, or an improvement, which must be depreciated over the life of the property. You are likeliest of all to have a large number of judgment calls if you are in business for yourself or if you work as an independent contractor, as many salesmen and real estate agents do. Such items as a car leased for business and expenses for travel and entertainment frequently lead to questions from the IRS. Keeping careful records and saving all your receipts can help make you more secure in taking such deductions, as your tax preparer should advise you.

Discussions with your preparer ought to embrace not only this year's return but future ones as well. In fact, tax planning may well be the service to which preparers typically give the shortest shrift because many clients view tax preparation as just an annual event. A conscientious adviser should take the initiative to alert you to possible long-range strategies to cut your tax bills.

The best way to keep the planning tips flowing is to nudge your tax pro periodically, asking whether there is anything you should be doing. If you believe some tax planning is in order, schedule a meeting with your adviser for May or June—after the tax-filing season—to go over it in more detail. You will, of course, pay for the session at the preparer's hourly rate. But if you schedule such sessions only when you really need them, you will probably save far more in taxes than the fees involved.

To get the best service from your tax pro,

keep his or her schedule and the press of the tax season in mind. Call in the fall to discuss whether there are moves you can make to cut your taxes for the current year. Be sure to mention anything new in your tax situation since the previous year's filing. Some accountants will begin to prepare preliminary projections for clients at this point, using intelligent estimates if they have to wait for necessary records to show up. With or without that device, your goal should be to start thinking through the coming return with your tax preparer and spot any potential new deductions or special problems. Then, schedule a formal session to go over the return early in the new year.

A Tax Vocabulary

Key terms you should know include:

Adjusted gross income. Your income minus any adjustments such as IRA contributions and alimony payments.

Alternative minimum tax (AMT). A special tax designed to compel people with sizable deductions to pay at least some income tax. The AMT rate is 21%.

Capital gains or losses. Your profits or losses from selling investments. If you sell your house for a profit, you also could owe capital-gains taxes.

Credit. A tax break that you subtract dollar for dollar from your tax liability.

Deduction. An expense that you subtract from your adjusted gross income in determining your tax liability. You can claim individual deductions only if you have enough to itemize on Schedule A.

Estimated tax. A quarterly tax payment that is required when you do not have enough taxes withheld from your income.

What the Pros Don't Know Can Hurt You

When 50 preparers took Money's *tax-return test, the results were even worse than the 1988 exam—and there were no excuses this time around.*

In 1988, *Money* asked 50 tax professionals to complete a 23-form 1040 return for a hypothetical family. The results were unnerving; no two preparers computed the same tax due. Worse, the answers varied by as much as 50%. The preparers had an excuse, however: The Tax Reform Act of 1986 was ridiculously complex and so new that the Internal Revenue Service had not yet published important regulations.

Since then, preparers have had the benefit of a year's worth of sorting out the new rules and of studying critical regulations the IRS issued. Yet in 1989, when *Money* asked another 50 preparers who volunteered to compute the tax owed by a new hypothetical family, the answers were more off the mark than before. The abundance of mistakes suggests that the pros are not as knowledgeable about the tax law as they are supposed to be. For example:

● Again, each participant computed a different tax for the family. The bottom line ranged astonishingly from a low of $12,539 to a high of $35,813.

● The accountant who designed the test (and gave the correct tax as $23,393) and 10 others made no significant errors. But all the rest did make mistakes, some missing such basics as dependency exemptions, the penalty tax on early pension distributions, and the wash-sale rule on stock sales.

● Preparers' fees for the 11 accurate returns ranged from $325 to $2,500, and the time spent completing the forms varied from four to 20 hours. Four preparers who made major mistakes charged more than $1,500, and two of the four worked on the problem for 20 hours or more.

● The errors, which of course could expose the family to an IRS audit and penalties, tended to cut the family's tax bill. That's why the $21,729 average tax due among the 50 participants is well below the $23,393 arrived at by the test's author, Wesley Fitzpatrick, a senior tax partner in the Portland, Oregon office of the national accounting firm of Grant Thornton.

Fitzpatrick's computation of $23,393 for the family's tax is not the only possible correct answer. The 10 other participants who made no mistakes calculated taxes of up to $24,493. (For simplicity's sake, the test assumed no withholdings.) The variation arises because the tax law is still unclear in some situations. Thus, more aggressive preparers like Fitzpatrick could legitimately deduct larger amounts while others played it more conservatively. Some small variations also arose out of independent assumptions that the preparers made about details not spelled out in the hypothetical profile. Many participants, for example, deemed a third home owned by the family to be investment property rather than real estate used for personal purposes—a decision that affected interest deductions. The preparers, however, had been urged to call *Money*'s referees if they had questions or needed help interpreting the problem.

The participants included 30 certified public accountants from local firms, three C.P.A.s from national accounting companies, 12 preparers from franchise outlets such as H&R Block, and five independent enrolled agents (who are licensed to practice by the Internal Revenue Service). With the exception of Arthur Young, none of the Big Eight firms agreed to take part. The Big Eight company

Touche Ross initially agreed to take part but dropped out eight days after the two-week deadline for completing the returns had elapsed. Nationwide Income Tax Service, a Michigan-based tax preparation chain, also backed out after having the test for more than two weeks.

Other than Fitzpatrick, the only preparers who made no major mistakes were five C.P.A.s from independent local firms; one enrolled agent; one preparer from Triple Check Income Tax Service, a 37-state chain; and all three participants from the Jackson Hewitt chain. But Jackson Hewitt's results are no guarantee that one of the outfit's outlets will fill out your return impeccably. John Hewitt, chief executive of the company, personally handled the hypothetical profile and then discussed its problems with the other two Jackson Hewitt participants. The three returns showed

The IRS Doesn't Know Either

Remember 1988's tax-filing season? There, amid the shrieks and bloodletting of your first encounter with the new tax law, stood IRS Commissioner Lawrence Gibbs, serenely confessing that the people down at the IRS who answered your tax questions by telephone were not really helpful. They were nearly as befuddled over the new law as you were. Gibbs promised vast improvements—notably, that the service's temporary phone workers had been hired full time and would be trained for months. Be patient, 1989 would be much better.

Alas, a *Money* test conducted last year reveals that the IRS' phone assistors are giving wrong answers a ridiculously high 41% of the time. That's only four points better than the IRS' score on a similar *Money* survey in January 1988. As we did then, we placed a total of 100 calls to assistors all across the country in January. Each assistor was asked one of 10 questions, and each question was posed to 10 different IRS employees. The dismal toll: 59 correct answers.

The queries were not deliberate brain benders; they were typical of what the assistors were likely to encounter. Example: Can a taxpayer count a subscription to *Money* as a miscellaneous deduction if he or she uses the magazine to help with investment and tax planning decisions? (Only two out of 10 correctly answered yes.) The new taxpayer's bill of rights waives the penalties on any such IRS-inspired mistakes that show up on your tax form—but only if you can prove that the IRS misled you by producing written documentation of the blunder.

Good luck. Who ever heard of a bureaucracy that willingly put it in writing? Whenever we asked for documentation of the answers we got, the IRS assistors said we had to mail in our questions first. Twice, when we requested written verification of a wrong answer, the assistor transferred us to a supervisor who provided the right one. But another time, when we asked for confirmation of a correct reply, we were transferred to a supervisor who changed the answer to a wrong one.

The six H&R Block participants all submitted remarkably similar returns as well. Each of their 1040s contained only one mistake. They all listed a high depreciation deduction that test author Fitzpatrick challenged based on a congressional report and other publications. The uniformity in the Block returns suggested that the firm's home office coached the six individuals who took part. But a company spokesperson asserted that headquarters merely assisted in developing answers for particular isolated questions that the various participants raised about the problem.

Fees, it turned out, were no clue to accuracy. The average participant would have charged $865. But the bills ranged from a mere $250 for an H&R Block preparer to $2,500 for Steven Caldwell of Blum Shapiro & Company in Farmington, Connecticut, who, to his credit, submitted one of the few flub-free returns. Yet Gino Paliaroli of Hayse & Paliaroli in Sterling Heights, Michigan also got a top score and would have charged only $340. On average, the C.P.A.s, who cater mainly to wealthier individuals and corporate clients, would have asked for $1,081. That compares with only $559 for the enrolled agents and $382 for the franchise outlets, which generally charge by the form rather than by billable hours.

Who was this hypothetical family that so baffled the pros? Meet the Clanceys, a couple who earned $56,400 in salaries and who both collected lump-sum pension distributions upon quitting their respective jobs. Wife Shannon worked out of her home and started a tool-sharpening business in September 1988, while husband Sean spent the second half of the year negotiating to buy his own company. They owned a variety of investments, plus a second home, and inherited a third home upon the death of Shannon's mother. Here are the specific issues that befuddled the participants, listed in order of greatest impact on the family's tax bill:

Lump-sum distributions. Because Shannon and her husband, Sean, were younger than 55, both should have owed a 10% early-withdrawal penalty on their $72,000 combined lump-sum pension distributions. Seven preparers failed to include any penalty at all, five counted a penalty only on Shannon's smaller $12,000 payment, and one applied the penalty solely to Sean's $60,000 distribution. The couple could have avoided the fines by rolling over the lump sums into Individual Retirement Accounts, but the hypothetical case made it clear that neither spouse elected rollovers. Neglecting the penalty reduced the Clanceys' tax bill by as much as $7,200. But if the IRS caught the mistake, as it likely would through computer matchups, the family would eventually have owed additional interest and possibly penalties.

Sean, aged 53—but not Shannon, 46—was old enough to cut his tax bill by applying a calculation known as 10-year forward averaging to his lump sum. All but one preparer correctly used forward averaging on Sean's payment and saved the Clanceys an extra $10,988 in tax. But two preparers wrongly applied forward averaging to Shannon's lump sum as well as Sean's, even though she was not eligible for the preferred treatment.

Inherited savings bonds. Shannon's mother bequeathed to the Clanceys U.S. savings bonds with accumulated interest of $10,000. Under a 1968 IRS revenue ruling, the personal representative of an estate—in this case, Shannon—has the option of counting the previously untaxed income on the deceased's final 1040. In this example, no tax would be owed on the $10,000 if it were included on the mother's return because the earnings could be offset by her $15,000 in deductible medical expenses. Yet 12 participants listed the money on the Clanceys' return, increasing the family's tax bill by $3,300.

Wash sale. In 1988, the Clanceys bought 100 shares of a specified stock on March 1 at $6,000 and another 100 on November 30 at $4,200, then sold 100 on December 10 at $3,000. Fourteen preparers mistakenly deducted a $3,000 loss for the transaction. They were wrong because the IRS wash-sale rule, dating back to 1921, states that you cannot deduct a loss on securities bought within 30 days before or after the same investment was sold. The error reduced the Clanceys' taxes by $990.

Dependents. Sean's mother, Erin, lived with the Clanceys for the entire year, and the couple paid more than half of her support. But she cannot be counted as a dependent on the Clanceys' return because she earned $3,000 in rent from her old residence. In addition, adults are not dependents if their gross income is more than $1,950. Ten participants wrongly claimed her as a dependent because they computed Erin's net income to be $200 after subtracting her expenses on the home. The error slashed the Clanceys' taxes by $644.

Interest deductions. The tax laws under this heading are an utter muddle, so the preparers should not be chastised for the wide divergence in write-offs they submitted for home mortgage, investment, and personal interest. Most of the confusion arose because Shannon's mother left her house to the Clanceys when she died, which gave the family a total of three properties. By law, full mortgage-interest deductions can be taken on only two homes. That left it to the preparers to decide which two houses to count. They also had to determine how much of the interest on the third property could be deducted, a consideration that was further complicated by other factors. Although the interest issues gave the preparers their worst migraines, their decisions generally ended up having a relatively minor impact on the tax bill. Most of the $1,422 variation in the amount of tax owed among the 11 mistake-free preparers resulted from differing tactics on the interest write-offs.

Master limited partnerships. Thirteen participants erroneously counted income from a publicly traded master limited partnership as so-called passive income. As a result, they wrongly cut the Clanceys' tax bill by $396. Congress enacted a law in 1987 stipulating that income from master limited partnerships cannot be offset by losses from passive investments such as tax shelters.

Depreciation. When Shannon started her business in September 1988, she bought a $10,000 tool-sharpening machine. Nineteen preparers, including the six from H&R Block, deducted a full year's depreciation on the machine, or $1,429. But IRS publications and a congressional report indicate that the deduction should apply only to the third of the year that she was in business.

The kiddie tax. The Clanceys' 13-year-old son, Colin, earned $600 from mowing lawns during the 1988 tax year. Does he have to file a return? Yes, because any self-employment income in excess of $400 is subject to tax, which in this case amounted to $78. Most of the 16 preparers who did not file a return for Colin conceded that they erred. Several said they assumed he would have had more than $200 in deductible business expenses, although no such costs were specified in our hypothetical write-up. Another preparer justified the omission by asserting that periodic lawn mowing does not constitute a trade or business. That, too, would be a difficult position to defend before the IRS.

If professional preparers are so susceptible to mistakes, should you fill out your own return instead? Not necessarily. For one thing, pros provide tax planning advice that can keep you from owing as much tax as the Clanceys would have paid. Just don't assume that hiring a preparer will keep you out of trouble with the IRS. If a mistake is caught, you are the one who legally owes interest and penalties—even though some firms like H&R Block and Jackson Hewitt promise to pay for their errors.

Your preparer might owe fines, too, if the IRS decides the mistakes on your return are a consequence of negligence or intentional disregard of rules and regulations. But in most cases the penalty amounts to only $100.

Penalties against preparers may be little consolation if you end up paying for their mistakes. But you can always sue for negligence. If *Money*'s test is any indication, the courts may soon be awash with taxpayers seeking retribution for their tax preparers' high-priced foul-ups.

Tax Information You Need to Collect

Sometimes the biggest job is pulling it all together.

Before you can even figure out how much tax you owe, you will need to shovel deftly through the ever-mounting blizzard of paperwork. All taxpayers must document earnings, from wages to tips to dividends. And if you itemize, each deduction, from babysitting expenses to gambling losses, must be substantiated with standard forms, receipts, statements, diaries, and canceled checks. The job must be done not only to determine what you owe—or what Uncle Sam owes you—but also to justify the return in case of an audit.

Even if you plan to hire a preparer to do your return, do this part of the job yourself. Only you can know what each chit of paper represents; otherwise, a deduction might be overlooked. Furthermore, if you hand the paper pile to your accountant, he or she will bill you perhaps hundreds of dollars to do the sorting.

Here is what you will generally need to assemble, depending on your sources of income, deductions, and expenses:

Income and Losses

The W-2 form (showing salary, wages, and taxes withheld) and the W-2P (for monthly distributions from a pension) must be attached to your return. Another form, the 1099, documents most other income such as self-employment income, interest, royalty income, dividends, lump-sum payments from pensions and annuities, state and local tax refunds, and mutual fund earnings and gains. Capital gains and losses are also reported on 1099s: one

form is mailed to you, one to the Internal Revenue Service.

The IRS uses a computer matching system that spots discrepancies between income statements on your return and the 1099s they have received. A 1099 needs to be attached to the return only in the event that tax has been withheld. (Income from tips should be backed up with Forms 4070-A, 4070, and 4137. Income and losses from partnerships, estates and trusts, and S corporations are documented on Schedule K-l.)

The IRS requires that both W-2 forms and 1099s be sent to taxpayers by January 31. The law does not require, however, that K-l schedules be available by April 15 (April 16 in 1990). If the party responsible—such as a brokerage, bank, or even the company you work for—does not mail your schedules on time, call and pester those offices. If you do not receive them by the April filing deadline, tax experts recommend that you file for an automatic extension and complete your return when you have the required information.

Expenses

Mortgage interest. Form 1098, which the lender sends you, covers this.

Consumer interest. You will need statements from creditors showing interest paid in 1989 (and subsequent years); normally, it is printed on the first page of your December or January statement. Only 20% of consumer interest is deductible in 1989. The write-off drops to 10% in 1990 and disappears thereafter.

Dependent-care payments. Keep canceled checks and statements from caretakers, baby-sitters, or child-care organizations.

Charitable contributions. Any charitable deduction for items worth $500 or more must be supported by statements from receiving organizations verifying the fair market value of the property. For items over $5,000, you need a professional appraisal. Old clothes should be valued at what a buyer might reasonably pay in a thrift shop or secondhand outlet. You should have a log for out-of-pocket costs on service done for a charity.

Medical expenses not reimbursed by insurance. To be deductible, expenses must exceed 7.5% of your adjusted gross income. One exception is the cost of premiums paid by self-employed taxpayers for medical- and dental-care coverage. Twenty-five percent of those expenses are deductible from your self-employment income. The 75% balance is subject to the 7.5% floor. Pull together receipts for prescription medicine or special health equipment authorized by your doctor and bills from doctors, clinics, and the like for treatment. If travel was necessary for medical treatment, you will want lodging (up to $50 a night) and meal receipts.

Miscellaneous expenses. Document these with receipts for expenditures such as union dues, safe-deposit box rental, investment advice, membership dues for a professional organization, and business publications. A comprehensive listing is included in the 1040 instruction booklet. Generally, they must be more than 2% of your adjusted gross income. Employee business expenses that are not reimbursed are treated as miscellaneous expenses. You may deduct 80% of entertainment bills. Collect receipts showing the date, cost, place of entertainment, name of those entertained, and purpose of the event. Travel expenses are fully deductible if substantiated by receipts. A log will document business car trips and mileage, on which you may deduct 24¢ a mile up to 15,000 miles and 11¢ for each additional mile.

Rental-property expenses. Collect your real estate tax bill and itemized receipts for repairs and maintenance. Back up the depreciation deduction with the closing statement from your purchase of the property. If you plan to deduct expenses connected with a vacation house that you rent out for a minimum of 14 days, you must have a log showing the number of days you rented the property and how many days you used it yourself.

Mistakes to Avoid This Year

Besides traps set by a complex tax code, beware of everyday forgetfulness.

More than one in five tax returns filed with the IRS in recent years contained some type of error—a Social Security number that was omitted, a math error in calculating tax, or perhaps a missing form. The IRS does not keep tabs on every kind of elaborate mistake, but it estimates that the number is enormous. These slipups cause overpayments (money out of your pocket) and underpayments (which often lead to penalties and/or fines). To alert you to some common pitfalls, *Money* consulted several knowledgeable tax preparers as well as the IRS to compile this list of 10 tax-return blunders:

Failure to take the standard deduction. The standard deduction is what the government considers a reasonable amount for deductible expenses. If your actual deductible expenses are greater than the standard deduction, itemize and claim them on Schedule A. Before 1987, the standard deduction was factored into the figures on the tax tables. Now those tables no longer include it; you must claim it on line 34 of the 1040 form. For 1989, the deduction is $5,000 for a married couple filing jointly, $4,400 for a head of household and $3,000 for a single taxpayer.

Incorrect calculation of capital gain from a mutual fund. All you have to do is subtract the purchase price of your shares from what you sold them for, right? Wrong. Most mutual fund shareholders elect to have their dividends reinvested in new shares in the fund. The shareholder pays taxes each year on the dividends, which are shown on the fund's annual final statement. When you sell shares, you are actually receiving a profit that includes dividends and distributions (on which tax has already been paid) and untaxed gains. In order to arrive at the taxable gain, you must total the dividends and distributions reported on the final fund statement for each intervening year from the time of purchase. That sum is added to the purchase price and then subtracted from the sales price to get the capital gain.

Overlooking taxable mutual fund sales and redemptions. Many taxpayers don't realize when they pick up the phone and switch from, say, a stock fund to a money-market fund in the same family, they are actually selling shares in the equity fund and can be realizing taxable gains. But the IRS knows because the fund sends a 1099 information form on the transaction to the service. Just as tricky are income funds with check-writing privileges. Each check you write is a redemption of principal and therefore a potentially taxable event.

If you have switched between funds in a fund family or written checks on a fund, go over your 1099 forms and final statements and add up all gains you have realized. You may have to pay tax on more gains than you thought.

Clerical errors. The IRS will charge you a $5 penalty for not including the Social Security number (taxpayer identification number) of a dependent child over five years old on your return. Failure to fill out Form 8606 for a nondeductible contribution to your Individual Retirement Account will result in a $50 penalty. If the spouse claiming a deduction for alimony payments does not record the Social Security number of the ex-spouse receiving the money on the return, there will be a $50 penalty. Forget to enter a spouse's Social Security number and the IRS will send you a letter asking for the number. There won't be a penalty, but any refund you are due can be delayed for as long as several months.

Failure to consider the alternative minimum tax. Filers who take substantial deductions for such items as real estate taxes, state and local taxes, or depreciation should calculate what their tax would be under the alternative minimum tax (AMT), which has a rate of 21%, using Form 6251. You pay whichever is greater, the amount calculated for regular tax or your AMT computation. It is unlikely that a taxpayer who does not itemize will be liable for the AMT, but the possibility exists for any couple filing jointly with adjusted gross income of more than $40,000—or more than $30,000 for single taxpayers or heads of household. If you do not make the calculation and the IRS concludes that you should have paid additional tax under the AMT rules, you will pay interest on the amount you underpaid.

Failure to pay tax on early IRA withdrawals. Any money taken from IRAs before age 59½—and not rolled over into another IRA within 60 days—is subject to income tax plus a 10% penalty. There are exceptions: If the individual dies or is totally disabled, or if the money is rolled over into an annuity at early retirement. There are no hardship provisions that allow penalty-free withdrawals from IRAs as there are for 401(k) savings plans.

Forgetting to pay self-employment tax. This Social Security levy paid by the self-employed often trips up salaried workers who moonlight. If the salary income on your W-2 is less than $48,000—the maximum subject to the Social Security tax in 1990—you must pay self-employment tax on the non-W-2 earnings from which Social Security (FICA) tax has not been withheld. The rate is 13.02% versus just 7.5% for FICA withheld from your paycheck (your employer pays the difference). So be sure to deduct any expenses connected to earning that freelance income, such as travel, meals, and supplies. The self-employment tax is levied on net earnings after subtracting expenses.

Incorrectly allocating state and local taxes and refunds. State and local taxes are deductible in the year you pay them, and refunds are income in the year you receive them. The IRS computer will catch any discrepancy.

Parents and kids both claiming the child's dependency exemption. Parents and children may no longer both take this benefit. If the parents are eligible to claim the child as a dependent, they must do it and the child may not. Generally, the parents claim the child as a dependent if the parents contribute more than half of the child's support, the child does not have an adjusted gross income greater than one exemption amount ($2,100 for 1989), and is not married and filing a joint return with someone else.

Taking a deduction for a nondeductible IRA contribution. Couples often mistakenly think that if one of them is not covered by a company retirement plan, then that spouse can take a deduction for an IRA contribution. In fact, they may claim a full deduction only if neither is covered and/or their combined income is less than $40,000. The deduction phases out over the next $10,000 so that no deduction is allowed for couples with a combined income of $50,000.

Ways to Slash Your Taxes

Reformers left open some great loopholes. Each can save you big bucks on your federal return.

Despite the radical changes imposed by the Tax Reform Act of 1986, there are still legal ways to save thousands of dollars on your federal taxes. True, the day is long gone when any accountant worth his green eyeshade could give you a trustworthy way to slash your yearly tax bill to zero. But don't assume that the architects of reform created a watertight tax structure. The law's authors left intact several loopholes that can be used by almost any middle- or upper-bracket taxpayer. Moreover, these are legitimate techniques that won't cost you any sleep worrying about being audited.

A few of the devices are fairly simple and could even help you cut this year's tax bill if you act by December 31. Others are more complicated and could well require months to be put in place with the help of a tax attorney, an accountant, or other specialist. Such expert help does not come cheap. For instance, the charitable remainder trust described on page 67 costs some $5,000 in legal and consulting fees. But the tax benefits to the couple who established the trust—and to their heirs—will keep rolling in year after year. Here is a close look at the last of the great tax loopholes:

Your Children

The kiddie tax curbed many maneuvers once commonly used by well-heeled parents to transfer income-producing assets to young children in low tax brackets. Today, kids under 14 pay no tax on $500 or less of unearned income: interest, dividends, and capital gains from investment sales. They are taxed at their own rate, typically 15%, on the next $500. Any unearned income above $1,000 is taxed at their parents' maximum marginal rate, which tops out at 33%. But you can still profit from two tax-cutting techniques that emerged unscathed from tax reform.

The annual gift-tax exclusion. This simple strategy allows you to make a tax-free gift of as much as $10,000 a year—$20,000 if the money is given jointly with your spouse—to anyone you please, including each of your children. Parents who use this device often have future college bills in mind (see "Meeting the High Cost of College" on page 86). But gifts can pay off in other ways because they no longer count as part of the parents' taxable estate.

You can make tax-free gifts of property as well as cash. Take one example of a married couple with two children, ages 8 and 11. The couple, whose combined taxable income of some $70,000 a year puts them in the 28% bracket, recently inherited a rental property and set aside the income from it for their children's college tuition. Their tax attorney advised the couple, instead, to give each child an annual gift of shares in the property worth $20,000. The shares are held in trust for the kids, with the parents as trustees so they can maintain full control over the property. The children's portion of the rental income, $2,160 a year recently, also goes into the trusts and is invested in bank money-market deposit accounts. The first $500 of income to the children is tax-free, and the rest is taxed at the trust's rate, which is only 15% on the first $5,000 of income. The bottom line: An annual tax saving for the parents of nearly $1,000.

Gifts of appreciated stock. Instead of selling a profitable investment yourself, you can give it to a child who is 14 or older. Then, when the child sells it, the capital gain will be taxed at his or her rate rather than yours. Consider, for example, the tax savings achieved by a mother who had planned to sell stock on which she had an $11-a-share gain and give the proceeds to her 16-year-old daughter. At the urging of her accountant, the woman avoided paying taxes on the gain at 28% by transferring the stock to her daughter. When the teenager subsequently sold the shares, the profit was taxed at her rate of 15%.

Your Property

Those real estate tax shelters that wealthy Americans once found so delectable are now only a memory. Still, investing in real estate remains one of the most rewarding ways in which middle- and upper-middle-income taxpayers can reduce their tax bills.

Rental property. You may be able to deduct up to $25,000 in losses from rental real estate against income from other sources and even your salary. To qualify for the full write-off, you must:

● Own at least 10% of the property.

● Actively participate in managing it—for example, by approving tenants and expenditures on maintenance.

● Have an adjusted gross income (AGI) for tax purposes of $100,000 or less. The deduction drops by 50¢ for every dollar that your AGI exceeds $100,000, phasing out entirely if it exceeds $150,000.

Like-kind exchanges. With this technique, you swap one piece of investment property for another and indefinitely postpone paying taxes on your profit from the first holding. In effect, you roll over your tax obligation into the new property, and you can do so again and again as you make future exchanges. When you eventually sell real estate acquired through a swap, you owe a capital-gains tax calculated on the basis of the cost of your first investment. In the meantime, your invested money grows tax-free.

Acquiring property through a like-kind exchange is complicated and filled with traps—one stumble and the IRS will hand you a tax bill that is payable on the spot. As a result, you will probably need expert help in making such swaps. But the payoff can be substantial. Consider, for example, the tax savings achieved by a Washington, D.C. man who wanted to sell a rental property worth $335,000 that he had bought 10 years earlier for just $145,000. Rather than take cash from the buyer—a move that would force him to pay taxes on his $190,000 profit—the man asked his real estate broker to find someone who would buy another rental property with about the same market value and exchange it for his. The search turned up a woman who wanted the man's property and was willing to serve as the intermediary. She bought the second property and then made the exchange, enabling the man to postpone some $62,700 in taxes.

Your Own Business

If you have income from self-employment, you are eligible for a multitude of attractive tax breaks. These write-offs were among the fattest targets of tax reform, but Congress didn't abolish them all.

Moonlighting. The deductions made possible by a sideline business can entirely offset the taxes due on your extra earnings. If you operate the business from your home, you may be entitled to write off a portion of your home mortgage interest, property taxes, and utility bills. To qualify for these deductions, you must use your home office exclusively for business, and the space must be your principal office for that work. Home-office deductions can trigger

an audit, however, so seek an accountant's advice on what you can legitimately claim and the documentation required. A sideline business also entitles you to a Keogh account, a generous, tax-deferred retirement plan for people with self-employment income. Even if you are covered by a pension plan at work, you can deduct contributions up to 20% of your earnings from moonlighting in a Keogh to a maximum of $30,000 a year. That's about 15 times the limit on what you can put in an Individual Retirement Account.

Full-time self-employment. If running your own business is your only employment, you can take advantage of a great number of tax benefits. Consider, for example, a Florida chiropractor who set up his own professional corporation to get all the tax breaks in perfect alignment. He constructed his first tax shelter in 1983, when he erected a much bigger office building than he needed so that he could lease space to other tenants. Since the chiropractor owns the building personally, his professional corporation can legitimately pay $2,400-a-month rent to himself as the landlord. Rental income from two other office suites brings him $1,150 a month.

To keep as much as possible of his practice's earnings in the family, the chiropractor employs his wife as his bookkeeper, his oldest son as a massage therapist, and his youngest son as a file clerk. He writes off their salaries—some $23,140 a year—as regular business expenses. All told, he estimates that his strategies shave about 13% from his corporation's taxable earnings and some 15% from his personal taxable income.

Gifts to Charity

Many taxpayers satisfy their charitable impulses with an annual contribution to their college alumni fund and a year-end donation of old clothes to the Salvation Army. While such gifts reward you with a modest break on your taxes, there are other ways to help your favorite charitable cause that yield considerably greater income and estate-tax benefits.

Land conservation easements. These are basically the tax code's way of rewarding a land-owner who is willing to preserve his or her land from development for conservation purposes. To qualify for a tax-saving land easement, your property must be worth preserving from development for one or more of these reasons:

● It is scenic—for example, it includes farmland or forest that provide beautiful vistas enjoyed by the public.

● Development would destroy a natural habitat of fish, wildlife, plants, or other ecosystems.

● The property includes an historically important structure as defined by a local or national registry of historic places.

● The property offers the public opportunities for outdoor recreation or education.

In exchange for the easement, owners get a charitable tax deduction equal to the difference between the land's value to developers and the lesser amount it will be worth if left untouched.

Such easements can greatly cut estate-tax liability and can be especially intriguing to people whose land has been in the family for years and is suddenly desirable to developers. Take the case of a Massachusetts widow in her seventies who owns a 60-acre farm in Middleborough. The community was turning into an outlying suburb of Boston, and developers were offering her a staggering $1 million for the land. But the widow was concerned about her three children, all of whom had families of their own and wanted her to keep the farm unspoiled and in the family.

Her accountant's solution was a land conservation easement that restricted further development of the farm but allowed the widow, and someday her children, to continue to own and enjoy the property. The widow's charitable deduction from the easement amounted to more than $500,000, which she could spread over six years. Even so, her income was not high enough over the period to allow her to

make full use of the deduction. But perhaps more important to the family, the easement also reduces the widow's estate-tax liability to zero because it diminished the market value of the property by close to half a million dollars.

The charitable remainder trust. With this device, you can donate cash, stock, or other property to charity and continue to earn income from your gift for life. Rather than making a contribution directly to your chosen charity, you put your gift into an irrevocable trust—meaning that you can't change your mind—designating the charity as your beneficiary. The trust, which is best set up with the help of an accountant and a tax lawyer, is managed by an appointee of your choice who invests your donation and pays you income annually out of the assets. You must receive at least 5% of the value of the assets in the trust every year, and you may elect to take greater amounts. In addition, you can deduct a portion of your contribution on your tax return. The size of the write-off depends on the amount of income you will be drawing from the trust and your life expectancy according to IRS actuarial tables. After your death, the charity receives the balance of the assets in the trust.

Charitable remainder trusts are particularly useful for older taxpayers looking to supplement their current income while reducing the size of their taxable estates. The trusts are equally well suited to taxpayers holding stocks or other investments that have appreciated greatly in value—assets that they would like to tap for income without being subject to stiff capital-gains tax. Reason: While individuals must pay taxes on the profits from a stock sale, a charitable trust does not.

These various advantages appealed to a Phoenix couple in their late sixties with stock worth $300,000 that they had bought years ago for $46,000. If they sold it themselves, they would have owed $71,000 in capital-gains taxes. Instead, they put their shares into a charitable trust for their favorite cause, the Firearms Civil Rights Legal Defense Fund of the National Rifle Association. The trust then sold the stock and invested the proceeds in

Treasury securities paying 8% a year, from which the couple receive $24,000 annually. The donation also entitled them to a charitable deduction of $108,506. They elected to spread the write-off over the allowable six-year period, thereby cutting their taxes by $18,084 in each of those years.

Your Estate Plan

Most taxpayers, unless they are wealthy, give little thought to federal estate taxes, which range from 37% on estates just over $600,000 to a maximum of 60% on multimillion-dollar ones. They are vaguely aware that they can leave their heirs as much as $600,000—or give away that much during their lifetimes—with no gift or estate-tax liability. And they know that they can leave everything to their spouses, no matter how much, free of taxes.

Unfortunately, if you take that relaxed approach to estate planning, what you eventually leave your heirs can be diminished by a staggering load of taxes. To underscore that point, compare the federal taxes on two $600,000 estates with those on one of $1.2 million. Each $600,000 estate passes tax-free. But the $1.2 million estate pays $235,000 in taxes. Every dollar of that could be avoided by paying a lawyer roughly $150 to $500 to draft wills for the husband and wife that include simple bypass trusts.

Lest you think an estate of more than $600,000 is out of the question, carefully consider the assets you currently hold. First, add up the equity in your home and the balances in your checking and savings accounts, as well as the value of any stocks, bonds, and other investments that you own. If you then tack on the proceeds due your heirs from life insurance policies and your pension plan, 401(k), and other retirement accounts, you may well find that your taxable estate easily exceeds $600,000. If so, you might want to consider the following perfectly legal ways to reduce the taxes on your estate, possibly to zero:

Trusts. These should be set up by a lawyer. First, you should consider a bypass trust. Let's assume a woman holds assets of $1.2 million. True, upon her death, everything could pass to her husband tax-free under the unlimited marital deduction. But when the husband dies, his estate would be exposed to the ferocious estate taxes cited earlier. Instead, the wife could provide in her will that upon her death, $600,000 of her estate will go into a bypass trust. The husband can receive all, part, or none of the trust's income, depending on the will's provisions. The rest of the wife's assets can pass to the husband tax-free under the marital deduction. When he dies, the trust will be dissolved and the remaining assets distributed to the heirs named by his wife in her will. His estate, assuming it does not exceed the $600,000 left to him by his wife, will go tax-free to his beneficiaries. And all $1.2 million of the wife's assets will escape estate taxes.

Another device to safeguard money from estate taxes is a life insurance trust, which should be considered by anyone whose life insurance might swell his or her taxable estate to more than $600,000. This involves transferring to the trust the ownership of your insurance policies. When you die, the policies' proceeds will be paid to the trust, clear of estate taxes, and can be invested to pay income to someone of your choosing, typically your spouse. Upon his or her death, the principal will pass to the beneficiaries of your choice.

Split-interest purchases. This is one of the few surviving legal ways that children and parents can work together to keep sizable assets out of the parent's estate. With a split-interest purchase, parent and child jointly buy an investment property. Each invests a percentage determined by an IRS actuarial table. It assumes that the younger the parent is, the longer he will live and benefit from the income generated by the property, so the greater the amount that he is required to invest. The parent buys a life interest in the property, meaning that he receives his proportionate share of its income during his lifetime. When he dies, the entire property passes directly to the child, avoiding the parent's estate. If the land appreciates during the parent's lifetime, the family will realize an estate-tax savings.

Your Safest—and Riskiest—Write-Offs

Not only did tax reform mow down deductions like a computer-driven grim reaper, but many of those that are left are wired to set off audit alarms at the IRS. So, here is a guide through the remaining write-offs. The safe ones tend to be the most commonly used and easily verified. Those freighted with peril lend themselves to padding or are difficult to calculate, leading to errors that can quickly spotlight your return. IRS computers are also primed to bleep at deductions that are unusually large or bizarre.

The Riskiest

Tax shelters. You are allowed to deduct 20% of your shelter losses against 1989 ordinary income. Although that's all perfectly legal, the sheer size of the deduction, not to mention the IRS' longstanding fixation on tax shelters, may red-flag your return.

Business expenses. The IRS wants to nab both the self-employed and employees who pad their travel and entertainment bills or who write off home offices that are not used regularly and exclusively as primary places of business.

Depreciation. Keep careful records if you plan to deduct the wear and tear on the car or computer you use for business. These include a daily log and receipts, plus, in the case of a computer, your employer's statement that it is essential to performing your job.

Charitable gifts. Document your donations with canceled checks or qualified appraisals. If you give tangible personal property such as art, antiques, or collectibles, get a letter from the charity stating that the gift will be used only to further the charity's stated purpose and not simply resold to raise money.

Hobby losses. To prove that your pastime is for profit, not pleasure, you must be in the black for three of the past five years or keep a copious record of your efforts to turn a profit.

Vacation rental losses. Byzantine compliance regulations can do you in.

Alimony. Regardless of what your divorce decree calls it, any alimony that actually pays for child support is not deductible.

The Safest

Mortgage interest. Limited in general only by the purchase price of your house plus improvements, this is still the most sizable and secure deduction left.

Medical and dental expenses. The trick is getting them above the requisite 7.5% of your adjusted gross income. Try ganging big-ticket expenses—like braces for the kids—you can plan every two years.

State and local taxes. But don't overreach; reporting is tightly monitored for both income and real estate taxes.

Individual Retirement Account. Your contribution is fully deductible if your employer or your spouse's does not offer a pension plan or if your combined adjusted gross income is less than $40,000 ($25,000 for singles).

Secrets of Profitable Home Ownership

In the good old days—back in the 1970s—house prices rose sharply, outpacing inflation. Lately, however, many homeowners have seen the values of their properties fail to keep up with the cost of living. In the 12 months that ended in March 1989, the median sales price of existing houses lagged inflation in 23 of the 50 largest U.S. metropolitan areas.

Whether you are thinking of buying a house or now own one, new and harsh rules of home economics apply. This information may be jarring to those still dreaming of the house-price spirals of the past. But the realities of real estate in the 1990s may well force you to revise your strategies for financing a house, borrowing against it, and undertaking remodeling projects. You can no longer depend on your biggest investment to be your best. In the 1980s, the median-price house rose in value by only 5.6% a year. By comparison, growth stock mutual funds gained on average 14.3% a year and bond funds were up 10.9% annually.

Four factors account for this softness in housing markets across the country and suggest why the trend should continue:

Changing demographics. The massive house buying by 76 million baby boomers in the 1970s and early 1980s is giving way to more careful shopping by the relatively few 41 million baby busters.

Squeezed first-time home buyers. Prices have outstripped would-be buyers' incomes, especially those of young couples. In Boston, for example, a family with the median income of $40,253 is $400 a month short of qualifying for a mortgage on the median-price $181,239 home. And today's relatively high mortgage rates only make matters worse.

Fear of debt. A 1989 survey by the International Association for Financial Planning said that mortgage payments have become the top financial concern of Americans, ahead of taxes.

Mortgage-deduction jitters. It's unlikely that Congress will restrict this write-off soon. Still, a 1989 Congressional Budget Office report pointed out to revenue-hungry lawmakers that slashing the maximum annual deduction to $12,000 ($20,000 for couples) would raise $7.5 billion over five years.

As a result of these factors, many economists expect housing appreciation to remain low through the 1990s, matching inflation or at best beating it by a slim percentage point or so. In other words, we're in for a repeat of the no-growth 1980s—but this time around, the grim reality will sink in.

It's Time to Rethink Your Biggest Investment

Use these new strategies to protect yourself when you buy, improve, or sell your home.

More and more Americans are shedding outdated notions about house-price appreciation. In a 1988 national survey, only 34% of homeowners said they had bought for investment reasons versus 45% in 1987. And today's helter-skelter real estate markets are the reason: In many parts of the country, housing offers only sporadic gains plus the threat that the value of your home may even fall for extended periods. Indeed, as an inflation fighter, the typical American house has been a loser during much of the last decade. The recent median house price of $96,400 is actually lower than 1980's median of $62,200 after adjusting for inflation.

Furthermore, the WEFA Group, an economics forecasting firm in Bala Cynwyd, Pennsylvania, predicts that between April 1989 and April 1990 inflation will have risen at least a percentage point more than home prices nationwide. If a recession develops, house values would take an even bigger hit. Don't expect widespread home-icide, however, as predicted by Comstock Partners, an influential Wall Street advisory firm. Comstock sees the possibility of a rapid decline in house prices nationwide and a crash of as much as 50% in some places over the next five years. But such a drop ignores the resilience of local markets. Real estate experts point out that the only time housing prices fell across the country was during the Great Depression. It probably would take a similar deflationary bust for history to repeat itself.

Nevertheless, real estate analysts expect to see more scattered areas in which house prices fall for a while. Usually housing deflation occurs when a region's economy cools, reducing demand for houses. The New York City metropolitan area, where prices have dropped by 10% to 15% since the October 1987 stock market crash, is a case in point. Even sellers in healthy local economies are not immune to price cutting. Builders sometimes flood such areas with so many new housing developments that the supply outstrips demand. In Atlanta, for example, a new house and condo glut has made selling for a profit almost impossible. Brokers there say that it's common for savvy buyers to get hard-pressed sellers to pay their 5% closing costs.

You can also expect to continue seeing pockets of the country where house prices go through the roof—temporarily. Southern California has lately held this honor. Prices in some cities there have climbed nearly 50% since 1987. In Beverly Hills, land-hungry buyers buy big houses, tear them down, and build huge ones—what local brokers cheerfully call "scraping." Prospective owners have been known to pay line-sitters $500 or more in San Diego to reserve places at new-home developments. Some of this crazed price inflation, however, is merely catch-up. From 1981 to 1986, Los Angeles home prices rose a mere 2% a year, a third below the national rate.

To help you take advantage of—or reduce your exposure to—today's ho-hum housing markets, *Money* interviewed dozens of analysts, real estate brokers, lenders, and financial planners. Here are guidelines for this new era:

Advice for Home Buyers

Consider renting instead. It usually takes three years of appreciation of more than 3% annually just to cover closing costs and sales commissions. So if you are likely to move in a few years, you may be better off as a tenant than an owner. The case for renting is even stronger if the monthly rent on nearby houses is less than 1% of their market value and you expect local home prices to lag inflation. Compare the after-tax costs of renting (utilities, insurance, and rent) to those of owning (mortgage, property taxes, utilities, insurance, maintenance, and repairs) over at least five years. You will have to factor in the value of write-offs for mortgage interest and property taxes, likely rent increases, housing appreciation, and the investment income from what would be your down payment. For about $25, you can order a personalized analysis of renting versus buying from a computer software company called Educom (7552 New Castle Drive, Department S, Annandale, VA 22003).

Don't stretch too much to buy a bigger, more expensive house. Since housing appreciation after inflation is less than guaranteed, buy what you need rather than all you can grab. Instead of spending an extra $500 a month for a house that's 1,000 square feet larger, stash that cash in liquid investments such as stocks, bonds, and mutual funds.

Beware of creative—read risky—financing. It is now a frightening possibility that when you sell your house, after subtracting the broker's commission, the sales proceeds might fall short of paying off your mortgage. As a result, you could have to drain your savings to pay the lender. One way to avoid this nightmare is to reject a graduated-payment mortgage. This offers initially—and artificially—low monthly payments that usually don't cover the interest expense in the early years. Thus, your mortgage balance will grow, not shrink. Such negative amortization increases the possibility that you'll have to write a check to the lender when you sell.

Advice for Homeowners

Be cautious about taking out a home-equity loan. Although borrowing against the market value of your home (less your mortgage outstanding) is tempting, this increasingly popular tactic could inadvertently deplete your equity. For example, if you have a $90,000 mortgage

The New Realities of Remodeling

"Sweat equity" was one of the catchwords of the last bull market in real estate. Refurbish your home, promised fix-up gurus, and a feverish buyer would pay you several times the cost when you sold. In reality, sellers of remodeled homes often owed any profits they collected more to inflation than to carpentry. Now that prices are softening nationwide, does remodeling make investment sense?

Unfortunately, not very often. The amount a remodeling project might add to the value of your home depends on the type of house and the preferences of home buyers in your area. But most experts agree that, in general, remodeling a single-family home is not a profitable venture.

The major exceptions to this rule are minor cosmetic facelifts undertaken just before you put your home on the market. Fresh paint on the walls or new carpet on the floor typically adds as much as 25% more than it costs to the value of your home. Sprucing up the exterior is particularly effective. If your lawn is brown or patchy, a bag of fertilizer might be the best remodeling investment you could make.

By contrast, involved remodeling projects rarely pay you back fully. In fact, a common mistake is to "overimprove" by adding, say, 1,500 square feet of space if you live in a neighborhood of 2,500-square-foot houses. Better improvements are those that enhance your home's practicality by updating, for example, an obsolescent kitchen. The idea is to present your house in the best possible light, not to turn it into something it isn't.

Adding space or amenities you need to a current house makes the most sense if it keeps you from having to move, particularly if you hold an older, low-interest mortgage. Otherwise, say experts, the bottom line on remodeling is the project's emotional reward. If you are going to stay there for five years or so, you should focus on the enjoyment your home improvements will bring rather than the return.

The Return on Your Improvements

With few exceptions, the best you can expect from a remodeling project is to get your money back when you sell your home. Most of the time, unfortunately, you won't break even. *Money* polled appraisers to find out how much homeowners should expect to recoup on six common projects. Adding a standard bath and updating the kitchen generally pay off best. But in-ground swimming pools add little or no value to your home in resale.

Project	Average cost nationally	Percentage of cost recovered when home is sold		
		Boston	Chicago	Los Angeles
Add a full bathroom	$3,450	100-125	35-75	75-100
Remodel the kitchen	6,830	100-125	40-100	50-100
Add a fireplace	3,010	50-100	40-70	75-100
Add a family room	11,240	75-100	25-65	40-50
Refinish the basement	6,580	50	30-70	N.A.*
Install an in-ground swimming pool	15,400	10-25	0-20	40-50

Sources: R. S. Means Co., Kingston, Mass.; Marshall & Swift, Los Angeles; and local appraisers' estimates.
* Since basements are rare in Los Angeles, no estimates are given here.

on a house now appraised at $150,000, a lender may let you borrow as much as $48,000. But if prices dipped 10%, the new value of your house ($135,000) would be less than your debt ($138,000). If you sold the house and paid a standard 6% broker's commission, you would owe $11,100.

Don't count on future appreciation to fund your retirement. More and more financial advisers are counseling clients against making their home equity a major part of their retirement planning. Because house prices in many areas are such an unknown, you will have to hit the market just right to get your money back. More suitable retirement investments are diversified, tax-sheltered income producers such as Individual Retirement Accounts and company savings plans like 401(k)s.

Go slow on home improvements. Remodeling may add space or panache to your house, but it is unlikely to add a lot of value (see "The New Realities of Remodeling" on the opposite page). Bryan Patchan, director of the National Association of Home Builders Remodelors Council, advises against any remodeling that would elevate the value of your home, plus the cost of improvements, to 20% or more above comparable houses in your area.

Advice for Home Sellers

Take pricing cues from market activity. Before listing your house, ask your real estate broker for a competitive market analysis. This will tell you what similar houses nearby have sold for recently. If prices have been moving up briskly—say, 1% a month or so—set your price roughly 10% above the market analysis. But if prices are trending downward and the market appears soft, you should ask no more than 2% to 5% above recent sales. If you need to unload quickly, set a low price.

Negotiate with your employer for relocation benefits. If a job transfer could force you to sell your residence in a depressed market and buy where home prices are jumping, you may be able to convince your employer to share any loss you may suffer. Roughly a third of the 1,000 major companies that belong to the Employee Relocation Council, a national trade group, compensate employees at least partially. Some firms dole out this perk on a case-by-case basis. Others may limit the reimbursement to a percentage of the seller's loss, say 85%, or impose a dollar cap ranging from $5,000 to $20,000. Ask about your company's policy. If there is none, try to convince your benefits department to create one for you.

Buying Your First House

You can still reach your goal by tapping sources of low-cost cash, including Mom and Dad.

Many discouraged young people feel like giving up on the American dream of home ownership. Incomes in most areas have not kept pace with rising house prices. Lenders have tightened mortgage-qualification standards. And you need a pile of cash for the down payment—typically, 10% to 20% of the purchase price—plus closing costs. These costs can total 5% of house prices and include a year's property taxes as well as fees for the lender's administrative expenses and a title search. The bottom line: With the median house price about $96,400, renters often need at least $20,000 or so in savings to become buyers. No wonder that, according to a recent study by the National Association of Realtors, more than 80% of renters under 35 say they don't have the money to become homeowners.

If you are among them, don't get mad, get busy. If you're willing to do the necessary legwork, you can cut your costs by finding lenders who accept down payments of less than 20%, locating a house selling for a below-market price, and making use of government or employer assistance programs for first-time buyers.

Interviews with real estate agents, mortgage lenders, and other housing analysts reveal a variety of creative ways to help you buy your first house. (For tips on choosing your first mortgage, see "Shopping for Banking Services" on page 125.) Before you look at a single home, it's also essential to figure out how much house you can carry. The table below will help. So will these guidelines used by many mortgage lenders:

● The price should not exceed 2.5 times your annual gross income.

● Your total annual payments for a mortgage, homeowners insurance, and property taxes should be no more than 28% of your gross income.

● Your total housing payments plus your long-term debts and such major fixed expenses as alimony should not exceed 36% of your income (33% if you make a down payment of less than 20%).

Consequently, for many people the first step toward buying a house is lowering their debt loads to qualify for a mortgage. Another way to break out of the rental rut is to save rigorously. First-time buyers spend an average of 2.5 years tucking away cash for a down payment, according to a survey by Chicago Title Insurance. One savings technique used by tenants is to pay themselves extra rent each month. For example, if your actual rent is $600, budget $750 and deposit the extra $150 in a money-market fund (recently yielding around 8%). After two years, you'll have about $3,890.

You can also make home ownership more affordable by looking for a condominium or

How Much House Can You Afford?

This table shows the financial realities of home ownership, with a 30-year, fixed-rate mortgage. Many lenders require that your monthly mortgage payments not exceed 28% of your gross income. A general rule is that the price of a home should be less than 2½ times your annual gross income. For a more precise estimate of home ownership costs, add the annual homeowners insurance premium and real estate taxes to your mortgage payments. If you haven't yet bought a home, ask your real estate agent for estimates.

For a house that costs . . .	with a down payment of . . .	here is your monthly payment at:			
		8%	10%	12%	14%
$80,000	$8,000	$528	$632	$741	$853
	16,000	470	562	658	785
120,000	12,000	793	948	1,111	1,280
	24,000	704	842	987	1,138
200,000	20,000	1,321	1,580	1,851	2,133
	40,000	1,174	1,404	1,646	1,896

Housing Costs Around the Country

In the year that ended in March 1989, the median-price existing house failed to keep up with inflation in 23 of the 50 largest population centers, listed here alphabetically. The WEFA Group, an economics forecasting firm in Bala Cynwyd, Pennsylvania, expects the homes to bounce back somewhat. It forecasts that house prices in only three of the spots will rise less than its projected 4.9% inflation rate over the next year: Detroit, New Orleans, and Oklahoma City. If inflation hits 6%, homeowners in Dallas/Fort Worth and Denver would be losers, too.

Riverside, California and Buffalo are projected to have the strongest housing markets over the next year. Why? Prospective buyers squeezed out of homes around Los Angeles and Orange County are making the hour-or-so commute to Riverside, where the median-price house sells for 52% less than in Orange County. Buffalo's prices are fueled by a bustling economy plus expected growth from the recent trade agreement between Canada and the U.S.

Metropolitan	Estimated median sales price in first quarter 1989	Inflation-adjusted return for first quarter 1988-first quarter 1989	Projected sales price for first quarter 1990	Projected inflation-adjusted return for first quarter 1989-first quarter 1990
Atlanta	$100,944	−3.8%	$107,669	+1.8%
Baltimore	90,954	+3.8	97,835	+2.7
Bergen/Passaic counties, N.J.	199,929	+6.1	212,633	+1.5
Boston	181,239	−2.5	194,033	+2.2
Buffalo	69,098	+2.8	75,950	+5.0
Charlotte	84,870	−2.1	91,076	+2.4
Chicago	99,896	+2.6	106,964	+2.2
Cincinnati	71,298	+1.9	76,537	+2.4
Cleveland	70,340	+0.8	75,284	+2.1
Columbus	75,891	+9.6	82,185	+3.4
Dallas/Fort Worth	84,056	−7.1	88,607	+0.5
Denver	80,709	−8.6	85,310	+0.8
Detroit	73,930	−1.6	77,036	−0.7
Fort Lauderdale	83,051	+0.7	89,577	+3.0
Hartford	167,239	−4.5	178,363	+1.8
Houston	57,870	−8.9	62,470	+3.0
Indianapolis	67,299	+3.9	72,088	+2.2
Kansas City	70,417	−6.0	75,619	+2.5
Long Island	172,904	+12.9	186,182	+2.8
Los Angeles/Long Beach	194,285	+16.5	210,128	+3.3
Louisville	55,935	+2.2	59,749	+1.9
Memphis	75,647	−7.4	81,539	+2.9
Miami	85,554	+4.7	91,684	+2.3
Milwaukee	73,891	−3.2	78,653	+1.5
Minneapolis/St. Paul	87,888	−0.9	94,052	+2.1
Monmouth/Ocean counties, N.J.	163,626	+2.4	176,237	+2.8
Nashville	77,408	−5.0	82,056	+1.1
Newark	195,375	+3.8	208,574	+1.9
New Orleans	76,650	0.0	79,562	−1.1
New York City	182,017	−7.7	195,851	+2.7
Norfolk	98,286	−3.8	105,551	+2.5
Oklahoma City	54,031	−9.4	56,630	−0.1
Orange County, Calif.	235,915	+23.4	255,957	+3.6
Orlando	79,517	−4.0	86,110	+3.4
Philadelphia	105,646	+3.1	113,080	+2.1
Phoenix	81,236	−2.2	88,036	+3.5
Pittsburgh	63,772	−0.3	67,950	+1.7
Portland, Ore.	66,485	+0.7	71,139	+2.1
Riverside, Calif.	112,407	+3.7	123,484	+5.0
Rochester	77,690	+1.1	83,670	+2.8
Sacramento	134,821	+0.4	147,094	+4.2
St. Louis	76,767	−1.4	81,923	+1.8
Salt Lake City	68,584	0.0	73,623	+2.4
San Antonio	63,206	−5.0	67,159	+1.4
San Diego	160,644	+14.5	174,333	+3.6
San Francisco	176,843	−6.4	188,405	+1.6
San Jose	196,786	+8.2	213,211	+3.4
Seattle	95,080	+2.8	102,401	+2.8
Tampa/St. Petersburg	67,422	+7.0	72,600	+2.8
Washington, D.C.	132,256	−5.0	141,846	+2.4

SOURCES: THE WEFA GROUP, NATIONAL ASSOCIATION OF REALTORS

townhouse, which can cost $10,000 to $40,000 less than a comparable single-family detached house in the same area. A condo is an apartment that you own. Condo owners often hold mortgages and pay monthly fees to their condominium associations for upkeep of public areas, such as lawns, tennis courts, and swimming pools. A townhouse is one of a row of houses attached to one another but separately owned, usually with no maintenance fees.

In addition, foreclosed properties offer bargains at prices that are frequently 10% to 80% lower than those of similar houses. Despite what you may think, buying a foreclosed house doesn't necessarily mean taking advantage of someone else's misfortune. Generally, foreclosed homes are sold through real estate brokers or at auctions long after their owners have moved out. To get a list of any foreclosed homes currently for sale in your area by the Federal Mortgage Association, call the company at 800-553-4636.

If you're truly a hungry home buyer, you should not overlook the following primary

12 Steps to Home Ownership

Once you find a house you want to buy, follow these steps to get it:

- Sign a binder agreement with the seller noting the house price and the date when you will sign a contract, which is usually set for a few days later. Give the seller's lawyer or real estate agent a good-faith deposit, typically 1% of the purchase price.

- Hire a lawyer or closing company to review—and amend, if necessary—the contract before you sign it.

- Sign the contract and make a second deposit, usually 9% of the house price.

- Shop for a mortgage (see the story on page 75) and gather the necessary documents to fill out the loan application. Pull out last year's W-2 form and receipts for self-employment earnings; statements with your bank, brokerage, mutual fund, and company savings plan balances; credit-card statements; and payment books for personal loans.

- Give the lender your completed application and documents.

- Arrange for homeowners insurance (see "Don't Leave Home Without It" on page 81).

- Have a professional engineer inspect the house for structural problems. Make sure the sales contract is contingent upon the inspector's written assurances that the foundation, the roof, and the electrical, plumbing, and heating systems are all sound. Typical cost of an inspection: $175 to $500. For an impartial report, you can hire one of the 600 building inspectors nationwide who belong to the American Society of Home Inspectors (ASHI) and sell nothing aside from their assessments. If the inspector turns up any problems, ask the seller to make the necessary repairs before the closing.

- A week before the closing, meet again with your lawyer or closing company representative to prepare for settlement day.

- A few days later, get certified checks from your bank for the closing.

- On closing day, give the house a final inspection.

- At the closing, write checks for assorted fees and escrow accounts and will receive from the lender a check for the mortgage, which you will sign over to the seller.

- Accept the keys to the house from the seller—a practical necessity but also a token of your new status as a homeowner.

sources in your search for financial help. The extra effort often pays off:

Your family. Should your parents or other relatives be willing to chip in, ask them to make a gift and not a loan. Otherwise, a lender will add their loan to your other long-term debts in determining how much of a mortgage you can carry. The extra debt could be just enough to disqualify you from getting the loan you want. A mother and father can give their child and his or her spouse up to $40,000 a year without owing federal gift taxes.

Lenders with low-down-payment, insured mortgages. Insured mortgages require less than 20% down and often have liberal mortgage-qualification rules. For example, if you're a member of the armed services, a veteran, or the spouse of a deceased vet, look into mortgages backed by the Veterans Administration—nothing-down, 30-year, fixed-rate loans of up to $144,000. The VA sets its interest rate, recently around 9.5%, at or slightly below the level of conventional loans; many mortgage lenders also offer VA loans. To apply, you need a certificate verifying your military service or your deceased spouse's. You can get the certificate and a list of nearby VA lenders from your local VA office.

Anyone can apply for Federal Housing Administration-insured loans, which demand down payments of 3% to 5%. The FHA insures mortgages of as much as $67,500, or $101,250 in the areas defined as high cost by the FHA. Most mortgage lenders offer FHA loans, charging interest rates at or below market level. FHA mortgages come with either fixed rates (lately about 10.5%) or adjustable rates (about 9%) that cannot rise or fall by more than one percentage point a year or five points over the life of the loan.

If you buy private mortgage insurance (PMI), many lenders will let you make a down payment of as low as 5% on a conventional mortgage. This insurance, sold by the lender, covers the difference between your down payment and what the lender usually demands, typically 20%. The cost of PMI is a one-time fee of 1% to 1.25% of the mortgage plus an annual charge, included in your monthly mortgage payment, of about 0.3% to 0.4% of the mortgage. So for a $90,000 mortgage, PMI might cost $900 initially, plus $23 a month. You stop paying PMI premiums when your equity—the amount of the house you own outright—equals 20% of its market value. This usually takes seven to nine years, less if your home appreciates rapidly.

Lenders charging multiple points. Part of the closing costs are lender's points or loan-administrative fees. Each point equals 1% of the mortgage amount. Typically, borrowers pay one to three points. But many lenders will lower a borrower's points in exchange for a higher mortgage rate over the life of the loan. This trade can be the ticket to a house if you are cash poor but can make the higher monthly payments. For example, paying one point rather than three would reduce your up-front costs by $2,400 on a $120,000 mortgage.

Your boss. Increasingly, employers who want to hire or keep talented employees are helping them reduce their home-ownership costs. Such programs are offered by Colgate-Palmolive, Hartz Mountain, and Mutual Benefit Life Insurance; ask your employee-benefits department about any programs where you work. Some companies pay for their employees' PMI or closing costs. Others will get local lenders to shave mortgage rates by one to two percentage points. But don't assume that such a rate is the best in town. You may be able to find a lender with even better terms.

If your debts are low and you have an employee savings plan such as a 401(k), ask your employer about borrowing against your account for a down payment. You usually have 10 years to repay the loan. The rate you will pay is typically the rate on short-term Treasury notes, or within two points of the prime lending rate. Both are well below what most banks charge for personal loans. Avoid *withdrawing* money for a down payment from your company savings plan. If you're younger than 59½, you'll have to pay tax on the withdrawal as well as a 10% penalty, just as you would for taking money prematurely out of the Individual Retirement Account.

Your state or local housing agency. More than 180 public agencies provide financial aid for first-time buyers. Generally, both your family's income and the price of the house you want must be at or near the medians in your area for you to qualify for the subsidy, which sometimes comes in the form of low-rate mortgages. In other cases, state housing agencies lend money toward a down payment.

The seller. Fees for a house survey, appraisal, and title search normally top $1,000. But you often can reduce them by hiring the companies the seller used since they have already done much of the work.

The Benefits of Using a Real Estate Broker

In a soft market, buyers and sellers may get a better deal with professional help.

Whether you are a buyer or seller, one way to lessen the stress of house trading is to work with a seasoned real estate broker. A professional can help you get a feel for the local housing market, which will improve your chances of getting the best deal. As a rule, brokers represent sellers and get paid by them—even though they may seem to work for buyers. Typical commission: 6% to 7% of a house's sales price. The buyer is a customer rather than a client. For example, if a buyer tells a seller's broker that he will bid $120,000 for a house but would go as high as $150,000, the broker is legally bound to report this to the homeowner.

A tiny but growing group of so-called buyer's brokers are hired by home buyers and have no obligation to sellers. A buyer's broker tells his or her client when a house has problems and negotiates on the buyer's behalf.

When hunting either a buyer's or a seller's broker, start by asking friends or business associates for the names of reliable agencies as well as individual brokers. (For referrals to buyer's brokers in your area, you can also call the Real Estate Buyer's Agent Council in Denver at 303-759-2211.) Then, after brief telephone conversations with likely brokers about their backgrounds and experience, arrange to meet with the two or three most promising candidates. In your face-to-face interviews, consider the following:

Advice for home buyers. If you are willing to pay for a buyer's broker, find out how you will be billed. Buyer's brokers charge either flat fees, hourly rates, or a portion of the commissions sellers pay their own brokers. The best deal is a flat fee, typically $2,500 to $7,000.

Be certain that the broker participates in a local multiple-listing service, which will assure you of seeing as many houses as possible in your price range. Avoid brokers who show buyers only houses listed by their own agencies to avoid splitting commissions with other agencies. Also, use extreme caution before signing up with a mortgage lender suggested to you by your broker. By federal law, brokers cannot receive kickbacks from lenders. Increasingly, though, major mortgage lenders are striking cozy deals with brokers. The lender generally splits with the broker the points or loan-origination fee that will be charged to the buyer.

Advice for home sellers. You should sign a two- or three-month exclusive right-to-sell contract with a broker. But don't be taken in by a broker who gushes about your house just to secure a listing. Instead, invite several brokers to your house and say: "Tell me what this property is worth—and tell me why." A competent broker should be able to assess your home in comparison with others that recently have sold. Your house probably has some structural or cosmetic problems. Whose doesn't? So after describing them to your broker, ask how the flaws will be played down in the sales pitch. If the broker is stumped, you need one with more imagination.

In negotiating fees with a broker, you will have the most leverage if the house is expensive or in an active market. Some brokers, for example, will accept fees as low as 3% to 4% of a home's sales price. Insist that at least once every two to three weeks the broker hold an open house for would-be buyers and other brokers. The broker should also promote your house weekly in a multiple-listing service and provide you with progress reports on the sales campaign. If you get no nibbles from the first 10 showings, the problem could be an unrealistic asking price, especially if your place is in disrepair. Or the fault may lie not in your stairs but in your broker. In that case, get yourself a savvier salesman when your sales contract expires.

Don't Leave Home Without It

Adequate homeowners insurance can mean the difference between peace of mind and disaster.

As soon as your mortgage is approved, start shopping for homeowners insurance. Without it, you can't take possession of the house. The policy will protect you if your house is damaged or destroyed; if your possessions are damaged, destroyed, or stolen; and if someone other than a family member is injured while on your property.

Your annual homeowners premium—the overall cost of the policy—will depend on a variety of factors. These include the amount of coverage, the age and construction material of your house, the local crime rate, whether your home is in a high-risk zone for hurricanes or earthquakes, and the size of your deductible (the maximum amount you agree to pay for a loss before your insurance kicks in). In general, a $100,000 policy with the standard $250 deductible will cost $300 to $500 a year. A $500 deductible can cut your annual premium by about 10%. (For more information, see "A Smart Shoppers Guide to Insurance" on page 100.)

When choosing a policy, phone three or four agents for price quotes. Some salespeople work for only one company. Ask them the following questions:

What types of damages will be covered? Basic homeowners policies protect you against damage only from perils such as fire, smoke, windstorms, vandalism, and lightning. Ask for the most comprehensive policy, which will cover losses from all causes except those specifically excluded in the contract. Flood damage is never covered, so if you live in a flood-prone area, ask about policies sold through the government's insurance program.

How much coverage should I get? Your policy ought to cover at least 80% of the value of the house. Try to get what's called a guaranteed-replacement endorsement, which will reimburse you for up to 100% of the cost of rebuilding the house. Replacement-value coverage will add 10% to 15% to the cost of your premium.

How will my coverage rise with inflation? Don't accept a policy unless it comes with an inflation endorsement that will keep your coverage in line with construction costs. Ask for an endorsement that is tied to a state or regional index, rather than a national one.

What about my possessions? Personal belongings are generally insured for up to half the amount of your coverage for the structure. A $100,000 policy, for example, typically provides $50,000 in contents coverage. Insuring your possessions for their replacement cost, not just their actual cash value, will add 10% to 15% to your premium. Most policies provide theft coverage of only $1,000 for jewelry and furs and $2,500 for silverware. For more insurance on valuables, buy what are called floaters. Each floater covers one category, such as silver, and costs roughly 30¢ to $4 annually for every $100 of valuables you insure. If you have, say, a stamp or coin collection with no single item of great value, consider buying a blanket policy. Typical cost: $60 to $70 a year to cover collectibles for up to $1,000 or $2,000 apiece and the entire set up to $5,000.

What will happen if someone gets hurt on my property? The standard homeowners policy includes personal liability coverage against lawsuits of up to $100,000 for members of your household and $1,000 in medical payments for others injured while on your property. In these sue-crazy times, you might want higher limits. Ask for limits of $500,000 for liability and $5,000 for medical payments; the extra cost will be about $25 to $50 a year. If you work at home part time, pay the $15 a year or so for incidental business coverage of up to $5,000 against damage to work-related property and up to $300,000 for any work-related accidents in your home.

Vacation Home Bargains

The hills and beaches are alive with the sounds of savvy buyers picking up properties for a song.

From ski cabins in Park City, Utah to condos on Padre Island, Texas, sellers of vacation homes are willing to accept 10% to 50% less for their properties than they would have in the mid-1980s. The softness is blamed on overbuilding, slumping regional economies, and tax reform's restrictions on rental write-offs. (One big tax break remains: If your adjusted gross income is $100,000 or less, you can deduct as much as $25,000 in losses from a vacation home you rent out against income from other sources.)

Many real estate analysts regard today's depressed prices as only temporary, however. Reason: The same baby boomers who bid up prices of first homes will cause a similar run on vacation homes in the coming decade. Before rushing off to make an offer on a vacation retreat, you'll need to figure out whether you can really afford a second home. Mortgage lenders suggest you first answer these important questions:

Do you have enough income? Your combined mortgage payments, homeowners insurance, and property taxes for your primary and vacation homes should not exceed 28% of your gross annual income. In addition, payments on your mortgages and other long-term debts should not top 36% of your gross.

Can you afford the down payment? It probably will be 20% of the purchase price versus as little as 10% for a primary residence. You may be required to put down 25% if you plan to rent out the property.

Have you allowed for the extra costs of a vacation home? You may be charged one-quarter to one-half of a percentage point more for a mortgage on a second home than for one on a primary residence. Because the getaway place may be remote and often unoccupied, your total insurance costs can run 50% higher than for a similarly priced principal residence. For example, beachfront properties often require flood insurance, which can cost $500 a year for $100,000 in coverage. And if you rent out your second home, you will pay roughly 20% extra to cover damage while tenants are there.

Resist the temptation to look for a house in a resort area merely because you enjoyed your vacation there this past summer. Instead, take a reality check. For instance, if the trip back and forth from your principal home would be unbearably long on a regular basis, you need to scout out a more accessible vacation spot. And be certain that you will get enough use out of the place for what you'll pay. If you only make the trip once a year, staying in a hotel will be cheaper.

Once you settle on an area, it pays to retain a knowledgeable local real estate agent. The agent can tell you, for example, whether the location you love is becoming heavily populated with year-round residents—a red flag that you could be stuck with escalating taxes to pay for schools you won't use. Local government officials can also provide valuable information. In a waterfront community, they can supply a study of the shoreline's erosion pattern, which could prevent you from buying a house that might one day need a $10,000 retaining wall. In winter resort areas, a highway department officer can cite the priority assigned by the town to snowplowing specific roads; some owners of secluded homes may not see plows for days.

When you find a house, a real estate agent can help you make a reasonable bid. Ask him or her for the average number of days houses are on the market compared with a year ago—two to four months is typical—and how much the seller has dropped the asking price. Sellers in languishing markets will often accept low bids. In areas such as Lake Winnipesaukee, New Hampshire, where properties took an average of 45 days longer to sell in 1989 than a year earlier, vacation homes go for as much as 30% below their list prices.

Be sure to ask your agent about auctions. They are fast becoming a favorite way to find buyers quickly for banks with foreclosed homes, developers with unsold properties, and even anxious homeowners. Auctioned homes typically go for 10% to 45% less than their asking prices. When bidding at an auction, you must bring a certified check—usually ranging from $2,500 to $10,000—and deposit any remaining balance on 10% of the purchase price in about a week. Then you will have 45 to 60 days to get a mortgage. Vacation homes listed with agents by a decedent's estate can also offer terrific buys. Families often are so eager to unload these houses that they may offer to help you with financing.

Taking Care of
Your Family

What really motivates people to get their finances in order? Oftentimes, the catalyst is the birth of their first child, a happy turning point in life that raises many sobering financial issues for parents. Chief among them are the costs of a college education, a growing family's insurance protection, and the parent's estate planning—all of which are covered in this chapter.

Providing for college. This is perhaps the most daunting task confronting today's families. Unlike saving for a house and retirement, in which the cost is spread over many years, a college education can consume upwards of $70,000 in just four short years. Moreover, it is an expense that is likely to rise more swiftly than the cost of living. (To stay abreast, see "Meeting the High Cost of College," beginning on page 86.)

You have every reason to hope that the choice of a college will be careful and reasoned. Yet the process of entering selective schools has become a frustrating fright of passage for many young people. Competitive pressures have always existed, of course. But now they have been needlessly exacerbated by colleges fearful of baby-bust enrollment declines. The solution: Colleges have embraced slick marketing techniques that sell education as if it were a new credit card, with fistfuls of direct mail, focus groups, and celebrity endorsements. As a result, students often wind up tailoring their resumes to a task in which the goal is not to get educated but to get accepted.

Insuring against financial crisis. A well-designed insurance program includes many different types of policies—auto, homeowners or tenants, excess liability, life, disability, and health. Such a package should shield you against disaster, not against the cost of every inflamed tooth or dented fender. Like a good soldier, you should recognize that no protection is perfect and too much of it can weigh you down. Thus, the policies you buy should cover only the perils, likely or not, that can drain your assets the most, as described in "A Smart Shoppers Guide to Insurance," beginning on page 100.

Keeping it all in the family. Whatever your age, you can always find reasons to put off estate planning. There is the hassle of finding a lawyer, the expense and, worst of all, the unsettling feeling you get from thinking about your own death. Yet none of these excuses justifies the price—in both money and frustration—that your survivors will pay if you don't plan ahead. If you die without a will, you leave your family's financial security to the mercy of inflexible state laws, plodding courts, and sometimes greedy lawyers. You could also wind up bequeathing far more than necessary to Uncle Sam. To sidestep these pitfalls, see "Putting Your Estate in Order," beginning on page 109. It explains how most families can pass their legacies on with a minimum of red tape—and zero federal estate tax.

Meeting the High Cost of College

There are cost-saving steps you can take now whether your child is five or 15.

If you are a parent, the goal of raising the money to send your child to college may seem achingly unattainable. After all, four years at a private college now costs more than $45,000 on average ($18,000 at public colleges). If the price keeps growing by 6% annually, as many economists expect, a coveted bachelor's degree for today's newborn could cost nearly $140,000. But the situation is far from hopeless. Consider the following points:

● Not all schools charge $20,000 a year. The very top schools receive most of the attention when it comes to costs. And projections of future costs are misleading because they ignore the fact that income will grow, too. The reality is that you can send a youngster to a prestigious school for two-thirds of what the most expensive colleges cost. Excellent

educations are also available at good but glamourless schools for less than half the cost of the priciest institutions.

● Roughly 50% of *Money* subscribers (median household income: $60,700) would be eligible under current rules for some financial aid. Even with income as high as $75,000, you may qualify for assistance—particularly at higher-priced schools.

● If you qualify for little or no aid, there are many strategies and investments that will help you amass the cash you need.

Of course, this is not to dismiss the painful fact that tuition during the 1980s increased 52%, in constant dollars, at private universities and 31% at public ones while median income rose just 6%. The only thing that has increased faster than tuition is the public's perception of the cost of higher education. According to a recent poll, the average person thinks that the full cost of attending a four-year public college is 57% higher than it actually is and that private colleges are 11% more expensive than they are.

Pressure on college costs will continue in the 1990s, despite the likelihood of declining enrollment. Some schools have discovered that raising prices actually attracts more applicants by creating the impression that an institution is more exclusive—administrators call this the Chivas Regal effect. But many experts don't expect costs to escalate at double the inflation rate as they did in the early 1980s. Increases of only 6% to 7% annually are more likely in this decade.

Furthermore, many families do not understand the financial aid system. One myth that often encourages parental paralysis is that by saving, a family will drastically reduce its chances for aid. It's true that a formula is applied to family income and assets, and that the more you have, the larger the share of the financial burden you will be expected to carry. But the formula assigns the greatest weight to income, and only about 5.6% of assets held in the parents' names is counted. So, if you save $10,000, you will be expected to contribute $560 of it in college costs, leaving you $9,440 farther ahead than someone who didn't save at all.

Parents convinced of the value of saving for education, however, feel that they face a painful choice: to invest for their children's college or their own retirement. Financial planners counsel young families to put retirement first, especially if they have 401(k)s to which their companies make matching contributions. Parents of young children should consider contributing the maximum to such plans even if it means no college savings for a few years. If they "overfund" retirement accounts now, they can kick in less later when money is needed for college expenses.

One funding source you don't want to overlook is grandparents. They can make a cash gift in any amount and pay no gift tax, as long as the money goes for tuition and is paid directly to the college. To pay for room and board, each grandparent can give an additional $10,000 free of gift tax. Grandparents can also lend a combined $10,000 without charging interest.

While it's never too early to start preparing for college, neither is it ever too late. The following strategies and financial products are appropriate for families who are just beginning to plan, but at different stages: when their youngsters are entering grade school; when they are exiting junior high; and when they are commencing their senior year of high school.

Getting Underway in Grade School

Families with more than 10 years until they ship their children off to college have time—the best savings tool that money can't buy. They have time to set dollars aside, and those dollars have time to compound. Say you're planning on sending a youngster to a school that costs $5,000 a year today, and assume that costs will increase 6% annually. If you begin saving when the child is five years old, you would need to set aside about $150 each month. But if you wait until age 10, you would have to come up with about $300 monthly. And if you don't start until the child's 15th birthday, it will take more than $1,000 a month to meet the goal.

Given the long lead time that parents of grade-schoolers have, they should think in terms of investing not just saving. Many people are reluctant to put their college savings at risk and stick to conservative vehicles. But with more than a decade until freshman year, low-yielding savings instruments leave you vulnerable to inflation. Thus, you should deploy some of your college portfolio—perhaps half—in riskier growth investments promising higher returns than those available on such traditional college-savings vehicles as Series EE bonds, certificates of deposit, and zero-coupon bonds.

The worksheet on page 88 will help you figure out how much money you need to save now to meet your college goal. The next question to confront is whether you should keep college funds in your name or your children's. While traditional wisdom has held that a custodial account is the way to go, many thoughtful parents are rejecting that strategy. For starters, money put in a custodial account is irrevocable. And after a certain age—usually 18 or 21—the youngster is free to do what he or she wants with it.

In addition, a custodial account is no longer the tax haven it was before 1986, when the kiddie tax reduced the advantages of shifting money into a child's name. If your child is under 14, the first $500 of investment income in his or her name is tax-free; the next $500 is taxed at his or her rate, probably 15%. Anything above $1,000 will be taxed at your rate. Once a child hits 14, all earnings on assets in his or her name are taxed at the child's rate. Also keep in mind that the formula for calculating financial aid is another reason to keep money out of the child's name. Colleges expect 35% of any money in a child's name to go toward school, whereas only 5.6% of money in the parents' name counts (see "Playing the Financial Aid Game" on page 93).

What follows is a closer look at some financial products and strategies designed for families with college-bound children. Since most of the investments offer low risk and low returns, they are most appropriate for the conservative half of a college portfolio:

Series EE savings bonds. These supersafe government bonds have always been exempt from state and local taxes. But beginning in 1990, EE bonds bought to finance college are also free of federal tax for many parents. Interest is fully tax-free for married couples filing jointly with $60,000 or less in adjusted gross income (modified to include Social Security benefits, retirement contributions, and passive investment losses). The cutoff is $40,000 for single parents. The tax break phases out beyond these levels and disappears

A Savings Plan to Cover Tuition

The worksheet below will help you calculate what you need to sock away this and every year to meet future college costs. It assumes that you have no college savings yet, that costs will grow by 6.5% annually, and that your investments will earn 8% after taxes.

1. Number of years before college (18 minus child's age) _____

2. Present annual college costs (use $4,733 average for public school, $12,635 for private, or the cost of a particular school) _____

3. Future cost of first year of college (line 2 times factor from column A in the table) _____

4. Future total cost of college (4.69 times line 3) _____

5. Amount you need to invest each year to meet that goal (line 4 times factor from column B) _____

Years to College	A	B
1	1.07	.926
2	1.13	.445
3	1.21	.285
4	1.29	.205
5	1.37	.158
6	1.46	.126
7	1.55	.104
8	1.65	.087
9	1.76	.074
10	1.88	.064
11	2.00	.056
12	2.13	.049
13	2.27	.043
14	2.41	.038
15	2.57	.034
16	2.74	.031
17	2.92	.027
18	3.11	.025

entirely at $90,000 for couples and $55,000 for singles. (Note: These amounts are revised annually to keep pace with inflation.)

EE bonds pay a variable rate, recently around 8%. A taxpayer in the 28% bracket who pays only federal taxes would need to get a taxable yield of nearly 11% to beat the EE bond's recent rate. For taxpayers in high tax states, the taxable equivalent would be as much as 12.5%. Although EE bond yields are guaranteed not to drop below 6%, you must hold them for five years or you will receive a return below 6%.

Baccalaureate bonds. Zero-coupon municipal bonds—nicknamed baccalaureate, B.A., or college savings bonds—pay no interest until they mature. Instead, zeros are sold at a sizable discount from the face value you collect at maturity. Thus, they offer parents the security of knowing exactly how much cash will be available when a child enters college. Like most munis, these are exempt from federal taxes and, for state residents, from state and local taxes as well. Recent yields on B.A. bonds were 6.5% to 7% on maturities of 10 years or more—the equivalent of a taxable 9% to 9.7%.

These B.A. bonds have a big advantage over other munis, however. They generally cannot be called, or redeemed prematurely by the issuer, in the event that interest rates decline. States that have issued B.A. bonds are Connecticut, Delaware, Hawaii, Illinois, Iowa, Missouri, North Carolina, North Dakota, Oregon, Rhode Island, Virginia, and Washington. Arkansas, Colorado, New Hampshire, and Tennessee are likely to offer them soon. If your broker can't find you a noncallable zero muni with an attractive yield, you may consider taxable zero-coupon Treasuries. They are exempt from state and local taxes and recently yielded 8% on 15-year maturities.

Universal life insurance. Universal life offers yet another tax-advantaged way to save but makes sense only if you also need insurance. With such policies, part of your premium is deposited in an account where it compounds tax deferred at a recent rate of 9%. When your child is ready to go to college, you can

withdraw the cash balance or borrow against it. But because up-front commissions are usually steep, your cash value is minimal in the early years. Two low-load insurers whose products allow you to build up cash value quickly are USAA and Ameritas. Insurance agents like to point out that cash-value life insurance provides a mechanism for savings. But if you are a disciplined saver, you may be better off buying cheaper term insurance and investing the difference in other tax-advantaged assets.

Prepayment plans. These allow you to pay now the cost of sending your child to school later, thereby eliminating the risk that inflation will put college out of your reach. Offered only in Florida, Michigan, and Wyoming, the best prepayment plan is that available in Michigan. In 1989, parents of a six-year-old put up $7,500—or 82% of the current costs—and their child's tuition is guaranteed at any Michigan state school in 12 years. When the child enrolls in 2001, he or she will have to pay taxes on the difference between his parents' prepayment and the current tuition. If tuition rises 6% a year, four years at a Michigan school will cost $18,512, so the child's tax, assuming the 15% bracket, would be $1,652. Meanwhile, if the same parents put their $7,500 in a 12-year zero muni, recently paying 6.5%, the bond would pay $2,348 less at maturity than the $18,512 tuition.

The deeper the prepayment's discount from current price, the better the deal. Florida's plan includes no discount. Wyoming's discount is 17% for a six-year-old, but there is only one four-year public college in the state. Moreover, if your child opts for a private or out-of-state school, Michigan refunds the average cost of Michigan state schools, but Wyoming returns just your principal plus 4%, and Florida refunds principal only.

Hemar Education Corporation of America, a private company involved in educational financing, is awaiting an SEC ruling on a prepayment plan that would offer a choice of a wide range of schools nationwide. Brandeis and George Washington University are among the well-known institutions considering participating. Also awaiting a go-ahead from the SEC is the nonprofit Tuition Maintenance Organization's College Prepayment Fund. Under this program, your prepayment would go into a new no-load mutual fund managed by Kemper and would guarantee your tuition at participating colleges. If, come college time, your investment is greater than the tuition, you would get to keep the excess.

A High-Speed Start in High School

Don't feel too guilty if your child is headed for high school and you're only just beginning to think about college. Most families wait until senior year. And if you have the feeling that there's nothing you can do at this late date that will make a dent in future tuition bills, you're wrong. Many of the moves you make now will have a substantial impact on your ability to finance higher education.

Before you do anything else, you should determine whether you are likely to get financial aid (see the worksheet on page 94). Colleges use a formula that takes into account family income and assets to determine what the family will be expected to contribute to college costs. Schools, especially expensive ones, try to make up the difference between their sticker price and the expected contribution; a family that qualifies for aid may pay no more for an elite school than for a middling one. Thus, getting a rough idea of your expected contribution several years in advance will help you

Applying for a Stafford Loan

Formerly called Federal Guaranteed Student Loans, Stafford Loans are available to all college undergraduates, graduate students, and vocational-education students demonstrating financial need. The maximum loan is $2,625 a year for first- and second-year students, $4,000 for upperclassmen, and $7,500 for grad students. A borrower has up to 10 years after graduation to pay back the loan. Interest recently started at 8% annually, rising to 10% in the fourth year of repayment. To apply for a Stafford, a high school senior and his or her parents should take these steps:

● Soon after January 1, fill out the federal financial aid forms required by the colleges to which you are applying. You can get the forms from your high school guidance counselor or the financial aid officers at the colleges. Ask at the colleges whether they require you to complete their own aid forms, too. Male applicants must have registered with the Selective Service System.

● Send the forms to the companies that process them. The College Scholarship Service issues the Financial Aid Form (FAF); American College Testing handles the Family Financial Statement (FFS).

● In the spring, after you receive your letters of acceptance, you will find out how large a Stafford Loan you can get at each college. Some schools send this information to you; others wait for you to ask their financial aid officers.

● Soon after you decide which college to attend, choose a Stafford lender—a bank, S&L, or credit union. If you have trouble locating a Stafford lender, phone the college's financial aid office for names. If this fails, call the Federal Student Aid Information Center at 800-333-4636 for the phone number of the state agency that can supply the names. By federal law, lenders can charge an insurance fee of up to 3% of the loan amount. Fill out the lender's loan application and the promissory note and mail the form to the financial aid office.

● You will be notified by letter within eight weeks if your application is approved. The lender will send the money to the college in the fall.

set savings goals and consider schools you had assumed to be out of your price range.

You may be tempted to turn to a professional for help at this point. Alas, financial advisers who are highly knowledgeable about investments are often uninformed when it comes to financial aid. For instance, many accountants and planners routinely advise parents to shift money into a child's name at age 14 when the kid is no longer hit with the kiddie tax—even though the maneuver may jeopardize aid.

Don't give up if what you will need to pay for the college of your choice or to meet your family's contribution seems an impossible amount to raise. Keep in mind that you do not have to save it all. You will be able to borrow some part and manage another portion out of current cash flow while your child is at college. Now, however, is the time to start thinking about cutting a few corners and adopting automatic savings habits. If you have been contributing to your pension plan over the years, you might consider reducing your contributions—or even ceasing contributions for a few years—and directing that cash toward college savings, particularly if your company plan does not allow borrowing.

Don't trust your instincts if they tell you to make up for lost time by putting your savings into risky investments. The fact is, the closer you are to needing the funds, the more conservative you should be. Indeed, the bulk of your portfolio should be investments that guarantee return of principal, such as bank CDs, zero-coupon bonds, and Series EE bonds. Stagger bond maturities to correspond with tuition-due dates. Also, many banks offer so-called designer CDs of three years or more that mature on the date of your choosing.

If financial aid is not an issue, you can save taxes on income-producing investments by placing them in your child's name. Popular vehicles include double-A-rated corporate zero bonds or ordinary corporates sold at a discount. Recent yields on five-year maturities averaged about 8.5%. Feel free to be generous at this time with a tax-free gift of up to $20,000 to your kid ($10,000 per parent) so that earnings can enjoy the lower tax bite. A

technique for realizing the tax break one year early: Just after the child's 13th birthday, buy a one-year CD that pays all interest at maturity. Such CDs lately yielded 8% to 9.5%.

For investments in your own name, start with EE savings bonds if you qualify for the federal tax break (explained earlier on page 88). Noncallable zero munis are also an excellent choice, though they are sometimes hard to find. You might also consider an intermediate-term bond fund. But realize that with a bond fund your principal is not guaranteed, nor is the yield locked in, as it is with individual bonds. For that reason, you should shift out of a fund about two years before you need the money. Keep in mind that you won't need all your savings in the first year, and that a child entering ninth grade still has six years before he or she is at the midpoint of a college career. You may therefore want to strive for some growth, keeping about 10% to 30% of your college portfolio in fairly conservative mutual funds that invest for total return.

Unprepared in Senior Year

With your budding scholar just one year away from introductory astrophysics, you may now be contemplating a new definition of infinite: The distance between the amount of money you have on hand to meet college costs and what you and your child will actually need.

Fortunately, there is hope for strapped families. Many of you will qualify for some form of financial aid, and even if you don't, help abounds. Among your choices will be three time-tested ways to get a good education at below-market cost. Cooperative education programs, in which students split their time between academe and the workplace, can allow students to pay the cost of tuition with their own earnings. The Reserve Officers Training Corps (ROTC) of the Army, Air Force, and Navy offer competitive programs that can cover almost all school costs. And don't overlook public schools, including ones outside your own state. Several regional consortiums of state school systems offer ways for students to attend colleges in nearby states at less than out-of-state prices.

For most people, though, the solution will be borrowing. Federal student loans are available to children from families with fairly high incomes, assuming the applicants demonstrate financial need. So don't skip applying for loans just because you think your family's income is too high for you to qualify. Each college interprets a family's financial data differently. Sometimes, high-income families who have extenuating circumstances—say, heavy medical costs or several children in college—can receive aid that they would not otherwise get. Indeed, students whose parents earn $60,000 or more may qualify for Stafford Loans, which are described on page 90.

There are other types of attractive loans for people who don't qualify for these federally subsidized student ones. Most other loans require parents to take responsibility for repayment, though all or some payments can usually be deferred until the student has graduated. Following are some of the options:

401(k) loans. You may want to borrow against the buildup in your 401(k) retirement account, if your plan allows you to do so. The major advantage of these loans (which can be for up to 10 years) is that interest payments go into your own account instead of into a bank's coffers.

Home-equity loans. If you can't borrow against a 401(k), this is probably your best loan option because of its tax benefits. Other education loans will be only 10% deductible in 1990 and not at all after that. But you can write off 100% of the interest on home-equity loans of up to $100,000. With rates recently averaging about 12.25%, a home-equity loan actually costs a borrower in the 28% tax bracket only about 8.8%.

Government-sponsored loans. Some states have educational loan programs that make money widely available at below-market rates. Massachusetts, for example, offers a 15-year, fixed-rate loan, recently 9.5%, to families of students attending 48 schools within its

borders. A 6% origination fee brings the actual annual percentage rate to 10.6%. Parents with one child in college can earn as much as $120,000 a year and still qualify. To find out about such loans, check with a local college financial aid office or one in the state where your child will attend school. The federal government also sponsors low-cost loans issued without regard for need through commercial lenders. The Education Department's PLUS loan carries an interest rate set 3.25 points above the average rate of 52-week Treasury bills, with a maximum of 12%. Two drawbacks: The PLUS spigot is turned off after $4,000 a year, and depending on the state in which you apply, you may pay an insurance fee of as much as 3%.

If $4,000 is not enough, turn to the Family Ed loans, underwritten by the federally chartered Student Loan Marketing Association (call 800-831-5626 for information). You can borrow up to $10,000 a year or the annual tuition and take up to 10 years to repay. The variable rate is set at 3.5 points above the 13-week T-bill, or about 12% recently. A 2% origination fee raises the annual percentage rate to 12.4%.

School-sponsored loans. Colleges also sometimes offer loans to families above the financial aid cutoff at attractive rates. Among the best is Duke's 8% fixed-rate loan of up to $2,500 a year. One of the University of Pennsylvania's offerings is more typical: A variable-rate line of credit pegged one point above the prime rate, recently 10.5%, that banks charge their best commercial customers. Always ask whether college or state loans offer the option of securing the debt with your home equity, thus allowing a tax write-off.

Loans from nonprofit underwriters. If you are seeking large sums, private nonprofit organizations that make low-interest, flexible loans for education may better meet your needs. Among the leading programs are the Education Resources Institute, or TERI (800-255-8374), and Consern: Loans for Education (202-331-9350). TERI, which also underwrites loans under the names Share and Excel, offers

20-year, variable-rate loans of as much as $20,000 a year at up to two points above the prime rate, after you pay an up-front 4% fee. Consern generally limits borrowers to $15,000, charges 4.1 points above its own index of commercial paper rates, nips you for 4% up front and allows you only 12 years to repay. Recent rate: 13.5%. Consern offers a better deal through employee benefits programs.

Commercial loans. Many banks and finance companies are peddling high-priced education loans under cutesy names. Some commercial offerings deserve careful consideration, though. Knight Tuition Payment Plans (800-225-6783), a Boston company, offers variable and fixed-rate loans that give even the non-profit lenders a run for their money. Knight's Extended Repayment loan is 4.5 points above T-bill rates (recently 7.5%) and carries a 10-year repayment schedule. Fleet Education Funding Corporation (800-456-1213), which is based in Rhode Island, also offers competitive prices on college loans.

Playing the Financial Aid Game

Reduce your income? Cut your assets? Welcome to the wild world of college assistance.

Lewis Carroll didn't design the rules of college financial aid, but surely he would have appreciated their downside-up logic. Such virtues as thrift, generosity, hard work, and common sense do not always pay off in this looking-glass universe. What seems expensive can be cheap; the more you give away, the more you save; and the more you make, the more you can lose. So get ready for unconventional thinking.

Understand first that the game is definitely worth playing. Fully half the students who attend college in 1990 will get some part of the estimated $27 billion that schools and government agencies hand out. Surprisingly, even families with incomes upwards of $75,000 sometimes qualify for aid. Like our tax system, however, the college aid game penalizes those who ignore its rules. So you can maximize the aid package your student receives only by following the game's curious twists and turns.

The object of this game is not to find schools whose stated tuitions are within the grasp of your budget—at least not if you qualify for aid. The reason is that no matter how expensive a college is, financial aid officers will analyze your aid application and put roughly the same ceiling on how much you must pay. They will then try to offer enough aid to make up the rest. Indeed, the aid offers from first-rank schools are so uniform that the Justice Department is investigating whether they violate antitrust laws.

For example, say your share comes to $8,000. Most schools with even higher price tags will charge you only that amount or slightly more—whether you choose Harvard University ($19,395) or Hastings College ($9,500). So look for schools that are well enough endowed to provide aid, especially outright gifts (called grants) rather than work-study programs or loans. One good guide is the annual *Peterson's College Money Handbook* ($18.95; P.O. Box 2123, Princeton, NJ 08543), which includes data on more than 1,700 schools.

Do not let yourself be mesmerized by those seemingly lucrative special scholarships that corporations, churches, and social groups offer. If your student wins such an award—a long shot, at best—most colleges will use the money to replace aid that you would otherwise receive from the school. Instead, try for government- and school-sponsored programs, which together make up at least 90% of all aid. You can fill out a standardized form, such as the Financial Aid Form (FAF) or the Family Financial Statement (FFS), both available at many high school guidance offices, and have your answers sent to several colleges at once. But submit the form early. Schools sometimes run out of money before they run out of eligible applicants.

Don't wait for the schools to tell you how much to pay. Estimate your likely share using either the worksheet below, the one in

What Colleges Will Expect You to Pay

Even if your child is years from college, it helps your long-range planning to know how much your family will be expected to pay when he or she gets there. And if the prospective scholar is at the school's doorstep, knowing that figure is essential to drawing your budget for next year. This worksheet, a simplified form of the complex one used by college financial aid officers, will give you a rough idea.

Complete sections 1 and 2 to calculate the parents' income and assets, respectively. Then use those figures to look up the parents' expected contribution in the table (the result will vary depending on your family size) and enter that in section 3. Finally, complete sections 4 and 5 to figure the student's expected contribution and your total family liability. If the result is less than the cost of the first year at your college of choice, financial aid may help you close the gap. But if your family's expected contribution exceeds that cost, you are not likely to qualify for aid.

1. PARENTS' PRETAX INCOME:
Enter your 1989 adjusted gross income reported on your IRS Form 1040, line 31. _____
Enter the sum of all nontaxable income (for example, Social Security, child support, tax-exempt bond interest). _____
If both parents work, or if the head of your household is single and working, subtract $2,130. _____
Enter the total here. _____

2. PARENTS' ASSETS:
Enter the equity in your home (its value minus any

unpaid balance on your mortgage
or home-equity loan).** _____
Enter the sum of all cash, bank, and money-market accounts. _____
Enter the value of investments such as stocks, bonds, mutual funds, or real estate (other than your home). _____
Enter the total here. _____

3. PARENTS' CONTRIBUTION:
Enter the value from the table that most closely fits your answers in sections 1 and 2 and your family size (include yourselves and all dependents). _____

4. STUDENT'S CONTRIBUTION:
Enter 70% of the student's 1989 pretax and nontaxable income or $700, whichever is greater. _____
Enter 35% of assets, including cash, bank, and money-market accounts and investments. _____
Enter the total here. _____

5. TOTAL FAMILY CONTRIBUTION:
Enter the sum of section 3 and section 4. _____

If the number seems high, don't despair. Colleges may be willing to reduce your bill if you own a business or farm, are near retirement, have more than six people in your family, or pay other school tution or high medical bills.

Peterson's, or the more detailed version in *Don't Miss Out: The Ambitious Student's Guide to Financial Aid* ($6.25 a copy from Octameron Associates, P.O. Box 3437, Alexandria, VA 22302). After adjustments for taxes and other considerations, aid officers expect students to contribute 70% of their income and 35% of their assets each year, and parents to add as much as 47% of their income and 5.6% of their assets. For example, a hypothetical four-member family with $55,000 in income and $75,000 equity in their house might have to come up with $11,500 a year to send one child to school. If both kids are in college, however, the family's share drops to about half that amount per child. This points up another example of backward logic. Although it makes fiscal sense to plan your family so that no two kids are in school at once, it makes better financial aid sense to bunch them together to

Assets	Family size	Parents' pretax income					
		$30,000	$40,000	$50,000	$60,000	$70,000	$80,000
$40,000	3	$2,768	$5,576	$8,444	$11,452	$14,460	$17,468
	4	2,119	4,487	7,474	10,482	13,490	16,498
	5	1,508	3,595	6,570	9,578	12,586	15,594
	6	1,056	2,767	5,534	8,542	11,550	14,558
$60,000	3	3,574	6,704	9,572	12,580	15,588	18,596
	4	2,792	5,615	8,602	11,610	14,618	17,626
	5	2,174	4,592	7,698	10,706	13,714	16,722
	6	1,584	3,573	6,662	9,670	12,678	15,686
$80,000	3	4,566	7,832	10,700	13,708	16,716	19,724
	4	3,607	6,743	9,730	12,738	15,746	18,754
	5	2,859	5,720	8,826	11,834	14,842	17,850
	6	2,160	4,565	7,790	10,798	13,806	16,814
$100,000	3	5,694	8,960	11,828	14,836	17,844	20,852
	4	4,605	7,871	10,858	13,866	16,844	19,882
	5	3,696	6,848	9,954	12,962	15,970	18,978
	6	2,840	5,693	8,918	11,926	14,934	17,942
$120,000	3	6,822	10,088	12,956	15,964	18,972	21,980
	4	5,733	8,999	11,986	14,994	18,002	21,010
	5	4,710	7,976	11,082	14,090	17,098	20,106
	6	3,673	6,821	10,046	13,054	16,062	19,070
$140,000	3	7,950	11,216	14,084	17,092	20,100	23,108
	4	6,861	10,127	13,114	16,122	19,130	22,138
	5	5,838	9,104	12,210	15,218	18,226	21,234
	6	4,683	7,949	11,174	14,182	17,190	20,198

SOURCES: PETERSON'S COLLEGE MONEY HANDBOOK 1990 AND PETERSON'S COLLEGE DATABASE. © 1989 PETERSON'S GUIDES INC.

enhance each child's chance of aid.

There are also a number of seemingly contrary financial strategies that you can legitimately employ to lower your share. The one proviso is that these moves make sense *only* if your child will likely receive aid. But if that's the case, you may well want to:

Reduce your student's income. Freshmen on aid are expected to contribute at least $700 from money they earn themselves; upperclassmen, $900. But a student who earns $4,000 after taxes from a summer job will be asked to hand over $2,800 (70% of $4,000). So much for the rewards of hard work. As for thrift, if that same summer-job money winds up in a savings account, it can also be counted as student assets—a ridiculous form of double jeopardy. This is not to say that students shouldn't work, just that they and their families should not forget that the school has a hand in their pocket, too. Students might, for instance, take a lower-paying or even a volunteer job if it is more satisfying or offers career experience.

Reduce the parents' income. That income includes after-tax profits realized from investments such as stocks, bonds, or real estate. If you hold mutual fund shares with a $5,000 unrealized capital gain, for example, only 5.6%—or $280—will count toward your family's contribution. But if you take your profit, most schools will expect you to hand over as much as 47%. Assuming you are in the 28% tax bracket, this will amount to $1,692 (47% of your after-tax gain of $3,600). Thus, you should take your gains early enough so that they don't show up on the tax return for the year preceding the one in which you apply for aid (you will have to supply tax data for that year as part of your application). Alternatively, defer taking the gains until after your child has reached his or her senior year.

Reduce the student's assets. Parents and other relatives who give money to students may unwittingly raise their college costs. For example, if Grandma writes a $10,000 graduation check to your high school senior, colleges will calculate their cut at the student's 35% rate, or

$3,500. Ask her to give the money to Mom and Dad instead. In that case, the family's contribution will rise by only $560—5.6% of $10,000—at most.

For the same reason, if your child is a candidate for financial aid, don't invest savings in his or her name because extra college costs could far outweigh any tax benefits. If you've already shifted assets to a child, spend that money before you spend your own. Say your daughter has $10,000 in savings and is asked to contribute 35%—$3,500—toward her freshman year. Use the remaining $6,500 in her account to pay the parents' expected share, leaving your assets intact. When she reapplies for aid the following year, most schools will figure your contribution from assets at the parents' more favorable 5.6% rate.

Reduce the parents' assets. Earnings put into a tax-sheltered retirement account—such as a 401(k), an IRA, or a Keogh—during the year before you apply for aid are counted by colleges as income. But they ignore assets that you already hold in such accounts. If you think your child will be a candidate for financial aid in a few years, it makes eminent sense to invest as much as you can in these accounts—assuming you have enough left over to meet emergencies and interim goals. Money in these plans not only will grow tax deferred but also reduce your college bill.

Replace sizable car loans or credit-card balances with a home-equity loan. Colleges ignore consumer loans in figuring your net worth. By contrast, when you give up equity in your home, they consider you poorer. Borrow $20,000 against your home to pay down consumer debts, and your contribution over four years might shrink by $4,500. Similarly, if you plan to make major purchases or gifts while your child is in college, pay cash or borrow against your home. And do it before you file for aid. A $10,000 gift to an elderly parent might qualify your student for more than $2,000 in additional aid over four years.

Be aware that schools and governments sometimes change the rules for a family in special circumstances. For example, if the parents are divorced, most schools will calculate aid based solely on the finances of the parent with whom the child is living. But others, notably in the Ivy League, consider the resources of both parents. Also, if you're supporting children by a previous marriage, elderly parents, or disabled family members, ask whether the school will give you a break.

Another bargaining chip is a particularly bright child. The school probably will not reduce your payment, but it may load up the aid package with grants instead of loans. Schools may also adjust an award to reflect death, divorce, or unemployment in a family. If a misfortune befalls you, write, call, or visit a financial aid officer. Describe clearly the change in your financial status, and make specific proposals. Don't beg, whine, or wheedle. And absent a genuine disaster, don't expect much relief—or even sympathy. With few exceptions, salaries for financial aid officers top out at around $35,000.

The Failure of the College Admissions System

The process is often capricious, excessively expensive, and fails to match students with colleges where they are most likely to flourish.

In a better world, every high school senior would know precisely what he or she wanted out of higher education. College admissions directors would honestly and openly identify the kind of students who would excel on their campuses. Parents would seek not the most prestigious schools, but the ones that best serve their child's needs. And no one would ever suppose the process of getting into college to be anything other than reasonable and fair.

But as any student who has recently applied to a selective college can tell you, the real world does not work that way. Instead, the process of turning high school graduates into college freshmen has become increasingly confusing, frustrating, and expensive. For too many 17-year-olds and their parents, it has become the family's first bitter taste of defeat and cynicism. The unavoidable fact is that our national system of college admissions is failing on many important levels. To be specific:

It is needlessly stressful. Far too much attention is focused on the hundred-plus most prestigious colleges. The other 3,000 or so are mindlessly written off as slow tracks to nowhere. As a result, a lot of kids are being set up for failure. Students are convinced that the only colleges worth applying to are those that are most likely to reject them.

It is capricious. Admissions officers at selective colleges like to say that choosing freshmen is an art, not a science. But even the professionals admit that communicating the rationales for the fine distinctions made among hundreds of similar candidates is often impossible. "While one answer used to hold for all the Ivies," says Anne Ferguson, director of college counseling at Hathaway Brown School in Cleveland, "now a student gets a mixed response: one acceptance, one waiting list, and several rejections. The message is that if I apply to all eight Ivies my chances of getting into at least one are better."

It is expensive. Even when a student applies to only five or six colleges, as most guidance counselors suggest, the cost in application fees alone can top $250 to $300. You could easily spend several thousand dollars more in travel costs to visit colleges, fees for Scholastic Aptitude Test (SAT) prep courses, and private guidance counseling—all of which some families see as providing an increasingly necessary edge in competitive admissions.

It is inefficient. For all the pain that applicants and their families undergo, the system does not do the job it is meant to do: match graduating high school seniors with colleges where they will flourish. If this year's freshmen follow their predecessors' pattern, nearly half will drop out before graduating.

The problems begin at home with achievement-oriented parents who are themselves members of the first generation to be widely college educated. They see a prestigious school's acceptance letter as a personal vindication, an A+ on the final exam of parenthood. They are abetted by SAT coaches and private guidance "consultants" who prey on the insecurities of college-bound seniors and their families. The result is that students are egged on to what for most will be a losing battle.

The way into the selective schools threads through an obstacle course of standardized aptitude tests, achievement exams, personal essays, and interviews. The preliminary judgment about a candidate's merit is likely to be the work of one or more associate admissions officers, typically recent college graduates who can afford to devote no more than 10 to 15 minutes to each file. The senior admissions director may rule on an applicant if the associates disagree. But often candidates are so closely matched that the decision to accept or deny is little more than a hunch about who is a "good kid."

Besides, merit is not the only—or even the most important—criterion admissions officers have to consider. At most colleges, the children of alumni are not held to the same strict admissions standards as other applicants. At Duke, for instance, 40% of alumni children are admitted, compared with just over 20% for applicants as a whole. Other groups of students such as athletes, musicians, and minorities also get favored treatment. Admissions officers say there is little parents can do to nudge the odds in their child's favor other than to encourage them to do their homework and to develop interests outside school. But even that tiny flicker of hope has created opportunities for eager entrepreneurs.

At $500 to $650, SAT coaching sessions have become an unquestioned rite of passage for many teens. These six- to 11-week courses, designed to hone the student's test-taking skills, promise to raise their SAT scores by 100 to 150 points. A Federal Trade Commission study in the late 1970s found that the courses actually increased scores by an average of 50 points. Some students do better than that, but 50 points has only a negligible impact on an applicant's chances.

At fees of $400 for a once-over to $9,000 for two years of hand-holding, the independent college consultant will happily help. Often former college admissions officers or high school guidance counselors, the consultants can step in to provide personal attention on choosing a college and polishing an application, which overloaded high school counselors often cannot.

But while consultants can improve an applicant's decision-making, they cannot get a student into college. Says Daniel Murray, former director of admissions at Boston University: "No recommendation from an independent—who was paid for the service—was ever read with the same credibility as one that came from school counselors who had known the applicant for years."

Far from assuaging students' and parents' fears, colleges actually exacerbate them. The inscrutable admissions committees, with their arcane and shifting selection criteria, contribute hugely to the feeling of futility. Most admissions departments spend the bulk of their energies on commercial marketing techniques to lure new applicants rather than trying to identify students who could benefit from studying there. "The colleges lead students on, making them think they'll be accepted," says Jim McClure, director of guidance at T. C. Williams High School in Alexandria, Virginia. "Then, in April, they start boasting to their alumni about how many kids they turned down."

Indeed, a war for bragging rights has broken out among colleges generally, not just among the selective ones. The proximate cause is a shrinking pool of high school graduates—the baby bust of the 1970s will not work its way through the college years until 1992. With applications down as much as 20% in 1989, the most favored schools fear that their high rates of selectivity are endangered, and the lesser lights of academe fear extinction. (In 1988, 11 colleges closed.)

All are aware that tuition shock has made it harder to justify charging up to $15,000 a year, and all are selling themselves more aggressively to more students than ever before. Anyone who remembers applying to college during the 1960s and 1970s will be amazed by the slickness of today's recruitment campaigns, with their massive direct-mail assaults, flashy brochures, and personal sells from admissions officers and alumni.

The heart of college marketing is junk mail. To attract a freshman class of 500, a college might send out 22,000 brochures to a list of student names collected from the standardized testing services such as the College Board and the American College Testing Service.

Practically any C student can expect at least 50 pieces of collegiate junk to show up in his or her mailbox beginning in the spring of junior year. A top student, an athlete, or a member of an ethnic minority may get as many as 500. A student who responds to the direct-mail is sent the college's annual viewbook, a lavishly-illustrated publication meant to describe the school and inspire prospects to submit an application. (The cost of a typical production run of 100,000 books is $200,000.)

Some viewbooks offer a good deal of useful information, such as a thorough profile of their freshman class against which high schoolers can match their own credentials. But most booklets are short on substance and careful to respect the limited attention span of the video generation.

Indeed, most colleges are quick to brandish a five- to 15-minute recruiting video to lend to prospects directly or through their high school counselors. Drake University's MTV-quality effort—made at a reported cost of $80,000—depicts students at the Des Moines university playing sports, flirting, staging pie-eating contests, tapping away at classroom computers, and visiting an off-campus disco. Almost no one does anything as unphotogenic as crack a book.

For parents, there is a particularly galling aspect to all this marketing hype. Over the course of your children's education, you will pay a portion of your tuition bill to crank out the viewbooks, videos, and tens of thousands of direct-mail pieces that are needed to bring in their freshmen classes.

But the real cost of the marketing war is more subtle, and potentially much steeper. Dorms, fancy lab equipment, fitness facilities, groundskeeping, and subsidized rock concerts are all part of the battle to stay attractive to the widest possible number of 17-year-olds.

And no college dares to stop escalating the competition. If Princeton installs a new Olympic swimming pool, how long can Cornell get by with its dank 1953 facility? Although the cost has nothing to do with education, experts estimate that this spiral adds two percentage points annually to the inflation in college prices.

Worse, colleges increasingly are afflicted by their own Gresham's law: As marketing drives up the price of higher education, it tends to drive down its quality. Good marketing and good teaching are incompatible; one requires that you find out what the customer wants and provide it, the other that you demand things of students that they may prefer not to do. The danger is that in battling with each other to give students what they want, the colleges are losing sight of their more important task: to give students what they need.

A Smart Shoppers Guide to Insurance

This essential purchase costs about $3,000 a year, yet is often misunderstood.

In the soap opera called life, no one can count on uninterrupted health or freedom from accidents. That's why you need to protect your assets and your family from risks by getting the proper insurance policies—namely auto, homeowners or tenants, excess liability, life, disability, and health. Yet, few people feel comfortable shopping for them because agents talk in jargon and policies are loaded with legalese.

Your home-study course in Insurance 101 should begin with a lesson covering the terms "deductible" and "premium" and the relationship between them. A deductible is the maximum amount you must pay before your insurance kicks in. If, for example, you accept a $500 annual deductible on a health insurance policy, your insurer will not pay any of your medical bills until you have shelled out $500 for them during the year. Insurers often let you choose among a range of deductibles. As a rule, the bigger the deductible, the smaller the premium—the price you pay for a policy.

Before you buy any type of insurance, be sure you can answer these four important questions:

- How much insurance do I need?

- What kind of policy is most suitable?

- Whom should I buy it from?

- How much should I pay?

Starting with the first question, the overriding principle should be to insure only against losses you couldn't absorb without wrecking your financial plans. Paying high premiums for costs you can easily handle is a waste of money. For example, you can probably afford that $500 a year in medical bills, but a catastrophic illness would wipe you out financially. So you are well advised to take a $500 deductible, rather than a $100 deductible, because you can then get coverage at a more affordable price.

Before answering the second question—what kind of policy to buy—you should address the final two. When choosing an insurance company, satisfy yourself that it is financially capable of paying your benefits when necessary. It doesn't matter whether you use an independent agent who can sell policies from a variety of companies or an agent who works for just one insurer. Either way, tell the agent you want policies only from companies rated A+ for the past 10 years by *Best's Insurance Reports*, a publication from the A.M. Best financial rating service.

As for price, one rule applies as much to insurance as to most other commodities—save money by buying in bulk. That means taking the most comprehensive coverage and spurning narrow policies such as flight insurance, credit insurance, burial insurance, and health plans that cover only single diseases such as cancer. Premiums for those policies may look small, but they usually mask extremely high rates per year or per $1,000 of coverage. You can also keep down your insurance costs by looking for ways to reduce life's risks. If you smoke or overeat, shed tobacco or pounds. Equip your house with smoke detectors, dead bolts, and burglar alarms. These steps can reduce your premiums by 5% to 20%.

Now take up the question, What kind of policy is most suitable? Answering it is the most vexing task when buying insurance. But making the right choices will be easier if you study the following descriptions of common policies and heed the tips on cutting your premium costs.

Auto Insurance

Smart shopping for this variety of coverage has become mandatory now that auto insurance premiums are rising at double-digit annual rates on average and some companies have stopped selling policies altogether in a few states. According to a survey by A.M. Best, the average motorist paid nearly $487 in 1987 to insure a car. Annual premiums in big cities such as New York and Chicago often exceed $1,000, as do those for teenaged boys in many suburbs. You should capitalize on premium-paring discounts by asking your agent whether you qualify for the savings listed in the table on page 102, which can lighten premiums by 5% to 60%.

To get the most for your dollar, be sure you are familiar with the anatomy of a policy. Car insurance comes in a package that consists of the following provisions:

Liability protection. This is the main reason for buying auto insurance. Liability coverage protects you against claims for injury and property damage brought by other drivers, pedestrians, or property owners who allege that you were at fault in an accident. Your insurer will defend you in or out of court against any claims. The insurance company pays the legal expenses and, if necessary, the damages up to the dollar limits set in your policy.

Policies may either have a single limit for all liability or three separate limits for: each person injured in an accident, all people injured

in the same accident, and property damage. In industry shorthand, a policy covering $25,000 of liability per person, $50,000 per accident, and $10,000 for property damage is referred to as 25/50/10 coverage. Those are typical minimum limits in the 38 states that require car owners to carry liability coverage. Laws in the other 12 states strongly encourage such coverage for most people. The cost of buying 25/50/10 liability coverage for a 45-year-old driving a mid-size automobile lately ranged from $120 a year in Bloomington, Indiana to about $840 in Los Angeles. You probably should buy liability protection of at least 100/300/50, which will cost only about 20% to 30% more than the minimum coverage.

Uninsured motorist coverage. This provision means your insurer will pay if you or a passenger in your car is hurt by either a motorist without auto insurance or by a hit-and-run driver. You can buy as much coverage as you carry under the liability section of your policy. The premium for coverage of $25,000 of liability per person and $50,000 per accident is often $20 to $30 a year. You can also buy underinsured motorist coverage, which protects you if the other driver's liability coverage is inadequate. It generally costs an additional $30 to $50 a year.

Collision and comprehensive coverage. If you carry these, your insurer will reimburse you for repair costs resulting from a crash (collision) or from fire, storm, vandalism, or theft (comprehensive). Collision is expensive—it typically represents about a third of your total premium—but comprehensive is far less costly. Banks and finance companies usually require you to buy collision and comprehensive coverage before approving you for a car loan. You typically will be responsible for annual deductibles of at least the first $100 of repairs under both collision and comprehensive coverage. By raising your deductibles to $500, you can cut your collision premium by about a third; $1,000 deductibles slash the cost about in half. Increasing your comprehensive deductible will have a smaller effect on your premium.

Unless you deliberately smash or torch your

car, your insurer will pay your claims up to the amount of your car's resale value. Once that value falls below $2,000 or so, consider dropping collision and comprehensive coverage. Otherwise, you can wind up paying more for the insurance than you could get in benefits.

Car Insurance Discounts

You can slash your total auto insurance premiums dramatically if you can qualify for discounts by, for example, insuring two cars with the same company or taking driver-training or defensive-driving courses. Insurance company rules vary on who qualifies for some discounts, such as the ones for good students and senior citizens. The price cuts listed below generally apply to charges for each type of auto coverage. Usually, however, there are no discounts for uninsured motorist coverage.

Qualification for discount	Premium discount
Air bags in front seats	30 to 60%
Automatic front-seat belts	10 to 30
Farmer	10 to 30
Multicar coverage	10 to 25
Car pool participant	10 to 20
Good student	5 to 25
Senior citizen	5 to 20
Student away at school	10 to 15
High school course in driver training	5 to 15
Auto antithief devices	5 to 15
Defensive-driving course	5 to 15
Female, age 30 to 64, as only driver	5 to 10

SOURCE: INSURANCE INFORMATION INSTITUTE

Additional types of coverage. Some extra protections cost only a few dollars a year. One is medical-payments coverage, which will commonly pay up to $5,000 to anyone in your car who is hurt in an accident. A less desirable option is towing coverage, which pays as much as $75 for getting your incapacitated car to a repair shop. This coverage violates the rule against buying insurance for small losses. And if you belong to an auto club, you probably already have towing coverage.

Personal injury protection (PIP). Residents of the 14 states with no-fault automobile insurance must buy this type of coverage. With PIP, if you are driving anywhere in the U.S. and are injured in an accident, your insurer will pay your medical expenses whether or not your driving contributed to the smashup. In return, you can't sue the other driver for additional compensation for pain and suffering unless your injuries are severe or your medical expenses exceed a threshold amount set by the state.

The best shortcut for finding a suitable, affordable automobile policy is to decide what coverage you want. Next, get a price quote from an agent for State Farm, the nation's largest auto insurer. While State Farm's policies are not necessarily the cheapest, they set a standard for the industry. Then call other agents to see whether you can find a better deal elsewhere.

Homeowners and Tenants Insurance

Like car policies, homeowners and tenants plans have liability protection. But your prime concern should be coverage of your personal possessions against theft and of your property against damage by fire and other perils. Expect to pay $200 to $3,000 a year for a policy with a deductible of $100 to $1,000. The premium depends on a multitude of factors, including the value of your house, its age, whether the area is prone to hurricanes or earthquakes, the local crime rate, and the type of construction of the house. Wood-frame houses, for example, cost more to insure than do ones made of fire-resistant brick or stone. Homeowners insurance comes in the following standard versions, known as forms:

● Basic covers damage by fire, lightning, windstorm, hail, explosion, riots, aircraft, other people's vehicles, smoke, vandalism, and volcanic eruption. The basic form also pays for theft and glass breakage.

● Broad adds these perils to the ones included in the basic form: falling objects; the weight of ice or snow; water or steam escaping from the plumbing; heating or air-conditioning systems; the freezing of those systems and home appliances; and damage from short circuits or power surges.

● Special is the most popular. In addition to the perils covered by the basic and broad forms, it guards your house against all others not specifically excluded by the policy. Among the common exclusions are damage from floods, earthquakes, sewer and drain backups, war and nuclear accidents. (To get the same coverage for your personal property, you may have to buy what's known as an endorsement.) Some companies add exclusions in certain locations. For example, if you live on the Gulf of Mexico, your house might not be insured against hurricane damage. You can usually insure against such assaults by nature at extra cost, however. No homeowners policy includes flood coverage. So if you want flood insurance, ask your agent about policies supervised by the federal government's National Flood Insurance program.

● Tenants forms generally cover only furnishings and personal possessions.

● Condominium and cooperative apartment forms provide the same coverage as tenants policies. Also, they insure home additions and alterations that are not covered by your homeowners association's insurance policy.

The tricky thing about homeowners insurance is setting the correct dollar figure of coverage. It should, of course, be large enough to pay for rebuilding your house if it is leveled by fire or storm. It should also fully cover much likelier partial losses. Insurers will typically pay you the cost of repairing any structural damage up to the dollar limit of your policy, as long as that limit equals 80% or more of the cost of rebuilding your house. Should your policy turn out to be too small (say, the coverage is only 60% of the replacement value of your home), the insurer will pay a portion of the cost to replace the damaged property (in this case, 75%) or its depreciated value, whichever is more.

If you buy a highly desirable feature called guaranteed replacement cost, which adds only a few dollars to your annual premium, you can be sure of recovering almost the full cost of repairs. When you get this option, the insurance agent will make sure that you buy enough insurance to cover any damage by appraising the replacement value of your house on a special estimating form developed by his company. Moreover, your coverage and its price will rise yearly with inflation.

Not every house is eligible for guaranteed replacement-cost coverage, though. Some insurers won't provide the benefit for homes that are more than 35 or 40 years old or so. One reason is that it may be quite expensive, if not impossible, to replace the handiwork in old houses. Owners of such homes must settle for lesser coverage.

All standard policies will cover your home's contents for half the dollar limit you place on the house. But that doesn't mean you can collect enough to replace any piece of furniture. If a five-year-old couch, say, is destroyed in a fire, you may get only the cash value of a used couch. For this reason, pay a little extra for replacement-value coverage on the contents of your home. Then if your old couch burns up, your insurance will pay for a new one. This option will cost an additional $1 to $2 per $1,000 of coverage each year.

You can buy additional insurance for valuables such as jewelry, furs, or silverware beyond the standard policy limits of $1,000 to $2,500. These so-called floaters generally cost roughly $8 a year for $2,500 of coverage on silver and about $90 to $270 to cover $10,000 of jewelry. If you have a collection of stamps or coins with no single item of great value, consider buying a blanket policy. The typical cost is about $60 to $70 a year to cover collectibles for up to $1,000 or $2,000 apiece and the entire set up to a total of $5,000.

The standard homeowners insurance package also provides $100,000 of personal-liability protection for members of your household and up to $500 of compensation for damage to trees and shrubs. If your credit cards are stolen, your policy will protect you against $500 or more in charges run up by the thief.

Excess Liability Insurance

If you have substantial assets and are therefore an easy target for a big lawsuit, you may want to supplement your auto and homeowners insurance with an excess liability policy, also called an umbrella policy. This coverage, sold by homeowners and auto insurance companies, provides $1 million to $5 million in protection for you and members of your household for claims because of negligence, as well as such wrongs as libel, slander, or defamation.

The premium for an excess liability policy depends on where you live and factors such as the number of cars, homes, and boats you own. A suburban family with two cars and a typical house might pay $150 a year for a $1 million policy, $225 for $2 million in coverage, and $350 for $5 million. You may have to increase your liability coverage to high levels on your homeowners and auto insurance policies in order to buy excess liability coverage. One tip: By getting your auto, homeowners, and excess liability insurance from one company, you may be able to knock 15% off your umbrella policy premium.

Life Insurance

You may have heard that life insurance can be a terrific tax shelter or a wonderful way to force yourself to save. Both statements are

true. But the prime reason for insuring your life is to protect your dependents financially if you die prematurely. That's doubly true for two-income families—both working spouses should have coverage to ensure that their present standard of living can be sustained and their financial goals met if one of them dies.

Bear in mind that fully insuring your family can cost a bundle. Take the case of a husband, 42, and a wife, 40, who plan to send their two children, now 4 and 6, to college. Assume the father earns $55,000, the mother $45,000, and both work for companies that provide group life insurance equal to their salaries. Finally, assume the parents have $50,000 in savings and investments and expect to retire comfortably at 65. By a conservative estimate, the husband should buy $300,000 in additional life insurance and the wife needs almost as much extra coverage. They could pay between $850 and $10,000 a year for the two policies, depending on the kind that they buy.

How much life insurance do *you* need? That's a difficult question to answer accurately unless you are handy with a compound-interest calculator and understand such concepts as the present value of future cash flows. Furthermore, you should ignore simplistic rules of thumb such as the one that says you should insure yourself for five times your annual income. Instead, meet with a life insurance agent or financial planner who will do the calculations to match your situation. The National Association of Life Underwriters, a group that represents agents across the country (telephone 202-331-6034), can direct you to a local association that will give you names of members in your area.

If you're married and the only breadwinner, your life insurance policy's death benefit, together with your other ready assets, should be large enough to deliver lifetime income for your spouse. If you have children, you'll need to provide income for them, too, until they leave home, as well as a tuition fund if you intend to send them to college. But if you're single and have no dependents, you need only enough in savings or insurance coverage to pay your final expenses at death.

There are essentially two types of life

policies: term insurance and cash-value insurance. One is not necessarily better than the other. With both, a portion of your premium pays the agent's commission and the company's overhead and profit. In a term policy, the remainder of your premium provides a guaranteed death benefit for your survivors. With cash-value insurance, part of your premium goes toward the death benefit and a large slice goes into a tax-deferred investment fund; you can borrow against your balance and sometimes withdraw your cash value.

In the early years of the policy, term insurance has the advantage of being by far the least expensive per $1,000 of coverage, regardless of your age. The most common form of term insurance is called annual renewable

term. Its premium rises each year as you age, but you generally cannot renew the policy after age 70. If, for instance, the 42-year-old man in the previous example were to buy a $300,000 annual renewable term policy, he'd pay about $550; when he reaches 50, his annual premium might double; and by the time he is 60, it would be roughly $3,000. Term insurance, however, can be made to conform to the typical pattern of coverage that families usually need. While the premium rate for term keeps rising, the amount of coverage a family should carry levels off and declines. As the children grow up and savings accumulate in pension and retirement funds and outside investments, people typically need to own less insurance, not more. They can then cut back

Top Picks Among Term Life Insurance Policies

These were the least expensive term life insurance policies submitted by five quote services for a hypothetical New York State couple, both healthy nonsmokers in their forties. Of all the policies the companies sell, these offer the lowest premiums over 10 years with options to renew for another 10 years without huge premium increases. These policies, all convertible to cash-value plans, probably won't be the best for you if you live

in another state or don't meet the specifications of the couple in the example. Four of the five services are free: InsuranceQuote (800-972-1104), LifeQuote (800-776-7873), SelectQuote (800-343-1985) and TermQuote (800-444-8376). They make their profits as agents for the insurers they decide are most competitive. The fifth service, Insurance Information (800-472-5800), sells only price quotes, at $50 a report.

	Insurer/policy	Quote service	First year's premium	Premiums over 10 years
$500,000 Policy For A Man Aged 47	Equitable Life of N.Y. *Equitable Term*	SelectQuote	$1,000	$15,010
	Berkshire Life *Art-100*	Insurance Information	995	15,055
	Bankers Security Life *Five-Year Term*	LifeQuote, SelectQuote, TermQuote	1,325	16,500
$500,000 Policy For A Woman Aged 44	North American Co. for Life & Health of N.Y. *Leveler*	SelectQuote	945	8,970
	T-100	Insurance Information, SelectQuote	415	9,950
	William Penn Life *Penn Term II*	Insurance Information, InsuranceQuote, LifeQuote	330	9,605

on their term insurance coverage.

By contrast, the much higher premium for a typical cash-value policy stays the same each year, and the insurance can be kept in force until you're at least 95. At that point, the insurer will pay you the money your beneficiaries would have received if you had died.

A cash-value policy can be invested in a variety of securities. A whole life policy, the traditional form of cash-value insurance, invests in bonds and mortgages and earns a fixed, modest rate of return—recently about 7.25%. Universal life policies let you adjust your premium and death benefit each year to suit your changing circumstances. Part of your premiums are invested in short-term securities similar to those in money-market funds. Lately, such policies yielded 8% to 9%. Variable life invests your cash value in your choice of stock, bond, or other funds. Returns fluctuate according to changing market conditions and the fund manager's investing skill.

Disability Insurance

The need for six-figure amounts of life insurance is a reminder that your earning power is an enormous asset. Insurance experts recommend that you carry enough disability coverage to pay you 60% of your gross income while you are laid up by a long illness or injury.

Your emergency reserve fund in a savings account or money-market fund should cover short periods of disability. Sick-leave benefits and employer-sponsored disability insurance may help, too. Social Security offers disability benefits, but only if you can prove you won't be able to work for more than a year or that your disability will result in death. Even then, you'll have to wait five months for the first check. In 1990, the maximum Social Security disability benefit for someone aged 45 with two children is $1,540 a month, or less than $18,500 a year. But the benefits rise annually to keep pace with inflation.

Disability policies are sold by many life insurance companies. To buy the highest-quality coverage you can get, look for benefits that will continue until you can work full-time again or reach age 65. The costliest policies define as a disability any medical condition that keeps you from performing your own occupation. You can keep receiving benefits—even if you earn money doing something else—as long as you are under a doctor's care. By taking disability insurance that will pay benefits if you are unable to work at an occupation suitable to your training and experience, you can save 5% to 15% in premiums.

The basic premium for disability insurance depends on your age, occupation, and how much income you want replaced. In a 1989 *Money* survey of the five largest sellers of top-flight disability plans, the maximum benefit available to a 40-year-old, nonsmoking, $40,000-a-year corporate manager was about $2,300 a month. Annual premiums for a policy that had a 30-day waiting period—the time between the day you are laid up and the day benefits start—ranged from roughly $1,000 to $1,500. You will pay less by shouldering a longer waiting period. For example, you can cut your cost by 30% or more if you accept a 90-day waiting period. In some other areas, however, you probably shouldn't economize. Among the options you should seek:

Noncancelable contract. This means that the company must insure you as long as you pay the premium. Equally important, the insurer cannot raise your premium.

Residual benefits. This policy feature means that while you are recuperating, you can return to work part time for partial pay and collect some benefits.

Annual cost-of-living adjustments. If you become disabled, your benefits will rise, preferably in step with the consumer price index.

Among other valuable options are a $500-a-month supplement to your disability income until your Social Security benefits begin, periodic opportunities to boost your insurance coverage in line with salary increases, and lifetime benefits. These add-ons can raise your premiums by 4% to 33%.

Health Insurance

Count yourself lucky if you belong to a group health insurance plan at work or through a professional or fraternal association. For an average $600 annual fee, such policies typically pay 80% of your medical expenses after you pay an annual deductible of, say, $100. Many group plans limit your annual share of the bills to $1,000. There is often no annual or lifetime maximum on the amount the insurer will pay.

If you don't have group coverage, you may have serious trouble finding affordable health insurance. Look first at policies sold by associations you belong to or could join, such as religious, professional, or college alumni groups. Their coverage is often far more comprehensive and less expensive than what you could buy on your own. Should you be forced to buy an individual health insurance policy, try to find one that follows the group plan model. The premium for a family of four whose parents are 35 and 40 can range from $1,200 to $4,600 a year. This cost may seem exorbitant, but it is less than what you would pay for the average hospital stay. Such a plan would cover 80% or more of your expenses above an annual deductible of $500.

Avoid indemnity policies, the kind often pitched on TV that pay a fixed amount per medical procedure or a flat dollar amount for each day in the hospital. The benefits from policies can fall woefully short of your actual health expenses and don't protect you against medical-cost inflation that has been running at about 12% a year. One alternative to traditional medical insurance worth considering is a health maintenance organization (HMO), a medical group that provides services for a flat annual fee, typically between $2,500 and $3,600 for a family of four. This charge may exceed what you'd pay for a health insurance policy. But you won't have to pay much more than your annual fee for medical treatment covered by the HMO contract.

Making Certain You Collect on a Homeowners or Auto Claim

Knowing how to file can protect you from stingy insurers who don't want to pay you what you deserve.

In the summer of 1986, a North Carolina woman drove slowly homeward during a torrential downpour to find a swarm of reporters, cameramen, and curiosity seekers gawking at her three-bedroom house—or what was left of it. A neighbor's giant oak had toppled onto the house, canting the walls at fun-house angles. The house (at an estimated value of around $70,000) and most of its contents were destroyed, including dozens of her paintings and other works of art.

Her insurer, North Carolina Farm Bureau, demanded an inventory of her lost personal belongings as well as proof of their value. So over a six-week period, the woman carted water-stained clothes to merchants for cost estimates and collected sales receipts for previously sold artworks as evidence of the value of her lost paintings. The company rejected her five-figure claim and offered $4,000 less.

Her lawyer pressed for a better award, pointing out that her inventory was unusually thorough. After two days of negotiations, the company raised its offer by $3,000 and the woman accepted. Still enraged, she says: "When you file a claim, you find out about all the loopholes in the policy that benefit the insurance company."

Caught in a profit squeeze caused largely by a 100% rise in personal-injury and auto claim payouts from 1978 to 1987, property and casualty insurers have been increasingly using exclusions. But by knowing how to file an airtight claim and, if necessary, challenge an inadequate settlement offer, you can keep a financial insult from being added to your injury.

Spend an hour or so now, before trouble occurs, carefully reading your auto and homeowners insurance contracts to find out what is not covered. Some insurers, for example, will not cover an auto accident if a family member other than the policyholder was driving. Next, take an inventory of your belongings. Keep it in your bank safe-deposit box. Include the following:

● A description of possessions that matter a lot to you. Also list the makes and model number of electronic equipment and appliances.

● Photographs or a videotape showing the condition and quality of your valuables.

● Appraisals of expensive items such as antiques, artwork, furs, and jewelry.

● Receipts to establish the original value of your belongings. If you've lost them, a canceled check or charge-card statement should be enough.

Should you have to file a claim, follow this procedure: First, in the case of a theft or an accident, file a report with the police. If you don't, the insurer will deny your claim. As soon as possible, write a detailed account of what happened to make sure you don't forget important details. If you are in a car accident, take photos of your car before it's repaired.

Similarly, take photos of damage to your house.

Next, notify your agent by phone and send him or her a copy of the police report. Ask the agent what steps you should take to prevent further loss or damage. If a door lock has been broken, the insurer could deny any part of your loss that could have resulted after the break-in. Some agents will send you a one- or two-page claim form to fill out. Others will ask you questions over the phone and enter your claim themselves. Either way, don't rush to complete this chore. Take time to assess the damage and collect all the backup documents you need.

For a homeowners claim, an adjuster for the insurance company will evaluate the loss within a week. If your car is damaged, your insurer may require you to get two or three repair estimates from body shops of its choosing. Large auto insurers such as Allstate and State Farm will often send you to their own drive-in centers for an estimate. Routine claims are settled on the spot, but more complicated ones usually take from one to three months.

If you decide the insurer's offer is stingy, ask for a written explanation of how the company calculated it. You may also want to hire a lawyer who is knowledgeable about dealing with insurers. A letter or call from your lawyer, at a fee of $50 to $200, may persuade the insurer that it will be cheaper to raise its offer than to fight.

Some claims are ideal candidates for challenges. Three examples:

● When you disagree with an insurer's interpretation of murky wording in its policy. If language is vague, your odds of winning are enhanced. Courts routinely side with customers who dispute ambiguous language in policies.

● When your insurer's offer is based on a repair estimate from a shop that you have visited and think does shoddy work. In this case, get an estimate or two from firms you choose to prove that the insurer gave you a lowball figure.

• When your insurer's adjuster neglected important evidence concerning your claim. For instance, if your car was totaled, the adjuster will probably use the NADA Official Used Car Guide or the Kelley Blue Book to estimate the car's pre-crash value. But if your car has low mileage or you have records of improvements, such as a new paint job or new tires, you might get a better settlement.

Whatever the reason for challenging an award, appeal first to your agent. If you're still not satisfied, call the insurer's claims department manager. Follow up with a letter describing the dispute, cataloguing your evidence, and summarizing the phone conversation. Attach pertinent documentation such as a police report, inventory, or photos.

Still no resolution? Your next move should be mediation or binding arbitration. Here, you and the insurance company hire a mediator or arbitrator (your cost: normally $150 to $650), whom you can find by calling an arbitration group such as Arbitration Forums (800-426-8889). Go to court only as a last resort. Small-claims courts let you defend yourself, although disputes typically must not exceed $1,000 to $5,000. A lawyer who represents you in a district court will probably collect 25% to 33% of any award you receive.

Putting Your Estate in Order

Regardless of your age or assets, you need a will. If you have children or substantial property, you may need much more.

Spend a moment answering these questions: If you died tomorrow, would your family know what they should about your finances? Would they know how you want your estate divided? Would they know your wishes about a funeral and burial? If you answered no to any of these questions, you're in good company. Probably more people procrastinate over putting their estates in order than over anything else in personal finance. Believe it or not, three out of four Americans die without wills.

Some people question the need for a will, thinking naively that they are too young or have too few assets for it to matter. Moreover, if you die intestate—without a will—your property will be divvied up according to your state's law no matter what your unwritten intentions. Take, for example, a New York family with two young children. The husband might want to leave most of his estate to his wife and the rest to the kids. But if he dies intestate, state law gives $4,000 plus a third of the remaining estate to his spouse and two-thirds to the children. The kids' share will be held by a guardian until they reach age 18, whether or not they're able to handle the money. The kids could squander their inheritance and then come back to Mom, who has a legal obligation to support them until they're 21.

Besides, you may have more to be divided among your heirs than you realize. The size of your taxable estate is based on a combination of the current market value of the property held in your name, your share of any jointly owned property, the death benefit of any life insurance policy you own, and any assets you have placed in what's known as a revocable living trust. State death taxes and other fees connected with the settlement of your estate are subtracted from the total.

So, if you now have a house, two cars, a life insurance policy, some mutual funds, a few IRAs, and a company savings plan, your estate could easily exceed $600,000—the threshold that triggers federal estate taxes. The first dollar of an estate over $600,000 is taxed at 37%, while any amount above $3 million is taxed at 55%.

At a minimum, making plans for the day when you won't be around will provide peace of mind. Beyond that, it will alleviate the financial burdens your survivors may face. Make sure that your survivors will have enough money. An emergency reserve fund can take care of their living expenses for a few months if your life insurance policy's death benefits are delayed, which is rare but common enough to be a concern.

You should carry sufficient life insurance for your family's living expenses as well as any estate taxes and the cost of probate—the court process of validating your will. Probate, which may take six months to two years, can cost 5% to 10% of your estate. However, by taking the proper steps, you can simplify the process greatly.

Before you draft a will, you should ask someone to act as your executor, or personal representative, when the time comes. This person will be in charge of getting your assets appraised, paying your taxes and debts, and distributing the remainder of your estate to the beneficiaries.

If your estate is now less than $600,000 and tax problems will be minimal, you can ask your spouse, an adult child, or another relative to be the executor. That way your family can avoid paying an executor's fees, which could be $20,000 on a $600,000 estate. If your estate is larger and likely to owe federal estate taxes, consider naming co-executors. One could be your spouse or another close relative and the other your accountant, banker, or some other trustworthy person who is adept at financial matters.

Parents should also ask someone to become the guardian of their minor children—those under age 18 in most states—just in case both parents die at the same time. You might choose your sister, brother, parents, or a close friend who shares your philosophy about raising children and has the time and energy to take care of yours.

Now you're ready to draw up your will. This document will spell out your choices as executor and guardian and set forth your wishes for the disposition of your estate. Wills come in basically two varieties: witnessed and holographic. (For advice on drafting a living will, which specifies the medical situations in which you would not want to be kept alive, see the story on the opposite page.)

You are probably better off with a witnessed will because it will be recognized by courts in every state. As the name suggests, you will have to get at least two adults to witness your signing of the document; neither of them should be beneficiaries. You write a holographic will by hand and sign the paper without witnesses. Be forewarned that only 26 states accept holographic wills as legal documents; the rest consider them the equivalent of dying intestate. Someone at your probate court can tell you whether your state permits holographic wills.

Do you really need a lawyer to draft your will? Thousands of people apparently think not, since Norman Dacey's do-it-yourself guide, *How to Avoid Probate!*, remains popular in bookstores. Quite simply, if your assets consist of nothing more than a stereo, a couple of worn Beatles albums, and a small life insurance policy, you probably can write your own will with the aid of a book that's more up to date than Dacey's, such as the *Simple Will Book* (Nolo Press, $14.95).

If you live in California, Maine, Michigan, or Wisconsin, you can also get standard will forms and instructions that have been approved by your state legislature. Check with your state representative's office for details. But if your estate is any larger or more complex, don't take chances. Spend $100 or more to have a lawyer draw up a proper will.

Be sure to keep your will current. Revise it if you get married or divorced, have a baby,

The Case for a Living Will

Everyone aged 21 or older should consider writing a living will, which spells out the medical situations in which you would not want your life artificially prolonged. The importance of this document is to make your instructions as clear and binding as possible. In 41 states that have laws recognizing living wills (the exceptions: Kentucky, Massachusetts, Michigan, Nebraska, New Jersey, New York, Ohio, Pennsylvania, and South Dakota), hospitals and doctors usually comply with them, although a few of these laws, like Florida's, require that all patients be fed. Scattered other states recognize durable powers of attorney for health care or health-care proxies, both of which are legal documents in which you give your next of kin or some other trusted person the power to decide, when you cannot, whether you should be kept alive by heroic means, such as heart resuscitation.

You don't even need a lawyer to help you. Thanks to groups like Concern for Dying, the nonprofit educational organization that originated the living will, you can fashion a valid document for yourself. Concern for Dying (250 West 57th Street, New York, NY 10107) will send you a set of forms at no charge, though it welcomes donations. Its kit includes a general form of living will, which is designed to win acceptance under whatever law applies, and a second document conforming to the law in your home state. You also get a durable power of attorney or a health-care proxy. To overcome potential legal obstacles in as many states as possible, be sure to fill out all these forms.

Concern for Dying suggests language that, for example, welcomes medical steps to relieve pain but rejects heart resuscitation, mechanical respiration, or tubal feeding. There is an argument to be made, however, for specifying that you do not want feeding stopped. In April 1989, a judge in Albany, New York authorized a hospital to stop feeding an 86-year-old stroke patient whose doctors testified that she was in an irreversibly vegetative state. A few days later, she regained consciousness and said she would "like to wait" before deciding whether she wanted her feeding tube removed.

To give your documents maximum authority, sign them in the presence of two witnesses who are not your relatives and have all signatures notarized. Also:

● Choose a person to make medical decisions for you if necessary. A friend may be more persuasive to a judge than a relative who is also your heir. Discuss your feelings with this representative before signing your living will, and periodically afterward, to make sure you are both in accord. Give this person a copy.

● Give copies to your family, your physician, attorney, and clergyman. Inform them of your wishes so they won't interfere if the time comes to invoke your living will.

● If your doctor disagrees with any key term in your living will, you might want to change physicians. But do not give your doctor decision-making powers. As a rule, he or she cannot act as both your proxy and your physician.

● When choosing a hospital or nursing home, ask the institution to agree in writing to comply with your living will.

● Don't keep the original document in a safe-deposit box. It may become inaccessible to others if you are stricken. Put your living will with other important papers, or have your attorney put it in his or her vault.

● Redate and re-sign your living will once a year. At least every five years, do the same before witnesses and a notary. Not only will a recent reaffirmation of your wishes carry extra weight with doctors, hospitals, and judges, but it will also force you to reconsider your position. The idea of clinging to a life you cannot enjoy may be abhorrent to you now, but who knows? In 10 or 20 years, any thread of life may seem precious.

move to another state, or have a substantial change in the value of your estate. Any big change in tax laws warrants a review, too. Otherwise, read your will every year or so to be certain it still reflects your wishes. When you decide to change the will, ask your lawyer to write an amendment—known as a codicil—or, if necessary, a brand-new will.

For many people with specific goals in mind, a will is not enough. You may also want a lawyer to draw up one or more trusts to do the following:

● Set aside a specified amount of money from your estate for your children. If they are young, the cash could go to them when they are mature enough to manage their finances. Disabled children might get special trusts to ensure they're taken care of after you're gone.

● Reduce your estate's tax bill. For instance, a husband who puts cash in a bypass trust for a child prevents the money from becoming part of his wife's estate, so the child will receive the principal free of federal estate taxes upon her death.

● Keep your assets out of probate court so the money will get into the hands of your survivors more quickly and without court fees.

There are two types of trusts. The first is called a living trust, and it may be revocable or irrevocable. A revocable living trust lets you receive its income while you are alive and pass the property to the trust's beneficiaries upon your death without going through probate. You can alter or cancel a revocable living trust at any time. You fund an irrevocable trust permanently with assets while you are alive, and the money or property goes to a beneficiary according to your instructions. You cannot alter or cancel an irrevocable living trust.

The second type of trust is called a testamentary trust, and it is set up in your will to take effect after you die. To determine whether you need a trust and what type is best for you, ask your lawyer. You can expect to pay $750 or more for the drafting of either type of trust.

Once your will and any trust agreements are written, don't put them in your safe-deposit box. Your family may need a court order to get into the box after you die, and that could take days. File the originals with a probate court (one-time fee: about $5) or a bank trust department.

A household file cabinet should hold all your other essential financial records. To be sure you do not forget any of them, get an estate-planning questionnaire from your lawyer, financial planner, or the trust department of your bank. Among the important records that belong in your cabinet:

● Birth and marriage certificates

● The past seven years' tax returns

● All of your life insurance policies

● Real estate deeds and contracts

● Cemetery deeds

● Titles to your cars

● Military discharge papers

Then, write a letter of instruction to your family (as explained in the box on the opposite page) about steps they should take upon your death. Include in the letter the names and addresses of your financial advisers and all the beneficiaries of your estate, as well as the birthdates of any minors in your family. One of the biggest delays in probate is when the lawyer is looking for names and addresses of relatives who might be receiving benefits. You can expedite the process by leaving behind a family tree. Remember: The more details you clear up now, the easier it will be when it is time to settle your estate.

After tidying up your estate plans and writing the appropriate instructions, call together your family or other close relatives. Tell them exactly what you've done. You might see a few squeamish expressions, but you can be certain your loved ones will ultimately be grateful for your forethought.

Leaving Instructions for Your Family

An essential part of putting your affairs in order is writing a detailed list of instructions to guide your family or executor in handling your finances after your death. The letter, though not legally binding, should give the location of your financial documents and what you'd like done about your burial. Before writing the letter, put all of your essential personal papers in a file cabinet at home so your family can get to them easily. Your letter should include the following:

The people who should be notified of your death. Give the names, addresses, and phone numbers of your beneficiaries, closest relatives, clergyman, accountant, broker, financial planner, insurance agent, lawyer, and employee-benefits counselor.

Your wishes concerning your funeral and burial. If you own a cemetery plot, write down the name and location of the cemetery and the plot number. Also indicate whether you wish to donate your organs for transplant or medical research.

The location and number of your safe-deposit box. Be sure to list the contents of the box and say where you have put the key so it can be found easily.

The death benefits to which your family is entitled. Don't forget to include group life insurance, a pension, a profit-sharing account, and deferred compensation at work. Also jot down your Social Security number and the location of your veteran's discharge papers (if you served in the armed forces) so that your family can file for government benefits.

Your bank accounts, investments, and other assets. Alongside each, note the location and any account numbers. Identify the type, location, and estimated value of jewelry, silverware, and antiques. If anyone owes you money, give the debtor's name, address, and the amount.

Your liabilities. These include a mortgage, charge cards, and other personal debts. The list will help your survivors decide which loans to pay off quickly to prevent foreclosure or repossession.

Update this letter yearly and keep a copy at home in your file cabinet. If your children are young, give a copy to their potential guardian.

Managing Credit and Debt

Sweet rewards will come to those who find ways to save more and borrow less for the 1990s. For many it may be essential to prospering in the decade. Would-be savers should consider the rising cost of college, their own retirement, and, in some cases, their aging parents, who may need financial assistance. Relentless debtors should also remember that Congress is trying to discourage borrowing with the tax-reform law that ends the deductibility of interest on personal loans and credit cards after this year.

At the office, you no doubt are the very model of a modern manager. Your department perennially shows an operating surplus, and your suppliers can rely on you to pay their invoices in 30 days. At home, however, you seem to be caught in a financial treadmill. While you usually have enough cash to pay your monthly bills, you rarely have anything extra to stash in savings or investments. Don't despair. This chapter will show you how to start managing your money as well as you do your employer's.

Track your cash flow. As any successful administrator knows, the key to ensuring greater inflows than outflows is a budget that you can live with. Creating a family budget can be much more challenging than putting one together at work. You have to map the myriad directions your money has gone in the past without the help of even one hotshot M.B.A. to hold your hand. Then you may come to the depressing conclusion that your cash has only trickled toward your financial goals. That will call for some difficult adjustments, as detailed in "Getting Control of Your Cash Flow," beginning on page 116. The toughest part of the job could be enlisting the support of your spouse and children—you can't threaten to fire them.

Get on top of your debt. Losing control of your finances is easier than regaining it. Getting yourself out of hock means changing borrowing habits built up over years and, in many cases, accepting a standard of living that is lower, at least temporarily, than you were accustomed to. While there is no painless way to undo the effect of years of overborrowing, "Cutting Your Debt," beginning on page 119, provides sure-footed steps to help you climb out of the hole.

Find ways to save more. Like a tap dancer, a saver needs a fixed routine and the discipline to practice it. The secret to building up your cash reserves can be summed up with a single rule: Always strive to pay yourself first. The simplest way is to put a set amount of your paycheck into savings each month. If doing that requires more willpower than you can muster, turn to "How to Save Automatically" on page 124. There you will find advice about enrolling in your company's payroll savings plan or arranging for your bank to shift a specified sum each month from your checking to savings account.

Getting Control of Your Cash Flow

Plugging leaks in your wallet is easy—once you find out where they are.

Almost everyone needs to find ways to curtail spending, freeing cash to meet short- and long-term financial goals. But how? And how much? For the answers, you'll have to learn the most basic process of managing your cash flow, which is the stream of money that passes through your hands before taxes. The "Where the Money Goes" worksheet on the opposite page will help you create a personal income and outgo statement and compare your spending with recommended ranges for middle-income couples and singles. Also consult "Figuring Your Net Worth" on page 118 to determine what you own versus what you owe.

The simplest way to track income and outgo is to focus on the past calendar year; you already gathered much of the necessary information when preparing your taxes. But if your financial life has changed significantly since December—you took out a new loan, received a windfall, got divorced—don't forget to make appropriate allowances in the worksheet. Plan to spend several hours collecting the data and plugging in the numbers. In addition to your tax return, your check register should be a mother lode of information. Also, haul out your store and credit-card statements. Most creditors will send you copies of any that you are missing. And you should pull together your bank statements for a record of your electronic cash withdrawals.

To fill in the final cash-flow numbers, you may need to keep an expense diary for a month to learn where your walk-around money ends up. You may be shocked at the dollars siphoned off by impulse purchases, routine expenditures such as dry-cleaning costs, and those impromptu evenings out when

Where the Money Goes

Fill out this worksheet to start monitoring your income and outgo. Capital gains are your profits from selling investments; mystery cash is money that you spent but can't account for. You can compare your spending in each category with the recommended ranges for three types of households: singles with gross income of $30,000; childless couples with gross incomes of $40,000 to $60,000; and two-children families with gross incomes of $50,000 to $75,000.

ANNUAL INCOME	
Earnings From Job	$
Investment Income And Capital Gains	
Gifts, Inheritances	
Alimony, Child Support, Other	
Total Income	$

ANNUAL EXPENSES

Suggested spending (% of gross income)

Single	Married, no kids	Married with kids		
20-23	23-25	22-25	Housing, Utilities	$
17-19	18-20	19-21	Taxes	
8-9	8-10	8-10	Savings, Investments	
8-9	8-9	7-8	Food	
8-9	4-5	1-2	Debt Payments	
7-9	7-8	5	Vacations, Entertainment, Hobbies	
7-8	6-7	4-5	Transportation	
4-5	2-3	3-4	Insurance	
4	4-5	5-6	Clothing, Personal Care	
3-4	5-7	5-6	Gifts, Contributions	
1-2	2-3	2-3	Medical Expenses	
1-2	1	7-8	Child Care, Education	
1-2	1-2	1-2	Unreimbursed Business Expenses	
1	1	1	Mystery Cash	
0-4	0-4	0-4	Alimony, Child Support	
			Total Expenses	$

SOURCE: SHIRES FINANCIAL GROUP, LITTLETON, COLO.

no one feels like cooking at home. Once you've assembled all the requisite data, fill in the income part of the worksheet and arrive at the total. Be sure to include interest from tax-free municipal bonds or muni-bond mutual funds.

Next, turn to expenses. Divide them into discrete spending categories such as the ones appearing in the worksheet. You'll probably wind up with between 12 and 20 categories. Be as precise as possible: you might subdivide household expenses down to his clothing, her clothing, and kids' clothing, for example. In time, as you isolate your spending excesses, you'll probably be able to whittle down the number of groups. But be sure to include a category for mystery cash—the money you spent but cannot account for.

Trying to nail down the exact amounts for variable expenses such as groceries, meals in restaurants, and medical bills can drive you crazy. For sanity's sake, analyze your payments for them over the past six months and multiply by two for a yearly total. As for the expenses without receipts that you tracked in the diary of your walk-around money, annualize the amounts and apportion them into the appropriate outgo categories. Don't worry about the pennies. Round the amounts to the nearest $10.

When this time-and-motion study of your spending habits is complete, take a deep breath and add up all your taxes and expenses, then subtract them from your gross income. Ideally, the bottom line will show a hefty cash surplus that you stashed in savings and investments. Keep this habit up each year and your cash flow will be under control. Or the worksheet may indicate that you broke even, which suggests a need for spending reform. If you paid out more than you took in, you'd better start mending your spending now. You either went into debt or drew on savings to make ends meet.

If you are not among the fortunate few who save regularly, you must find ways to rein in spending. Chances are, about 70% of your income is earmarked for taxes, housing, and other relatively immutable costs. So you'll have to squeeze the remaining 30%. A few areas are usually ripe: clothing, dinners out, spending

on electronic gear and kitchen gadgets, as well as overuse of credit cards with finance charges that can top 18% a year. You'll get more ideas by looking at the worksheet and comparing your spending as a percentage of gross income

Figuring Your Net Worth

The difference between what you own (assets) and what you owe (liabilities) is your net worth. By finding ways to control your spending, reduce your debt, and increase your savings and investments, you will make your net worth grow and have an easier time reaching your financial goals. To figure your net worth, take out a note pad and follow these steps:

1. List the name of everything you own, including your checking and savings accounts, certificates of deposit, money-market fund accounts, cars, furnishings and appliances, artwork and antiques, clothing, jewelry, vested holdings in company savings and pension plans, Individual Retirement Accounts, Keoghs, other investments, cash-value life insurance, and your house, condominium, or cooperative apartment.

2. Next to the name of each asset, write down its present market value. For your life insurance, note any cash value.

3. Total your assets.

4. On another page, list the names of your creditors, including your credit-card and charge accounts and the holders of your home mortgage, home-equity line of credit, and any other loans, such as ones for cars, college, and investments.

5. Next to each creditor's name, write the principal amount still due.

6. Total your liabilities.

7. Subtract your liabilities from your assets to arrive at your net worth.

with the suggested ranges for people like you.

For example, mystery cash is often the most troublesome category to control. If more than 30% of your take-home pay is spent in cash outlays, try writing checks for all purchases of $10 or more to create a paper trail of your expenses. Also take a look at your insurance policies. Raising your auto and homeowners insurance deductibles—the amounts you agree to pay each year before benefits kick in—might easily save you 20% of your premiums.

No matter how sound the spending plan you devise, be prepared to fight temptation. Forgive yourself for an occasional lapse. But if the spending bug starts threatening your resolve to save, you might need to adopt these countermeasures:

● Make fewer shopping trips and buy only from lists you prepare in advance.

● Consider the entire cost of an expensive item, not just its retail price. Factor in the interest you'll owe on credit payments as well as any upkeep expenses.

● When you decide to make a purchase, check prices at three or more stores first.

Once you have devised a comfortable spending plan, follow it for three months. Then conduct the first of three quarterly reviews. At each, you may want to restore certain luxuries and curtail others. You could also find that some ordinary expenses are not costing as much as you anticipated. For example, your clothing bills may be lower than in the past, allowing you to add the unexpected cash to savings. After 12 months, your spending habits should be so impressive that you may need only an annual checkup.

Cutting Your Debt

Whether you are cautious about credit or already in the hole, follow these important rules.

Americans, like their government, have become hooked on deficit spending during the 1980s. Consumer borrowing recently amounted to 19% of the after-tax income of U.S. households, up from 14% in 1982. Personal bankruptcy filings are at an all-time high, reaching about 550,000 in 1988. Credit counseling services report huge increases in the number of clients coming in for help. This surge in the ranks of the debt-lorn, predictable enough in bad times, looks all the more ominous coming as it has in an era of prosperity.

In addition to the inherent risk of going into hock, borrowing is no longer the wise financial strategy that it was in the late 1970s. Then, steep inflation practically demanded people buy now and pay later in cheaper dollars. Most loans had fixed interest rates whose payments wouldn't rise with inflation. Interest was fully tax deductible. Now, inflation has moderated and most lenders build inflation into their interest rates or charge adjustable rates. In the meantime, the tax incentive for borrowing is going, going, gone. You can still deduct all the interest on mortgages up to $1 million and home-equity loans up to $100,000. Otherwise, Americans have one year left to get out of debt before losing the last penny of interest deductions. In 1990, you can write off only 10% of the cost of consumer loans and purchases.

Next year, the deduction disappears. So, for a host of reasons, it's time to curb your borrowing. If you don't, racking up debts will force you to fall short of important financial goals. And what if your income dries up so you can't pay your debts on time? Even temporary delinquency can cripple your ability to borrow, buy insurance, or get a job. Lenders will stamp you as a deadbeat, and the stigma can cling to your credit record for years.

Where to begin? Before cutting up all your credit cards, take the time to determine how much debt you can realistically afford to carry (see "Are You Carrying Too Much Debt?" on the opposite page). If you're over your limit, don't borrow anymore. You will also need to map out a debt offensive. If possible, lead this brigade by just saying no to future invitations to borrow. At the very least, look for ways to reduce your current debt load. And if you are truly unable to make your payments, find ways to stall for time. These eight rules show you how to win the war against debt:

Don't borrow to pay for anything as perishable as a vacation. Finance only the kinds of purchases that pay long-term returns. Short of a house or car, try to buy anything else with cash. If you must take out your charge card, be sure you'll have the cash to pay the bill in full when it arrives.

Liquidate your costliest debts first. Do this by drawing up a table with columns for: the names of all your creditors, the balance owed to each, the monthly payment, and the interest rate. You may find that you owe interest at, say, 21% on credit cards, 15% on a personal loan, 12% on a mortgage, 10% on a car loan, and nothing on money borrowed from relatives. With no disrespect to relatives, they tend to be the most flexible lenders. So, pay off the credit cards first. Put your mortgage last on your debt liquidation list because the interest is tax deductible. If you are in the 28% tax bracket, a 12% mortgage costs only 8.6% after taxes.

Get a grip on your plastic. Most credit-card issuers charge annual interest rates of 18% to 21%, making the cards among the most expensive ways to borrow. One method of slicing your credit-card debt is by cutting up unnecessary cards. You need only one or two cards for personal use and perhaps another for business expenses.

Always try to pay off the monthly bill in full. Never pay merely the bare minimum; that just saddles you with more debt. For advice on how to choose the right credit card for you, see "Shopping for Banking Services," beginning on page 125.

Avoid debt-consolidation loans. The pitch is time honored: borrow from us by making one easy monthly payment and we'll pay off your other loans. Generally, though, debt consolidators are likely to charge a higher interest rate than you were paying, and they might fail to settle your old debts as promised. You may be thinking about consolidating your debts yourself using a home-equity loan as your sole borrowing source and paying off your credit-card bills and personal loans for good. But resist this temptation unless you're a paradigm of self-discipline.

Consider refinancing your mortgage to reduce your debt payments. By trading in your current mortgage for a new one with a lower interest rate, you can slash your monthly payment and thus your borrowing costs. Say you've been paying a 12%, 30-year, fixed-rate loan for five years and you still owe $100,000. If mortgage rates have fallen to 10% and you refinance the balance of your mortgage, you could lower your payments by more than $100 a month, from $1,029 to $926. Refinancing only makes sense, however, if today's going rate is at least two percentage points below yours. Otherwise, you'll find that the fees charged for refinancing—known as closing costs—will eat up any savings on your monthly payment. Over the long run, you could wind up paying more than the cost of your original mortgage.

Telephone your creditors if you can't meet your payments. Like a bad muffler on a car, a debt you cannot pay is a hard problem to ignore. Insistent letters come in demanding money, bill collectors keep your nerves jangling, and your credit rating plummets. So if you're unable to pay lenders on time, be upfront with them. Say what the problem is and what you think you can pay per month to get the debt out of the way.

The creditor probably has repayment guidelines based on how long you have been a customer, how much you owe, how long you have been delinquent, and your past payment record. For example, at Abraham & Straus, a department store chain in the New York City area, a customer with an excellent credit record who loses his or her job might be able to negotiate a two-month breathing spell that will cut monthly charge-card payments by 25%. By the third month, however, he or she would

have to resume normal payments and catch up on the arrears.

When a creditor refuses to negotiate further, seek outside help. Head for the nearest non-profit credit counseling service, which you can find by calling the National Foundation for Consumer Credit (301-589-5600) in Silver Spring, Maryland. A credit counselor will review your debts and your ability to pay them and help you set up a supervised payment plan. The first consultation is often free. After that, you'll be charged according to your ability to pay. The average fee is $10 a month; some people are not charged at all.

Counselors, typically, devise a two- to three-year schedule for liquidating your debts. They determine how much you can afford to pay

Are You Carrying Too Much Debt?

Every family should set its own tolerance for consumer debt. You do so by limiting debt to a fixed percentage of your household's disposable income—that is, monthly take-home pay minus taxes and all other deductions. Depending on the stability of your family's income, your stage of life, and your cash on hand, this ratio of installments to income might be held to a cautious 10% or, more typically, 15% to 20%. The top of the range gets risky unless you have exceptionally strong job security and lots of life, health, and disability-income insurance. If your borrowing costs exceed 20% of after-tax income, you are entering the danger zone.

Gauging the amount of debt you can handle and how close you are to your personal debt limit is a simple process:

1. Add up your debt payments. These are the monthly installments you pay on car loans, credit cards, charge accounts, student loans, home-equity loans, and all other nonmortgage and nonbusiness debts.

2. Figure out your monthly take-home pay. Get your latest pay stub and multiply the net

income amount by the number of pay periods in the year. Divide the result by 12. Do not include bonuses, since you can't depend on them. Unless you are living on investment income, exclude your dividends, interest, and capital gains, too.

3. Now you can calculate your debt limit. Multiply your take-home pay by .10 if you live on a fixed income, have recently changed jobs, or are the only person in your household who is earning an income.

Multiply by .20 if your household has two incomes and you are spending a lot to furnish a house. Do the same if you have enough cash on hand to cover three months of living expenses in an emergency. Multiply your take-home pay by .15 if you seem to fall in between these two guidelines.

4. Determine your additional borrowing power. If your debt limit in Step 3 exceeds your current debt payments in Step 1, the difference is the extra carrying charges you can afford on new debt. If there's a deficit, borrow no more.

each month and allot a fair share of the total to each of your creditors. They then notify your lenders to get them off your back. Each month, you write a check to the counseling agency for the overall specified repayment amount, and counselors mail out separate checks to your creditors. Do not confuse these legitimate counseling programs with so-called credit repair services, alias credit clinics or credit doctors. These operatives promise to remove adverse data from your credit report—and even get you a credit card—for a fee of as much as $2,000. But they cannot deliver.

If all else fails, file for bankruptcy. The time to start weighing this desperate measure is when creditors threaten to seize part of your wages through a court process called garnishment. Bankruptcy stops creditors from hounding you by putting you under the protection of the U.S. Bankruptcy Court. And bankruptcy's recent popularity—at last count, filings were up 90% since 1984—perhaps proves that it is not the disgrace it used to be.

Filing for bankruptcy, of course, has some ugly drawbacks. First, you'll have to liquidate most of your assets, probably including your house if you have one. Then, a record of the bankruptcy will show up in your credit bureau files for as long as a decade. You won't have to wear a scarlet letter, but you will be sentenced to a long term of paying cash for practically everything. Getting a mortgage or car loan will be all but impossible for at least seven years.

There are two forms of personal bankruptcy: the wage-earner plan and straight bankruptcy. Under the wage-earner plan, called Chapter 13, a court trustee supervises the full or partial repayment of your debts, usually over three to five years. Under a straight, or Chapter 7, bankruptcy, the court apportions most of your assets among creditors. Federal law, unless overruled by stricter state limits, protects $7,500 ($15,000 for a married couple) of the equity in a home and about $4,000 of furnishings and clothing, plus a few designated items such as life insurance cash value and tools of your trade worth up to $750. The balance of your debts gets wiped out. Exceptions include alimony, child support, three years' back taxes, and some government-subsidized student loans.

How to Start Saving

Here are some fairly painless ways to increase your stash of cash.

When it comes to saving, nearly everyone procrastinates. Yet, you get the biggest bang from your first bucks because they compound the longest. If, for example, you steadfastly socked away $2,000 at the start of a year for 10 years, then upped the ante to $5,000 annually for 20 years, you would accumulate $392,960, assuming an 8% return. But if you omit that first $20,000 in contributions, your nest egg shrivels to $247,114—a drop of 37%.

The challenge, of course, is to create a savings routine that you can realistically live with. A technique that helps is to have some of your money taken out of your hands before you get a chance to spend it. One way to do that is to establish some form of automatic savings program. You may be able to do this at work through an employer-sponsored savings plan,

U.S. savings bond program, or a credit union payroll plan. Otherwise, you'll have to devise your own system to transfer, on a regular basis, a specific amount from your checking account into a savings account or mutual fund. (For more information, see "How to Save Automatically" on page 124.)

Rookie savers often wonder how much is enough. A general guideline is that you should try to put aside 10% of gross income each year. If that goal seems too ambitious, consider a strategy of saving 4% to 8% of your income in your twenties and doubling the percentage during your thirties and forties. In your fifties, when your children's college bills have been paid off and your retirement looms, you may be able to squirrel away 20% of your pay.

Rules are fine, but reality sometimes gets in the way. Take the common household tug-of-war between spending now and saving for later. If Cheryl Cheapskate marries Sam Spendthrift, the newlyweds may face some thorny decisions. Suppose that Cheryl and Sam have $2,000 of spare cash each year, coming in at the rate of about $165 a month. Cheryl would like to tuck the bucks in an Individual Retirement Account, while Sam would rather spend the money on dinners out. One solution is to alternate between funding the IRA one month and going out to dinner the next. If this combo plan sounds appealing, be prepared to make some compromises down the road. After all, you will end up with a smaller pool of savings than if you didn't spend some of the cash. The trade-off for fond memories of all those nights out could well be postponement of your retirement for several years.

One way to ensure that you stick to any savings plan you devise is to set specific objectives for the money—some short term, some long term, and some just for fun. To figure out how much you'll need to save to reach a specific goal, use the Rule of 72: Divide 72 by the interest rate you expect your savings to earn. The answer will be the number of years your savings stash will take to double, before taxes. For instance, if you earn 8%, the money will double in nine years.

Your first savings goal should be an emergency cash reserve to see you through illness, unemployment, or any other financial setback. This fund should equal at least three to six months of living expenses. Fine-tune the amount to your own circumstances by considering what misfortunes could occur that would not be covered by your health and disability insurance. Since the emergency fund should carry you through any periods of unemployment, its optimal size will also depend on your employability. For example, if you are a highly paid executive in a slow-growth industry, you may need a year's worth of living expenses in your reserve fund. But if your skills are in great demand and you have ample insurance, then just two months' worth of expenses may be sufficient. In the event of a disability, the emergency fund should pay living expenses until your insurance coverage kicks in, which might take from two to six months.

Whatever its size, keep your emergency cache in a safe place where you can get to it quickly. If you have only several hundred dollars or less, put it in a bank savings account. As your fund grows, you can switch to a higher-yielding, money-market deposit account, which typically requires a $1,000 minimum investment, or transfer the cash to a money-market fund. This is a type of mutual fund that resembles a bank money-market account but is not federally insured. Lately, money funds have been yielding about 8.75%, roughly 2.25 percentage points higher than the rate on many money-market accounts. Most money funds have no sales charges and will take $500 to $1,000 as an initial deposit, $50 and up for subsequent additions. You can deposit and withdraw cash either by mail or through wire transfers from your bank.

Don't be disturbed that money funds are not federally insured. The securities they hold are usually so conservative—Treasury bills, short-term corporate IOUs, and the like—that the extra risk is quite small. Before opening a taxable money fund account, however, you may want to consider the tax-exempt variety. These funds buy short-term municipal bonds whose interest is free from federal income taxes.

Deciding whether to save with a taxable or tax-free money fund is easy. First, find out the current yields on tax-free money funds by checking the weekly average in *Barron's*. Then subtract your income tax bracket from 100 and divide the remainder into the tax-free yield you are considering. The result is what's called the equivalent taxable yield. Suppose 5.5% is the average tax-free money fund yield and you are in the 28% tax bracket. You would have to find a taxable money fund yielding 7.6% to earn more than with the tax-free fund (100 minus 28 equals 72; that divided into 5.5 equals 7.6%). For a list of the top-performing taxable and tax-free money funds and their toll-free phone numbers, see the Fund Watch column monthly in *Money*.

Once you have your emergency fund in place, you are ready to start putting away so-called discretionary savings—funds for buying a house, paying for a child's college education, and funding your retirement (for specific advice about each, refer to the respective chapters in this book). Since you probably won't touch these dollars for awhile, you can afford to deposit them in savings and investment havens with higher returns. Your alternatives include company savings plans, U.S. Treasury securities, bank certificates of deposit, and growth stock mutual funds.

How to Save Automatically

Sometimes the best way to save is by placing the process in someone else's hands. Your employee-benefits department can tell you how to sign up for tax-deferred savings plans managed by your company. Other types of automatic savings plans to consider:

U.S. savings bond payroll-deduction plans. If your employer lets you buy Series EE bonds with deductions from your paychecks, ask your benefits department for the enrollment form. You decide how much you want to have withheld, though your employer sets the minimum amount. The bonds will cost you $25 to $5,000, half of what they will be worth at maturity in 12 years. Most companies will give you the actual certificates for the bonds as you buy them, but a few will hold the bonds in escrow until you ask for them. Allow one or two pay periods after you sign up for withholding to begin.

Credit union payroll plans. If you belong to a credit union at work, a slice of your paycheck—as much as you wish—can be automatically deposited into your share account, which is the credit union equivalent of a bank savings account. Your benefits department can supply you with information and an authorization form. After you commit to a plan, the deposits will begin in one or two pay periods.

Automatic transfers from a checking account to a savings account. Most banks and savings and loans will automatically transfer as little as $25 a month or as much as you want from your checking account to a savings account. There is usually no charge for the service, and the money can go into a passbook or statement savings account, or occasionally into a money-market deposit account. Filling out the authorization form takes only a few minutes. Your first transfer can be made within a week.

Automatic transfers from a bank account to a mutual fund. Stock and bond funds typically accept automatic transfers of $50 and up, as often as every other week or as infrequently as once a year. Some banks permit transfers only from checking or NOW accounts, others from savings accounts as well. There is generally no fee for this service. If your mutual fund is a no-load, call its toll-free number and ask for an application. When you get it, fill in the name of the fund, the location and number of your bank account, and the amount and frequency of your planned transfers. In addition, attach a personal check (write VOID on it) or a savings deposit slip. If you invest in funds through a stockbroker or financial planner, get the materials from him or her. Expect the transfers to begin in two to four weeks.

Most financial planners consider employer-sponsored plans unbeatable for long-term savings. Each year you and your employer can put aside up to 25% of your pay or $30,000, whichever is less. The earnings on your contributions will grow tax-free until you take the money out, usually when you retire or change jobs. Your employer's matching contributions, if any, will produce an automatic return on your savings. But perhaps the greatest plus of a company plan is that saving becomes mechanical—since you never get your hands on the money, its absence causes minimal pain.

Most company plans offer a variety of investment choices. You, typically, can select among the company's stock, fixed-income or growth-stock mutual funds, and guaranteed investment contracts, which are basically certificates of deposit sold by insurance companies (but not insured by the federal government). If you have a savings program known as a 401(k) plan, your employer can take some of your pay before it's taxed and put it into a savings fund. Most employers match part of an employee's 401(k) contributions, often kicking in $1 for every $2 invested.

You usually cannot withdraw savings from your company plan except in an emergency, though. Even then, you will be hit with a 10% early-withdrawal penalty. However, some companies let you borrow against your account.

More than 47,000 companies also offer employees payroll-deduction plans to buy U.S. savings bonds. Interest on Series EE bonds is exempt from state and local income taxes. Moreover, interest is entirely free from federal taxes for savings bonds bought after 1989 and used for college by couples earning less than $60,000 a year (under $40,000 if you're single). By holding bonds for five years or longer, you will get at least a guaranteed rate (6% in early 1989) or a higher return (7.35% in early 1989) if the average yield of Treasury securities maturing in five years exceeds the guaranteed rate. Redeem your bonds within five years, however, and you will get a puny rate of return—as low as 4.16% in 1989.

One more forced savings plan worth considering is cash-value life insurance. Here, a portion of your annual premium goes into your insurance policy's savings fund. When you die, the insurance will pay your survivors a death benefit. But while you're alive, your cash value will grow tax deferred at a rate that will depend on the type of policy and the cash fund's investment performance. You can borrow against the cash value, and sometimes even withdraw it, if you need the savings.

Shopping for Banking Services

By seeking out the best deals, you can boost your savings yields and cut your borrowing costs.

Accarding to the ads, one-stop banking is the only way to go. The promise: Sign on with the right bank, savings and loan or credit union and never again will you have to spend time hunting for the best deal on a checking account, savings account, certificate of deposit, credit card, car loan, or any other bank service. Bankers call this "relationship banking"—creating an incentive for customers to consolidate their banking services.

Occasionally, the relationship can work in your favor. For example, if you have a savings or checking account at some banks, they will waive any annual credit-card fee. By restricting yourself to one institution, however, you may end up paying more for some services, such as checking and borrowing, or receiving lower returns on others, like savings. Only if you sample the offerings of several banks can you be sure of getting the lowest fees, the highest yields, and the services that suit you best. A no-fee credit card is no bargain if it carries a 21% interest rate and your balance is consistently high. And a bank that charges $5 if your checking account balance dips below $1,000 may be perfect for you, but not for your spouse.

Before shopping for any bank account, loan, or credit card, jot down the services and terms you want. Let's say you are looking for a savings account or CD. In that case, put federal insurance at the top of your list. At nearly all banks, S&Ls, and credit unions, balances of up to $100,000 are insured by a U.S. agency. In these uncertain times, accept nothing less.

Then, start your hunt for the account paying the highest interest. Read ads and brochures of competing institutions. Don't overlook the footnotes, and always look for the asterisk that invariably corresponds to a disclaimer of some sort. Don't ignore so-called nonbanks either. Sometimes brokerages and mutual funds offer better rates than banks do on CDs and home-equity lines of credit. Expand your search beyond your hometown, too. Each month the Investor's Scorecard department in *Money* publishes the names and toll-free phone numbers of the institutions with the best deals in the country on savings accounts, CDs, and credit cards.

What follows are specific guidelines to help you find your way through the maze of choices in bank services:

Checking Accounts

Like cars, checking accounts come in a variety of styles that range from no frills to super-deluxe. You may find different names—NOW accounts at banks and S&Ls, and share-draft accounts at credit unions—but the models all

serve the same function of letting you park your cash safely and draw checks on it at will. The most suitable account depends on two factors: the size of your monthly balance and the number of checks you write. As a rule, the higher your balance, the lower your fees, and the better your chances of finding an account that will pay you interest on your money.

Balances are figured in different ways, so be sure to ask a bank officer about the institution's method before opening an account. Some banks charge service fees according to your lowest balance during the month. Others base them on your average daily balance, which is preferable. Take, for example, two banks requiring minimum monthly balances of $1,000 for free checking and a customer at each whose account balance drops to $800 for a day. With the first method, the unfortunate depositor could be stuck with a service fee of $4 or $5 and possibly additional charges for each check. The other customer will make it through the entire month fee-free.

If you write few checks (the monthly average is 19) and your balance is usually small, look for a basic account that permits limited transactions at low cost. With a minimum balance of about $250, for example, you will probably be allowed to write 10 free checks a month; additional checks might cost 25¢ to 50¢ each. If your account falls below the minimum, expect to pay a $2 to $3 monthly service charge. If you can keep a $500 minimum balance, open a regular account with unlimited free checking but no interest. When your balance drops below the minimum, the bank will charge a monthly fee of $4 or $5 and your checks will cost 15¢ to 25¢ each.

A heavy check writer who keeps a volatile balance ought to ask about a flat-fee account, which does not pay interest. You'll typically get 20 to 30 free checks each month for a flat monthly fee of $3 or $4. Additional checks will cost 20¢ to 45¢ each. Generally, you must keep a minimum balance of around $1,000 to earn interest on your checking in another type of account called a NOW—for negotiable order of withdrawal. Recent interest rates: 4.5% to 5.75%. In a month when your balance falls below the minimum, the bank or S&L will charge a service fee of $5 to $10 and 20¢ to 25¢ for each check.

Savings Accounts

For generations, these accounts have been the first choice of young savers whose needs outgrew their piggy banks. A savings account keeps your money safe but readily available for withdrawal either at a teller's window or through an automatic teller machine. Sometimes you can even write checks against your savings. Generally, the more you can keep in your savings account, the higher your interest rate will be.

Most institutions that accept deposits of any kind offer traditional savings accounts—the type that used to require a passbook but now often sends you a monthly statement instead. Credit unions call them share accounts. For an initial deposit of $100 or less, you can open a savings account that pays about 5.5% a year. If your balance falls below the institution's minimum, there could be a monthly or quarterly maintenance charge of a few dollars.

Most banking institutions also offer money-market deposit accounts, which often require minimum deposits of $1,000 or more but normally pay higher rates than those on traditional savings accounts. Yields on bank money-market accounts, recently averaging about 6.4%, rise and fall with other short-term interest rates. Unlike traditional savings accounts, money-market accounts let you write checks. Many institutions limit this privilege to three checks a month, however, to prevent the accounts from becoming high-yielding checking accounts. A few banks offer savings accounts that pay more than money-market accounts, but do not permit check writing.

Unless you expect to keep more than $5,000 in savings, don't spend much time searching for the highest-yielding account. The differences don't amount to much on small balances. But be sure to analyze yields carefully, because methods vary for compounding interest. One way to cut through the technicalities is to ask each bank for the effective annual return on a sum after your interest is compounded. You

might, for example, inquire: "What would $1,000 deposited today be worth in a year if all my interest is left on deposit?" Then go with the bank whose answer is highest.

If you can trade a whisker of flexibility for an appreciably higher return, shop for rates nationally and do your saving by mail. A few banks and S&Ls lately paid up to 2.25 points more on money-market accounts than the national average. Institutions that court out-of-state depositors often have toll-free numbers; call or write to request terms and application forms. Don't mail any money until the bank sends you written confirmation of its rates and minimum deposit.

Some of the top-yielding institutions are financially shaky. If a troubled federally-insured institution were to shut down, as much as $100,000 in your principal and interest to date would be secure. The government might close your account or CD, however, and pay you the money for it.

An alternative to a bank money-market account is a money-market mutual fund. This savings haven is not federally insured, but money funds are extremely safe because they invest in conservative, short-term securities such as Treasury bills. And the funds can yield as much as 2.5 percentage points more than bank money-market accounts. With a money fund, you deposit and withdraw cash by mail; withdrawals can also be wired to your bank savings or checking account. Money-market funds usually accept initial deposits of at least $500 to $1,000. Most also offer unlimited free check writing, though checks frequently must be for $500 or more.

Certificates of Deposit

Unlike a savings account, a CD has a fixed maturity. When you buy a CD (typical minimum: $500), you promise to leave the money on deposit for a set period, commonly three months to five years. In return, you will receive a higher yield than you could get from a savings account. Usually, the longer the maturity of a CD, the higher the yield. In late 1989, for example, the national average for six-month CDs was 8.1%; for five-year CDs it was 8.8%. Some institutions pay higher interest for deposits of more than $10,000 or so. If you are willing to bank by mail, you may be able to find an out-of-state bank or S&L paying higher yields than local institutions.

Many issuers impose early-withdrawal penalties. Do not accept a CD from an institution that will withhold more than six months' interest if you have to withdraw your cash before maturity. Some banks let CD savers make one early withdrawal, penalty-free, after they have held the certificates for at least seven days. But you may have to give up a quarter of a percent in interest for such a feature. Another interesting wrinkle is called an add-on CD. This type of certificate allows you to make subsequent contributions that will earn interest at your initial rate. Locking in a yield in this way can be advantageous if interest rates begin to fall.

Perhaps the best combination of high yield and convenience is available from a so-called brokered CD, offered by large securities firms. Brokerages get CDs from banks and S&Ls for their individual investors and then sell them in minimum amounts of $1,000 to $10,000 and at higher yields than those on certificates bought directly from most banks and S&Ls. If you need funds before your brokered CD matures, you might have to pay an early-withdrawal penalty of sorts. When a broker resells a CD, it trades the way a bond does. So, if interest rates have risen, the value of your CD will have declined and you may lose some principal. Conversely, if rates have fallen, you could reap a capital gain.

Stay away from CDs that smack of gimmickry. For instance, some banks sell CDs whose yields rise or fall with the performance of local professional teams or the stock market. CDs are for saving, not speculating.

Credit Cards

While savers will often shop till they drop to capture the highest CD returns, heavy spenders rarely compare costs on MasterCard and Visa, the ubiquitous bank credit cards. This can be an expensive mistake, not just for the 60% of cardholders who owe interest on the balances they carry from one month to the next, but also for customers who swallow high annual fees of $20 or more. You may be surprised to learn that bank-card rates, fees, and repayment terms vary enormously. Visa and MasterCard are actually umbrella organizations comprising independent financial institutions that issue cards and set their own terms for borrowers.

The perfect bank credit card carries no annual fee, has at least a 25-day grace period (the time before finance charges kick in), and has an interest rate below 15%. Although such an exemplar is virtually nonexistent, you can find either a card with an interest rate below the national average of 18% or one that charges no annual fee. Low-rate cards are appropriate if you tend to carry a balance from month to month; some of these cards have variable interest rates. No-fee cards are best if you pay off your charges in full at the end of each month.

These bargain bank cards are part of an elusive and endangered species that you are unlikely to find in your own backyard. Still, you can hunt one down by expanding your search across state lines. A nonprofit group called Bankcard Holders of America (460 Spring Park Place, Suite 1000, Herndon, VA 22070) offers consumers a list of more than 50 banks and S&Ls across the country with cards whose annual rates are below 16.2%, as well as a list of about 25 institutions that charge no annual fees for their cards. Send $1.50 for each list.

Many issuers also hawk gold and other premium bank cards. Such cards cost up to $50 a year and sometimes come with slightly reduced interest rates. But the additional costs probably are not justified unless you expect to use the cards' extra services, such as emergency cash advances or discounts on selected hotels and rental cars. As for other types of credit cards:

● If you drive extensively, get oil-company cards that charge no annual fee. If you don't pay your monthly bills in full, you'll be charged interest of about 17% to 18%.

● Credit cards from national retailers such as Sears and J.C. Penney usually carry no annual fee (interest rates on unpaid balances range from 11.5% to 21%). Don't confuse these cards with the Discover card from Sears (interest rate: 19.8%). With Discover, you get a cash rebate of up to 1% on purchases you charge.

● If you travel widely, particularly overseas, you may want to get a travel and entertainment card such as American Express, Diners Club, or Carte Blanche. These cards usually have no interest charges because you are expected to pay them in full each month. (Extended payments for some purchases trigger an annualized finance charge of 12% to 18.5%.) Pay late, and you may be assessed a fee of 2.5% of the amount due. Do it often enough and you may be drummed out of the corps.

These so-called T&E cards don't come cheap. Annual fee: $40 to $55 for the basic models, $75 for the American Express Gold Card and $300 for its Platinum. If you have owned an American Express card for a year or longer, you can apply for the company's Optima card. Optima costs $15 a year, and it could be a suitable replacement for your Visa or MasterCard. The interest charge fluctuates at 5.75 points above the prime rate that banks charge their best corporate customers. In late 1989, the Optima rate was 16.75%.

Personal Loans

Even if you stick faithfully to a budget, the day may come when you need to borrow for a towering expense. One option, if your need is short term, might be a personal loan. Banks are generally willing to lend qualified borrowers $2,000 to $25,000, payable over one to five years. You can deduct 10% of the interest you pay on a personal loan in 1990, but nothing after that.

There are basically two types of personal loans. The first, a secured loan, requires you to pledge as collateral an asset worth at least as much as the loan. If you fail to make your payments, the lender can claim the collateral.

The second type, an unsecured loan, requires no collateral. Because collateral makes a debt less risky to a lender, interest rates on secured loans are lower—13.4% on average in late 1989 versus 16.1% for unsecured loans. For bargain loan rates, you should look for the following deals:

● A personal loan secured by your certificate of deposit. Many lenders will charge you only two or three percentage points over the rate on CDs, or roughly 9% in late 1989.

● A credit union loan, which generally costs about half a point less than a loan from a bank or S&L.

● A reduced-rate loan at the bank or S&L where you have your checking or savings account. Bank of America, for example, snips a quarter-point off its personal-loan rates for customers who agree to have the monthly payments automatically withdrawn from their accounts.

Consider a revolving credit line if you would prefer to borrow a portion of your loan at a time. This way, you can avoid paying interest on money you won't need for awhile. A revolving credit line might be appropriate, for example, when you expect to pay a building contractor in installments over a period of a year or so. The flexibility of a revolving credit line comes with a price: The interest rate can be several points higher than that on a secured personal loan. Some lenders have tougher rules for credit lines than for other personal loans. They may, for instance, restrict credit lines to borrowers who have annual incomes of more than $25,000.

Auto Loans

When you shop for a car, salespeople may suggest that you finance it with them rather than with a bank. In fact, your dealer may quote one overall figure when you plan to trade in your old car, buy a new model, and finance it with them. Don't fall for this one-price ploy. Instead, ask for a breakdown. Check with at least three local lenders, including the one where you have a checking or savings account, to see who has the best deal.

In late 1989, some dealers' financing arms offered loans at 4.9% to 9.9% versus 11.9% on average at banks. But the dealers' loans often come with three strings: they are available only on certain models; you cannot qualify for a dealer's cash rebate if you accept the financing; and you can usually receive the lowest rate only by signing up for a loan of no more than two years or so.

Before applying for a car loan, decide on the length of term you want. The shortest loan is two years, but you may be able to stretch out payments for as long as 10 years. Keep in that the shorter the loan's term, the lower its interest rate but the higher your monthly car payments. For example, a $14,500 car loan at 4.9% over two years costs $635.48 a month; borrowing the same amount with a four-year loan at 11% costs $374.76 a month. Ask whether there will be any penalty if you pay off the loan early. And stay away from auto loans with terms longer than five years, despite their relatively low monthly payments. By the fifth year, the amount you still owe could be more than the depreciating market value of the car. If you sell the car, you might have to come up with additional cash to pay off the loan. A few more tips:

● Ask a lending officer at your bank or S&L whether depositors get special breaks on car loans. At some institutions, you can get a quarter-point discount on the rate if your payments are automatically deducted from your checking account each month.

● Mention your credit history if it's spotless, particularly when you borrow from a car dealer. Some Ford and General Motors dealers, for example, shave as much as three to four percentage points off their regular loan rates—about 10% in late 1989—for solid-citizen borrowers.

● Try to make at least a 20% down payment. Lenders frequently add a quarter of a point to their rates for borrowers making 10% down payments. On a four-year loan for a $15,000 car, the extra interest can amount to $500.

Mortgages

Searching for a home mortgage isn't nearly as complicated as it was when no two lenders seemed to offer the same loan. Even so, you must still sift through a jumble of interest rates and other loan terms to find the right mortgage for you. Do so carefully; a mistake could cost you thousands of dollars. Mercifully, no matter what type of mortgage you select, the interest will be fully tax deductible as long as the loan does not exceed $1 million.

Ask your real estate agent to recommend lenders. But don't stop there; some agents get paid by lenders to steer customers to them. Get names from friends and review the mortgage advertisements in your newspaper's real estate section. Then call half a dozen banks, S&Ls, and mortgage bankers for current rates and terms. Many companies routinely publish lists with data on mortgages offered by dozens of lenders in the same area. For example, every week HSH Associates (1200 Route 23, Butler, NJ 07405; 800-873-2837) puts together surveys of 25 to 80 lenders for home buyers in 36 states. Cost: $18 for two surveys.

There are two types of basic mortgages. Fixed-rate loans have interest rates that don't change. Most such loans have 30- or 15-year terms. In late 1989, the national average rate for fixed-rate mortgages was 11.3%. Variable or adjustable-rate mortgages (ARMs) come with rates that can rise or fall along with other interest rates. Most ARMs have 30- or 15-year terms. An ARM's rate generally cannot rise by more than two percentage points a year or six points over the life of the loan. ARM rates almost always start about two percentage points lower than those of comparable fixed-rate loans, which makes it easier to qualify for an ARM. In 1989, the national average rate for ARMs with annual adjustments was 10.6%.

The initial interest rate on an ARM is typically locked in for six months or a year. Then every year or so, the lender will raise or lower the rate in tandem with an index, such as the one-year Treasury bill rate. The first-year ARM rate is set at a discount from the index, so that even if interest rates remain flat, a borrower's ARM would rise in a year.

Choosing between a fixed-rate loan and an ARM really comes down to your financial situation. You may have to sign up for an ARM if your income is too low to qualify for a fixed rate. If you can make a choice and want to budget a specific amount each month for your mortgage payment, take a fixed-rate loan. If you don't expect to own the house for more than a few years, an ARM can be appealing because there is little risk that your rate will rise substantially.

The second big decision is whether to take a 30- or a 15-year mortgage. A 15-year loan has two big attractions: your rate will probably be about a quarter point lower than that of a comparable 30-year loan and your total interest payments will be cut in half. The drawback is the 15-year loan's higher monthly payment. For example, if you borrow $75,000 at a fixed rate, you would pay $829 a month on a 15-year mortgage at 10.5% versus $700 on a 30-year loan at 10.75%.

There are two other mortgage variations worth considering. The biweekly loan requires you to make payments every two weeks, thereby slashing your total interest costs over time. For example, over 30 years you could save $90,561 in interest with biweekly payments on a fixed-rate, $100,000 loan at 10.75%. Or check out a convertible loan, which starts out as an ARM but gives you the option of switching to a fixed rate between the second and fifth years of the loan. The interest rate is initially about one percentage point higher than that of a comparable ARM, though still lower than what you'd pay for a fixed-rate mortgage. At conversion, you will owe a fee of about $250 and will then owe the going rate on fixed loans.

Once you've been approved for a loan, take a shot at predicting which way mortgage rates are headed over the next few months. If you think rates will rise, tell the lender you want to lock in the current rate on your loan. Most lenders will let you do it for two to three months, but you may have to pay a fee equal to one percent of the loan amount—known as a point. But be sure you can close on the house in time. Otherwise, if the lock-in period ends and market rates have risen, the lender can boost your rate, too.

Home-Equity Loans

These loans against the value of your house constitute one of the few remaining tax loopholes. You can fully deduct interest on a loan of up to $100,000. As a result, banks, S&Ls, and stockbrokers are pushing the loans hard, sometimes with deceptive come-ons. So don't sign up unless you clearly understand the loan agreement. More so than with any other kind of debt, a home-equity loan should be used cautiously. Since you put up your house as collateral, you risk foreclosure if you fall behind on the loan payments. Reserve this debt for big-ticket bills such as college tuition or home renovation.

A home-equity loan can be taken all at once or as a credit line that you draw on over time. A lump-sum loan typically must be repaid within 10 to 20 years. You borrow against a home-equity credit line by writing a check or using a special credit card. These credit lines have a variety of repayment options, but the amount you borrow must be paid off within 30 years. With both types of home-equity loans, the maximum amount you can borrow depends on the appraised value of your home; the lender will handle the appraisal. You can frequently borrow as much as 75% to 80% of the house's value, minus the balance on your mortgage.

Home-equity loans can have either fixed rates—about 12.6% in late 1989—or variable rates. The variable loans are often set at 1.5 to 2 percentage points above the prime rate, around 10.5% in late 1989. When shopping for a variable-rate loan, restrict your search to ones whose rates can rise no more than two percentage points annually and five to six points over the life of the loan.

Home-equity credit lines usually have interest rates that can fluctuate monthly. Your rate also will be 1.5 to 2 percentage points above the prime. As with variable loans, borrow only from those lenders whose rates cannot rise by more than five or six points over their lifetime.

Be sure your monthly payment will cover a portion of both your loan's interest and principal. Some home-equity loans look inexpensive because you pay only the interest each month. But the true cost is clear when the loan is due and you must come up with the balance to pay off the principal.

Before taking out a home-equity loan or credit line, analyze its fees, including:

An application fee. This charge averages $100 and is often nonrefundable. Some lenders who are hungry for business will waive this fee.

Assorted closing costs. When borrowing against your home equity, you must pay many of the same closing costs that go with a mortgage such as attorney's fees, an appraisal, and a title search. The total of these expenses can run from $400 to $2,000.

Annual fees. Loans have no annual fees. But some of the equity lines charge $25 to $50 a year, even when you are not drawing on them. Don't accept such costs unless the other terms are attractive enough to compensate you.

Fast Ways to Raise Rainy-Day Cash

You can use your assets to obtain reasonably priced loans.

You hear it as regularly as church bells: Set aside three to six months of living expenses for emergencies, and keep the money liquid in a bank account or money-market fund. That suggests tying up a goodly sum—a minimum of $6,500 or so for someone earning $50,000 a year. Fortunately, the definition of liquidity has some stretch to it. There are ways to have your cash and invest much of it, too.

Liquidity generally means keeping money where you can get it back quickly without the risk of a sizable loss or an early-withdrawal penalty. But no investment is ruled out as part of an emergency fund if you can use it as collateral for a reasonably priced loan on short notice. Of course, borrowing of any kind should rank as a last resort in coping with emergencies. And you should always keep at least one month's worth of expenses as close as your checkbook. But provided you retain

borrowing rights, the rest of your rainy-day funds can work harder for you somewhere else. Check out the following:

Salary withholding plans at work. Tax law prohibits withdrawals from 401(k) retirement plans and parallel 403(b) plans, except in narrowly defined emergencies. Most employers, however, will let you borrow all of your untaxed contributions to the plan and often the employer's contributions to your account as well. Borrowers pay a fixed interest rate based on the then current prime rate—what banks charge their best corporate customers for loans—or some other index. In late 1989, loan rates ranged from 9.25% to 14%. By leaving their retirement funds in place, borrowers generally pay no more interest, and often less, than their money is earning in the plan.

Before relying on your 401(k) plan as an

emergency fund, ask your benefits counselor about the borrowing rules. Most important is the waiting time for a loan. While some plans process applications in a week or less, a month is more typical. One plan in 10 takes more than seven weeks to produce the money.

Life insurance loans. If you need more insurance anyway, it may make sense to buy a cash-value policy that can double as part of your emergency fund. Should you have to borrow against the policy, you can get the money in a week or two.

Note, however, that Congress has stripped holders of single-premium and some other types of life insurance of the right to borrow investment earnings tax-free from policies bought after June 21, 1988. Even so, you can still build lots of tax-free borrowing power in a few years with other policies.

Take, for example, a 35-year-old man who qualifies for the lowest premium rate on a universal life contract called Variable Appreciable Life, sold by Prudential. For a yearly premium of $4,000, he can buy $102,644 of insurance. Assuming a net investment return of 8%, his tax-free loan values—the amount he could borrow—will start at $2,693 the first year and rise to just under $20,000 in the fifth year. After that, if he exercises his option to stop paying money into the policy, his borrowing power will still grow to almost $60,000 in 20 years. His death benefit, minus loans, will remain constant for 11 years, then start to rise again, even if the loan is not repaid.

Prudential would charge 5.5% interest on the loan and cut earnings on the amount borrowed to 4%. The policyholder has the choice of repaying the loan in installments, paying just the interest, or paying nothing and borrowing the interest from the policy. The last approach, however, would eat further into the death benefit.

Certificates of deposit. To get money out of CDs in an emergency, you can cash them in and pay a penalty of as much as six months' interest. Or, at many banks and savings institutions, you can borrow 90% to 100% of your CDs' face value. Banks and S&Ls usually set the interest rate at one to four points more than the CD is earning. In late 1989, typical CD loan rates ranged from 10.5% to 14.5%. Many banks let you pay only the interest on CD-backed loans. Some will let you skip payments altogether. Either way, the bank will deduct what you owe from your principal when the certificate matures. There are no other fees, and bankers say they can usually hand you a check in 15 minutes to an hour.

Brokerage accounts. If you open a margin or asset-management account with your broker and have your stocks and bonds re-registered in the firm's street name, you can gain immediate access to part of your securities' value through a margin loan. The interest rate will fluctuate in line with the call-money rate, which banks charge brokers. Margin rates run one-half to 2½ points above the call-money rate, recently around 10%.

Such loans, however, carry a special hazard known as a margin call. Federal rules limit borrowing against securities to a set fraction of their value—50% in the case of stocks. If the share price drops sharply and your account falls below the minimum, your broker will demand more money. If you don't have it, your securities will be sold to restore your account's equity (or net worth) to the minimum allowed.

Spending Wisely

Inspired shopping involves much more than consulting *Consumers' Report* or timing purchases to take advantage of retailers' seasonal sales. The keys to paying less for the best are market intelligence—the shoppers' equivalent of inside information—and strategies to ensure that you get what you bargained for. This chapter serves as your guide to these and other topics:

Pitfalls of fine print. These days everything from bank certificates of deposit to parking lot tickets comes with minute legalese that could cause you big headaches if something goes wrong. For example, does that health club membership form you signed obligate you to make payments to your health club even if you move? Does your personal loan let the bank demand payment in full at any time? Fortunately, there are many effective countermeasures that consumers can deploy to protect themselves from the old adage, "The big print giveth, and the fine print taketh away." Also be wary of the no-print ploy used by some contractors, caterers, and photographers.

Gaining by complaining. Consumers love to gripe about unreliable products, lousy service, and snooty salespersons. Don't get mad, get busy. With a little patience and a lot of moxie, you can get all or part of your money back by brushing up on the art of creative kvetching. The discipline requires that you know your rights, document your case, and demand redress from the proper authorities, including small-claims courts. (Refer to page 142 for advice about seeking—and collecting on—small-claims judgments in 50 states and the District of Columbia.)

Trading in your car. Curbstone wisdom holds that cars should be replaced after about four years or 40,000 miles—the rough averages for buyers of new American-made autos—to avoid the expense of major repairs. But if you are set on saving money, then age or a magic number on the odometer should take a back seat, as explained in "Hang On to Your Old Heap," beginning on page 144.

Savings on airfares. Vacationers increasingly feel frustrated and lost as the cost of air travel climbs and fares change at a moment's notice. *Money* provides you with new strategies to stay calm and find the hidden bargains on many popular routes.

Cutting medical bills. Although most people are covered by health insurance, you could still face sizable expenses if a member of your family becomes ill or injured. One way to trim your bill is to ask your doctor for a price break—if you think that the fee is out of line or that your patronage entitles you to a discount. Yes, physicians' fees are negotiable. We also provide advice from experts on how to determine whether the cost and benefits of elective surgery are warranted.

Reading the Fine Print

You can protect yourself if you know which contract clauses are most troublesome, which can be altered, and which can be ignored.

Practically every time you pay for something, you enter into an enforceable contract that limits your rights in meaningful ways. Ignore the terms of such everyday contracts and you could wind up surrendering valuable rights or agreeing to unconscionable terms that could cost you big money. Reason: Companies are seeking pre-emptive strikes against customers who might file lawsuits by marshalling arsenals of ever more complex legalese and finer print.

You can counter this contractual assault on your rights if you know how. For openers, the fine print is often negotiable, since there is no such thing as a "standard" agreement. The most neatly typeset contract can be amended by adding your own words or by deleting some

of its language. In addition, the legalese itself frequently has loopholes.

In some instances, the contract wording is flatly illegal or can be superseded by state or federal laws. For example, federal law stipulates that manufacturers cannot avoid liability no matter what their contracts may say. Twelve states, including Connecticut, Minnesota, and New York, now have laws requiring that plain English be used in some contracts, particularly for real estate transactions, loans, and insurance policies. You can also sometimes protect yourself by simply making a verbal statement in front of witnesses that you refuse to accept certain conditions or that you accept the terms only because of time or physical constraints.

Interviews with dozens of lawyers provided the following advice for sidestepping the pitfalls of fine print in some of the most common contracts:

Health club memberships. In years past, dance studios were notorious for the fancy footwork in their contracts. Today, the nasty tradition of fine print in membership contracts has spread to unethical health clubs. The big abuse found in these agreements is long-term membership without the right to cancel. Many of the contracts demand hefty initiation fees of $250 to $1,000 and then require monthly payments of $20 to $90 for long periods of time, perhaps for life. You could develop a health problem that keeps you from using the facilities, or you could move to another city, and still have to pay monthly membership fees.

As a result, consumer advocates say you should avoid a health club membership stretching more than three years. And make sure that the agreement offers you the right to cancel and receive a refund if you have a good reason. Also, take precautions before signing up for a club still under construction. If the opening is delayed, you could wind up paying dues even though you don't have use of the club. You can avoid this by inserting a clause that will give you the right to cancel your membership and receive a refund of your deposit if the club doesn't open within a few months. You could also defer making your first payment until the club begins operating or add a clause that will extend your membership by the length of any delay.

Apartment rental leases. Most preprinted lease forms are landlords' documents that restrict tenants' rights substantially. Watch out for four clauses:

• Use of the premises. Many leases limit the use of the apartment to residential purposes. If you have a home office, you are violating the lease and the landlord can terminate your agreement.

• Vacating the apartment. Some leases state that the landlord can charge three times the rent for any time spent in the premises after the lease expires.

• Defaulting on rent. There is often a re-entry clause that gives the landlord the right to enter the premises after a default, change the locks, and throw you out on the street, so long as he doesn't disturb the peace by doing it.

• Paying for repairs. Most tenants mistakenly assume that if there is a problem with their apartment, they can repair it and deduct the cost from the rent. Usually, however, this won't work because a clause commonly used by landlords separates your obligation to pay the rent from the landlord's obligation to make repairs.

Before signing an apartment rental contract, pay a lawyer $100 to $500 to review it and, if necessary, to strike out or amend some of the more heinous provisions. For example, a phrase could be added to the contract allowing the tenant, say, 30 days to correct any problems and requiring the landlord to wait at least that long before taking any action against the tenant.

Certificates of deposit. Aside from the now famous phrase "penalty for early withdrawal," you might not expect a CD contract to give you much trouble. Yet, many of these agreements contain a clause saying that unless the depositor provides other written instructions, when the CD comes due the bank or savings and loan will automatically roll it over into a new one. The new CD will have the same maturity as the former one, but its interest rate could be much lower if rates have fallen. Some institutions give customers a seven-day grace period after their CDs mature to notify them about rollovers.

Whenever you purchase a certificate of deposit, you should send a letter to the bank saying that the CD should not be rolled over without your specific direction. Indicate that if you have not specified what should be done with the funds at maturity, they should be placed in the bank's money-market account. The bank should notify you accordingly.

Personal loans. No banking document has caused more litigation nationally than the personal-loan agreement. And uniformly, the consumer has been the loser in court under the following, all-too-familiar scenarios:

You walk into your bank and sit down with an officer you have known and trusted for years. You tell him that you would like to borrow $10,000 and pay it back over 36 months. The friendly banker says, "Fine—but we don't do time loans. We'll just have you sign a demand note. It has no maturity date. But don't worry, we'll keep rolling it over on a regular basis." The lender doesn't mention that, as its name suggests, a demand note allows the bank to order you to pay off the balance of your loan—your remaining principal plus interest—at any time.

Suddenly, there is a change in policy or personnel at the bank. You get a letter saying that while the institution values your business, they have decided to call your loan note. Not only is the total amount due, but it is also possible that there was a clause indicating that a higher rate of interest will apply if the loan goes into default. This gives the bank additional leverage

Get It in Writing

While the fine print in many contracts may contain clauses hazardous to consumers, there are other types of agreements in which the absence of provisions can be just as dangerous. Hiring a contractor for home renovation or a caterer or photographer for a party all enter into this "no-print" danger zone. If things go wrong, the result can be especially upsetting because the work often involves once-in-a-life-time events. The rule to remember: Get everything in writing. A guide to dealing with no-print businesses:

Home contractors. The appearance of your home is too important to leave to faith. Never hire a painter, plumber, electrician, carpenter, or other contractor without signing a detailed work agreement. Before signing an agreement, determine all the work you will need and find out which contractor can handle each of your projects. Then, review contracts from every person you employ. Be certain that each specifically spells out the services that will be provided, their costs, and the work-completion date.

Caterers. The first clause to insert in a caterer's contract is that the chef who prepares your sample food will be the same chef who makes the actual meal. There should also be a provision that says if an additional guest shows up unexpectedly, the caterer will charge the same fee as for the other guests and not a surcharge. Be sure the contract also specifies the amount and types of food and liquor to be served, what will happen to the leftovers, and the number and appearance of the caterer's employees who will work for you. Include in the contract a clause saying you will pay 10% less than the agreed price if meals are served late. Be sure to define "late."

Photographers. When photographers offer contracts, their documents are generally short, vague, and one-sided. Don't sign one. Instead, get in writing that the photographer responsible for the sample shots you reviewed will be the one who takes the photos or the videotape of your event. All contracts should specify the number of rolls of film that will be used, the percentages of candid and posed pictures, and any special effects you want included. Find out the cost of buying the proofs and negatives, and have the photographer include it in the contract. Finally, be sure the contract provides some recourse if the photos don't turn out, such as having the photographer reshoot the pictures free of charge.

to negotiate. What about those verbal promises made by your friendly banker? They are worthless. To avoid such disasters, put all terms of a personal loan in writing and refuse to sign a demand-loan agreement. You've got a friend at the bank only if the agreement is in writing.

Mortgages and home-equity loans. Today's soft housing markets give borrowers some additional standing to negotiate contracts for mortgages and home-equity loans. For example, you can probably get more time for a home appraisal or other closing matters. If a contract says you have 30 days to get a loan commitment, change it to 45 or 60 days. This alteration is always advisable from your standpoint, but lenders in seller's markets are not always amenable.

Be aware, however, that many mortgage and home-equity loan contracts contain what are called acceleration clauses whose provisions are like those of demand loans. They can force you to pay off your remaining balance early. If the bank is looking for a reason to call the loan—perhaps it was made when interest rates were low—it is apt to take advantage of the opportunity to invoke an acceleration clause. There are generally three factors that could trigger such clauses:

● If you rent out your house without the lender's permission.

● If you fail to make your property tax or homeowners insurance payments.

● If you are late making a loan payment.

Most of these clauses appear so the bank can easily sell the loan to another financial institution in what is called the secondary mortgage market. If the lender intends to sell, you probably won't be able to alter the terms much. Therefore, if you think you might want to rent out your home someday, borrow only from a lender whose institution plans to hold your mortgage or home-equity loan until it matures. Small and foreign banks are more likely to hold these types of loans than sell them.

Home-equity loans contain other offensive clauses, too. In a 1989 survey conducted by Consumers Union, 62% of lenders said they had the power to change their home-equity loan terms at any time. Among the unilateral terms: The way the lender calculates its interest rate and repayment terms and, on home-equity credit lines, the size of the borrower's available credit line. A new federal law, fully effective in fall 1989, prevents lenders from changing a borrower's terms. Also, the law requires a lender to provide explicit disclosure of its terms and fees when you apply for a home-equity loan.

Automobile purchase agreements. While dealers and automakers are throwing rebates and low-cost financing at buyers today, there is a clause in their contracts stating that the purchase price is based on the date of delivery, not the date of purchase. Therefore, if the manufacturer raises prices between the time you order your car and the time you get it, you will probably have to pay the higher price.

Here today, gone tomorrow rebates and option packages also merit special scrutiny. There may have been a $1,000 rebate in effect on the day you signed the agreement. But if the rebate ran out before you took delivery of the car, it may no longer apply.

The solution is to strike out the offending clause, if you can. Otherwise, make an oral agreement with the dealer, in front of any witnesses—even your relatives—that the prices and terms you agree to will still hold when you accept delivery of the car.

Parking lot tickets. The simple act of parking a car in a lot and turning the keys over to an attendant in exchange for a receipt doesn't seem contractual. Yet, it is as binding an agreement as taking out a bank loan. In this case, the contract is known as a bailment. Parking lot owners are obligated to see that your car remains safe in their custody. You are obligated not to leave valuables on the seat of an unlocked car as well as to pay for the parking service. Within that agreement, the parking lot owners usually try to limit their liability by posting signs or printing disclaimers on the back of their parking receipts.

The most common disclaimer is that the company is not responsible for the theft or loss of any items left in your vehicle. Some lots go further, requiring customers to make any claims for damages before leaving. They may also demand that a car damaged in the lot be repaired by a mechanic chosen by the parking garage. In addition, garage owners sometimes try to limit the time within which you can sue them, place the burden of proof on you, and reduce their financial exposure to a ridiculously low amount such as the price of the parking ticket.

Don't be cowed. Despite claims to the contrary, the burden of proof is on the lot owner to show that he wasn't negligent. If anything significant happens to a car in a lot, no one should assume that posted signs or printed disclaimers are valid. In some states, if you leave the keys with an attendant, the disclaimer probably doesn't apply. And if there is a theft or damage, the owner of the parking lot is entirely liable.

To be on the safe side, if your car or something in it has special value, tell the parking attendant in advance. The warning carries legal weight. This will give the garage the option to take special care of your car and provide an added level of security or refuse to park it.

Airline tickets. The purchase of an airline ticket constitutes a contractual relationship between the passenger and the carrier that is extremely disadvantageous to you. Airlines make every effort to limit their liability, particularly for baggage containing cameras, jewelry, and artwork. In addition, flight schedules, times of arrival, even the final destination of the plane are all excluded. The contracts also give the carriers the right to overbook flights and force passengers off planes.

Other elements of an airline's liabilities vary depending on whether the scheduled flight is domestic or foreign. Domestic flights fall under state or federal regulations. These rules are generally more liberal than ones for foreign flights, which are subject to an agreement known as the Warsaw Convention that regulates airline travel all over the globe. Don't assume that your flight is domestic even if you board in New York City and exit in Miami. If the flight continues on to Mexico, it is considered foreign for passengers who stay on.

The difference can add up. Domestic airline tickets have no liability limit in the event of personal injury or death. International airline travel provides a restricted liability threshold of $75,000.

There is a catch, though. The fine print on the ticket notes that the $75,000 includes legal fees and costs. In April 1989, the U.S. Supreme Court, in effect, allowed airlines to use print with especially tiny type. The court affirmed the right of Korean Air Lines to limit its per-passenger liability to $75,000 even though the print on its tickets was smaller than required by U.S. regulations.

Parts of the airline contract, incidentally, appear in different places: on the back of the ticket; in the envelope surrounding it; and in the airline's rule book called "Conditions of Contract of Carriage." Unfortunately, there aren't many opportunities for consumers to even out imbalances in the airline/passenger relationship.

If you alter the terms of the ticket, the airline can refuse you passage. In fact, there is a clause that specifically says no oral changes are binding and that the representative behind the counter has no right to make or accept written changes.

The only defense is to travel informed. No passenger can be forced off a plane for overbooking until the airline has asked for volunteers and offered compensation. If there are no volunteers and you are told to leave the plane, you have to comply. The airline has to compensate you, though. By law, the carrier must offer as much as $400 in cash to someone forced to surrender his seat. Some airlines pay for a night at a hotel or for a meal, or offer reduced fares on subsequent flights. Despite all the liability protections for the airlines, there is something of a loophole for the consumer. If you can prove willful misconduct, all the limitations on an airline's liability are thrown out the window.

How to Get Your Money Back

Our service economy doesn't always serve us. But with some pluck, you can collect on a foul-up.

How can you get some or all of your money back when you get ripped off or are just dissatisfied with a local member of the service economy? Complaining to the business at fault—or to some higher authority—is usually the best policy, if you know what to do. Yet fewer than 10% of unsatisfied customers take their complaints to a third party with clout—a government agency, a mediation or arbitration program, or a small-claims court. More should. Many people in that not-so-silent minority who turn to these referees walk away as satisfied customers. Here's what to do:

Define the problem precisely. For example: "I paid $5,000 for a procedure that most doctors in this area charge half as much for." Or: "The catalogue said this stereo came with a cassette deck, but when it arrived there wasn't one." Weak expressions of disappointment—"the catered meal wasn't very tasty"—are definite nonstarters.

Demand the proper remedy. Do you deserve a full refund? A partial one? A refund plus damages? If you lounged around for two weeks in a beach house, horrid though it was, you are clearly not entitled to get back your entire rent.

Document your case. Collect all receipts, repair orders, leases, tickets, warranties, canceled checks, and contracts. Hang on to copies of correspondence, and keep notes of any conversations you had about correcting the problem. Be sure to compile evidence of any actual financial loss resulting from the foul-up, such as essential car rentals and hotel tabs.

Find out your rights. Don't just read the contract or warranty. Call the government agency that licenses or regulates the service. If you don't know where to turn, start with your state consumer protection agency or attorney general's office. Whichever agency you call, ask to speak with the staffer who handles your type of problem and request any written information that will help you get your money back.

Now you are ready to take action. In a case of suspected fraud, go straight to your city or county government agency. Otherwise, begin by registering your complaint with a pleasant and polite call to the person who performed the service. You may find this direct approach will be all it takes for success. When you make your pitch, run through the complaint succinctly in an authoritative tone. Say exactly what you want and give a deadline (two weeks is usually reasonable). Demonstrate that it is in the company's interest to satisfy you.

If round one is a draw, keep fighting. Ask for the local manager and then the vice president for consumer affairs, if one exists, or the manager of customer service. Should the VP give you the runaround, place a call to Mr. or Ms. Big. Top honchos or their subordinates often will tell you to put your demand in writing. Fine. Keep the letter to one page and enclose copies of relevant documents. If you are writing to someone you don't intend to

Collecting from Small-Claims Court

As every Judge Wapner fan might suspect, taking your case to small-claims court can be fast and inexpensive. Cases are typically heard within a month after they are filed, and rulings are handed down by judges or arbitrators either on the spot or within two weeks. Fees usually range from $5 to $25 to file a petition and from $5 to $20 to serve the defendant with a summons. But viewers of Wapner's *People's Court* may not know two key facts:

Small-claims court rules vary from state to state. Most states limit claims to between $1,000 to $5,000. In Tennessee, however, you can bring a case for $10,000, and Virginia considers $7,000 a small claim. Most states allow lawyers to represent plaintiffs, but 11 do not. Courts in some states, including Alaska, Michigan, and Vermont, provide free booklets on their procedures.

It can be difficult to collect on a judgment. Victors stand the best chance of getting their cash when defendants earn salaries, have bank accounts, own property, or run businesses. But when defendants don't show up in court or their business has gone bankrupt, your odds are slimmer than a dime.

Sometimes judgments are issued immediately after the hearing. If you get an on-the-spot decision, ask the judge to set up a pay schedule. When a judgment is handed down, write to the defendant to collect. If you get no response, return to small-claims court and file a writ of execution authorizing the sheriff or marshal to go after the defendant's property. If you know where the person works, ask the sheriff to file a garnishment form with the employer authorizing withholding up to 25% of the defendant's salary to pay the claim. Your cost: $5 to $50. Unemployment checks and Social Security checks cannot be garnisheed. Some states also limit garnishment to 10% of net pay, however. And a few states, such as North Carolina, Pennsylvania, and Texas, prohibit garnishment of wages altogether. If you can't attach wages for one reason or another, consider asking the sheriff or marshal about seizing the defendant's property. But this technique is tricky and rarely recommended. For example, it won't pay off if you are seeking a small sum because you must often pay fees equal to 10% of the value of the property to get your money back. Those expenses could exceed your original claim. Furniture and appliances usually can't be seized. You can often take a defendant's car, but states frequently protect up to $2,000 of its value to insure that the defendant is left with some financial assets. If he or she uses the car for business, the exclusion can even be higher, and in some states you then may not be able to seize the auto.

Another alternative is to seek a lien on the defendant's property through the county recorder's office. But you won't get your money back until the debtor comes up with the cash or the sheriff holds a public auction—a process that can take up to a year. Before an auction is held, you will probably be required by law to advertise it publicly—and that could cost you $300 or so. If you don't know whether the defendant owns any assets, ask the court for an order of examination. This requires debtors to appear in court to file a list of assets; if they refuse to appear, they face arrest.

As a last resort, try collecting your money by making the defendant's life miserable. You can:

● Notify credit-reporting services of the judgment. The defendant may be forced to pay you in order to qualify for a new loan or a credit card.

● Call or write the local bureau of motor vehicles if your case involved a car accident. In some states, the defendant's license will be suspended until the judgment is paid.

● If the defendant owns a business, ask the local consumer affairs department to consider suspending the business operating license.

turn to again, let the recipient know that you're mailing or faxing copies to a few well-chosen authorities with a direct interest in the matter, such as your insurer or the appropriate regulator. Otherwise, forget the threatening carbons.

Even after you have wheedled, cajoled, and hinted darkly in every manner possible, you may get little or no response. Write one more time, and put the company on notice that you will pursue the matter further if you get an insufficient response. This time, signal that you'll be notifying a bit more of the western world.

If this step also fails, don't despair. You must push on by seeking help from the agency, person, or group with the most experience handling your type of problem. These, essentially, are your choices:

A local or state government agency. The agency's fraud-busters ostensibly use their clout to provide free, speedy relief to victimized constituents. In reality, some government consumer officials are godsends; others are worthless. There's no way of knowing until you try. In all cases, expect the agency to be understaffed and overworked. And plan to fill out a mound of paperwork. Understand, too, that once you file your case in small-claims court, the government agency will drop your complaint.

If you don't know which agency to turn to, start by calling City Hall and asking for the person who handles your type of complaint. You will be directed to the proper authority. Chances are, if your beef is with an insurance company or agent, a bank, a utility company, a car dealer, or a garage, there's a state consumer agency that specializes in your problem.

Better Business Bureau mediation or arbitration. The Better Business Bureau is a private, nonprofit group comprising local consumer-protection programs across the country. BBBs are funded by their member businesses, but they often rule in the little guy's favor. For example, consumers who used the BBB to arbitrate car problems in 1987 reported that they were satisfied with the outcome around

60% of the time. Most BBBs have such Auto-line programs specifically to arbitrate disputes between consumers and car manufacturers other than Chrysler and Ford, which have their own complaint systems.

You begin by calling the nearest BBB chapter for a complaint form. Once you fill it out and send it back, the agency will give the business a copy and will await a response. Within two weeks, a BBB employee will try mediating the dispute for you.

If mediation fails, you can ask for an arbitrator or sometimes a panel of two or three referees. Some local BBBs determine whether their members can refuse to arbitrate complaints other than Autoline; others make arbitration mandatory. The BBB usually also lets consumers ask for consequential damages (the cost of replacing a $100 sweater ruined in the course of a $3 cleaning job) as well as a refund or a new performance of the service itself. Most BBBs guarantee to deliver arbitration decisions within 10 days of a hearing. When a BBB arbitration panel rules in your favor, there's little chance that the business owner will stiff you. BBB members know this is part of the bargain for membership in the group.

Trade association arbitration. You can sometimes take your case to a national trade association's consumer arbitration panel (CAP) specializing in complaints about your type of service. Car dealers, funeral homes, interstate movers, and manufacturers of furniture and heavy appliances run CAPs. As with BBBs, consumers don't always come away winners. In 1987, the car dealers' panel, AUTOCAP, resolved only 44% of its nearly 4,000 complaints in favor of car owners. You will likely have to pay a filing fee of $40 to $300 or so when using a CAP. This outlay is usually refundable if you win.

Independent arbitration. If your case exceeds the limit of small-claims courts where you live and involves a complicated contractual matter such as a major renovation, consider turning to one of a dozen or so independent arbitration organizations. The largest, the American Arbitration Association, has 32 regional offices around the country. The AAA doesn't come cheaply, however. Cases involving up to $20,000 require an administrative fee of 3% of the amount you are asking, with a minimum charge of $300. The business owners must agree to an AAA hearing and they usually will, to avoid an expensive, drawn-out court proceeding. You may need a lawyer; many independent arbitration cases are complex and turn on fine legal points.

Mediation and arbitration by professional groups and licensing agencies. If your beef is with your doctor, lawyer, or stockbroker, consider going to a professional group or licensing agency. But don't expect to win a refund if you are merely unhappy with the outcome of your divorce, real estate suit, or criminal trial.

County medical societies have judicial committees that handle written complaints—many concern overcharging and improper treatment—against members. The committees initially try mediating disputes by helping the parties come to a mutual decision. Should mediation fail, the committee will arbitrate, independently ruling whether the doctor should give you a refund.

If you don't think the local medical association will give you a fair hearing, take your complaint to the appropriate government licensing agency. Here, outsiders rule on complaints, and the agencies are given legal authority to enforce judgments. Many states now have what are known as client security funds to cover losses if a lawyer cheats you. Maximum amounts typically range from $25,000 to $100,000.

As a result of a recent Supreme Court ruling, most contracts that investors sign with brokers now call for binding arbitration. At last count, 11 different panels conduct such hearings: the self-regulatory bodies of the nine stock exchanges, the National Association of Securities Dealers (NASD), and the American Arbitration Association. Your contract will specify which arbitrators you can use. The most objective ones are those run by the AAA and the NASD.

Small-claims court. Going to small-claims court can often be the best route when you have exhausted all other possibilities to recover your cash in a dispute over no more than $1,500 or so, the usual court limit. Compared with higher courts, small-claims court is fast, easy to navigate, and inexpensive (expect a $5 to $25 filing fee). But be forewarned that small claims judgments are notoriously difficult to collect from defendants. (See "Collecting from Small-Claims Court," page 142.)

Hang On to Your Old Heap

Given the high cost of new wheels, trading in could be an expensive mistake.

She has faithfully hauled you to work and play these past four years. The new-car odor is long gone, as well as most of the bugs that somehow got installed at the factory when she was built. The ineradicable squeaks and rattles have taken on the status of background noise, if not music. But you've still got reliable transportation—or so you think, until that day when your friendly mechanic turns menacing. "She needs new shocks, brake pads, tires, and a battery, and maybe a little valve work," he says. "Figure $1,000, maybe $1,500." Man and machine have betrayed you.

If your impulses resemble those of the typical motorist, you balk at sinking that much into an old car and head for the showroom. According to a Hertz Corporation survey of American-made cars—the conclusions generally apply to foreign vehicles as well—new cars change owners after an average of 4½ years and 41,140 miles. Trading in so soon, however, can be an expensive mistake because there is plenty of dependable life left in a well-maintained 4½-year-old auto.

Hertz's figures on used cars show that they last an average of nearly 10 years and 102,600 miles from U.S. factory to scrap heap. Furthermore, the fixed costs of owning a car—such as those recommended by your heartless mechanic—fall sharply as it ages. Gas, oil, routine repairs, and other operating costs go up along with the miles registered on the odometer, but nowhere near as swiftly as the fixed costs are going down. A car loses most of its trade-in value in its first four years, and you pay most, if not all, of the interest on your car loan in those years.

Rising repair bills naturally will sound a warning siren in the minds of all people who depend on wheels to carry them to work, chauffeur the kids, and get around town. What good is economy in a car that won't start or that might conk out on the interstate, you might well ask. Why not buy a new machine and be done with it? Alas, the factory smell of a new car is no guarantee that it won't break down, especially in the first days of ownership. Design defects or sloppy workmanship put plenty of autos out of commission soon after they touch asphalt.

The considerable financial advantage of hanging on to a car for at least eight years has been demonstrated by Runzheimer International of Rochester, Wisconsin, a worldwide transportation consultant to corporations. In 1988, Runzheimer's analysts posed two choices for the owner of a mid-size, six-cylinder 1984 Chevrolet Celebrity, then four years old and free of debt: Drive it another four years or trade it in on a 1988 model and drive that car

for the next four years. The main finding was that the owner would stand to save $5,036 by sticking with the 1984 Chevy—despite the analysts' estimate that repair costs for the older car would exceed those of the new car by $1,179 and that the 1984 model would consume $428 more gas and oil.

There are offsetting economies. One is modestly lower insurance premiums on an old car. As an auto loses trade-in value, you pay less to insure it for theft and collision damage. But that lost value, together with financing costs, is what knocks the new car out of contention. Those two items could be expected to account for nearly 55% of the total costs of keeping a 1988 Celebrity on the road during its first four years of life. On the debt-free 1984 model, depreciation would total just 35% of expenses. And in this regard, a Chevy is no different from a Ford, Cadillac, or Mercedes.

The road must end for every auto—but when? Many experts belong to the six-figure

Sometimes the Old Car Is Best

Let's say you have just made the last payment on the car—in our example, a 1984 Chevy Celebrity that you bought in the fall of 1983. You're trying to decide whether to keep it or trade it in on a new model. Broken out below are estimated differences in expenses that go with that decision. The old car cost $9,243. You can get $3,790 for it on a trade-in for a 1988 Celebrity selling for $12,301 and can borrow the difference with a four-year loan at 8.9%.

Four-Year Cost of Ownership	Old Car	New Car
Loan payments (interest and principal)	$0	$10,166
Gas and oil	3,428	3,000
Insurance	2,213	2,403
Repairs, maintenance, and tires	2,562	1,383
Total expenses	8,203	16,952
Trade-in value	924	4,637
Net cost of ownership	$7,279	12,315
Saved by not trading in	5,036	

Source: Runzheimer International

school: With required maintenance, most cars are designed to go 100,000 miles before you have to worry about major repairs. Corrosion is another matter. Mechanics can replace just about any part, but no amount of putty and paint can restore a rust bucket to respectability. The onset of rust spots in the paint tells you not to make the next $1,000 repair. Normally, you should not see such disturbing signs until your car is at least six years old. And since 1986, most automobile manufacturers have anticipated the dreaded rust disease by offering six-year corrosion warranties.

For most motorists, of course, the pulsing need for a new car becomes overpowering long before the first sign of rust on the old one. Eight years, owners reason, should be just about enough for any car.

By then, inflation will have put quite a distance between 1984 purchase and 1992 replacement prices. If General Motors, for example, continues to tack on an average of 4.35% annually to the price of its Celebrity (renamed the Lumina), a 1992 model will sell for $14,585. But the steadfast owner of a 1984 who tucks away his or her savings will have taken a giant stride toward beating inflation and car replacement costs. The money, if invested at 7% after taxes, would grow to $9,751. Together with $924 of estimated trade-in value on the old heap, that would cover all but $3,910 of the replacement price.

Beating High-Flying Airfares

These strategies will help you stay cool and find the real bargains.

With a record 455 million people flying in 1988—nearly double the number just a decade earlier—you might think that U.S. airlines would be reaping windfall profits. They're not, and that's the reason for the turbulence in air fares that is frustrating price-conscious travelers.

Nevertheless, with airlines under pressure to punch up profits and skies perhaps a little too friendly now that eight carriers dominate 90% of domestic travel, the cost of flying is trending skyward. In fact, 1988 marked the first year in the previous eight that air fares (which rose about 7%) outpaced inflation (about 4%). Part of the increase came from "yield management," a technique under which airline computers change fares more than 200,000 times daily to maximize revenue. As a result, booking has become a cruel lottery in which you must strive to avoid being the one person in 10 who gets stuck paying full price.

So, whether you are making a day's business jaunt to Pittsburgh or planning the European tour of a lifetime, here are tips to help you avoid getting taken for a ride:

Check for split-ticket bargains. For example, it's considerably cheaper to fly Delta from Dallas to Albuquerque and then Albuquerque to Los Angeles than to book a full-fare flight from Dallas to L.A. The reason is that Delta competes with Southwest and America West in Albuquerque. Other cities with split-ticket breaks: Phoenix and Las Vegas.

Consider the "nested maxsaver" strategy. Suppose you are facing a quick hop from New York to Los Angeles at the full-fare price. You can fight back by purchasing two pairs of discounted round-trip tickets that include Saturday night stays and total about 60% of the full-fare charge. For example, the first might take you from New York to Los Angeles on February 7 with a return on February 16; the second would be from L.A. to New York on February 9 and back to L.A. on February 14. Using only the first half of each round-trip ticket, you'd go out February 7, come back February 9. And the second half of each ticket could take you back to L.A.—out on the 14th, back on the 16th—practically for free.

Look for "hidden city" routes. This time you are flying one-way from Salt Lake City to New York. But you buy Pan Am's M fare from Salt Lake City to Washington, D.C. via New York's John F. Kennedy airport and save about 35% of the full fare simply by getting off the plane at JFK. The carriers don't like this, of course, and are trying to close these loopholes. But hidden cities still abound, especially at airline hubs. If you don't want to sniff them out yourself, check the monthly listings in *Best Fares* (phone 800-635-3033; $68 a year). Two cautions: Use the ploy only one way, since the airline will cancel your return ticket if it catches you. And don't check any bags—they'll wind up in D.C.

Establish an ongoing relationship with a travel agent. Some 63% of fliers book through an agent versus 34% who call airlines directly—but not all use the same agent trip after trip. Finding bargains takes work, so you get your best service from one who is eager for more business.

Book early. The deepest discounts require 7, 14, or 30 days' notice. And fly off-season: January and February for lowest rates overall; Easter until Thanksgiving for warm-weather destinations; November–March for Europe.

Ask which computerized reservation system your travel agent uses. All five big ones are owned by airlines (the Sabre system by American; Apollo principally by United; Pars by TWA and Northwest; System-One by Texas

Air; and Datas II by Delta). Both the General Accounting Office and Department of Transportation have complained that agents using these systems may tend to favor the owner airlines. If your travel agent uses Sabre, and you always wind up on American, get a competing price quote next time.

Double-check your agent by calling an airline or two. Often carriers don't release discounted seats to a competitor's computer, so a follow-up call may unearth bargains.

If your travel plans are flexible, stress that. You'll have to give a rough idea of when you want to fly, but don't get pinned to a precise day or time. Instead, ask the agent to call up the fare-finder screen, spot any discounts and explain them to you. Try flying to an alternative airport (Midway instead of O'Hare in Chicago, for example). Or change planes.

Fly home Sunday. Since the best deals often require you to stay a Saturday night, some travelers find it cheaper to book a hotel room for the extra day or two.

Book the cheapest seat available but keep calling back. New discounts can crop up at any time. Or reserve a cheap but unrestricted fare (one with no penalty for a change in plans) for another day and head to the airport on the day you really want to fly. Chances are you will find a vacant seat, since planes are usually only 60% full.

Ask about discounts. US Air, for example, gives anyone over 65 a 10% price break; Continental slices unrestricted fares 20% for children between the ages of two and 11.

For overseas flights, seek out an agent with an international rate desk that can find discounts on multistop trips. Take a traveler going from New York to Stockholm to Vienna to Innsbruck to New York. He or she could save about 50% over full fare by booking an Apex ticket to Vienna with a stopover in Stockholm and return from Innsbruck, plus a one-way fare from Vienna to Innsbruck.

Ask Your Doctor about Costs

Fees vary dramatically for the same services even among the best physicians.

Most of us can talk to our physicians about the most intimate subjects, but there is something about the doctor-patient relationship that makes it hard to raise the matter of money. Yet it is hard *not* to worry about that issue these days. Physicians' fee hikes have exceeded the inflation rate for each of the past eight years. Employers and insurance companies are asking patients to shoulder an ever-larger share of the load. The average U.S. family spent $720 a year in unreimbursed medical expenses in 1980; that figure had nearly doubled to $1,300 by 1988. Worse, since tax reform, only health costs exceeding 7.5% of your adjusted gross income are deductible.

Of course, quality is still the most important criterion in choosing a doctor. But top drawer doesn't have to mean top dollar. Physicians' charges vary dramatically even within a single community (see the table at right). And the cost-management company that gathered this data, MedFacts of Miami, found no correlation between a doctor's fee and whether he was board certified in his specialty or trained in the U.S. or abroad. The point is not that a doctor's price is set arbitrarily but that you may have more room to negotiate than you think.

The only way to find out is to raise the issue of fees yourself. If you're looking for a new doctor, assemble a recommended list and then call the office of each to ask about his first-visit and subsequent fees. If you choose a doctor whose scale is reasonable, tell him when you meet that his pricing was part of your criteria.

On the other hand, if you've already settled on a doctor you like but wish his fees were lower, don't be afraid to point out your problem. One tactic: Send him some insurance reimbursement statements to show how much extra he is costing you. Or if his fees aren't out of line but you are having trouble keeping up, put together a brief account of your circumstances and a suggested payment.

If your doctor won't budge, ask whether there's any other way he can help lower the overall bill. Take, for example, tests for back

A Doctor/Customer Relationship

Maybe you'll feel less reticent about discussing fees with your doctor if you realize how dramatically they can vary for the same service. Med-Facts, a cost-containment firm serving employers, uncovered the following four-and fivefold disparities in charges in one not atypical Florida county (Dade). The "mid-range" figure for the office visit is the median cost; for the surgeries, it's the "usual, customary and reasonable" fee as defined by insurers.

Service	Fees		
	Lowest	Mid-range	Highest
First visit (internist)	$30	$60	$175
Appendectomy	500	1,400	2,100
D&C (diagnostic)	250	800	1,100

pain. Ask whether a less expensive CAT scan can do instead of a mylogram. By doing some research and mentioning cost cutting, you'll get your doctor thinking about the subject. That's helpful because physicians sometimes own the diagnostic facilities they use—a questionable practice open to conflicts of interest. Your seeming knowledge and frankness are warning shots to the doctor that you are aware of current trends toward overtesting. Your feistiness may also encourage him to bargain for you with outside services and practitioners he recommends.

When you have incurred a large bill, it's hard, but not impossible, to lower it after the fact. Let the doctor know in person and in writing that you feel the bill is more than you can afford, and chances are good he'll try to find a way to satisfy you. This might mean a fee reduction or creative alternatives, such as stretching your bill over installments.

As a last resort, and especially if you are unhappy with a doctor's treatment and not just his bill, you can always complain to the local medical society or state licensing agency, or take your case to arbitration. (Such routes of recourse are explained in "How to Get Your Money Back" on page 141.) If you are still convinced that you deserve a better deal from your doctor, consider that about half the U.S. physicians already, in effect, offer discounts through pre-priced medical plans like health maintenance organizations. Why? Because they want the business and are willing to bargain for it. By 1995, that fraction is expected to swell to perhaps 75%. So remember, when you dare to talk money with your doctor, the tide's on your side.

What Price Surgery?

You need thorough research and expert guidance before you decide whether you should go under the knife.

Some 16 million Americans undergo operations each year, 40% more than the number who did so in 1971. Yet more and more doctors worry that the national passion for surgery has cut too deeply. In particular, they worry that too many patients are having various kinds of elective surgery—operations that people choose to have rather than ones undertaken to save their lives.

One 1988 study in the *Journal of the American Medical Association*, for example, estimated that nearly half of all coronary artery bypasses (open-heart surgery) are done for questionable or inappropriate reasons. Another study came to a similar conclusion about a third of the 85,000 carotid endarterectomies (operations intended to prevent stroke) performed each year. The American College of Obstetricians and Gynecologists has been concerned enough about reports of unnecessary hysterectomies (removal of the uterus) that it is reconsidering criteria for doing the operation. And an eye operation called radial keratotomy is the subject of continuing lawsuits and countersuits between surgeons who perform it and the American Academy of Ophthalmology, which calls the procedure "investigational."

If you are facing such surgery, consider your decision carefully. You should begin by learning enough to make informed choices about your own care, take part in decisions, and play an active role in deciding what's right for you, rather than just being a passive recipient of whatever care you are given. Most people, for example, choose the first surgeon who is recommended to them and go to the hospital he happens to be affiliated with. That may work for a simple operation like a hernia repair. But it could be dangerous with a complicated procedure such as bypass surgery, for which mortality rates at U.S. hospitals vary from less than 1% to as high as 20%.

Even the question of whether you need surgery at all may be answered differently depending on what city you live in. One study found that a person living in New Haven is about twice as likely to have a coronary bypass operation as someone living in Boston—though both cities have excellent teaching hospitals, comparable rates of heart disease, and populations of similar ethnic and cultural background. For carotid endarterectomy, the situation is reversed: people in New Haven are only half as likely to have them. And equally puzzling regional discrepancies have turned up in studies of other often-elective procedures, including knee and hip replacement, hysterectomy, and back surgery.

A Consumer's Guide to Elective Surgery

Here are thumbnail sketches of seven surgeries that are frequently done electively—meaning they are intended to improve the quality of a person's life, not save it. In cases where these operations are not mandatory, it is especially important that the patient weigh the pros and cons of surgery carefully and gather as much information as possible from medical and consumer sources, some of which are listed below. The cost estimates are national averages and are subject to wide regional variation. Medicare and standard health insurance cover all the procedures except radial keratotomy—if a second surgeon confirms the operation is needed.

Operation	Number in 1987 (in 1980)	What surgeons do	Estimated cost Surgeon's fee	Estimated cost Total cost	Possible alternative treatments
Hysterectomy	655,000 (649,000)	Remove the uterus and sometimes also the cervix, ovaries, or fallopian tubes	$1,500 to $2,000	$6,000 to $8,000	Partial surgery (myomectomy), laser ablation therapy, drugs
Cholecystectomy	536,000 (458,000)	Remove the gallbladder as a treatment for gallstones	1,000 to 1,500	5,000 to 7,000	Drugs, lithotripsy (in which doctors use sound waves to destroy the stones)
Prostatectomy	410,000 (335,000)	Remove part of enlarged prostate gland to restore urinary flow	2,500 to 3,000	6,500 to 8,000	Drugs, balloon dilation, modified surgery
Coronary artery bypass	332,000 (137,000)	Bypass clogged arteries in the heart by grafting new blood vessels from the leg or chest	3,500 to 4,000	25,000 to 35,000	Balloon angioplasty (a tiny balloon is inserted and inflated to open blocked arteries), drugs
Lumbar laminectomy	264,000 (189,000)	Remove fragments of herniated disk in the lower back, easing pressure on spinal nerves	2,500 to 3,000	9,000 to 11,000	Microsurgery, anti-flammatory drugs, rest, corrective corset or brace, exercise therapy
Knee arthroscopy	247,000 (169,000)	Inspect, remove, or repair torn cartilage in the knee using a fiber-optic instrument	600 to 1,800	600 to 1,800	Total knee replacement, traditional open surgery, or, in some cases, physical therapy
Radial keratotomy	50,000 (5,000)	Correct nearsightedness by making a series of tiny incisions in the cornea	1,000 to 2,000 (one eye)	1,500 to 4,000 (one eye)	Eyeglasses, contact lenses

Why the discrepancies? No one really knows beyond the obvious—that well-meaning doctors cannot agree on when to cut. Drug companies pour $1.5 billion a year into clinical studies of new drugs, but virtually nothing goes into comparing the effectiveness of surgery and other forms of treatment. In the absence of objective criteria with which to judge, surgeons adapt to regional patterns that are as strong as geographic differences in accent, taste, and slang.

For the patient, the fact that doctors disagree over when to operate should be a strong warning sign. It means that style of practice rather than objective scientific information may be responsible for your physician's recommendation. And it means that you, as the one who cares most about the outcome, are the one most likely to make the best decision. In the case of elective surgery, the first question is whether an operation is necessary at all. Here are some steps to help you decide:

Learn as much as possible about the procedure. Start with your physician or surgeon. Ask him or her to describe the operation and

Comments	Sources for more information
Since many hysterectomy patients are young (median age: 38), some may want to ask whether they can have less radical surgery that preserves fertility.	American College of Obstetricians and Gynecologists (202-638-5577); American College of Surgeons (312-664-4050); HERS Foundation (215-667-7757); *Hysterectomy: Before & After* by Winnifred B. Cutler (Harper & Row, $19.95)
Studies show that with "silent gallstones" (those with no pain) there is no pressing need for surgery.	American Digestive Disease Society (301-652-9293); brochure *About Cholecystectomy* by the American College of Surgeons (312-664-4050)
This is often done through the urethra with microsurgical tools rather than by open incision; complications can include incontinence or impotence.	*About Prostatectomy*, a 10-page brochure available free from the American College of Surgeons (312-664-4050); *The Prostate Book* by Stephen N. Rous, M.D. (Norton, $18.95)
Balloon angioplasty is often preferred in cases of partial blockage, but some 5% of balloon treatments fail and require emergency bypass.	The American Heart Association (check your phone book for the nearest of the 1,800 local chapters); *The Healing Heart; Antidotes to Panic and Helplessness* by Norman Cousins (Avon, $4.50)
Microsurgery, though not endorsed by all physicians, requires only a small incision and thus may speed healing.	*Low Back Pain*, free brochure by the American Academy of Orthopaedic Surgeons (312-823-7186); *About Low-Back Pain*, free brochure by the American College of Surgeons (312-644-4050)
For young, athletic people, repair—rather than removal—of cartilage is preferred, although full recovery can take months rather than weeks.	*Arthroscopy*, free brochure by the American Academy of Orthopaedic Surgeons (312-823-7186); *Save Your Knees* by James Fox and Rick McGuire (Dell, $6.95)
Few health plans reimburse you for it; those that do often cover it only if neither glasses nor contact lenses can correct your vision to 20/50.	The American Academy of Ophthalmology (P.O. Box 7424, San Francisco, CA 94120); a list of surgeons who perform the operation is available from the Keratorefractive Society (P.O. Box 145, Denison, TX 75021)

the intended result in detail. Ask about possible complications from the procedure, their likelihood, and how to deal with them should they arise. Find out whether less radical surgery would accomplish the same thing. For example, many surgeons now prefer to do a myomectomy—which removes only portions of the uterus—rather than a hysterectomy for women with benign growths called fibroids when those women want to retain the capacity to bear children.

Investigate any nonsurgical alternatives. Remember that surgeons have a natural bias for their specialty—they are trained to operate. But as most surgery is irreversible, it is usually best to exhaust other treatments such as drugs, diets, exercise, and so forth before seeking surgery as a last resort.

Get a second opinion. According to one study, this all-important option is exercised by fewer than 5% of participants in voluntary second-opinion programs—those where the insurer will pay for a second opinion but the patient doesn't have to get one. This is a serious mistake. Even minor surgery is dangerous enough that you should not contemplate it unless two independent experts believe it's worthwhile. Be as thorough in your questions to the second surgeon as you were with the first. You don't want a rubber-stamp confirmation of what you've been told. You want an independent evaluation. For this reason, you should get the second opinion from someone who is not an associate of the first surgeon.

Fortunately, a growing number of public and private agencies can help you find another physician to review your case. Many employers' health insurance companies today require second opinions. And most major insurance companies, including Prudential, Metropolitan, Equitable, and many of the Blue Cross/Blue Shield groups, can refer you to someone. The U.S. Department of Health and Human Services (800-638-6833, 800-492-6603 in Maryland) makes referrals free of charge. Local Social Security offices will refer Medicare recipients; welfare offices do the same for those on Medicaid.

If you decide to have surgery, the following steps should help you select the right surgeon:

Ask your primary physician to recommend two surgeons and describe the relative strengths and weaknesses of each. This will enable you to see how candid and comprehensive he is. If he sees both as equal and fully acceptable and can make no effective comparisons, then there is more cause to suspect the validity of the recommendation.

Get advice from other physicians. Ask whom they would recommend if you could go anywhere in the country for treatment, and also whom they would suggest if you decided to stay in your state or community. For simple operations like hernia repair, you probably don't need a world-renowned specialist, but for a quadruple bypass you might want one.

Be cautious about the advice of friends and relatives. While the experience of others is informative, it can also be misleading. One tip-off: Find out how thorough a search your friend conducted before picking a doctor. If he or she was methodical, place greater faith in the choice.

Check the surgeon's professional qualifications. The American College of Surgeons (55 East Erie Street, Chicago, IL 60611; 312-664-4050) can recommend members in your area. You may want to limit your search to those who are board certified in the specialty you need. This designation means the doctor is more likely to be aware of recent trends in his field, though it is not a guarantee of surgical skill. You can look up a physician's training and credentials in the *Directory of Medical Specialists*, available in most public libraries.

Ask what your surgeon's success rate is for this type of operation. The best doctors never mind being questioned because they know that better-informed patients are generally better patients. If a doctor takes offense at questions about the operation and his skill, that's a red flag that maybe you ought to find another doctor.

Select a doctor affiliated with a topnotch hospital. The best care for complicated operations is likely to be at a large, university-affiliated teaching hospital whose expert surgeons treat hundreds of cases like yours a year, not just a dozen or so. If yours is relatively uncomplicated surgery, however, you can often find a warmer atmosphere and better service at a smaller community hospital. In any event, pick one that is accredited by the Joint Commission on the Accreditation of Hospitals, which has tougher standards than most state licensing boards.

Finally, don't be afraid to raise the issue of cost, though that is not usually a big factor for people with good health insurance. Surgeons' fees aren't set in stone. What they charge often depends on the individual's insurance and his capacity to pay.

Shopping by Mail

Hold the phone until you read this catalogue shopping survey.

As any postman will attest, the mail-order catalogue business is booming. The reason for this explosive growth is simple: Shopping by phone is meant to be easier than ordinary shopping. No waiting on long cashier lines. No communal dressing rooms. No racks of clothes in every size but yours.

But do catalogue houses really deliver on their promise to provide no-hassle service? To find out, *Money* tested 20 of the nation's leading direct-mail retailers. Ten of the 20 were chosen because they do a high sales volume. The other 10 made the list because they carry trendy or interesting merchandise such as high-fashion sporting apparel (Patagonia), children's books (Telltales), and plants, trees, and garden supplies (Spring Hill). Five *Money* testers, scattered around the country, requested catalogues from all 20 firms. Each of the five attempted to place one order with all 20, and kept track of how easy it was to order, how cooperative the operators were, how quickly the goods arrived, and whether they were as promised.

Then the testers did something they hope you never have to do: they returned every order. In some cases, they told the customer service representative that the item was the wrong size or color; other times, they just said they had changed their minds. The testers did this not to try the operators' patience but simply to analyze, by actual example, each company's return policy. What emerged from the six-month study was an intriguing snapshot of the catalogue business today, plus many practical tips for taking advantage of its strengths and dealing with its foibles.

For example, companies such as Eddie Bauer, Lands' End, L.L. Bean, and Patagonia stood out because their catalogues were attractive and accurate, their operators were accommodating and informed, and their refunds arrived promptly. L.L. Bean, in particular, cheerfully accepted returns for any reason and always included the shipping charge in its price so that you never paid more than the figure listed next to the item in the catalogue.

Scoring low for service were companies such as Fingerhut and Spencer Gifts. At Fingerhut, which markets household goods, problems included rude operators and slow refunds (a credit for one item entailed a wait of more than 70 days). At Spencer Gifts, the problem was tardy service. One caller had to wait 49 days to get a catalogue; another, told to pay by check for an item that was below the $20 minimum credit charge, sent the check via overnight mail but still didn't receive the shipment until five weeks later. These two firms were not the only ones whose service sometimes lapsed. On the contrary, the problems just cited differed only in frequency—not in kind—from difficulties we encountered at many of the 20 firms surveyed.

To help you avoid or overcome such problems, *Money*'s testers compiled 10 of the most common hitches that occur during ordering by mail and offered some suggestions for how to cope with them:

You can't get the catalogue, or it's not free. You'd think a mail-order company would send you its catalogue readily. Not always. One tester waited as long as 108 days for Renovator's Supply catalogue. On four occasions (twice each from Fingerhut and Sharper Image), catalogues failed to come at all. Spring Hill, the plant- and tree-supply house, couldn't send its catalogue to two of the five testers because it had run out of copies.

The company has no toll-free number. Seven of the 20 firms expect you to pay for the phone call to place an order. If you're calling on your nickel, expedite the process by filling out the order form in advance, and have it in front of you when you dial. Or if you need advice on what to buy, call the operator, explain the situation, and ask the operator to call you back. If you're registering a complaint, ask for a callback or keep track of your phone charges and seek a reimbursement for them.

The operators are unhelpful, uninformed, or blatantly rude. This happened more often than you might imagine. The testers didn't expect the average order taker to be intimately familiar with every nuance of fishing lures (Orvis) or marine radios (Gander Mountain). On the other hand, efficient operators like those at Spiegel and Sharper Image illustrate that it is possible for a telephone sales force to master the contents of entire catalogues. One tip: If the order taker seems mystified by your questions, ask to speak to a supervisor or customer service representative. You'll usually get someone who has more knowledge and experience.

The item never arrives. Only two of the 100 orders went completely astray (one never arrived; another was canceled after it didn't come). Still, it's a good idea to keep a written record of what and when you order and always to ask by what date to expect delivery. If it doesn't come by that time, call immediately. At that point, you'll usually have the option to cancel and get a refund. If the company refuses to cancel and you placed your order by mail (not by phone), a Federal Trade Commission rule entitles you to a refund if the item wasn't shipped within 30 days of the order—unless the catalogue explicitly warns you to expect a longer delay. Alternatively, if you paid by credit card, you can protest the charge, provided you do so within 60 days of the billing date.

The merchandise is damaged or is not what you wanted. Save the box, its contents, and all packing materials, and call the company immediately. Reputable firms will issue you a credit or send you a replacement at their expense, although some ask that you return the damaged item (they should also pay the return postage). If you encounter any difficulties, see "How to Get Your Money Back" on page 141.

The items are not as described in the catalogue. Sometimes the discrepancy is open and shut, as was an order for a San Francisco Music Box miniature playing "It's a Small World After All." Instead, the tester received one that hummed Brahms' "Lullaby." Other times it was more of a judgment call, such as a rug described as blue in the catalogue that turned out to be turquoise-and-white striped. Your best protection here is to get as much information as possible from the operator before ordering, including what to do if the item is the wrong size or otherwise unsuitable. If the merchandise fails to live up to its advance notice, you are within your rights to return it for a refund. However, you can run into problems if . . .

The company will not credit you for your original postage, will not pay the return shipping charges, or both. Postage is a touchy subject for mail-order houses because shipping eats profits. The best companies, like Spiegel, L.L. Bean, and San Francisco Music Box, often pay transportation costs in both directions regardless of the reason for the return. That avoids disputes over who made the mistake in the first place. But most firms don't like to pay shipping charges if the error was yours—if you ordered the wrong size or you simply decided you didn't like it after it came, for example. If you do persuade the company to pay for the return, try asking the operator to arrange pre-paid UPS shipping. Several firms, including Brookstone, Eddie Bauer, Orvis, and Williams-Sonoma, will do this for you if you tell them it would be very inconvenient for you to return it yourself. With Penney's, you can also take things back to the chain's retail stores.

The company does not issue credit promptly. All the operations surveyed said they process credits as soon as an item is returned. That means a refund should appear on your credit-card bill within the next two billing periods, which was not the case with tardy credits from Fingerhut and F.A.O. Schwarz.

The company charges a high rate of interest on any unpaid balance. Spiegel and J.C. Penney impose annualized rates of interest as high as 21% in some states if you bill purchases to their charge cards. And Fingerhut demands an annualized 24% on bills that are not paid within 30 days.

You and the catalogue company get into a dispute. As with all consumer complaints, the key to winning is to keep careful records of what you did, when you did it, whom you spoke to, what they said, and of all bills, correspondence, checks, and the like. If you

charged your purchase to a credit card, you can protest that portion of your bill. Then, take your complaint to the catalogue's customer service department. Write a letter that states the problem, and include copies of supporting documents. If you haven't heard from the company in 30 days, file the same sort of protest with the Direct Marketing Association's Mail Order Action Line (6 East 43rd Street, New York, NY 10017). Another option is to complain to the Better Business Bureau in the city where the catalogue company is located. And if that doesn't work, complain to your local postal inspector, who will pass your comments on to the Postal Service headquarters. If after trying all these avenues you are still dissatisfied, you could take the matter to small-claims court.

This list of complaint procedures should not mislead you into thinking that ordering from catalogues is risky business. The testers often found the mail-order houses going out of their way to deliver service. A Brookstone customer service rep, for example, called to ask why an item was returned. Patagonia and Lands' End offer special phone lines for the hearing impaired. And Telltales, the children's book firm in Bath, Maine, will search for out-of-print books and then order them, all for a $5 fee.

Unfortunately, one of the main advantages of catalogue shopping—dodging state sales taxes—may one day become history. Congress is currently considering a law that would force the firms to collect sales tax, even if they do not have a retail store in your state (the only circumstance under which you would have to pay state tax today).

Even so, mail order will retain its relative convenience—especially as the number of catalogues proliferates and specialty houses emerge to serve your particular interests.

And if you're enough of a catalogue addict to want to shop for catalogues by catalogue, you can do that, too. Just send $3 for the *Great Catalogue Guide* from the Direct Marketing Association at the same address given above. It lists more than 1,000 catalogues from which you can order by mail or phone to your heart's delight.

A Guide to Shopping by Mail

The best catalogue houses offer round-the-clock toll-free information and ordering service, ship catalogues and items promptly, accept returns for any reason, and either pay or credit you for all postal charges when you send an item back. The only firm that met this standard rigidly was J.C. Penney, although Gander Mountain, Lands' End, and L.L. Bean came close. Those where service lagged included Fingerhut and Spencer Gifts.

Catalogue Companies	What they sell	Phone and hours in local time*	Credit cards accepted†	Days to receive catalogue
Brookstone *Peterborough, N.H.*	Hard-to-find tools	603-924-9541 8-5 M-F	A,M, O,V	2-20
Eddie Bauer *Redmond, Washington*	Clothing, outdoor gear	800-426-8020 24 hours a day	A,M,V	3-24
F.A.O. Schwarz *New York, N.Y.*	Toys, stuffed animals	800-426-TOYS 24 hours a day	A,DC, M,V	7-30
Fingerhut *St. Cloud, Minnesota*	Household items, bric-a-brac	612-259-2500 6-9:45 M-F 8-2 S	A,DC M,V	28-30
Gander Mountain *Wilmot, Wisconsin*	Apparel, sporting goods	800-558-9410 24 hours a day	D,M,V	13-35
J.C. Penney *Dallas, Texas*	Clothing, furniture, appliances	800-222-6161 24 hours a day	A,M, Penney, V	6-30
Lands' End *Dodgeville, Wisconsin*	Preppie clothing	800-356-4444 24 hours a day	A,M,V	2-16
Lillian Vernon *Mount Vernon, N.Y.*	Household items, bric-a-brac	914-633-6300 24 hours a day	A,D,DC, M,O,V	3-7
L.L. Bean *Freeport, Maine*	Sporting equipment, camp gear, clothing	800-221-4221 24 hours a day	A,M, O,V	8-21
Orvis *Manchester, Vermont*	Apparel, hunting supplies	800-548-9548 24 hours a day	A,M,V	17-35
Patagonia *Ventura, California*	Active apparel	800-638-6464 7-7 M-F, 9-5 S	A,M,V	5-14
Renovator's Supply *Millers Falls, Massachusetts*	Hardware, household supplies	413-659-2211 8-10:30 M-F, 8-5 S-S	M,V	14-108
San Francisco Music Box *San Francisco, California*	Music boxes, musical toys	800-227-2190 24 hours a day	A,D,DC, M,V	9-31
Sharper Image *San Francisco, California*	Electronic goods, gadgets	800-344-4444 24 hours a day	A,D,DC, M,V	15-35
Spencer Gifts *Williamsburg, Virginia*	Bric-a-brac	804-220-5966 8-8 M-F	A,M,V	12-49
Spiegel *Chicago, Illinois*	Apparel, furniture	800-345-4500 24 hours a day	A,M,O, Spiegel, V	12-24
Spring Hill *Tipp City, Ohio*	Plants, trees	309-691-4616 9-6 M-F	A,M,V	6-13
Telltales *Bath, Maine*	Children's books	800-922-READ 8-6 M-F	A,M,V	6-41
Victoria's Secret *Columbus, Ohio*	Lingerie, women's apparel	800-888-8200 24 hours a day	A, Limited, M,V	10-21
Williams-Sonoma *San Francisco, California*	Cooking supplies, serving pieces	415-421-4242 7-7 M-F, 8-4 S-S	A,M,V	8-32

*Toll-free numbers may differ for in-state calls. †Credit-card legend: A = American Express; D = Discover; DC = Diner's Club; M = MasterCard; O = Optima; V = Visa.

| Days to receive item | Paid, or gave credit, for: | | Comments |
	Original postage	Return postage	
6-37	Given on 5 of 5	Given on 1 of 5	Sends a helpful postcard to let you know items are back ordered; unfortunately, also charges your account at that time.
10-18	1 of 5	1 of 5	Operators seemed especially well informed about the merchandise and its availability.
4-42	2 of 5	2 of 5	Delightful toys, but two items came weeks late, and we got no credit for one return.
22-48	2 of 5	1 of 5	Order by mail, not by phone. Operators were rude and unhelpful, and we are still waiting for credit on one returned item.
7-32	5 of 5	3 of 5	Service was efficient, but the operators didn't know enough about outdoor gear.
2-7	5 of 5	5 of 5	The catalogue costs $5. You get a $5 gift certificate, too—but you can redeem it only by taking it to a Penney's store.
4-7	5 of 5	2 of 5	Good catalogue, friendly operators. One tip: They'll arrange a UPS pickup for some returns but only if you ask for it.
14-38	3 of 5	1 of 5	Has different items on sale each day; operators will pitch them to you.
2-30	5 of 5	2 of 5	The patriarch—and deservedly so—of catalogue companies; guarantees its products forever.
8-58	1 of 5	2 of 5	Need to order fishing tackle at 2 a.m. on a Sunday? Orvis is open for business.
5-22	1 of 5	2 of 5	The merchandise is classy and high-priced; the phone service was excellent.
7-22	1 of 5	1 of 5	One order was lost; we canceled another when it didn't come after 709 days.
5-15	4 of 5	2 of 5	Even the music you hear while waiting on hold comes from an antique music box.
7-24	4 of 5	1 of 5	We liked the goods, but the operators answered questions only reluctantly.
13-21	3 of 5	1 of 5	We encountered rude and uninformed operators; no charges on items under $20.
6-42	1 of 5	4 of 5	Spiegel is very efficient; operators always offer to arrange UPS pickup for returns.
13-21	Not applicable (no returns on plants)		You can place an order year round, but the company won't ship plants to cold-weather states during the winter.
5-11	1 of 5	0 of 5	Operators helped us search for out-of-print titles.
3-55	1 of 5	0 of 5	Minimum shipping charge is $5.95, so order multiple items all at once, not singly.
8-42	1 of 5	1 of 5	Some of this merchandise is fragile; always insure it if you make a return.

Financing a Secure Retirement

If you are in your prime retirement planning years—roughly ages 45 to 64—see whether this profile sounds anything like you:

• You look forward to a full life after work; you're not at all afraid to bid the workaday world good-bye; and you even intend to let go before you reach age 65.

• You are a superior saver, putting away an impressive 14% of your annual income (versus about 4% for the U.S. population at large).

• You don't plan to move to a less costly house after retirement, and you don't expect your standard of living to drop in step with your income.

• Your biggest worry is inflation, but your major form of investment is a savings account, the least inflation-resistant of all. You have little or no confidence in stocks, historically the best inflation hedge.

If those traits tend to fit you, it's no wonder. They are all shared by most of the 600 pre-retirees interviewed by telephone in a June 1988 study done for Merrill Lynch and released to *Money*. Among the most telling of the survey's other findings:

Estimating retirement costs. On average, pre-retirees figure that they will need 70% of their current income for a comfortable retirement. But some retirement planners contend that most early retirees will need 75% to 80% of current income. Reason: Each retiree could have 3,000 additional nonworking hours to fill every year—and part of that time will likely be spent in activities that cost money.

Social Security. Most believe that they will collect all the benefits to which they are entitled. But only half of the 45- to 49-year-olds feel that they can count on Social Security, compared with three-quarters of the 60- to 64-year-olds. Whatever your views, it is unrealistic to assume that what you collect from the government and your company pension will equal your savings contributions. Indeed, Social Security and your pension may provide only half of your future retirement income.

Long-term health care. Although the great majority of pre-retirees view this as an important issue, nearly two-thirds are untroubled about their ability to pay for long-term care. The explanation: Respondents believe that employers and the government should be responsible for three-quarters of long-term health-care costs. While long-term care is on the congressional agenda, employers are unlikely to expand benefits.

Figuring the Cost of Retirement

Financial independence won't come cheap. But if you know now what it will cost, paying for it later will be much easier.

How much money do you really need in savings to retire comfortably? Brace yourself: The figure is daunting. Let's say you and your spouse were to retire today at age 62. Social Security and your company pension would provide much of the income you require, but you would have to depend on your own investments for the rest. You must have $202,000 in capital to collect an inflation-proof $10,000 a year for the next 30 years. If you would like $20,000 a year, you would need to have saved more than $400,000. Obviously, you can't expect to build a nest egg of such proportions in just your last few years on the job. Instead, you must start regularly putting aside a chunk of your income many years in advance of your retirement.

The first step is to set a specific savings goal that reflects both the living standard you expect in retirement and the time remaining before you plan to leave work. Such a target will help to make you disciplined about saving—and perhaps keep you from realizing too late that you haven't saved enough.

To calculate your goal, use the retirement savings plan worksheet on page 162. The worksheet takes into account what you can expect from Social Security and your company pension and tells you how much you have to save each year, starting now, to build the retirement fund you'll need. To make the sums involved easier to comprehend, the worksheet automatically corrects for the effects of future inflation, thereby keeping all figures in 1989

Your Living Expenses

These tips will help you complete the worksheet to figure out your cost of living in retirement.

Line 1. Rent, mortgage, property taxes, utilities, home furnishings, household services, insurance, maintenance, and improvements.

Line 2. Include dining out, tobacco, and alcohol.

Line 3. Car loans, repair and maintenance, insurance, gas, commuting costs, parking.

Line 4. Federal, FICA, state, and local.

Line 5. Movies, plays, concerts, sports, cable TV, and video rental, plus hobbies.

Line 6. On average, the combined costs of medical insurance and out-of-pocket payments go up 20% to 30% in retirement.

Line 7. Expect to reduce your clothing costs by 30% if you're retiring to more informal habits.

Line 8. Travel expenses are likely to soar in the first three to five years of leisure.

Line 9. You may want to help children with a down payment or with the cost of an advanced degree.

Line 10. Put money aside—try for 15% of income—for emergencies and to offset inflation.

Line 11. Senior-age students are a growth industry on campuses.

Line 12. If your mortgage is paid and your spouse will be supported by your pension benefit, you may want to drop life coverage.

Line 13. Include charitable contributions and gifts to friends and family.

Line 14. Loans are a slate that you should try to wipe clean before you retire.

Divide your total expenditures in your early retirement by your current gross income. The result is the percentage of your current income you will need after retirement. Use the actual dollar amount to complete line 1—annual income needed in retirement—in the master worksheet on page 162. Use the percentage of income needed in late retirement for future planning.

Expenditures	In early retirement	In late retirement
1 Housing		
2 Food		
3 Transportation		
4 Taxes		
5 Recreation		
6 Medical		
7 Clothing and personal care		
8 Travel		
9 Support of relatives		
10 Savings		
11 Education		
12 Life insurance		
13 Gifts		
14 Loan repayments		
Total expenditures **(add lines 1 through 14)**		
Total expenditures divided by current gross income	%	%

How Much Should You Save?

This worksheet will help you estimate how much you must save each year for retirement. It assumes that your investments will earn 3% after inflation, about the historical average for a conservative portfolio of stocks, bonds, and cash. For extra safety, the worksheet also as-sumes that you will live to age 92, 10 years beyond the life expectancy of a 65-year-old in 1989. All amounts are in today's dollars. If you are less than 10 years from leaving work, update your calculation annually. If retirement is fur-ther off, do so every two years.

1 Annual income needed in retirement (Transfer your estimated living costs in retire-ment from the worksheet on page 161. If you haven't completed that worksheet and want only a rough estimate, use 70% of your current income.)

2 Expected Social Security benefit (Call the Social Security Administration at 800-234-5772 for a projection of your benefit. Or use one of these ball park estimates: $10,788 if you make more than $48,000, or an amount between $9,300 and $10,788 if your earnings are between $25,000 and $48,000.)

3 Expected pension benefit (Ask your benefits counselor at work to estimate your future pension, assuming that your salary remains the same until you retire. For a rough estimate, multiply 1.5% of your salary by the number of years you plan to stay on the job and then subtract half your projected Social Security benefit.)

4 Expected income from retirement benefits **(line 2 plus line 3)**

5 Annual retirement income needed from savings and investments **(line 1 minus line 4)**

6 Amount you must save by retirement in today's dollars **(line 5 times multiplier from line A below)**

7 Amount you have saved already:

A IRAs and Keoghs	**B** Employer savings plans (Include vested amounts in 401(k)s, ESOPs, SEPs, and profit-sharing plans.)	**C** Other investments (Include all CDs, mutual funds, bonds, stocks, in-vestment real es-tate, and any other assets avail-able for retire-ment.)	**D** Optional (If you wish to count a portion of your home's value as savings, enter its present value minus the anticipated cost of a new home in retirement.)	**E** Total retirement savings (Add lines a through d)

8 Value of your retirement savings at the time you retire **(line 7e times multiplier from line B below)**

9 Amount of retirement capital still needed **(line 6 minus line 8)**

10 Total annual savings still needed **(line 9 times multiplier from line C below)**

11 Annual employer contributions to your company savings plans (Include 401(k)s, ESOPs, SEPs, and profit-sharing plans.)

12 Annual amount you need to set aside in today's dollars **(line 10 minus line 11)**

Age at retirement	55	56	57	58	59	60	61	62	63	64	65	66	67
Multiplier A	22.8	22.5	22.1	21.8	21.4	21.0	20.6	20.2	19.8	19.3	18.9	18.4	17.9

Years until retirement	1	3	5	7	9	11	13	15	20	25	30
Multiplier B	1.03	1.09	1.16	1.23	1.30	1.38	1.47	1.56	1.81	2.09	2.43
Multiplier C	1.00	.324	.188	.131	.098	.078	.064	.054	.037	.027	.021

dollars. Start by estimating your annual retirement living expenses, using your imagination as well as arithmetic. According to a common rule of thumb, you will need about 70% of your current gross income to live as well in retirement as you do now. For a more precise estimate, fill out the cost-of-living worksheet on page 161.

Next, pin down what you can expect from the following sources:

Social Security. For an estimate of your future retirement benefit, call Social Security at 800-234-5772 and ask for Form SSA-7004, the Request for Earnings and Benefit Estimate Statement. After you return the self-addressed form, you should receive the estimate within six weeks.

Under Social Security's benefits formula, the more you earn over your career, the larger your benefit, up to a maximum in 1989 of $10,788. Because of this cap, high-income people shouldn't rely on Social Security to replace a substantial portion of their pre-retirement earnings. For instance, if you consistently earn the maximum wage covered by Social Security—$48,000 in 1989 and adjusted annually for inflation—your benefit under today's rules would replace about 23% of your pay. But if you retired from a $75,000-a-year job, the maximum benefit would replace only around 14% of your salary.

Your age at retirement also affects the size of your Social Security benefit. Today, you are entitled to a full benefit when you reach age 65. If you start collecting at age 62, which is the youngest you can do so, your monthly check will be permanently set at 80% of the full benefit.

Your spouse is entitled to a Social Security check, too, even if he or she didn't have a paying job. The spousal benefit equals 50% of your full benefit if your spouse starts collecting it at the standard retirement age. The payout drops to 37.5% if your spouse takes it at age 62. Of course, if your spouse worked and is entitled to a larger benefit, he or she can claim that benefit instead.

Whether Social Security will be able to maintain its projected level of benefits, however, is far from certain. Though the system is solvent for now, it could run into serious funding difficulties after the baby boomers start retiring in about 20 years. If you're already over age 50, you can probably count on getting the full benefit you have coming under today's law. If you're younger, some financial planners advise that you estimate your benefit using today's projections but review the calculation every two years. More cautious planners suggest that you omit Social Security entirely from your planning. Without it, you'll have to save more, but you'll gain a financial cushion that will keep your retirement plan sound no matter what happens to Social Security.

Your pension. A typical corporate pension might award you a benefit equal to 1.5% of your average salary over your last five years on the job, multiplied by the number of years you worked for the employer, minus roughly half your expected Social Security benefit. Most plans reduce your benefit if you retire before 65. If you joined up at age 35 and left at 55, for example, your benefit might be only 25% as much as if you had stayed to 65.

Since pension formulas vary, ask your company benefits counselor to figure the amount for you, based on the job tenure you anticipate and assuming that your salary remains the same until you retire. Performing the calculation this way keeps the estimate in today's dollars.

Your investments. Social Security and your pension will probably provide no more than 40% to 60% of the income you'll need in retirement. To make up the shortfall, you will have to depend on your savings in tax-deferred plans such as Individual Retirement Accounts and company-sponsored 401(k)s, as well as your after-tax investments and perhaps even the equity in your home.

Though the sums you'll need may seem unattainable, they can be within surprisingly easy reach if you start saving early. For example, assuming an investment return of three percentage points above inflation, a 35-year-old couple could amass a retirement fund of more than $200,000 in 1989 dollars by jointly saving

$350 a month until age 65. With the help of 401(k) plans in which their employers match their contributions 50¢ on the dollar, the couple's savings goal drops to just $233 a month. (Remember that this example is in 1989 dollars. The couple must increase their contributions each year by the inflation rate to save the equivalent of $200,000 in today's dollars.)

Your goal should be to accumulate a large enough stake to handle the twin perils of inflation and a long life. Half of today's 65-year-old men are expected to live past 80; half of the women should make it past 84. And most financial planners urge you to provide for the possibility that you will outlive your peers.

Though your Social Security benefit will rise with the cost of living, most pension benefits will not. In just 10 years, steady annual inflation of 5% would slash the spending power of a fixed monthly check by around 40%. Thus, your investments in retirement must return much more than you'll need for living costs in the early years after you stop working. You can then reinvest the surplus to keep your fund growing. (For investment advice, see "Investing Like a Pro," page 21.)

Eventually, even if you invest wisely, inflation may still push your expenses higher than your income. By that time, however, your fund will presumably be large enough for you to tap the principal without fear of outliving your money.

Making Sure You'll Have What You Need

You can't depend on Social Security or a pension for a comfortable old age. So start tucking away money now, preferrably in tax-deferred accounts.

Chances are, you will start receiving Social Security checks at retirement, though your benefits won't be big enough to live on. How about a corporate pension? You might get one if your employer has a plan and if you stay there long enough to qualify for benefits, which is known as vesting and generally takes at least five years. But most private pensions have fixed payments that do not increase with inflation. So you cannot rely on a pension to provide a cushy retirement if the cost of living rises sharply.

Thus, the core of your retirement plan must come from your own efforts. Perhaps you will use a variety of retirement-savings programs discussed below. Or you might fund one option to the max, such as an Individual Retirement Account or Keogh plan, and stick with it year after year. But you must begin piling up money for your retirement as soon as you can. Reason: Early savers have a silent partner called compounding that does half the work. If, for example, you are 25 and set aside $2,000 a year for 10 years in an IRA yielding an average of 8% annually, you'll have $198,000 at age 60. If you wait until 45 to begin the same savings plan, by 60 you'll have just $43,000. As a result, assuming an 8%

payout, the IRA would provide the late starter less than $3,400 a year in income after age 60 versus nearly $16,000 for the early saver. (To get a rough idea of how much you'll need for retirement, see the worksheet on page 162.)

Your nest egg will grow fastest in a tax-deferred account, such as an employee-savings plan at work or an IRA. That way, the income on your money won't be eaten by the tax moth until you make withdrawals. Naturally, there's a catch. Most tax-favored retirement accounts don't allow you easy access to your cash. And if you do get your hands on the money before age 59½, you must usually pay taxes on it, plus a 10% early-withdrawal penalty.

The easiest tax-sheltered outlet for most people is a payroll-deduction savings plan at work. Also called a defined-contribution plan, it lets you allocate a portion of your salary to your account, deferring taxes on the earnings until you take the money out. Companies often restrict employee contributions to 5% or 6% of pay, but the law generally allows you to save up to 25% of pay or $30,000, whichever is less. What's more, many employers match every dollar you invest with 50¢, sometimes even $1.

Of all the types of employer-sponsored savings plans, the most attractive is a 401(k), named for a provision in the tax code. It lets you salt away part of your paycheck before the money is taxed. In 1990, you can contribute up to $7,627 to a 401(k); the dollar limit rises annually with inflation. Many businesses, however, limit employee contributions to either that amount or 10% of pretax pay, whichever is less. A 401(k) prohibits any withdrawals before you quit or retire unless you can prove financial hardship. In that case, you must pay taxes and, almost always, a 10% penalty on the withdrawal if you are under age 59½. (See "Managing Your 401(k)" on page 169.)

If you are self-employed—or have any self-employment income—don't miss out on a roomy retirement shelter known as a Keogh plan, named after the congressman who created it. Each year, you can put in a Keogh up to 20% of your net self-employment income or $30,000, whichever is less, and deduct the contribution from your taxable income.

Earnings grow tax deferred until you withdraw them, and you can invest your Keogh in everything from Treasury bonds to real estate limited partnerships. Keoghs are available through banks, financial planners, insurance companies, mutual funds, and stockbrokers.

Whether you are self-employed or work for someone else, you might also consider an IRA, which you can establish at banks, brokerage firms, mutual funds, and insurance companies. Anyone with employment income is allowed to deduct contributions of as much as $2,000 a year—$4,000 for married, working couples and $2,250 for couples with one working spouse—if you meet one of the following qualifying rules:

● You (and your spouse, if you are married) are not covered by a pension plan at work.

● You are covered but earn less than $25,000 a year—$40,000 if you are married and file joint tax returns.

You can take a partial deduction if you are covered by a pension plan and are single with earnings of $25,000 to $35,000 or married with earnings of $40,000 to $50,000. If your income is higher than those limits, you can have an IRA and the money in it will grow tax deferred until withdrawn, but you can't deduct your contributions.

Should you make maximum use of an IRA? The answer is an unqualified yes if you can claim the $2,000 deduction. Otherwise, the answer depends on how disciplined you are. Some people invest each year in tax-free municipal bonds or muni-bond funds instead of an IRA, keeping a silent pledge to withdraw the money only at retirement or in an emergency. (With munis you can take out your money at any time without paying a tax penalty.) Other people need the institutionalized IRA and its early-withdrawal penalty to force them to save for retirement. If you're in the latter group, be absolutely certain you won't need your nondeductible IRA money before retirement.

Another way to save for your retirement and reduce your current tax bill is through a deferred annuity (as opposed to an immediate annuity, described on page 170). A deferred contract is sold by an insurance company for as little as $25 a month. Your investment is not tax deductible but it goes into one of the insurer's portfolios, where it grows tax deferred until withdrawn. Depending on the portfolio you select, your rate of return will be guaranteed for about a year or will fluctuate with the investment markets. Upon your retirement, the insurer will begin monthly payments, as specified in the contract. In addition, you can generally withdraw your investment and its earnings at any time, though you will owe taxes and a 10% penalty if you are under age 59½.

Before signing up for a deferred annuity, be sure you are familiar with the contract's terms. You'll probably pay a high up-front commission. Most insurers also charge surrender fees that generally start at 7% to 10% of the amount withdrawn if you cash out in the first year of the contract; the fees gradually shrink, disappearing after seven to 10 years.

The tilt of your investment portfolio for retirement should depend chiefly on how far you are from quitting work and on your tolerance for risk. It isn't enough simply to sock your money away; you also have to invest it wisely. With even a moderately risky growth portfolio, you should be prepared to ride out market drops that could be as grim as 30% in a year or as precipitous as October 1989's one-day, 7% rout. Financial planners and investment advisers offer these rules of thumb:

● If you are younger than 35, weight your portfolio toward growth. This means keeping as much as 70% of it in stocks or stock mutual funds; another 15% to 25% in fixed-income

Opening an IRA or Keogh

To be frank, the paperwork required to set up an Individual Retirement Account or a Keogh retirement plan can be annoying. You may have to fill out a couple of forms for an IRA; a Keogh can require half a dozen. The forms aren't difficult, though. And the potential payoff—a comfortable retirement—makes the process bearable. After choosing the type of investment that suits you, take the following steps:

Select an institution that sells your investment choice. You can open an IRA or Keogh account with any bank, savings and loan, credit union, brokerage, mutual fund or insurance company. Fees and commissions will vary. You are likely to pay $25 to $100 to set up a Keogh. Most banks, S&Ls and credit unions let you open an IRA for free; their competitors usually charge $25 or so. Annual maintenance fees are generally $10 to $50.

Do the paperwork. The institution will furnish you with its version of the forms that meet government regulations. You can easily handle the five or six questions on IRA forms concerning your investment choice and your beneficiary. The several dozen questions on Keogh forms are somewhat more demanding because they deal with your business. They cover such matters as your Keogh plan's vesting schedule and the appointment of an administrator of the plan—typically you, your accountant, or another financial adviser. You may want an accountant to help you handle the Keogh documents. If so, expect to pay him or her $100 to $300.

Meet the deadline. You must open a Keogh by December 31 and deposit usually at least $100 or so in order to claim the deduction for the year's entire contribution. But you don't have to come up with all the cash you intend to put away for the year until the day you file your tax return. For an IRA, you have until April 15 (April 16 in 1990 because the 15th falls on a Sunday) to both open and fund an account for the previous year.

investments such as bond funds, bank certificates of deposit, and money-market funds; and the rest in inflation fighters such as rental real estate or precious metals.

• In your late thirties and forties, you should start adjusting your portfolio's balance toward fixed-income investments. A good mix would be 40% to 70% in stocks; 30% to 40% in taxable and tax-free bonds, CDs, and money-market funds; and the rest in inflation hedges.

• In your early fifties, focus on preservation of your assets. For growth, stocks should represent at least 20% of your portfolio, with close to 70% in fixed-income investments, and the rest in inflation hedges. (For further information on investments, see "Where to Put Your Money Now" on page 9 and "Investing Like a Pro" on page 21.)

You may be living in your largest source of retirement cash. Home values, historically, have risen, on average, by at least a percentage point or two above the inflation rate. So, if you buy a house for $100,000 this year and it appreciates annually at a modest 5.5%, you could sell the property in 20 years for $292,000. Then some of the proceeds could be used for retirement income, and the rest could be spent on a smaller house or condominium or for rent on an apartment. Anyone age 55 or older can take a once-in-a-lifetime exclusion from income taxes of as much as $125,000 of the profit on the sale of a principal home. Another way to make use of your home as a storehouse of retirement cash is through a so-called reverse mortgage. This is a loan that pays a homeowner a fixed monthly amount and defers repayment of principal and interest until the house is sold, usually after the owner's death. (For details, see "Cashing In on Your Home" page 178.)

Don't forget what's potentially your most productive retirement asset: yourself. Cultivating a hobby or sideline business now can deliver retirement income later. Or you can develop a second career. For instance, you can take classes to learn the basics of another occupation that could bring in income during retirement—from making desserts that you could sell to working as a travel agent. The important thing is to have a lot of options as you head into retirement.

Moving Tax-Deferred Accounts

As with your other investments, it pays to periodically reassess the asset-allocation in your IRAs, Keoghs, and SEPs.

Every spring, banks, brokerages, and mutual funds face off with one another over shares of the estimated $25 billion that pours into tax-deferred retirement accounts before the mid-April tax deadline. Even if you swore off putting new money into IRAs after tax reform, this annual hype fest is still a good time to assess your existing tax-deferred accounts and see what reallocation may be in order. Is it time to ease some cash into stocks, for example, or to lock in the interest rates on Treasury notes? If so, make your move. But mind the following rules which apply equally to IRAs, simplified employee pensions (SEPs), or Keoghs.

The process is quite simple if you are planning to convey tax-deferred money from one mutual fund to another within a fund family, or from one investment to another within a brokerage account. In that case, simply call your fund or broker. Just make sure that the superior (or safer) returns you project on your new investment compensate you for any sales charges and commissions you may incur.

The process is more complicated if you want to shift some or all of an account from one custodian to another—for example, from a brokerage to a fund or from one fund company to another. First, you have to decide whether to have the two custodians carry out the move—a procedure known as a transfer—or to withdraw the money yourself and redeposit it in a new account. This process is called a rollover.

By transferring rather than rolling over, you avoid most of the tax-related pitfalls of moving tax-deferred money. For example, the law allows you to transfer assets as often as you wish, while it restricts rollovers to one per account within a 12-month period. In addition, when you withdraw money in a rollover, you must redeposit it in a new tax-deferred account within 60 days. Otherwise, the money turns into a pumpkin on which you will owe income taxes and, if you are under age 59½, a 10% early-withdrawal penalty. In a transfer, by contrast, your tax deferral is never in jeopardy because you never take possession of the funds.

On the other hand, you can execute a rollover in a matter of days, while transfers between custodians can take up to four weeks. Until the process is completed, the money remains invested in the original account, gaining (or losing) ground accordingly. Thus, a rollover may make sense if you are trying to catch a move in the stock market or if you are switching money out of a certificate of deposit.

Most banks allow you to withdraw assets from a certificate of deposit without penalty only during a seven-day window following the certificate's maturity. After that, the bank

simply plows the funds into another CD. So unless you initiate a transfer two to four weeks before your CD matures, a rollover may be the only way to be sure of extracting your money before it's reinvested.

The mechanics of transfers and rollovers are quite simple. To request a transfer, ask the bank, brokerage, or fund company to which you plan to relocate your money for an IRA application form and a so-called letter of acceptance. This paperwork establishes a tax-deferred account with the new custodian, and that company then sends your current custodian your signed letter of acceptance, directing that the specified amount be sent to your new account.

To avoid delays, check with the institution holding your current account to find out whether you face other requirements before the money can be sent. For example, most companies charge a fee for closing a discretionary tax-deferred account—that is, one in which you can switch among different investments. You have to pay $10, for instance, to pull your money out of the T. Rowe Price no-load fund group and $50 to get out of the brokerage Shearson Lehman Hutton. These fees are not tax deductible, and it is better to pay them out-of-pocket rather than from your tax-deferred account so that the fee does not deplete the earning power of your retirement savings.

To carry out a rollover, notify the custodian of your account that you wish to withdraw all or part of your money. You can do this either in person or by letter. (If you write, you will need to have your signature guaranteed by a bank or broker.)

The company will issue you a check within five days, and you then have 60 days from the date you receive it to open a new tax-deferred account wherever you choose. You can also split the old account into several different new ones. But if you open more than one Keogh, you will have to submit a separate IRS Form 5500 every year for each plan. It is much simpler to establish your Keogh at one mutual fund family or brokerage firm where you can take advantage of a variety of investments in one plan.

Managing Your 401(k)

You are responsible for deploying the funds in your retirement plan.

Once you decide to stash cash in a 401(k), you have to learn how to manage the account, since all the critical decisions will have to be yours. The following information on investment choices, hardship withdrawals, and loans will help you get the most out of your plan:

Asset allocation. Under most 401(k)s, you can apportion your contributions among at least three investment options, typically a stock mutual fund, shares in your company, and a guaranteed investment contract (GIC). GICs are by far the most popular choice because they are safe, which is crucially important to a host of amateur investors making critical decisions without professional advice. The insurance companies and banks that issue and back GICs promise to pay a fixed return for a specified period, usually one year. GICs generally yield slightly more than money-market funds, recently about 8.5%. This nominal yield advantage reflects GICs' longer average term—a year versus a month or so for money funds. But GICs are considered just as safe.

While GICs may be comforting, most retirement professionals advise against putting your entire nest egg there. For example, younger people can afford to bypass staid GICs and go for long-term gains in diversified stock funds. And employees of all ages should favor such funds over undiversified alternatives like company stock—the most popular form of company contribution to 401(k)s.

The best way to deploy your plan will depend on your age and tolerance for risk.

People who are a couple of decades or more away from retirement can comfortably put half to three-quarters of their 401(k) money in their plan's diversified stock fund. If your

Where Employees Put Their Money...

Percentage of 401(k) Contributions in:	
GICs	64%
Employer stock	33
Balanced mutual funds	28
Equity funds	23
Government bonds or other fixed-income funds	21
Short-term securities or money-market funds	19

(Percentages do not add up to 100% because not all plans offer all options.)

Source: Hewitt Associates

...and Where They Ought to Put It

In Your Twenties and Thirties:	GICs	25%
	Equity mutual funds	75
In Your Forties and Early Fifties:	GICs	25
	Equity and balanced funds	25
	Government bonds or other fixed-income funds	25
In Your Late Fifties and Sixties:	GICs	75
	Equity and balanced funds	25

Source: Westbrook Financial

employer offers several, make your allocation in accordance with your profile as an investor: an aggressive stock fund is for the most daring, followed by equity income, and then by balanced, which is a more sober mix of stocks and bonds. If, however, your company's stock fund performs poorly compared with similar funds, consider picking a conservative option like a GIC instead. Reason: If enough employees vote with their money, your company may switch fund managers. Also give greater weight to GICs and fixed-income funds as you get closer to retirement.

Hardship withdrawals and loans. It's tougher than ever to pry money out of a 401(k) before the requisite age 59½. You will have to convince your employer that you need the cash for medical expenses; a down payment on your principal residence; next term's tuition at a post-secondary school; avoiding eviction or foreclosure of your mortgage; or some other purpose specified in your company's plan. You must also prove that you cannot raise the money by selling assets or borrowing elsewhere at a reasonable interest rate. If you do manage to extract cash from your 401(k), such early withdrawals are subject to income tax plus a 10% tax penalty. (In cases involving catastrophic illness, however, the penalty may

be waived.) Mercifully, nearly two-thirds of companies allow employees to borrow against their 401(k)s at rates a percentage point or two above or below the prime rate, which is what banks charge their best customers. Generally, you must repay your employer within five years, but loans used to purchase a primary residence are usually due in 10 to 15 years. You can borrow as much as half of the vested amount in your account, up to $50,000. That limit is reduced by your highest outstanding loan balance over the past 12 months. If your vested account balance is less than $10,000, you can borrow it all. However, if you do, your employer may choose to impose additional limits.

If you must borrow against your retirement savings, bear in mind that most employers demand repayment in full when you quit your job. That may create a tax problem for you. Say you're under 59½ and leave your company with a 401(k) worth $15,000 and an outstanding balance of $5,000. If your employer keeps $5,000 of your lump sum to settle your debt, you'll still owe income tax and a 10% penalty on the $5,000. The only way to elude the tax man's grasp is to scrape up another $5,000, add it to the $10,000 you receive, and roll over the entire amount into another qualified retirement plan, such as an IRA.

Is an Immediate Annuity for You?

These insurance company products can offer high payouts, but rates vary sharply from one company to another.

If longevity seems in the cards or in your genes, you should consider investing some savings or part of a lump sum from a corporate retirement plan in a single-premium immediate annuity.

The best of these products, which are sold by insurance companies, offer a higher payout—as much as 13% for a 65-year-old male—than most other long-term investments. Annuities make particular sense if your health is good and your ancestors were long-lived. Since monthly payments to you are based on average life expectancy, an annuity turns out to be a terrific deal if you live longer than actuarially expected. Annuities have a major drawback, however: your monthly payment doesn't increase with inflation.

If an immediate annuity seems right for you, prepare to do some serious shopping—payout rates vary considerably from one insurance company to the next. For example, a 65-year-old man with $100,000 to invest could collect anywhere from $521 to $1,080 a month for the rest of his life, depending on the contract he buys.

Before searching for the highest yields, you should select a settlement option—the terms under which income is paid out. That's because a given insurer doesn't necessarily offer competitive payout rates for each settlement option. In general, the size of your monthly check will depend on your age and sex, how much you invest, and whether payments cease at your death or continue for a specified number of years or until the death of your beneficiary. Here's the menu that insurers typically offer:

• A straight-life or lifetime-only annuity pays you until you die, whether you last to 111 or expire shortly after signing the contract. Since straight-life annuities are risky, they come with the highest monthly payments. They make sense for people who need lofty monthly incomes and lack dependents or intend to provide for them some other way.

• A life-and-period-certain annuity pays you and a beneficiary for at least a specified number of years, typically 10, 15, or 20. For example, if you buy a 10-year-certain annuity and die after seven years, your beneficiary will receive monthly payments for another three years. But you pay a price for peace of mind. Ten-year-certain contracts usually pay 5% to 8% less than straight-life annuities.

• An installment-refund annuity pays back your original investment to your beneficiary if you die. Installment-refund annuities usually pay 4% to 5% less than the straight-life variety.

• A cash-refund annuity works like the installment-refund type, except that your survivor receives the balance of your premium in a lump sum. The advantage is that your beneficiary can reinvest the cash at current rates. The disadvantage is that cash-refund annuities usually pay 1% to 2% less than installment-refund annuities do.

What an Annuity Pays

This table shows the best and worst monthly payouts available for immediate annuities under five options for men and women aged 65 and 75 who invest $100,000.

| Option | Your age and sex | | | |
	65/male	65/female	75/male	75/female
Straight life	$780-$1,080	$705-$935	$1,001-$1,479	$857-$1,208
10-year certain	$521-$949	$712-$891	$903-$1,074	$823-$1,110
20-year certain	$663-$857	$645-$837	$722-$890	$717-$866
Installment refund	$730-$959	$677-$894	$903-$1,140	$818-$1,096
Cash refund	$720-$923	$671-$875	$879-$1,104	$808-$1,020

SOURCE: A.M. BEST CO.

• A joint-and-survivor annuity pays until both you and your beneficiary are dead. The amount of your monthly check is based on your survivor's age as well as your own. Insurers generally offer joint-and-survivor annuities that pay 100%, 67%, or 50% of your monthly benefit to your survivor.

Once you decide on a settlement option, ask two or three insurance agents or brokers for quotes on the type of contract you want. Rates change as often as weekly, so ask for quotes when you're ready to buy. You can get an idea of who pays the highest rates by consulting *Best's Retirement Income Guide,* a reference book available in most public libraries.

Even Houdini could not wriggle out of an annuity contract gone sour. So entrust your nest egg only to an insurer rated A+ or A for financial strength by Best's, particularly if you live in the District of Columbia or one of nine states (Alaska, Arkansas, California, Colorado, Louisiana, New Jersey, Ohio, South Dakota, or Wyoming) with no guaranty associations to make good on contracts issued by life insurers who go bust.

There is one comforting note: Your heirs get a tax break if you die before recovering all the money you invested in an annuity. The unrecovered amount is deductible on the income tax return that your executor files for you after you're gone.

Sizing Up a Company Offer

If you are ready, an early retirement incentive package can be an express ticket to freedom. But be sure it will carry you for life.

For hundreds of thousands of management-level employees, the golden handshake has replaced the gold watch as a token of retirement farewell. Employers see voluntary retirement offers—more formally known as early-retirement incentive packages or "windows" because they are typically available for only a limited time—as an effective and relatively humane way to cut payroll costs.

Though the packages have become somewhat less common now that the mid-1980s wave of corporate downsizing has subsided, a recession could bring them back en masse: nearly a third of the executives queried last year by the American Management Association said they would offer an incentive package next time they needed to shrink their managerial work forces.

For some employees, the packages are a windfall that suddenly fast-forwards the dream of financial independence into one's fifties and early sixties. For others, an early-retirement offer is a temptation all too often accepted in haste and repented at leisure.

One reason is that the packages are complicated and can look more generous than they really are. Worse yet, companies generally give you only a few months to weigh the difficult financial and emotional issues of retirement—adjustments that you might otherwise have made over a period of years.

If an early-retirement offer does show up on your desk, review it with a financial planner or accountant. This is one instance in which the counsel of an experienced financial adviser will be worth every penny it costs. At the same time, however, making a sound decision requires you to ask the right questions of your employer, your adviser—and yourself. Be sure you cover these areas:

Evaluating a package. First, find out the circumstances of the offer. What will happen if you reject it? After all, the incentive window may be the prelude to a reduction in force in which you will be laid off anyway or transferred to a less desirable job. If so, there may be little point in turning down the offer, whether you are ready to retire or not.

To find out what is behind the company's offer, you may have to do some independent sleuthing. Odds are your boss will not make any forecasts of what will happen if you reject the package, especially if the outlook is bleak, for fear of seeming to coerce you into accepting the deal. One clue: Is the offer widely available—say, to all employees 55 and older with 10 years of service—or is it limited to those at one plant or in one department? In general, the narrower the window, the more it presages significant changes for those who remain.

If you determine that you really are free to take the offer or leave it, examine the package itself more closely. The majority of early-retirement incentive offers adjust the company's basic pension formula to give you a higher benefit than you would otherwise receive by retiring early. A basic formula, for example, would reduce your monthly benefit by 5% or so for each year you took off before the plan's normal retirement age, typically 65. An incentive package might reduce or eliminate this early-retirement penalty. That alone could boost the pension available to a 60-year-old early retiree by 33%.

A company might also plug what are known as bonus years into an employee's pension calculation. This spring, for example, Unisys offered to figure early retirees' pensions as if the employees were two years older than they really were and had worked for the company two years longer than they really had. That would have increased the pension of a 60-year-old retiring after 20 years with a salary of around $40,000 by about 25%.

About half the offers include a lump-sum severance payment. That award could be, for example, a flat six months' or one year's salary for everyone who accepts the package. Or it may vary according to your length of service. In a 1986 package, for instance, Hewlett-Packard gave employees 55 and older with more than 15 years' service half a month's salary for each year they had worked for the company.

Some companies also offer a subsidy for retirees under 62, the age at which you can begin collecting Social Security. Under this provision, the company agrees to pay you an amount equal to all or part of your projected Social Security benefit until you are old enough to collect it from the government.

An important but often underrated feature of the most generous packages is continued medical benefits. Federal law already requires your employer to carry you in its group health plan at your expense for at least 18 months after you leave work. But some programs allow you to stay in the plan at the same subsidized rates you received as an employee until Medicare kicks in at age 65. A few companies also extend coverage under their group term life insurance policy until you hit 65, after which benefits begin to taper off, eventually disappearing by age 70.

If you are inclined to accept a package that omits a benefit you would like, ask for it. Terms may be more negotiable than you realize.

To help you evaluate a package, companies typically compare the offer with the benefits to which you would be entitled if you retired now without the incentives. By that standard, most packages look positively magnanimous. But a more useful comparison may be between the package and what you could expect if you stayed in your job as long as you originally intended. That will tell you what you are giving up in return for leaving early. (For an example of such a comparison, see the table on page 176.) And you almost certainly will be sacrificing *something*. No incentive package is going to be as valuable as continuing to earn a paycheck.

There are a couple of reasons for this, none of which your employer is likely to point out.

Taking a Lump Sum

Whether or not you can afford to retire early depends on more than just the munificence of your company's incentive package. No offer, however sweet, can see you through 25 or 30 years of financial independence by itself. You also need some broad-shouldered support from other sources, in particular your 401(k) and other tax-deferred savings plans sponsored by your employer.

The problem is, any amount in such plans that is large enough to fund early retirement is also large enough to start tax collectors salivating. Company-sponsored savings plans— technically called capital-accumulation plans—typically pay your benefit to you in a single grand lump sum. If you had to treat this wad as ordinary income—as you must do with an early-retirement severance check, for example—you could easily end up sharing a third to two-fifths of the money with the feds and your state.

Fortunately, the tax code provides some less wrenching ways to settle up with the tax men. We describe the alternatives below. All of them, however, are mined with penalties and excise taxes, deadlines, and irrevocable choices. So if you have a lump sum coming, seek advice from an accountant or financial planner *before* you retire.

The simplest way to minimize taxes on a lump sum is to roll over the money into an Individual Retirement Account. The principal can then grow tax-free, though you will, of course, pay taxes on any withdrawals plus a 10% penalty if you are under 59½. If you choose to roll over the money, you must complete the transfer within 60 days after you receive the payout.

Generally, if you can leave the money untouched in your IRA for three to five years, the tax-deferred buildup will more than compensate for your having to pay taxes on your withdrawals. But don't let your IRA bulk up too much: If the total distributions from your IRA and other retirement plans exceed $150,000 in any single year, you could be liable for a 15% tax on the excess, in addition to ordinary income tax.

If you decide that you can't afford an IRA rollover, you can reduce the taxes on your money with a special formula called forward averaging, which is reserved for lump-sum distributions from retirement plans. In forward averaging, you figure your tax liability as if you received the money over five years instead of all at once. The technique can significantly lower your tax bill. For example, without forward averaging, a married couple with $30,000 of ordinary income after deductions would pay $74,515 in taxes on a distribution of $250,000. With five-year forward averaging, they would pay $59,218. The benefits of averaging diminish, though, as distributions get larger; for any sum over $465,650, five-year averaging gives you exactly the same tax as the regular one-year calculation.

To use five-year forward averaging, you must generally meet these conditions: your payout must represent your entire interest in the plan; you must have participated in the plan for at least five years; and you must be 59½ or older.

There is one exception to the age requirement. If you were born before January 1, 1936, you can use five-year forward averaging even if you aren't yet 59½. (You may still be liable for the 10% early-withdrawal penalty, however, as explained in the box on page 177.)

Before using five-year averaging, check to make sure you wouldn't be better off using one of two other tax options available only to people born before January 1, 1936. The first is 10-year forward averaging. The basic rules are the same as for the five-year method, except that your sum is taxed as if it were received over 10 years. One twist, though: The tax rates that apply are those that were in effect in 1986, when tax brackets went as high as 50%. The 10-year-averaging treatment saves you more money than five-year averaging on payouts of up to about $474,000; on the $250,000 payout in the example cited earlier, the couple's tax would be only $50,770. With more than $474,000, you should use the five-year method because you then get the benefit of today's lower tax brackets.

The second option available if you were born before January 1, 1936, is a special capital-gains rate that can be applied to the portion of your lump sum that you accumulated prior to 1974. (Your benefits department can tell you exactly

how much that is.) If you are eligible, you can declare that money to be capital gains and pay taxes on it at 20%, which was the maximum capital tax rate in 1986. You can choose either five- or 10-year averaging for the rest of your payout.

To tell which method will provide you the most money in retirement, have your tax adviser run a comparison for you, as in the table below. This is one tax question that is too tricky to answer any other way.

The Best Lump-Sum Option: An IRA

When you take a lump-sum payout from your pension plan, you need to preserve as much of the money as possible from taxes. The impact can be considerable, as demonstrated in the table below. It shows what happens at current tax rates with each of the typical tax options on a $250,000 lump sum paid out to a 60-year-old couple with $30,000 a year of other taxable retirement income. The table assumes that the couple want the money to last until they are 90.

They must decide whether to pay an immediate tax on the money under one of three tax options and invest the balance at 6.8% tax-free in municipal bonds or roll the money over into an Individual Retirement Account, invested at a tax-deferred 9% in a corporate bond fund, and make annual taxable withdrawals. Because of the beneficial effects of tax deferral, the best option is to roll over the money into an IRA and wait five years before pulling any money out.

Option	Initial tax	Initial amount invested	After-tax income at age 60 to 65	After-tax income at age 65 to 90
Lump sum at ordinary tax rates	$75,020	$174,980	$13,819	$13,819
Lump sum with five-year averaging	59,218	190,782	15,067	15,067
Lump sum with 10-year averaging	50,770	199,230	15,734	15,734
IRA rollover (withdrawals start immediately)	0	250,000	17,644	17,644
IRA rollover (no withdrawals for five years)	0	250,000	0	28,319

One is that your 401(k), stock-ownership, and other retirement savings plans stop growing when you retire and the balance is paid to you. At many companies, your annual contributions to these savings plans plus your employer's can easily exceed 10% of your salary. The earnings on your account can also be substantial, depending on the investment performance and the size of your balance. Bountiful as a severance check may seem, it can rarely compete with a few more years' worth of contributions and compounded earnings in your savings plan.

As for your pension, even a sweetened early-retirement payout is likely to look stingy compared with the one you could expect if you continued to work. That's because at early retirement, your pension is likely to be based on the average of what you earned in your most recent three to five years rather than your presumably higher salary in the future. Most likely, not even a generous allocation of bonus years to your pension formula will make up the difference. Suppose, for example, your company's package credits you with five extra years of service—considered a generous bonus. For a 60-year-old covered by a typical pension plan for 25 years, that could increase the pension by as much as 60%. Nevertheless, if you kept on working for five years and received 5% raises annually, your pension would be 110% higher.

Does It Pay to Stay?

Even a generous early-retirement package, such as the hypothetical one outlined below, provides less retirement income than you could get by working until your company's normal retirement age. In this example, a 60-year-old manager with 25 years of service and an annual salary of $50,000 receives an early-retirement offer that includes these sweeteners:

1) Elimination of the early-retirement penalty in his pension formula
2) A two-year pension supplement equal to two-thirds of his Social Security benefit at age 62
3) Five years added to his length of service in calculating his pension

The inducements will boost his early-retirement income to a maximum of $29,800 a year. But even so, his income would still fall short of the $39,100 he would retire on were he to work until age 65, assuming he received raises of $2,000 a year and continued to contribute 3% of his salary to a company-sponsored retirement savings plan such as a 401(k). The reason is two-fold. First, his higher final salary and longer service at age 65 would entitle him to larger benefits from both his pension plan and Social Security. Second, the extra years of savings and compounded tax-deferred growth would lead to a larger payout from his company's savings plan.

INCOME

Age	Retirement at 60* (without package)	Retirement at 60** (with package)	Retirement at 65***
60	$13,500	$26,467	$50,000
61	13,500	26,467	52,000
62	23,500	29,800	54,000
63	23,500	29,800	56,000
64	23,500	29,800	58,000
65	23,500	29,800	39,100

*Consists of a $10,500 pension, $3,000 a year from a 401(k) and, starting at age 62, $10,000 annually from Social Security   **Consists of a $16,800 pension, $3,000 a year from a 401(k), a company-paid $6,667 Social Security supplement through age 61 and $10,000 annually from Social Security thereafter   ***Consists of salary until retirement at 65, a $21,300 pension, $4,800 a year from a 401(k) and $13,000 annually from Social Security thereafter

Source: Kwasha Lipton

Evaluating yourself. After reviewing an incentive package, you may decide that the extra years of leisure are worth the reduced pension. In that case, the critical issue is not how well the package compares with age-65 retirement benefits, but whether it is sufficient to meet your retirement income needs.

To answer that, you have to examine yourself. Think about the standard of living you would need to be content in retirement. Be honest. A lot of people say that they can live at a reduced standard of living in retirement, but

Avoiding the Early Retirement Tax

To most people, early retirement means taking leave of their jobs before 65; not, however, to the writers of the federal tax code. In their obscure wisdom, they have decreed that retirement age begins precisely at 59½. Only then can you get at the savings built up in your tax-deferred retirement accounts, such as your 40l(k), 403(b), IRA, or Keogh, without paying anything more than ordinary income taxes on the withdrawal. Take out a dollar one day sooner than that, and the IRS will slap you with a 10% penalty on top of the tax.

Thus, if you are still on the callow side of 59½, you have to include the early-withdrawal penalty in your evaluation of an early-retirement package. Luckily, there are ways to skate around it:

Roll your money over. The tax collectors can't penalize you if you deposit your retirement payout in an IRA or Keogh within 60 days of receiving it. If you plan to work for another company, you can transfer the money from your IRA or Keogh into your new employer's tax-deferred plan, if its rules permit rollovers. But make sure to keep this IRA or Keogh separate from other accounts if you intend to roll it over; once assets from your former employer's plan are mixed with money in other IRAs or Keoghs, you lose the chance to move the money to a new employer's program. Of course, a rollover makes sense only if you can afford to let the money percolate until you reach 59½.

Withdraw your company-plan money on retirement after age 55. The IRS waives the early-withdrawal penalty on distributions from employer-sponsored plans if you take early retirement after age 55. Unfortunately, this 4½-year grace period applies only to employer plans, such as 401(k)s and 403(b)s, and not to IRAs. One drawback: You can't use forward averaging to cut taxes before age 59½ (see the box on page 174).

Withdraw the money in equal annual installments based on your life expectancy. This is the widest of the escape hatches: it works no matter what your age, and it applies to IRAs and Keoghs as well as to employer plans. Essentially, you avoid the 10% penalty if you take out your money in yearly amounts adjusted according to your life expectancy or your joint life expectancy with a beneficiary (as determined by IRS tables). You have to continue the withdrawals for five years or until you reach age 59½, whichever comes later. After that, you can do whatever you want with your money free from the 10% penalty. You can increase the amount of your annual withdrawals, stop them entirely, or pull the money out all at once. Naturally, you will still have to pay ordinary taxes on it.

Odds are, however, that your employer won't let you withdraw your money piecemeal from the savings plan. Normally, these plans pay out all at once. But no matter: Simply roll over the lump sum into an IRA and make the installment withdrawals from there. Of course, you will still owe income taxes on the installments, and you must forgo forward averaging, since that technique is reserved for lump-sum payouts. Still, if the installment plan helps you get to your retirement money when you need it without a penalty, the price is worth paying.

when it comes time to cut back, they can't. (For help in estimating your living costs in retirement, see the worksheet on page 161.)

If you intend to work after leaving your present job, your incentive package and other savings need not supply all your retirement income. Indeed, many early-retirement offers include out-placement counseling for those tempted to accept the package but not yet ready to leave paid employment. But again, be honest: If you are a scientist or engineer with readily transferable skills, for example, you may have no trouble landing a new job. But if you are a middle manager, you will probably find yourself competing against younger, less expensive workers in the open market, where your former chief strength—your knowledge of your ex-employer's corporate culture— counts for little.

If the package is adequate to pay for your retirement, one question remains, perhaps the most crucial of all: Are you *psychologically* prepared to leave work? Incentive offers tend to arrive without warning, and a two- or three-month window is usually too short to prepare for an entirely new life.

Cashing In on Your Home

While the best way to draw money from your home is still the trade-down, the reverse mortgage is getting to be a better deal than it once was.

Le Corbusier, France's foremost 20th-century architect, called a house "a machine for living." For someone who bought one a decade or more ago, when inflation was bumping up prices at annual rates of 10% or more, a house has also been a machine for making money. As these lucky people approach retirement, they are discovering that their homes can be rich storehouses of cash that can be tapped when they need it.

But these mother lodes aren't quite as rich as they were in the 1970s. Since 1980, house prices nationally have lagged inflation by a third of a percentage point a year. At best, they are expected to beat the general inflation rate by a percentage point a year during the 1990s. The lesson for retirement planning today: Tread cautiously and carry a ready calculator.

By far the best way for house-rich retirees to extract cash from their real estate is by trading down—selling their present homes for ones that cost less. This strategy lowers living expenses, converts some equity into a lump sum that can be invested for income, and leaves a house that can be passed on to heirs. Yet financially savvy as trading down may be, older adults often find it emotionally unacceptable. Surveys by the American Association of Retired Persons and others show that most older adults want to stay in their own homes and neighborhoods, close to friends and relatives. If you are in this immobile majority, you may be able to turn to a reverse mortgage, which lets you pull cash from your home while you still live in it. Consider the choices:

Trading down. Begin planning a trade-down far enough ahead so that you can be sure to squeeze the maximum return from your prime asset. Unloading your house when prices are escalating and sellers have the upper hand not only improves your odds of getting top dollar, but also means selling in six to seven weeks versus as long as a year.

Right now, for instance, is a difficult time to sell in most places in the U.S. While the pace of home sales can vary dramatically by city—even by neighborhood—the housing market overall was sluggish in 1989. Sales by mid-summer 1989 were down 6.8% nationally compared with the same period in 1988. But with mortgage rates on a downward drift—the rate on 30-year loans fell from 10.6% in June 1989 to 9.8% in August—the balance of power already began to shift from buyers to sellers in August, when sales inched upward 3.3% from July.

In addition to timing the sale of your old house correctly, thorough long-range planning requires you to research the living costs as well as recreational and entertainment opportunities of the place where you are thinking of resettling. The best way is to use vacation time to test locales where you might want to live.

Paying cash for a new house is usually wise in a trade-down since it frees you from the yoke of carrying a mortgage on a reduced income. Also, unless your combined federal and state tax bracket is 33% or higher, allowing hefty deductions for mortgage interest payments, you might have to put the profit from selling your old house into risky, high-yield investments to produce income needed for mortgage payments. In the retirement stage of your life, you want predictability, not volatility.

If you can spare part of your profit, you might consider taking back a mortgage from the buyer of your old house. This way you convert your house to both cash and income. Ask for at least a 20% down payment, but consider such an arrangement only if the down payment exceeds your loan balance. Otherwise, you would have to dip into savings to pay off your mortgage. And by charging a competitive interest rate—10% or so for a fixed-rate loan—you earn more than you would on other low-risk investments.

If you or your spouse is over 55, you can cut your tax bill by excluding from taxes as much as $125,000 of the gain from the sale of the house. To qualify for the one-time exclusion, you must have lived in the house as your principal residence for at least three of the preceding five years. Exception: You need have lived there a total of only one if you spent the remaining four in a hospital or nursing home. If you are in the 28% tax bracket, the maximum exclusion would save you $35,000 in taxes.

The best way to prosper in a trade-down is to sell in an expensive market and buy in a cheap one. To find a suitable locale for your retirement, you can consult *Retirement Places Rated* (Prentice Hall, $14.95), which gives the living costs—including median house prices—in 131 cities.

Reverse mortgages. For homeowners who prefer to stay put, the challenge is to find ways of mining the equity in a home while continuing to live in it. One increasingly popular strategy is the reverse mortgage loan, which usually pays you a fixed monthly sum but postpones repayment of both the principal and interest until you move or die, in which case your estate repays the loan. With some reverse mortgages you can also set up a line of credit that allows you to draw additional funds for emergencies or other unexpected expenses.

Borrowers can either receive payments for the rest of their lives—with what is known as a life tenure reverse mortgage—or for a specific term, generally five to 20 years. A term loan is usually appropriate only if you plan to sell your house when the loan comes due, perhaps to move into a retirement community.

Your monthly stipend from either kind of reverse mortgage depends on the amount of equity you have in your home and the loan's term—the shorter the term, the higher your payments. With a life tenure loan, the payments are based on your life expectancy. For example, a 75-year-old who owns a $100,000 house with no mortgage could receive a monthly payment as high as $534 under the plan offered by Providential Home Income Plan of San Francisco.

You should consider a reverse mortgage only if you expect to stay in your home at least five years. Such mortgages are also extremely expensive for small amounts of money—say,

Where the Living is Easy and Taxes are Low

For 15 years, Howard Smith and his wife, Nancy, both in their sixties, never regretted retiring from smoggy Los Angeles to the sweet piney air, fabled salmon fishing, and easier cost of living of rural Washington State. They certainly didn't miss California's stiff income tax (top rate: 9.3%). Then, in 1989, the state of California blindsided the Smiths with a $1,157 tax bill on Howard's $26,000-a-year pension from the Los Angeles Police Department. While the Smiths protest the bill through repeated letters and phone calls, California has slapped them with a 50% penalty on the unpaid tax for failure to file and for lateness. Meanwhile, the bill grows at an interest rate of 10% a year. The state even told the couple it could put a lien on their house unless they paid up. Moral: When you retire, don't move to another state without first investigating the tax consequences. Most states publish tax guides for retirees, available by calling the state department of revenue. You should also ask your accountant how a move might affect your state-tax liability. Include the following in your research:

Your income. Only seven states impose no personal income tax: Alaska, Florida, Nevada, South Dakota, Texas, Washington, and Wyoming. Two others—New Hampshire and Tennessee—tax just dividends and interest. Connecticut taxes dividends, interest, and capital gains. But as the Smiths' experience shows, you can't always escape state income tax by relocating to one of these tax havens. California and at least four other states—Iowa, Montana, New Jersey, and Oregon—tax all or part of pensions accrued there, reasoning that pension income is taxable where earned, regardless of where you currently live. In what may come as an even ruder surprise, Social Security benefits that are subject to federal income tax are also taxed in 13 states.

Lastly, only the District of Columbia and three states—Indiana, New Mexico, and Utah— exempt interest from municipal bonds issued in another state from income tax. (North Dakota taxes the interest if you file the state's long form; Vermont exempts the first $5,000 of interest income for taxpayers aged 62 or older.) But before you rush to cash in your bonds, ask your accountant to figure out the tax consequences; one important matter to consider, for example, is that capital gains on munis are subject to tax at the federal level as well as in most states.

Your property. Because taxes on real estate vary dramatically within each state, ask a local real estate agent to project the tax liability on your new home. Be sure to find out whether rates or assessments are expected to rise soon. Many localities also tax tangible personal property, such as cars and boats. Again, ask the city or county assessor about rates. Some states will tax your intangible personal property as well. For example, Florida charges an annual levy of 0.1% of the fair market value of intangibles such as stocks and bonds, after an exemption of $40,000 if you are married and filing jointly, $20,000 if you are single.

Your estate. Twenty-five states impose estate or inheritance taxes of their own, which may expose even a modest estate to death taxes. Have an attorney in the state to which you want to move review your wills and trusts to make sure they conform to the state's laws. Should your estate plan call for making tax-free gifts, be aware that gift taxes are levied by seven states— Delaware, Louisiana, New York, North and South Carolina, Tennessee, and Wisconsin.

If you plan to maintain homes in two states, the tax complications can be Byzantine. To avoid having both states attempt to tax your entire estate, you must establish one state as your domicile. You can do that by living there for more than half of the year, transferring your bank accounts, changing your motor vehicle and voter registrations, and joining community organizations.

less than $10,000. In addition to yearly interest—typically 9.5% to 11.5%—some lenders charge so-called risk premiums of 2% to 7% of the house's value; like points on a regular mortgage, the premiums are charged up front. Other lenders take all or part of any appreciation in the value of your house that occurs after signing for the loan. As a result, the effective interest rate on a small loan or on one that is repaid in a few years is downright usurious, in some cases well over 100% a year.

In general, the longer the term of the loan and the less your home appreciates, the lower the effective interest rate you pay. For example, under Providential's program, at a 10% home-appreciation rate, the effective annual average interest rate is 18% on a 14-year loan. That rate drops to 7% if your house appreciates at just 5% and the loan term extends to 18 years.

Though reverse mortgages are still relatively scarce—only 4,000 or so have been made to date—borrowers may soon have a wide assortment of lenders to choose from. In a demonstration program that will run to September 30, 1991, the Federal Housing Administration is insuring 2,500 such loans made by private lenders. Unfortunately, demand has been so great that most lenders now have long waiting lists. That could change, however, now that legislation has been introduced in Congress to allow the FHA to boost the number of insured loans to 25,000. (For the names of lenders in your area that plan to offer FHA-backed loans, call the FHA at 800-245-2691.)

As more lenders offer such loans, Ken Scholen, Director of the National Center for Home Equity Conversion in Madison, Wisconsin, predicts that competition among lenders will eventually drive rates on FHA-backed reverse mortgages below those on conventional mortgages.

You might find that you are better off with a reverse mortgage that is not insured by the FHA. Reason: The maximum monthly payments on FHA reverse mortgages are linked to that agency's mortgage ceilings, which typically ranged from $67,500 to $101,250 in 1989. As a result, the top payment on a life tenure reverse mortgage at 10% for a 75-year-old ranged from $240 to $360. Homeowners whose equity exceeds the FHA ceilings may be better off with the bigger payments from non-FHA mortgages.

Good Coverage is the Best Policy

While Medicare may take care of nearly half your medical bills, paying the rest could be up to you. Here's how to make sure you are protected.

For an idea of your employer-paid health insurance coverage in retirement, consider what it is now. Chances are your company has been tinkering with your medical benefits lately, adding an option here, a cost there, forcing you to plan more and pay more. That's what retirement will hold—only much more so, as health-care costs continue to spin out of control. Says Harold Dankner, a partner at the accounting firm Coopers & Lybrand: "It's unrealistic for today's workers to expect anywhere near the benefits that current pensioners receive." His discomfiting prediction: "An employee at mid-career may get only half that coverage. He may get nothing."

Well, okay, you may say. There's always Medicare. True, but not until you're 65, which is no help if you retire early. Besides, Medicare pays only about half of a patient's total medical expenses. And you'll still need a way to take care of bills that Medicare doesn't cover.

Fortunately, at retirement you'll have lots of choices. You can buy private insurance, join a health maintenance organization, or move to a residential community that provides medical services. But the quality and price of these alternatives vary widely, so the smartest thing you can do in the last few years before retirement is to study the options to make sure you'll make the right choices.

Here's what everyone, no matter how far from retirement, should know:

Company coverage. If you're only a couple of years from retirement, your employer's benefits department may be able to give you a reasonable idea of the coverage you can expect. For employees of large corporations, that should be nearly as much as they now receive. If you're several years away, though, assume you'll get less.

Reductions are likely to be proportionate to your age. When Armstrong World Industries in Lancaster, Pennsylvania announced in June 1989 that it would no longer pay premiums on its group health plan for workers retiring after year's end, those older than 48 got a partial reprieve. Depending on their present age, when they retire they will pay 7% to 93% of premium costs, now $1,247 a year. Younger workers will have to pay all their premiums themselves or find their own insurance, which probably will cost them more and cover less than the company's group policy. To cushion the loss of coverage, Armstrong World will give its current employees company stock; the number of shares will depend on their ages and years of service. New hires will have to find coverage on their own after they retire.

Even if you have to pick up the whole tab, staying in a group plan is usually your best bet. Group rates are generally about 20% less than the cost of individual policies, and you don't have to pass any physical exams or wait to be covered for pre-existing conditions. And the coverage will probably be better than what you could buy on your own.

If you know you won't have company coverage as an early retiree, you may want to consider putting off your departure until age 65. Then Medicare will be the backbone of your protection against medical costs, no matter how much—or how little—coverage your company provides. Any company benefits you have will be coordinated with Medicare, providing protection against the gaps in its coverage.

Early retirees without company benefits will have to find coverage on their own. Federal regulations, however, stipulate that your employer must let you or your under-65 spouse stay on the company plan for at least 18 months, at your expense, typically $110 a month.

Individual coverage. If you have to go it on your own, expect to pay a lot. The policy you'll need, called comprehensive major-medical insurance, will cover most of your bills, including ones from your doctors, hospitals, and labs. The price? Consider Aetna's AetnaCare Xtra. In 1989, it cost a 62-year-old man and his 60-year-old wife an average of $5,950 a year, with a $1,000 yearly cap on their out-of-pocket expenses above a deductible of $500 each. Not-for-profit Blue Cross may be cheaper—a similar policy might cost $3,600 or so a year—but in parts of the country where medical costs are highest, premiums have been running about the same for Blue Cross as for commercial carriers.

You can reduce premiums by assuming more of the risk yourself. One way is to ask for the highest deductible you can afford. For instance, by doubling deductibles on the Aetna policy, you could reduce the annual premium to $4,367. Or you can buy a policy that covers only serious illnesses. One such policy, Prudential's Pru-Med, pays specified amounts for hospital, surgical, and other major expenses but provides benefits for lesser services, such as office visits to a doctor, only when your out-of-pocket costs exceed $1,000. The price of the policy depends on the maximum reimbursements you choose for daily hospital charges ($175 to $300) and surgical fees ($3,000 to $6,000). The higher the potential payback, the higher the cost. For maximum coverage, a 60-year-old of either sex would pay Pru-Med about $2,000 a year with a $300 deductible.

HMOs. As a less expensive alternative to insurance, you can join a health maintenance organization (HMO), which will provide most medical services for a flat monthly fee. In return for the greater coverage, you must patronize doctors, hospitals, and labs that have contracts with your HMO.

HMOs cover nearly 100% of your costs, usually with no deductibles or partial payments required from you. The organizations often wind up costing you less than comprehensive medical insurance would. In 1988, a typical HMO monthly premium was less than $100 for individuals under 65. About half of HMOs accept applicants over 65, and Medicare picks up most of the monthly fee. You'll owe only $30 or so a month for extras not covered by Medicare, like eyeglasses and hearing aids.

A study released in 1989 by the federal Health Care Financing Administration, which supervises Medicare, concluded that older people are more likely to receive top-quality care at HMOs than from practitioners with no connection to one another. The reasons: continuity and comprehensiveness of care.

Medigap insurance. If you're not in an HMO, and your company coverage is inadequate or nonexistent, you may want to buy Medigap insurance to supplement Medicare. There are two kinds of Medigap policies. The most common type pays only your share of costs covered by Medicare.

The second, more valuable type of Medigap policy pays excess charges for doctor bills and lab tests—meaning the charges that exceed Medicare's limits. Though these policies are sometimes no more expensive than the first type, they may require you to have an above-average medical history. For example, National Home Life of Valley Forge,

Pennsylvania rejects 10% to 15% of all applicants for health reasons, and Golden Rule in Indianapolis turns down 20% to 30% of those age 65 and nearly half of those 70 and older. Both companies sell competitively priced policies that cover excess fees. Home Life charges a 70-year-old woman $299 to $575 a year, depending on where she lives. A man the same age pays $359 to $671. A 70-year-old of either sex pays $579 a year for Golden Rule's policy in most parts of the U.S. By comparison, policies sold by Blue Cross in North Carolina and Maryland cost more than $700 and cover no excess charges.

There are several excellent consumer guides to Medigap coverage. Among the best are *The Consumer's Guide to Medicare Supplement Insurance* (free from the Health Insurance Association of America, P.O. Box 41455, Washington, D.C. 20018) and *Managing Your Health Care Finances* ($7.95 from United Seniors Health Cooperative, 1334 G Street NW, Washington, D.C. 20005).

Long-term care coverage. Neither Medicare nor Medigap insurance will be of much use if you need long-term care in a nursing home. Both cover only skilled nursing after illness or injury, not the custodial care required for deterioration caused by aging. With average annual costs at a nursing home topping $20,000, lengthy care could destroy a couple's financial security. As a result, more than 100 insurers now sell long-term-care policies to cover some of the cost of a stay in a nursing home and, sometimes, of care in your own home.

Sales of these policies have shot up 200% over the past two years, but panic, not prudence, may be motivating most people. For younger or healthier people, insurance may not be worth the cost.

Coverage is expensive—$300 to $400 a year for those in their fifties, $2,000 to $3,200 for those in their late seventies, depending on the amount of coverage—and no policy is comprehensive. For instance, most require that you be ill or injured before they'll pay, though physical frailty, not illness or injury, is the main reason for needing long-term care. Only a few companies—Travelers, Unum, and Mutual of

Omaha among them—offer coverage for care required by disability alone, and those policies are the most costly, up to $5,000 a year for a 75-year-old of either sex. Any policy worth buying covers Alzheimer's patients.

Another problem is inflation. The policies almost always pay only indemnity benefits—fixed daily amounts that don't rise with costs over the years. With nursing-home expenses climbing 5.5% a year, a typical benefit of $80 a day, adequate for nursing-home costs today, would cover less than two-thirds of them in 10 years and just a third in 20 years. Some policies have inflation riders that let you bump up the amount of your benefit by a few percentage points for a corresponding increase in your premium. But no policies have inflation riders that keep benefits entirely abreast of inflation.

Currently, three of the largest and most reliable insurers—Aetna, John Hancock, and Amex Life Assurance—offer high-quality policies with similar benefits of $80 per day. Hancock charges a 70-year-old $1,441 a year for six years of coverage, and Aetna asks the same person for $1,552 for only four years. Amex prices lifetime coverage at $1,134. The bottom line is, read every word and learn what to look for. You can get some help from *Long-Term Care: A Dollar and Sense Guide* ($6.95 from United Seniors Health Cooperative) and *The Consumers Guide to Long-Term Care Insurance* (free from the Health Insurance Association of America).

Continuing-care communities. If you are over 60 and in good health, you can cover all your health-care needs by spending the rest of your life in one of the country's 800 continuing-care retirement communities, also called life-care communities. Residents get private apartments and services such as housekeeping, meals, and medical care, including nursing-home care, as needed. Some communities exact a flat entrance fee—generally about $37,000 to $100,000, depending on the size of the apartment—and $730 to $1,100 a month for maintenance, meals, and health care. Residents receive whatever services they need at no additional cost. Other communities charge less—typically entrance fees of $27,000 to $85,000 and $650 to $750 a month—but residents must pay extra for services beyond the minimum specified in their contracts. For instance, a contract might limit home health care to 60 days or require residents to pay 80% of the cost of care in the community's nursing home. Communities with the lowest entrance and monthly fees—$21,000 to $56,000 and $570 to $690—usually charge extra for each service.

If you move to a community with separate fees for all or some services, you may still need Medigap and long-term-care insurance. The policies may be offered at group rates to residents and be 15% to 25% cheaper than if you bought them on your own. Increasingly, entrance fees at continuing-care communities are at least partially refundable if you change your mind at any time. Some communities refund all or part of the entrance fees to the estate upon a resident's death.

It's wise to make sure that there are no blemishes on the record of a facility you are considering; call or write the attorney general of the state in which the community is located. Accreditation sponsored by the American Association of Homes for the Aging, a trade group, is another indicator of sound management. But accreditation is voluntary, and only about 70 communities have met the standards so far. For a free list of accredited facilities, write AAHA, 1129 20th Street NW, Washington, D.C. 20036. For $4, you can also get the AAHA's guide to choosing a continuing-care community.

Mutual Fund Rankings

For most fund investors, the five years to June 22, 1989 have been like an Indiana Jones movie. There were quite a few close shaves: Remember those chilling scenes in October 1987 or, for bond fund investors, in the spring of that year as interest rates rose? But, like Indy himself, stock and bond fund players somehow not only survived but also prospered. Though the average stock and government bond fund failed to keep pace with the popular investment indexes, their five-year compound annual returns—16.1% and 11.8%, respectively—were generous by historical standards. The gains during those five years—an appropriate period for investment strategizing—weren't spread equally among all funds or fund groups, of course. A newsreel of performance thrills and spills might include:

Most stunning reversal. The top five-year gainer, Merrill Lynch Pacific (up 282%), logged the worst 1989 performance of any stock fund, losing 9.9% through June 22, the cutoff date for *Money*'s stock and taxable bond fund rankings. As a group, international stock funds, up 199.6%, led all categories during the five-year period. But, largely because a rising dollar cut into the value of their foreign holdings, they showed a puny 1989 gain of 4% through June 22, placing them next to last among the 20 fund subsets that *Money* followed.

Unlikeliest superstars. Moderate-risk growth and income funds posted a five-year gain of 124.8%, the best among all domestic stock fund groups. This normally solid but middle-of-the-pack category rode the stock market's blue-chip bull to nifty gains. But the U.S. market's dramatic rise in the first half of 1989 favored the bold. Growth funds (up 18% through June 22) and maximum-capital-gains funds (up 19.1%) turned in the best results of any categories. The hottest fund: gains-oriented Delaware Trend, up 38%.

Worst performance. Gold funds won this dubious five-year honor pans down. The glitter group rose just 9.5%—and that's *total*, not average annual, return. The worst individual performance was claimed by the Strategic Investments gold fund, down 57.5%.

The following pages of stock and bond fund rankings and alphabetical listings represent *Money*'s most comprehensive record of fund performance ever. Not only does this effort cover more funds—900, to be precise—but it also provides additional information to help you X-ray those you've either invested in or are considering. Starting on page 186 are rankings of the top funds in each of 20 stock, taxable bond, and tax-exempt bond fund categories for the five years through mid-1989. If a fund you're interested in doesn't rank among the top performers, you're likely to find it in the alphabetical listings, which begin on page 194.

The most direct way to see how a fund has fared is to look at its **percent gain (or loss) to June 22, 1989**. For an idea of how much a top-performing fund averaged annually, check out the **percent compound annual return**. But don't stop with either of these measures. Did the fund's performance justify the risks it took? To find out, examine the *Money*

risk-adjusted rating for each fund. Based on a formula developed by Stanford University finance professor William Sharpe, the rating rewards funds for high total returns and punishes them for nerve-testing volatility (defined here as the amount by which a fund's month-to-month returns deviated from its average monthly returns).

Armed with this tool, you can readily choose among funds that have delivered comparable gains in the past few years. If two funds scored similar total returns but have different risk-adjusted ratings, the one that subjected shareholders to fewer bumps was the more efficient investment. For purposes of this rating, tax-exempt bond funds compete with other tax-exempts; taxable bond entries with other taxables; and stock funds with similarly deployed portfolios. Specialized stock funds—namely, international and global funds as well as gold and sector funds—compete among themselves in two customized groupings.

To get the highest rating (★), a fund must rank in the top 10%; a ☆ goes to the upper-middle 20%; a ● to the middle 40%; a ○ to the lower-middle 20%; and a □ to the bottom 10%. A few very volatile top performers, like Scudder Capital Growth (the No. 2 stock fund overall), scored high risk-adjusted ratings by posting gains big enough to compensate for sharp setbacks along the way. An investor seeking to sidestep unpleasant surprises should check a fund's **five-year analysis**, which tells you how much the fund gained or lost during its best and worst quarters for the period that ended March 31, 1989.

Few investment strategies work well in all market conditions, and you can check for inconsistent results in the **Lipper Market Phase Rating**. It grades the top-performing stock and taxable bond funds during three distinct investment periods: the current phase (defined by Lipper Analytical as December 3, 1987 to June 22, 1989); the prior *up* phase (July 26, 1984 to August 20, 1987); and the

THE TOP PERFORMERS: TAX-EXEMPT BOND FUNDS

Ranked by five-year performance	Money risk-adjusted rating	% gain (or loss) to June 1, 1989				% compound annual return		Five-year analysis		Portfolio analysis		
		1989	Three years	Five years	10 years	Five years	10 years	Best quarter	Worst quarter	% yield	% rated A or better	Average maturity (years)
HIGH-YIELD TAX-EXEMPTS		**5.0**	**27.0**	**80.5**	**136.4**	**11.9**	**8.6**			**7.6**		
1. Vanguard Muni–High Yield	☆	6.1	31.9	100.1	113.1	14.1	7.6	9.8	(5.9)	7.2	60.0	17.9
2. SteinRoe High-Yield Munis	★	5.4	31.9	99.8	—	14.1	—	9.1	(4.3)	7.4	42.7	17.1
3. Fidelity High Yield Munis	☆	6.5	28.2	95.4	120.6	13.6	8.0	9.4	(5.9)	7.0	71.7	23.4
4. IDS High Yield Tax-Exempt	●	5.6	29.8	88.9	128.6	12.9	8.4	10.6	(4.9)	7.4	61.0	21.1
5. Merrill Lynch Muni–High Yield A	●	4.4	28.9	87.4	—	12.8	—	9.6	(4.4)	7.5	79.0	21.5
6. GIT Tax-Free High Yield	○	3.3	23.8	75.1	—	11.4	—	10.6	(4.1)	6.7	57.2	17.0
7. Mass. Fin. Managed High Yield*	●	5.5	24.3	72.6	—	11.1	—	6.3	(1.5)	8.3	29.7	20.0
HIGH-GRADE TAX-EXEMPTS		**5.1**	**27.7**	**88.9**	**111.4**	**12.9**	**7.5**			**6.9**		
1. United Municipal Bond	★	5.6	34.0	105.1	100.9	14.6	7.0	11.3	(6.5)	6.7	90.0	27.5
2. Financial Tax-Free Income Shares	☆	6.5	31.8	105.1	—	14.6	—	12.1	(7.5)	6.8	74.0	26.4
3. Delaware Grp. Tax-Free–USA	★	5.7	32.5	104.4	—	14.6	—	10.4	(6.2)	7.3	52.0	25.1
4. Seligman Tax-Exempt–National	★	5.2	31.1	104.3	—	14.6	—	10.8	(5.7)	6.8	76.4	23.5
5. Mutual of Omaha Tax-Free Inc.	☆	5.3	33.8	102.4	101.9	14.4	7.1	10.4	(6.0)	6.9	86.5	23.0
6. SteinRoe Managed Municipal	☆	4.9	30.3	100.9	138.0	14.2	8.8	12.2	(4.6)	6.6	84.3	18.0
7. Safeco Municipal Bond	☆	5.1	33.5	99.4	—	14.0	—	9.8	(4.2)	7.0	69.0	21.7
INTERMEDIATE-TERM TAX-EXEMPTS		**3.0**	**20.9**	**53.3**	**93.9**	**8.6**	**6.7**			**6.4**		
1. Vanguard Muni–Intermediate	●	4.8	28.2	79.0	90.0	11.8	6.5	7.4	(3.6)	6.8	83.0	9.5
2. Fidelity Limited Term Muni	○	3.4	23.3	70.3	105.0	10.8	7.2	7.4	(3.6)	6.6	92.3	10.8
3. USAA Tax Exempt–Intermediate	○	4.6	25.1	69.3	—	10.7	—	6.5	(2.8)	8.1	90.0	9.2
4. Dreyfus Intermed.-Term Tax Ex.	○	3.9	24.4	65.9	—	10.3	—	6.7	(2.8)	7.2	91.0	8.6
5. Scudder Tax-Free Target–1993	○	2.7	19.8	60.2	—	9.5	—	6.2	(2.1)	6.0	82.0	3.9
6. Scudder Tax-Free Target–1990	○	2.3	17.1	48.4	—	8.0	—	4.6	(1.5)	5.5	80.8	1.0
7. USAA Tax Exempt–Short Term	□	2.9	18.3	42.4	—	7.1	—	3.5	(0.3)	7.2	86.0	2.3
SHEARSON LEHMAN HUTTON MUNI INDEX		**5.2**	**29.5**	**92.4**	**131.8**	**14.0**	**9.3**			**7.8**		

*Currently closed to new investors

prior *down* phase (August 20, 1987 to December 3, 1987). For each market phase, the top 20% of funds in each of 11 stock categories and in the taxable bond group earned an A rating; the next 20%, a B; and so on to E, the rating assigned to the lowest 20%.

The **portfolio analysis** section of the tables profiles each fund's management approach. For both stock and bond funds, note the **percent yield** and **percent cash**. Stock funds with above-average yields tend to be conservative; for bond funds, the opposite is often true. A high cash level of 10% or more often reflects a defensive stance that can cut risks—and returns. For stock funds, there's also a **price/earnings ratio**—the higher the P/E ratio, the greater generally are the potential pitfalls and rewards. For bond funds, check the **average maturity**, which indicates the typical term of the issues in the portfolio. The lengthier that figure, the more shareholders stand to lose if interest rates rise—and the more they will gain if rates fall. For the top-performing tax-free

bond funds, the column headed **percent A-rated or better** indicates how heavily the fund invests in high-quality debt. The column marked **senior fund manager, age (years managing fund)** tells you whether the individual who built the fund's record is still on the job.

No amount of study can guarantee that you'll choose the most rewarding fund. But the **expense analysis** section will turn up funds that provide a solid headstart by keeping costs down. It shows the **percent maximum initial sales charge**, the load that many funds deduct from a shareholder's original investment. The **five-year projection** of expenses tells the total amount you will pay in sales charges and operating expenses, assuming you invest $1,000 at an annual return of 5%, reinvest all dividends and capital gains, and sell your shares after five years. A fund's **percent turnover** is also worth noting. If annual turnover is unusually high—say, 200% or more—commission costs and tax liabilities on transactions are likely to nibble at future gains.

Net assets (millions)	Senior fund manager, age (years managing fund)	% turnover	Expense analysis % maximum initial sales charge	Five-year projection	Minimum initial investment	Telephone Toll-free (800)	In state
						◀ CATEGORY AVERAGE	
$830.3	Ian A. MacKinnon, 41 (7)	40	None	$16	$3,000	662-7447	—
270.8	Thomas Conlin, 35 (5)	53	None	42	1,000	338-2550	—
1,686.8	Guy E. Wickwire, 41 (7)	47	None	40	1,000	544-6666	—
4,309.8	Kurt A. Larson, 49 (10)	13	5.0	82	2,000	328-8300	—
1,521.0	Vincent Giordano, 44 (9)	73	4.0	70	1,000	637-3863	—
40.6	Rick Gunn, 41 (4)	77	None	64	1,000	336-3063	—
457.4	Robin Huntley, 41 (5)	23	4.75	82	250	225-2606	617-954-5000 (Mass.)
						◀ CATEGORY AVERAGE	
570.2	John M. Holliday, 54 (8)	225	4.25	74	500	—	816-283-4122
141.0	William Veronda, 43 (5)	41	None	43	250	525-8085	—
492.1	J. Michael Pokorny, 50 (5)	25	4.75	88	1,000	523-4640	215-988-1333 (Pa.)
140.0	Thomas Moles, 47 (6)	41	4.75	91	1,000	221-2450	800-522-6869 (N.Y.)
343.4	Mark L. Winter, 37 (3)	73	8.0	113	1,000	228-9596	800-642-8112 (Neb.)
504.3	David Snowbeck, 46 (12)	28	None	36	1,000	338-2550	—
250.8	Stephen C. Bauer, 44 (8)	72	None	34	1,000	426-6730	800-562-6810 (Wash.)
						◀ CATEGORY AVERAGE	
939.2	Ian A. MacKinnon, 41 (7)	89	None	16	3,000	662-7447	—
427.5	John F. Haley Jr., N.A. (4)	30	None	41	2,500	544-6666	—
422.7	Kenneth E. Willmann, 43 (7)	139	None	31	3,000	531-8000	—
1,056.0	Monica Wieboldt, 38 (4)	49	None	41	2,500	645-6561	—
75.5	Donald C. Carleton, 54 (6)	54	None	44	1,000	225-2470	—
64.9	Donald C. Carleton, 54 (6)	31	None	44	1,000	225-2470	—
251.1	Steven D. Harrop, 40 (1)	148	None	31	3,000	531-8000	—

Key to rating symbols: ★ = Top 10% ☆ = Next 20% ● = Middle 40% ○ = Next 20% □ = Bottom 10%

Gains or losses are with all dividends reinvested.

THE TOP PERFORMERS: STOCK FUNDS

Ranked by five-year performance	Money risk-adjusted rating	% gain (or loss) to June 22, 1989				% compound annual return		Five-year analysis		Lipper market phase rating			assets (million)
		1989	Three years	Five years	10 years	Five years	10 years	Best quarter	Worst quarter	Current	Prior up	Prior down	
MAXIMUM CAPITAL GAINS		**19.1**	**33.6**	**118.6**	**440.9**	**15.8**	**17.0**						
1. Putnam Voyager	☆	24.4	46.2	173.2	484.8	20.6	18.1	24.3	(20.2)	B	A	C	$679
2. Pacific Horizon–Aggr. Growth	●	28.8	24.4	168.4	—	20.2	—	39.3	(20.1)	E	A	B	97
3. SteinRoe Special	☆	24.9	51.5	159.4	549.2	19.5	19.2	19.3	(19.5)	A	B	C	275
4. Neuberger & Berman Manhattan	☆	19.8	40.6	156.3	528.0	19.3	18.8	21.5	(26.0)	B	A	D	410
5. AIM Constellation	●	23.7	42.3	155.1	510.0	19.2	18.5	36.1	(26.9)	A	A	E	100
6. Twentieth Century Growth	●	30.4	43.9	150.9	576.0	18.8	19.6	32.0	(27.3)	C	A	E	1,427
7. Oppenheimer Time	☆	21.2	41.1	149.6	471.5	18.7	17.8	24.1	(19.6)	B	B	C	323
8. Lehman Opportunity	☆	19.5	46.6	149.3	505.0	18.7	18.4	16.2	(19.5)	B	C	A	114
9. Shearson Lehman Aggr. Growth	●	30.4	42.9	146.3	—	18.4	—	34.9	(23.7)	A	B	E	90
10. Keystone America Omega	●	17.6	39.5	144.5	232.8	18.3	12.2	26.9	(19.4)	B	A	D	37
GROWTH		**18.0**	**33.2**	**116.6**	**376.3**	**15.5**	**15.4**						
1. Fidelity Magellan	★	21.8	48.0	202.1	1,251.3	22.7	26.9	22.9	(24.7)	A	A	D	10,808
2. Scudder Capital Growth	★	29.6	62.6	184.6	499.0	21.5	18.3	18.5	(24.2)	A	B	D	815
3. IAI Regional	★	16.8	40.8	172.9	—	20.6	—	17.0	(16.0)	B	A	A	112
4. New York Venture	★	20.9	52.3	172.0	590.2	20.5	19.8	19.1	(18.4)	A	A	B	299
5. Guardian Park Avenue	☆	17.3	37.2	165.4	513.5	20.0	18.6	23.7	(20.6)	A	A	C	157
6. AIM Weingarten	☆	19.4	38.1	165.1	657.9	20.0	20.8	23.9	(21.8)	B	A	D	347
7. Thomson McKinnon–Growth	☆	26.7	53.4	162.8	—	19.8	—	23.0	(21.3)	C	A	C	359
8. Boston Co. Capital Appreciation	★	15.7	43.1	161.6	366.6	19.7	15.7	16.8	(19.8)	B	A	B	550
9. Fidelity Destiny I	☆	19.6	49.5	161.3	557.3	19.7	19.3	22.2	(24.2)	A	A	E	1,701
10. New Economy	☆	21.6	43.8	161.1	—	19.7	—	18.1	(19.6)	B	A	B	799
GROWTH & INCOME		**15.1**	**37.2**	**124.8**	**353.9**	**16.4**	**15.2**						
1. Vanguard Windsor*	★	15.4	56.1	180.0	558.8	21.1	19.3	16.3	(18.6)	A	A	C	7,670
2. Fundamental Investors	☆	18.1	46.3	160.9	421.0	19.6	16.9	20.9	(22.2)	B	A	E	724
3. Washington Mutual Investors	☆	18.0	46.5	160.4	486.2	19.6	18.1	16.9	(19.0)	B	A	C	3,428
4. Selected American Shares	★	19.7	45.5	159.9	389.7	19.6	16.2	16.1	(19.1)	A	B	C	341
5. Mutual Qualified*	★	12.7	62.7	156.1	—	19.2	—	15.5	(16.3)	A	D	A	1,453
6. Merrill Lynch Basic Value A	★	13.0	49.3	156.0	467.8	19.2	17.7	15.3	(18.2)	A	B	B	1,770
7. Investment Co. of America	★	17.4	44.0	154.6	422.2	19.1	16.9	17.5	(18.8)	C	A	B	4,810
8. Mutual Shares*	★	12.9	60.5	153.6	528.6	19.0	18.8	14.7	(16.3)	A	D	A	3,305
9. Merrill Lynch Phoenix A*	★	11.1	51.9	149.8	—	18.7	—	16.9	(18.6)	A	C	B	280
10. Merrill Lynch Capital A	★	12.4	41.7	149.3	428.5	18.7	17.0	16.0	(15.9)	C	B	B	803
EQUITY INCOME		**12.6**	**31.6**	**119.2**	**369.6**	**15.9**	**15.5**						
1. United Income	★	18.1	52.5	183.9	456.7	21.4	17.5	22.6	(11.2)	A	A	C	1,399
2. Vanguard High Yield Stock*	★	9.1	43.0	166.6	562.4	20.1	19.4	17.6	(16.0)	B	A	C	168
3. Delaware Group–Decatur I	☆	16.1	52.4	151.2	451.1	18.8	17.4	16.5	(18.9)	A	A	E	1,800
4. Financial Industrial Income	☆	16.9	38.2	141.8	400.0	18.0	16.4	17.6	(17.0)	B	A	D	408
5. National Total Income	★	14.0	40.8	141.1	375.2	18.0	15.9	13.5	(8.3)	C	C	A	164
6. Fidelity Puritan	★	14.5	41.9	140.5	418.0	17.9	16.8	12.8	(14.7)	B	B	C	4,652
7. Oppenheimer Equity Income	★	12.1	42.7	137.7	442.7	17.7	17.3	15.9	(12.6)	C	B	B	1,021
8. Fidelity Equity–Income	☆	15.6	43.0	137.1	524.2	17.6	18.7	14.9	(18.0)	A	B	D	4,768
9. Safeco Income	☆	13.2	31.0	128.5	388.2	16.9	16.2	14.4	(19.2)	B	A	D	227
10. Income Fund of America	★	14.4	38.5	127.5	332.9	16.8	14.9	11.4	(7.7)	D	D	A	1,140
BALANCED		**11.4**	**30.6**	**114.4**	**309.7**	**15.4**	**14.3**						
1. Loomis-Sayles Mutual	☆	14.4	37.5	161.0	354.4	19.7	15.4	19.6	(14.4)	D	A	E	299
2. Alliance Balanced	★	14.3	37.1	147.3	318.7	18.5	14.6	15.9	(12.0)	A	B	D	141
3. Mass. Fin. Total Return	★	13.2	41.4	142.7	346.1	18.1	15.2	14.4	(12.4)	B	A	C	587
4. IDS Mutual	★	12.1	44.5	136.6	322.9	17.6	14.7	13.3	(9.2)	B	C	B	1,593
5. Vanguard Wellington	☆	13.3	40.1	135.5	356.3	17.5	15.5	14.0	(12.4)	A	C	D	1,790
6. Phoenix Balanced	★	12.8	30.0	130.7	385.2	17.1	16.1	15.4	(8.8)	E	B	B	436
7. American Balanced	☆	13.4	38.1	127.3	300.3	16.8	14.1	14.1	(10.6)	B	C	C	246
8. Putnam (George) Fund of Boston	☆	12.6	35.2	126.3	308.6	16.7	14.3	14.1	(13.6)	B	B	D	404
9. Axe-Houghton Fund B	●	11.6	23.0	122.3	249.3	16.3	12.7	16.6	(18.4)	C	A	E	164
10. Delaware Fund	●	15.9	26.4	121.7	399.5	16.2	16.4	21.1	(27.3)	A	A	E	347
S&P 500-STOCK INDEX**		**16.5**	**40.4**	**149.8**	**381.0**	**20.1**	**17.6**						

*Currently closed to new investors   **Figures are to 7/1/89   †Fund may impose back-end load or exit fee.

Portfolio analysis			Senior fund manager, age (years managing fund)	Expense analysis			Minimum initial investment	Telephone	
% yield	P/E ratio	% cash		% turnover	% maximum initial sales charge	Five-year projection		Toll-free (800)	In state
1.5									◀ CATEGORY AVERAGE
0.4	26.6	8.2	Matthew A. Weatherbie, N.A.	66	8.5	$138	$500	225-1581	—
0.0	26.5	0.0	William Duncan Jr., 46 (5)	276	4.5	67	1,000	332-3863	—
1.1	23.2	8.1	Richard Weiss, 38 (6)	42	None	55	1,000	338-2550	—
1.5	17.6	1.9	Irwin Lainoff, 58 (10)	70	None	66	1,000	722-9876	—
0.0	16.1	0.0	Harry Hutzler, 65 (12)	131	5.5	139	1,000	231-0803	800-392-9681 (Texas)
2.0	20.3	3.5	James E. Stowers Jr., 65 (17)	143	None	55	None	345-2021	—
2.4	23.6	17.9	Donna Calder, 38 (2)	103	8.5	134	1,000	525-7048	—
2.0	16.3	10.1	Irving Brilliant, 70 (10)	29	None	66	1,000	221-5350	212-668-8578 (N.Y.)
0.0	42.8	0.9	Richard Freeman, 55 (6)	10	5.0	108	500	—	212-528-2744
0.7	12.8	6.9	Donald Dates, 54 (three months)	84	2.0†	97	1,000	343-2898	—
1.8									◀ CATEGORY AVERAGE
1.7	13.5	5.0	Peter Lynch, 45 (12)	101	3.0	91	1,000	544-6666	—
0.3	28.6	12.3	Andrew H. Massie, 41 (7)	49	None	53	1,000	225-2470	—
1.3	17.3	23.0	Bing Carlin, 52 (9)	85	None	55	5,000	—	612-371-2884
2.4	17.1	7.6	Shelby M.C. Davis, 52 (20)	38	4.75	110	1,000	545-2098	—
2.3	13.2	10.0	Charles E .Albers, 48 (17)	58	4.5	82	1,000	221-3253	—
1.0	16.7	1.0	Harry Hutzler, 65 (20)	93	5.5	116	1,000	231-0803	800-392-9681 (Texas)
0.4	12.3	5.3	Irwin Smith, 50 (3)	104	None†	117	1,000	628-1237	212-482-5894 (N.Y.)
1.8	12.0	8.0	Gerald Zukowski, 55 (6)	24	None	72	1,000	225-5267	—
1.8	11.8	4.2	George Vanderheiden, N.A. (8)	80	9.0	33	25	225-5270	—
1.9	23.3	16.7	Committee management	8	5.75	96	1,000	421-9900	714-671-7000 (Calif.)
3.3									◀ CATEGORY AVERAGE
4.3	8.4	8.8	John Neff, 57 (25)	24	None	26	10,000	662-7447	—
2.7	12.0	9.4	Committee management	8	5.75	97	250	421-9900	714-671-7000 (Calif.)
3.0	12.0	6.0	Committee management	12	5.75	96	250	421-9900	714-671-7000 (Calif.)
1.4	15.8	22.8	Donald A. Yacktman, 47 (6)	35	None	61	1,000	553-5533	—
2.9	22.7	27.3	Michael F. Price, 38 (8)	85	None	38	1,000	553-3014	—
4.2	11.1	25.0	Paul M. Hoffmann, 59 (12)	20	6.5	95	250	637-3863	—
3.7	12.9	20.4	Committee management	16	5.75	88	250	421-9900	714-671-7000 (Calif.)
2.2	22.3	27.7	Michael F. Price, 38 (13)	90	None	40	5,000	553-3014	—
3.4	22.4	36.0	Robert J. Martorelli, 35 (2)	51	6.5	125	1,000	637-3863	—
3.9	12.7	15.0	Ernest S. Watts, 56 (5)	85	6.5	96	250	637-3863	—
5.4									◀ CATEGORY AVERAGE
3.2	13.7	9.9	Russell E. Thompson, 49 (10)	49	8.5	119	500	—	816-283-4122
6.9	9.3	4.3	John Neff, 57 (14)	17	None	30	3,000	662-7447	—
4.3	15.0	7.2	Paul Ehrsam, 33 (6)	39	8.5	122	25	523-4640	215-988-1333 (Pa.)
3.9	13.9	7.2	John Kaweske, 46 (4)	148	None	43	250	525-8085	—
6.0	11.3	23.0	John Doney, 59 (2)	33	7.25	119	250	223-7757	203-863-5600 (Conn.)
6.4	13.8	7.6	Richard Fentin, 33 (2)	88	2.0	59	1,000	544-6666	—
5.1	15.6	17.0	Diane Jarmusz, 37 (7)	124	8.5	127	1,000	525-7048	—
5.3	14.4	4.1	C. Bruce Johnstone, 48 (17)	68	2.0	54	1,000	544-6666	—
5.0	12.7	0.3	Arley N. Hudson, 55 (11)	34	None	54	1,000	426-6730	800-562-6810 (Wash.)
6.3	11.9	14.2	Committee management	43	5.75	95	1,000	421-9900	714-671-7000 (Calif.)
4.8									◀ CATEGORY AVERAGE
4.9	17.3	3.7	G. Kenneth Heebner, 48 (13)	218	None	56	1,000	345-4048	617-578-1333 (Mass.)
3.2	17.5	17.2	J. Andrew Richey, 38 (2)	190	5.5	121	250	221-5672	—
5.5	14.1	8.0	Richard Dahlberg, 49 (5)	52	7.25	109	250	225-2606	617-954-5000 (Mass.)
6.0	9.4	6.0	Tom Medcalf, 41 (6)	60	5.0	87	2,000	328-8300	—
5.3	11.6	8.7	Vincent Bajakian, 58 (17)	28	None	26	3,000	662-7447	—
4.7	14.3	10.0	Patricia Bannan, 28 (3)	226	6.9	110	500	243-4361	—
5.4	12.8	13.1	Committee management	42	5.75	100	500	421-9900	714-671-7000 (Calif.)
5.4	11.3	2.7	Thomas V. Reilly, N.A.	139	8.5	126	500	225-1581	—
5.1	15.3	3.7	Porter H. Sutro, 51 (2)	251	None	74	1,000	366-0444	—
4.5	13.9	1.9	Stanton J. Feeley, 52 (1)	180	8.5	124	25	523-4640	215-988-1333 (Pa.)
3.5	**11.6**		**Key to rating symbols:** ★ = Top 10% ☆ = Next 20% ● = Middle 40% ○ = Next 20% □ = Bottom 10%						

Gains or losses are with all dividends reinvested.   N.A. Not available

THE TOP PERFORMERS: STOCK FUNDS

Ranked by five-year performance	Money risk-adjusted rating	% gain (or loss) to June 22, 1989				% compound annual return		Five-year analysis		Lipper market phase rating			Net assets (millio)
		1989	Three years	Five years	10 years	Five years	10 years	Best quarter	Worst quarter	Current	Prior up	Prior down	
SMALL-COMPANY GROWTH		**16.7**	**16.6**	**87.8**	**303.2**	**12.3**	**14.0**						
1. Alliance Quasar	●	28.0	35.4	170.9	—	20.4	—	29.6	(26.7)	A	A	D	$158
2. Acorn Fund	☆	17.0	50.3	163.5	429.9	19.9	17.0	17.1	(20.8)	B	A	A	733
3. Putnam OTC Emerging Growth	●	21.9	35.6	160.6	—	19.6	—	26.5	(23.1)	A	A	D	183
4. Nicholas II	☆	13.9	35.7	146.6	—	18.5	—	22.6	(16.8)	D	A	A	399
5. Babson Enterprise	●	17.8	30.8	132.1	—	17.2	—	21.9	(28.2)	A	B	B	72
6. New Beginning Growth	●	22.2	29.2	128.7	—	16.9	—	29.6	(22.0)	D	A	B	55
7. Neuwirth Fund	●	18.0	17.8	127.6	296.7	16.8	14.0	23.7	(27.8)	A	B	C	29.
OPTION INCOME		**10.6**	**31.7**	**91.9**	**237.1**	**13.2**	**12.2**						
1. Pru-Bache Option Growth	●	13.4	36.0	120.4	—	16.1	—	15.3	(16.6)	A	B	E	69
2. Putnam Option Income	○	13.7	33.9	91.9	230.2	13.2	12.1	13.3	(25.4)	A	A	E	1,025
3. Oppenheimer Premium Income	●	4.0	61.2	91.5	251.8	13.2	12.8	19.3	(5.0)	D	C	A	294
4. Franklin Option	●	12.1	33.6	91.5	312.8	13.2	14.4	10.6	(15.1)	B	B	C	45
5. Analytic Optioned Equity	●	9.8	36.9	85.2	224.9	12.5	12.0	9.2	(10.7)	C	C	B	105.
6. Gateway Option Index	○	7.4	25.9	71.0	165.7	10.9	9.9	7.0	(16.4)	C	E	B	27.
7. SLH Income–Option Income	—	11.7	31.5	—	—	—	—	12.5	(18.1)	A	—	C	590.
SECTORS		**17.3**	**35.3**	**112.5**	**288.0**	**14.8**	**13.7**						
1. Fidelity Select–Leisure	★	27.7	47.3	255.3	—	26.2	—	24.1	(25.0)	A	A	D	86.
2. Pru-Bache Utility	★	19.8	48.5	224.5	—	24.2	—	26.4	(10.7)	A	A	E	2,024.
3. Vanguard Special Port.–Health	★	15.5	44.3	182.1	—	21.3	—	23.7	(25.6)	B	B	B	61.
4. Fidelity Select–Health Care	☆	18.7	16.5	165.4	—	20.0	—	31.2	(28.5)	D	A	D	185.
5. Seligman Comm. & Information	☆	22.4	46.1	156.0	—	19.2	—	29.7	(19.3)	B	A	B	43.
6. Fidelity Select–Utilities	★	18.8	31.7	150.5	—	18.8	—	18.1	(8.4)	A	B	C	90.
7. Century Shares Trust	☆	21.2	20.2	145.1	329.3	18.3	14.8	21.4	(18.1)	C	A	B	126.
INTERNATIONAL		**4.0**	**59.4**	**199.6**	**411.0**	**22.4**	**16.3**						
1. Merrill Lynch Pacific	☆	(9.9)	67.3	282.1	713.3	27.7	21.5	29.6	(25.9)	B	A	E	286.
2. Japan Fund	★	(6.8)	72.9	259.7	—	26.4	—	27.8	(16.8)	C	B	A	374.
3. Vanguard Trustees' Com.–Intl.	★	3.9	78.6	229.0	—	24.5	—	19.4	(12.0)	B	C	B	493.
4. Kleinworth Benson Intl. Equity	●	4.4	60.4	221.7	357.7	24.1	15.5	24.5	(18.4)	B	C	B	62.
5. T. Rowe Price Intl. Stock	☆	5.2	66.8	218.4	—	23.8	—	22.6	(17.3)	B	B	C	693.
6. Vanguard World–Intl. Gro	☆	(0.6)	48.1	216.7	—	23.7	—	25.9	(13.0)	D	A	B	456.
7. Financial Strategic–Pacific Basin	●	2.6	75.1	210.1	—	23.3	—	23.1	(27.4)	A	A	E	23.
GLOBAL		**4.1**	**39.9**	**152.1**	**440.0**	**18.8**	**17.2**						
1. Paine Webber Classic Atlas	☆	3.2	41.9	209.0	—	23.2	—	20.1	(24.8)	B	A	D	193.
2. Putnam International Equities	☆	7.0	35.4	205.3	472.5	22.9	17.8	23.4	(18.0)	D	A	C	471.
3. Oppenheimer Global	○	14.9	50.0	170.1	510.6	20.4	18.5	25.7	(32.0)	A	B	E	442.
4. Pru-Bache Global	○	(0.1)	27.2	159.2	—	19.5	—	24.4	(21.5)	E	B	B	422.
5. New Perspective	●	10.3	54.8	153.0	431.5	19.0	17.1	18.3	(18.0)	C	B	B	1,097.
6. Templeton Growth	○	11.1	49.1	137.6	362.5	17.7	15.6	15.5	(22.2)	A	D	C	1,984.
7. Templeton World	○	12.4	43.0	137.1	422.9	17.6	16.9	16.4	(19.3)	A	E	C	4,359.
GOLD & PRECIOUS METALS		**2.8**	**56.6**	**9.5**	**215.0**	**0.4**	**11.1**						
1. Oppenheimer Gold & Spl. Min.	●	10.8	180.9	115.3	—	15.6	—	44.7	(17.7)	A	B	A	116.
2. Lexington Goldfund	○	0.0	60.9	37.2	185.3	6.4	10.6	42.7	(17.1)	C	A	B	85.
3. Franklin Gold	○	9.9	101.4	25.1	384.6	4.5	16.1	58.1	(22.7)	A	C	C	248.
4. Bull & Bear Gold Investors	○	0.5	48.1	20.2	149.0	3.7	9.2	44.5	(24.6)	C	A	D	37.
5. Vanguard Special. Port.–Gold	○	2.5	69.1	20.2	—	3.7	—	52.9	(22.6)	C	A	B	114.
6. International Investors	○	7.8	49.6	9.6	336.8	1.8	15.0	52.9	(21.8)	D	C	B	679.
7. Keystone Precious Metals	○	3.0	72.3	8.9	218.2	1.7	11.7	52.4	(24.8)	B	B	C	190.
S&P 500-STOCK INDEX**		**16.5**	**40.4**	**149.8**	**381.0**	**20.1**	**17.6**						

* *Figures are to 7/1/89

Portfolio analysis			Senior fund manager, age (years managing fund)	Expense analysis			Minimum initial investment	Telephone	
% yield	P/E ratio	% cash		% turnover	% maximum initial sales charge	Five-year projection		Toll-free (800)	In state
1.1									◀ CATEGORY AVERAGE
0.0	21.9	10.3	Paul H. Jenkel, 50 (17); Frank Burr, 52 (17)	58	5.5	$123	$250	221-5672	—
1.9	29.5	4.1	Ralph Wanger, 55 (19)	36	None	44	4,000	922-6769	—
0.0	27.1	8.5	Richard Jodka, N.A.	77	6.75	148	500	225-1581	—
1.6	16.5	8.7	Albert O. Nicholas, 58 (5)	18	None	43	1,000	—	414-272-6133
0.0	19.6	5.3	Peter Schliemann, 44 (4)	41	None	75	1,000	422-2766	816-471-5200 (Mo.)
1.2	33.3	10.0	Douglas C. Jones, 45 (8)	78	None	66	2,000	332-5580	—
0.1	19.6	5.5	James Engle, 31 (3 months)	108	None	104	1,000	225-8011	—
4.9									◀ CATEGORY AVERAGE
2.3	20.7	12.9	Leigh Goehring, 30 (3)	45	None†	102	1,000	225-1852	—
3.3	15.0	4.2	Robert S. Stephenson, N.A.	38	8.5	129	500	225-1581	—
6.8	23.4	10.2	Diane Jarmusz, 37 (1)	335	8.5	139	1,000	525-7048	—
2.8	14.4	13.4	Martin Weskemann, 62 (17)	80	4.0	85	100	342-5236	—
8.1	N.A.	7.0	Chuck Dobson, 47 (11)	66	None	64	5,000	—	714-833-0294
1.7	13.0	1.1	Peter W. Thayer, 40 (11)	10	None	82	500	354-6339	—
7.6	11.3	7.8	John Fullerton, N.A. (3)	56	None†	102	500	—	212-528-2744
2.2									◀ CATEGORY AVERAGE
0.0	27.8	27.0	Karen Firestone, N.A. (six months)	229	2.0†	135	1,000	544-6666	—
4.2	13.3	8.2	Warren Spitz, 34 (4)	66	None†	94	1,000	225-1852	—
1.7	22.1	8.5	Edward P. Owens, 42 (4)	18	None†	35	3,000	662-7447	—
0.7	23.1	8.0	Steven Kaye, N.A. (2)	122	2.0†	119	1,000	544-6666	—
0.0	27.1	1.8	Calvert Dooman, 62 (5)	117	4.75	131	1,000	221-2450	800-522-6869 (N.Y.)
2.3	14.5	5.2	Alan Berro, N.A. (2)	143	2.0†	134	1,000	544-5666	—
3.0	11.5	2.8	Allan W. Fulkerson, 55 (22)	3	None	48	500	321-1928	617-482-3060 (Mass.)
1.0									◀ CATEGORY AVERAGE
1.5	N.A.	7.0	Stephen I. Silverman, 38 (5)	39	6.5	118	250	637-3863	—
0.2	N.A.	9.0	Laura Luckyn-Malone, 36 (3)	39	None	56	1,000	535-2726	—
1.9	N.A.	7.4	John Callahan, 65 (5)	14	None	29	$10,000	662-7447	—
0.0	27.2	3.6	Henry deVismes, 42 (18)	55	None	141	1,000	233-9164	212-687-2515 (N.Y.)
2.4	21.0	7.9	Martin G. Wade, 45 (4)	42	None	64	2,500	638-5660	301-547-2308 (Md.)
1.5	N.A.	4.1	Richard R. Foulkes, 43 (7)	71	None	37	3,000	662-7447	—
0.0	32.0	7.7	William Keithler, 36 (2)	69	None	89	250	525-8085	—
4.7									◀ CATEGORY AVERAGE
2.9	N.A.	18.0	Nimrod Fachler, N.A. (2)	67	4.5	124	1,000	544-9300	—
1.6	16.6	5.1	Anthony W. Regan, N.A. (1)	103	8.5	165	500	225-1581	—
0.3	N.A.	0.7	Kenneth Oberman, 59 (8)	27	8.5	178	1,000	525-7048	—
3.2	N.A.	4.3	Peter Lehman, 30 (5)	82	None†	111	1,000	225-1852	—
2.9	13.1	16.4	Committee management	21	5.75	99	250	421-9900	714-671-7000 (Calif.)
3.1	11.5	7.4	John M. Templeton, 76 (34)	11	8.5	120	500	237-0738	—
2.4	11.4	2.4	John M. Templeton, 76 (11)	20	8.5	120	500	237-0738	—
2.2									◀ CATEGORY AVERAGE
1.4	13.8	21.1	Kenneth Oberman, 59 (1)	176	8.5	146	1,000	525-7048	—
1.0	22.2	8.7	Caesar M.P. Bryan, 33 (2)	20	None	87	1,000	526-0057	—
3.5	20.7	12.7	Martin Weskemann, 62 (17)	7	4.0	81	100	342-5236	—
0.3	N.A.	9.0	Robert W. Radsch, 46 (6)	42	None	125	1,000	847-4200	—
3.2	N.A.	8.2	David J. Hutchins, 28 (3)	14	None	27	3,000	662-7447	—
2.9	19.9	1.0	John Van Eck, 73 (34)	5	8.5	127	1,000	221-2220	212-687-5201 (N.Y.)
0.8	19.9	3.0	Frederick G.P. Thorne, 53 (14)	82	None†	100	250	343-2898	—

Key to rating symbols: ★ = **Top 10%** ☆ = **Next 20%** ● = **Middle 40%** ○ = **Next 20%** □ = **Bottom 10%**

Gains or losses are with all dividends reinvested. †Fund may impose back-end load or exit fee. N.A. Not available

THE TOP PERFORMERS: TAXABLE BOND FUNDS

Ranked by five-year performance	MONEY risk-adjusted rating	% gain (or loss) to June 22, 1989				% compound annual return		Five-year analysis		Lipper market phase rating			
		1989	Three years	Five years	10 years	Five years	10 years	Best quarter	Worst quarter	Current	Prior up	Prior down	
U.S. GOVERNMENT BOND FUNDS		**6.1**	**22.0**	**72.7**	**165.4**	**11.0**	**9.8**						
1. Lord Abbett U.S. Gov. Securities	●	6.8	28.0	88.4	201.2	12.9	11.2	10.6	(3.8)	C	B	A	$1.
2. Value Line U.S. Gov. Securities	☆	6.1	26.8	88.3	—	12.9	—	10.1	(4.1)	C	C	B	
3. Colonial Gov. Securities Plus	●	6.3	25.0	83.6	—	12.3	—	10.1	(5.3)	B	D	B	2.
4. AMEV U.S. Gov. Securities	●	6.4	27.2	83.5	173.6	12.3	10.2	8.4	(2.8)	C	C	B	
5. United Government Securities	●	5.0	18.1	77.1	—	11.6	—	10.0	(7.4)	D	D	B	
6. Fidelity Government Securities	●	6.0	22.1	75.5	179.7	11.4	10.4	7.5	(2.3)	D	D	B	
7. Carnegie Gov. Sec.—High Yield	○	6.0	22.4	74.9	—	11.3	—	9.2	(2.2)	E	D	A	
MORTGAGE-BACKED SECURITIES		**6.0**	**25.0**	**76.9**	**134.3**	**11.5**	**8.6**						
1. Vanguard Fixed Income—GNMA	●	7.0	29.9	88.2	—	12.8	—	8.9	(4.0)	B	C	B	1.
2. Kemper U.S. Gov. Securities	●	7.4	26.3	87.5	152.0	12.8	9.4	8.6	(3.0)	D	B	C	4.
3. Franklin U.S. Gov. Securities	☆	6.7	29.1	85.5	136.8	12.5	8.7	9.4	(3.5)	C	C	C	11.
4. Lexington GNMA Income	●	8.3	28.8	80.1	127.5	11.9	8.3	9.5	(4.8)	C	D	D	
5. Fund for U.S. Gov. Securities	●	7.2	28.9	77.8	150.7	11.7	9.3	9.1	(3.3)	C	D	C	1.
6. Putnam U.S. Gov. Guar. Secur.	☆	6.5	29.1	77.7	—	11.7	—	7.8	(4.0)	C	D	B	1.
7. Alliance Mortgage Securities	●	4.3	27.6	77.6	—	11.7	—	7.9	(2.6)	B	D	B	
HIGH-YIELD CORPORATES		**4.3**	**22.1**	**80.1**	**184.4**	**11.9**	**10.5**						
1. Kemper High Yield	★	4.7	39.6	110.2	252.7	15.1	12.8	8.4	(2.2)	A	A	D	1,
2. Delaware Group–Delchester I	★	4.6	33.3	106.7	203.4	14.8	11.3	8.4	(4.8)	A	A	D	
3. Financial Bond Shares–Hi. Yield	★	5.3	28.8	103.8	—	14.5	—	9.5	(1.8)	A	A	E	
4. Fidelity High Income	☆	4.6	26.6	101.6	239.2	14.3	12.4	9.2	(3.7)	A	A	E	1,
5. Cigna High Yield	★	5.1	31.1	100.4	213.5	14.1	11.6	7.8	(2.5)	A	A	E	
6. Investment Portfolio–High Yield	★	4.0	33.7	94.8	—	13.6	—	7.8	(1.4)	A	A	D	
7. Vanguard Fixed Inc.–High Yield	☆	3.7	29.2	94.2	203.6	13.5	11.3	7.4	(4.5)	A	A	E	1,
HIGH-GRADE CORPORATES		**6.2**	**25.0**	**88.9**	**174.8**	**12.9**	**10.2**						
1. Axe-Houghton Income	☆	5.0	23.8	107.3	208.8	14.9	11.4	12.0	(4.1)	B	A	D	
2. United Bond	★	7.1	30.5	105.7	184.8	14.7	10.6	10.2	(4.1)	B	A	B	
3. SLH Inv.–Investment Grade	●	8.6	22.6	102.6	—	14.4	—	13.5	(7.6)	C	A	C	
4. Bond Fund of America	☆	6.6	27.3	98.5	209.2	13.9	11.5	9.1	(3.8)	B	A	D	1,
5. American Capital Corporate Bond	★	4.2	29.2	96.4	165.3	13.7	9.9	9.3	(3.3)	A	A	D	
6. Alliance Bond—Monthly Inc. Port.	☆	5.7	25.9	95.8	161.9	13.7	9.7	10.6	(2.7)	C	A	C	
7. John Hancock Bond	☆	6.3	26.9	95.0	159.3	13.6	9.6	9.8	(3.5)	B	B	C	1,
FLEXIBLE INCOME		**6.9**	**27.9**	**99.5**	**205.5**	**14.0**	**11.3**						
1. Vanguard Wellesley Income	☆	11.5	33.4	121.4	283.7	16.2	13.7	12.0	(3.0)	A	A	C	6
2. Eaton Vance Income of Boston	★	6.0	33.9	111.4	232.6	15.3	12.2	10.8	(2.7)	A	A	E	
3. Northeast Investors Trust	★	2.9	25.3	106.9	205.2	14.8	11.3	9.9	(5.4)	A	A	E	
4. Seligman Income	●	9.9	23.1	102.9	243.9	14.4	12.5	12.2	(2.7)	C	C	C	
5. Mutual of Omaha Income	●	8.3	29.8	101.0	196.5	14.2	11.0	10.0	(4.5)	C	D	C	
6. USAA Mutual–Income	☆	8.4	34.2	92.6	201.3	13.3	11.2	9.3	(3.6)	B	C	D	
7. Scudder Income	●	6.7	26.2	89.7	168.4	13.0	10.0	8.5	(3.5)	B	B	C	2
SHORT-TERM TAXABLES		**4.7**	**20.9**	**65.1**	**155.7**	**10.1**	**9.5**						
1. John Hancock—U.S. Gov. Sec.	○	6.0	19.0	75.2	155.7	11.4	9.5	7.8	(2.9)	E	D	C	
2. Vanguard Fxd. Inc.—Short-Term	●	5.0	24.2	70.2	—	10.8	—	6.6	(0.2)	C	E	A	
3. Midwest Inc.—Int.-Term Gov.	○	4.7	19.0	59.6	—	9.5	—	5.7	(1.3)	E	E	A	
4. T. Rowe Price Short-Term Bond	○	4.0	21.2	55.4	—	8.9	—	4.7	(0.3)	D	E	A	2
5. Neuberger & Berman Ltd. Mat.	—	5.1	21.5	—	—	—	—	3.1	(0.4)	D	—	A	
6. IAI Reserve	—	4.2	21.2	—	—	—	—	1.9	1.3	C	—	B	
7. Delaware Grp. Treasury Rsvs.–I.S.	—	2.9	20.3	—	—	—	—	2.7	0.7	C	—	A	
SALOMON BROS. INVESTMENT-GRADE INDEX		**9.2**	**28.1**	**99.6**	**—**	**14.8**	**12.5**						

Portfolio analysis				Expense analysis				Telephone	
% yield	Average maturity (years)	% cash	Senior fund manager, age (years managing fund)	% turnover	% maximum initial sales charge	Five-year projection	Minimum initial investment	Toll-free (800)	In state
8.5									◀ CATEGORY AVERAGE
11.1	9.9	6.0	Carroll Coward, N.A. (1)	332	4.75	$94	$500	426-1130	212-848-1800 (N.Y.)
8.9	23.0	2.1	Milton C. Schlein, 56 (3)	54	None	37	1,000	223-0818	—
8.4	19.4	0.3	Robert Busby, 41 (1)	66	6.75	126	250	426-3750	—
9.5	15.6	5.2	Dennis M. Ott, 43 (3)	109	4.5	91	500	872-2638	—
8.3	17.4	1.1	Robert G. Alley, 41 (1)	238	4.25	83	500	—	816-283-4122
8.5	7.2	4.2	James Wolfson, N.A. (3)	283	None	44	1,000	544-6666	—
7.6	14.0	11.0	John Shriver, 33 (4)	26	4.5	112	1,000	321-2322	—
9.1									◀ CATEGORY AVERAGE
9.3	26.6	8.3	Paul Sullivan, 46 (8)	8	None	20	3,000	662-7447	—
10.1	6.3	1.0	Patrick Beimford, N.A. (8)	203	4.5	72	1,000	621-1048	—
10.1	28.0	3.0	Jack Lemein, 45 (5)	34	4.0	68	100	342-5236	—
8.6	19.3	18.0	Denis P. Jamison, 41 (8)	233	None	59	1,000	526-0057	—
9.2	23.0	2.2	Thomas N. Slonaker, 53 (5)	72	4.5	96	500	356-2805	—
10.0	9.7	8.4	Jaclyn S. Conrad, N.A.	55	4.75	81	500	225-1581	—
11.3	5.0	19.1	Paul Zoslchke, N.A. (1)	239	5.5	113	250	221-5672	—
12.1									◀ CATEGORY AVERAGE
9.9	5.6	8.0	William R. Buecking, 54 (11)	76	4.5	83	1,000	621-1048	—
9.1	10.8	3.8	J. Michael Pokorny, 50 (9)	139	6.75	112	25	523-4640	215-988-1333 (Pa.)
8.6	8.8	11.5	William Veronda, 43 (5)	42	None	46	250	525-5085	—
9.5	9.1	8.1	Margaret Eagle, N.A. (six months)	68	None	49	2,500	544-6666	—
10.5	9.0	6.0	Alan Peterson, 38 (6)	76	5.0	100	500	562-4462	—
9 5	5.7	2.0	William R. Buecking, 54 (5)	102	None†	123	250	621-1048	—
9.5	10.1	14.3	Earl E. McEvoy, 41 (4)	32	None	23	3,000	662-7447	—
9.0									◀ CATEGORY AVERAGE
9.9	6.5	15.4	Robert E. Manning, 52 (2)	258	None	80	1,000	366-0444	—
9.1	8.2	3.1	Robert G. Alley, 41 (4)	179	8.5	118	500	—	816-283-4122
8.6	25.8	1.4	George E. Mueller, 47 (4)	72	None†	99	500	—	212-528-2744
9.5	13.8	11.4	Committee management	93	4.75	85	1,000	421-9900	714-671-7000 (Calif.)
10.5	12.0	6.8	David Troth, 55 (10)	56	4.75	87	500	421-5666	—
9.5	7.5	21.9	Wayne D. Lyski, N.A. (2)	96	5.5	148	250	221-5672	—
9.5	14.9	3.0	James K. Ho, 37 (1)	66	8.5	127	1,000	225-5291	—
9.3									◀ CATEGORY AVERAGE
6.3	14.7	5.8	Earl E. McEvoy, 41 (7)	19	None	29	3,000	662-7447	—
13.2	9.8	6.6	Hooker Talcott Jr., 58 (3)	61	4.75	116	1,000	225-6265	—
13.6	10.1	0.0	Ernest E. Monrad, 59 (29)	17	None	42	1,000	225-6704	—
7.8	N.A.	8.4	J. Paul Rodriguez, 60 (5)	74	4.75	90	1,000	221-2450	800-522-6869 (N.Y.)
8.4	18.0	5.0	Eugenia M. Simpson, 33 (3)	87	8.0	120	250	228-9596	800-642-8112 (Neb.)
9.3	13.3	1.0	John W. Saunders Jr., 54 (3)	11	None	34	1,000	531-8000	—
8.5	8.7	1.1	William M. Hutchinson, 32 (2)	20	None	52	1,000	225-2470	—
8.3									◀ CATEGORY AVERAGE
8.7	4.0	2.0	David S. Turner, 43 (8)	12	8.5	137	500	225-5291	—
8.4	2.1	7.4	Ian A. MacKinnon, 41 (6)	88	None	19	3,000	662-7447	—
7.8	2.7	17.0	William J. Snider, 52 (2)	88	2.0	76	1,000	543-8721	800-582-7396 (Ohio)
8.5	2.8	63.3	Edward A. Taber, 45 (5)	309	None	53	2,500	638-5660	301-547-2308 (Md.)
7.9	1.7	17.7	Theresa Havell, 42 (3)	68	None	36	10,000	722-9876	—
7.3	0.4	15.0	Larry Hill, 37 (3)	0	None	47	5,000	—	612-371-2884
8.3	3.3	2.8	Dorothea M. Dutton, 42 (3)	146	None	50	1,000	523-4640	215-988-1333 (Pa.)

Key to rating symbols: ★ = Top 10%   ☆ = Next 20%   ● = Middle 40%   ○ = Next 20%   □ = Bottom 10%

Gains or losses are with all dividends reinvested.   † Fund may impose back-end load or exit fee.   N.A. Not available

The Alphabetical Guide to 900 Mutual Funds

ABBREVIATIONS

Bal Balanced; **Eql** Equity income; **Flx** Flexible income; **G&I** Growth & income; **Glo** Global; **Gold** Gold/metals; **Gro** Growth; **HGC** High-grade corporates; **HGT** High-grade tax-exempts; **HYC** High-yield corporates; **HYT** High-yield tax-exempts; **Intl** International; **ITT** Intermediate-term tax-exempts; **Max** Maximum capital gains; **MBS** Mortgage-backed securities; **OpInc** Option income; **SCG** Small-company growth; **Sec** Sector; **STT** Short-term taxables; **USG** U.S. Government bonds

BENCHMARKS FOR INVESTORS

	% gain (or loss) to July 1, 1989				
	1989	Three years	Five years	10 years	% yield
S&P 500-stock index	16.5	40.4	149.8	381.0	3.5
Dow Jones industrial average	15.0	43.8	163.4	371.0	—
Lipper growth fund index*	18.9	35.4	125.8	331.5	—
Lipper growth and income fund index*	14.9	42.6	129.9	343.9	—
Salomon Bros. investment-grade bond index	9.2	28.1	99.6	—	9.8
Shearson Lehman Hutton Treasury bond index*	10.4	24.6	136.2	194.0	10.2
Shearson Lehman Hutton municipal bond index**	5.2	29.5	92.4	131.8	7.8

*Figures are to June 22, 1989   **Figures are to June 1, 1989

STOCK FUNDS

FUND NAME	Type	MONEY risk-adjusted rating	% gain (or loss) to June 22, 1989				Portfolio analysis			Net assets (millions)	Expense analysis	
			1989	Three years	Five years	10 years	% yield	P/E ratio	% cash		% maximum initial sales charge	Five-year projection
ABT Growth & Income Trust	G&I	●	12.4	45.4	134.5	345.2	2.7	11.4	24.6	$106.8	4.75	$114
ABT Utility Income	Sec	☆	14.3	37.3	125.6	151.4	6.7	14.7	1.4	114.8	4.75	114
Acorn Fund	SCG	☆	17.0	50.3	163.5	429.6	1.9	29.5	4.1	733.2	None	44
Advest Advantage Growth	Gro	—	14.6	34.1	—	—	1.2	N.A.	12.4	27.7	None†	143
AIM Charter	G&I	●	23.4	38.9	121.0	375.9	2.9	16.5	2.0	68.4	5.5	132
AIM Constellation	Max	●	23.7	42.3	155.1	510.0	0.0	16.1	0.0	100.2	5.5	139
AIM Summit	Gro	○	18.7	27.0	107.9	—	1.7	N.A.	1.0	215.5	8.5	55
AIM Weingarten	Gro	☆	19.4	38.1	165.1	657.9	1.0	16.7	1.0	347.5	5.5	116
Alliance Balanced Shares	Bal	★	14.3	37.1	147.3	318.7	3.2	17.5	17.2	141.9	5.5	121
Alliance Canadian	Intl	□	17.6	69.8	121.8	246.7	0.4	9.8	1.1	31.2	5.5	150
Alliance Convertible	Eql	—	9.0	19.6	—	—	6.0	N.A.	1.4	77.0	5.5	134
Alliance Counterpoint	G&I	—	26.6	47.3	—	—	1.4	17.1	0.4	52.0	5.5	145
Alliance Dividend Shares	G&I	☆	15.5	37.3	142.9	354.1	2.6	14.6	12.4	368.1	5.5	112
Alliance Fund	Gro	○	17.1	37.1	119.5	288.8	1.2	20.8	4.8	855.4	5.5	98
Alliance International	Intl	—	12.1	56.5	—	—	0.7	N.A.	3.0	163.3	5.5	128

Key to rating symbols: ★ = Top 10%   ☆ = Next 20%   ● = Middle 40%   ○ = Next 20%   □ = Bottom 10%

†Fund may impose back-end load or exit fee.   N.A. Not available

STOCK FUNDS

FUND NAME	Type	MONEY risk-adjusted rating	% gain (or loss) to June 22, 1989				Portfolio analysis			Net assets (millions)	Expense analysis % maximum initial sales charge	Five-year projection
			1989	Three years	Five years	10 years	% yield	P/E ratio	% cash			
Alliance Quasar	SCG	●	28.0	35.4	170.9	—	0.0	21.9	10.3	$158.7	5.5	$123
Alliance Surveyor	Gro	●	25.6	39.7	131.9	326.5	0.0	23.7	1.3	111.6	5.5	134
Alliance Technology	Sec	●	7.1	25.5	83.8	—	0.0	19.2	12.8	169.2	5.5	128
AMA Classic Growth	Gro	○	11.6	13.1	83.9	160.6	3.4	14.1	11.1	34.4	None	89
AMA Global Growth	Glo	—	9.5	—	—	—	2.6	15.8	14.6	105.9	None	79
AMCAP Fund	Gro	●	19.9	46.4	120.8	445.9	1.8	19.6	14.6	1,932.8	5.75	99
American Balanced	Bal	☆	13.4	38.1	127.3	300.3	5.4	12.8	13.1	246.5	5.75	100
American Capital Comstock	Max	○	18.6	36.5	92.7	447.4	2.4	12.8	5.8	925.9	8.5	121
American Capital Enterprise	Gro	○	21.6	26.3	106.6	425.9	1.6	20.8	6.0	596.8	5.75	96
American Capital Harbor	EqI	○	15.1	26.0	92.1	346.3	6.0	10.5	6.0	368.5	5.75	95
American Capital OTC Securities	SCG	□	22.9	(24.2)	4.7	—	0.0	19.8	4.7	45.5	5.75	125
American Capital Pace	Max	○	18.3	34.1	97.1	574.2	2.2	13.0	6.3	2,461.0	5.75	93
American Capital Venture	Max	□	17.3	12.3	54.0	319.2	2.3	19.3	5.8	201.2	5.75	105
American Growth	Gro	□	7.1	13.4	50.1	237.4	4.9	15.0	32.8	61.0	8.5	150
American Investors Growth	Gro	□	25.5	27.1	54.8	82.4	0.7	17.1	1.0	67.0	8.5	162
American Leaders	G&I	☆	9.9	33.1	120.1	366.5	3.9	10.2	29.2	151.9	4.5	98
American Mutual	G&I	★	14.9	39.3	136.0	436.0	4.8	12.0	22.8	2,959.1	5.75	90
American National Growth	Gro	●	15.8	30.8	105.9	298.3	2.1	17.2	3.0	106.0	8.5	148
American National Income	EqI	○	14.2	27.6	85.5	332.2	3.4	13.9	10.0	67.0	8.5	143
AMEV Capital	G&I	●	24.8	27.9	130.8	575.8	1.4	27.0	7.6	127.1	8.5	141
AMEV Fiduciary	Gro	●	25.8	23.2	143.4	—	0.6	27.3	5.5	32.4	4.5	126
AMEV Growth	Max	●	27.6	28.2	128.9	585.4	0.5	27.4	3.2	224.9	8.5	138
Analytic Optioned Equity	OpInc	●	9.8	36.9	85.2	224.9	8.1	N.A.	7.0	105.0	None	64
Axe-Houghton Fund B	Bal	●	11.6	23.0	122.3	249.3	5.1	15.3	3.7	164.5	None	74
Axe-Houghton Stock	Gro	□	19.9	4.8	71.1	228.0	0.8	17.9	16.5	63.7	None	95
Babson Enterprise	SCG	●	17.8	30.8	132.1	—	0.0	19.6	5.3	72.0	None	75
Babson Growth	Gro	●	16.4	42.5	134.2	276.7	2.4	14.7	5.4	279.0	None	45
Bartlett Basic Value	G&I	●	9.5	29.6	104.7	—	4.1	20.1	8.0	107.0	None	68
Blanchard Strategic Growth	Max	—	6.9	43.7	—	—	1.0	N.A.	10.0	249.0	None††	164
Boston Co. Capital Appreciation	Gro	★	15.7	43.1	161.6	366.6	1.8	12.0	8.0	550.0	None	72
Boston Co. Special Growth	Gro	○	20.2	23.5	102.6	—	2.0	15.6	7.8	36.2	None	88
Bull & Bear Capital Growth	Gro	○	22.8	18.7	88.8	269.5	0.0	23.9	0.0	76.1	None	123
Bull & Bear Gold Investors	Gold	○	0.5	48.1	20.2	149.0	0.3	N.A.	9.0	37.2	None	125
Calvert Ariel Growth	SCG	—	17.2	—	—	—	0.5	14.3	17.0	82.5	4.5	126
Calvert Social Invest. Managed Growth	Bal	☆	11.1	25.6	113.5	—	5.1	14.8	34.0	194.2	4.5	115
Capital Income Builder	G&I	—	9.7	—	—	—	5.1	11.7	20.4	164.7	5.75	123
Capital World Bond	Glo	—	(1.3)	—	—	—	7.5	N.A.	4.1	32.7	4.75	121
Cardinal Fund	G&I	☆	12.5	31.1	130.1	379.4	3.6	10.8	13.0	151.0	8.5	121
Carnegie Cappiello–Growth	Gro	☆	22.4	47.4	140.5	—	1.7	N.A.	10.0	59.0	4.5	133
Carnegie Cappiello–Total Return	G&I	—	22.8	42.9	—	—	5.1	N.A.	3.0	70.2	4.5	132
Century Shares Trust	Sec	☆	21.2	20.2	145.1	329.3	3.0	11.5	2.8	126.3	None	48
Cigna Growth	Gro	○	15.4	29.0	102.2	286.7	1.6	14.9	3.0	185.6	5.0	102
Cigna Utilities	Sec	—	16.0	—	—	—	6.0	12.2	2.0	33.7	5.0	115
Cigna Value	G&I	●	18.2	51.1	118.8	—	1.6	15.4	8.0	68.9	5.0	102
Colonial Advanced Strategies Gold	Gold	—	(3.9)	61.7	—	—	2.8	25.8	1.4	72.0	6.75	156
Colonial Diversified Income	EqI	○	5.9	27.8	75.1	195.0	6.8	8.0	6.1	570.0	6.75	124
Colonial Fund	G&I	☆	12.8	42.0	135.9	340.3	4.4	14.4	8.8	298.0	6.75	115
Colonial Growth Shares	Gro	●	19.4	52.3	144.7	412.8	1.6	13.4	4.7	111.0	6.75	119
Colonial Income Plus	OpInc	—	11.0	22.9	—	—	3.2	13.6	26.8	111.0	6.75	124
Colonial Small Stock Index	SCG	—	15.5	—	—	—	0.3	17.8	3.6	48.0	4.75	136
Colonial U.S. Equity Index	G&I	—	17.0	—	—	—	2.0	14.4	1.9	34.0	4.75	125
Columbia Growth	Gro	●	18.2	37.4	131.8	488.8	2.1	20.8	12.7	239.0	None	57
Columbia Special	Max	—	23.3	55.9	—	—	0.0	19.0	7.0	61.8	None†	76
Common Sense Growth	Max	—	15.5	—	—	—	0.9	16.7	5.0	673.7	8.5	180

Key to rating symbols: ★ = Top 10% ☆ = Next 20% ● = Middle 40% ○ = Next 20% □ = Bottom 10%

†Fund may impose back-end load or exit fee. †† Fund charges $125 start-up fee. N.A. Not available.

STOCK FUNDS

FUND NAME	Type	MONEY risk-adjusted rating	1989	Three years	Five years	10 years	% yield	P/E ratio	% cash	Net assets (millions)	% maximum initial sales charge	Five-year projection
Common Sense Growth & Income	G&I	—	17.5	—	—	—	2.4	15.3	4.8	$225.3	8.5	$163
Composite Bond & Stock	Bal	●	10.2	29.1	97.6	254.1	4.8	11.7	4.4	71.5	4.0	128
Composite Growth	G&I	☆	11.8	34.9	122.4	363.7	2.9	12.0	7.8	72.7	4.0	102
Cowen Income & Growth	EqI	—	17.7	—	—	—	3.8	N.A.	3.0	40.8	4.85	133
Dean Witter American Value	Gro	●	16.6	30.6	117.7	—	2.2	19.5	1.1	91.0	None†	116
Dean Witter Convertible Securities	EqI	—	10.0	4.8	—	—	5.7	N.A.	3.2	866.0	None†	117
Dean Witter Developing Growth	SCG	□	10.8	6.4	38.0	—	0.0	17.5	31.2	94.0	None†	124
Dean Witter Dividend Growth	G&I	★	19.2	45.0	147.2	—	2.7	16.5	5.8	2,128.0	None†	104
Dean Witter Natural Resources Devel.	Sec	●	14.9	60.2	78.2	—	1.6	18.1	0.0	139.0	None†	124
Dean Witter Option Income	OpInc	—	13.3	21.3	—	—	4.3	15.8	2.1	244.0	None†	127
Dean Witter World Wide	Glo	○	2.6	33.1	133.6	—	1.1	N.A.	9.0	306.0	None†	137
Delaware Fund	Bal	●	15.9	26.4	121.7	399.5	4.5	13.9	1.9	347.0	8.5	124
Delaware Group–Decatur I	EqI	☆	16.1	52.4	151.2	451.1	4.3	15.0	7.2	1,800.0	8.5	122
Delaware Group–Decatur II	EqI	—	16.0	—	—	—	3.8	15.0	4.9	252.6	4.75	114
Delaware Group–Delcap I	Max	—	24.6	120.2	—	—	0.7	23.1	18.9	120.9	4.75	128
Delaware Group–Trend	Max	●	38.0	33.5	118.5	448.1	0.0	26.3	0.0	66.7	8.5	145
Drexel Burnham Fund	G&I	★	12.7	39.2	140.8	375.9	5.4	18.4	12.0	177.0	5.0	106
Dreyfus Capital Value	Max	—	14.7	48.2	—	—	5.7	N.A.	0.8	533.8	4.5	117
Dreyfus Convertible Securities	EqI	☆	10.7	38.4	125.6	292.2	4.5	N.A.	6.6	261.6	None	47
Dreyfus Fund	G&I	●	12.2	34.7	113.2	319.5	3.9	16.9	9.3	2,503.4	None	43
Dreyfus General Aggressive Growth	Max	●	14.2	20.5	124.8	—	1.4	N.A.	8.6	42.0	None	94
Dreyfus Growth Opportunity	Gro	●	12.5	42.5	108.8	304.9	3.7	16.7	5.3	670.9	None	50
Dreyfus Leverage	Max	●	11.1	29.7	124.6	343.2	4.3	16.0	(5.5)	466.4	4.5	114
Dreyfus New Leaders	SCG	—	17.2	17.4	—	—	0.8	N.A.	18.5	120.5	None	82
Dreyfus Strategic Aggressive Investing	Max	—	9.5	—	—	—	0.0	N.A.	(4.5)††	143.8	3.0	134
Dreyfus Strategic Investing	Max	—	20.4	—	—	—	7.4	N.A.	0.4	105.6	4.5	152
Dreyfus Third Century	Gro	●	9.6	35.7	108.1	288.4	4.6	15.9	26.0	168.6	None	56
Eaton Vance Growth	Gro	●	17.5	34.2	123.4	341.3	1.0	19.9	15.9	88.0	4.75	100
Eaton Vance Investors	Bal	●	11.1	29.1	103.5	279.2	5.2	11.6	8.0	209.0	4.75	95
Eaton Vance Special Equities	Gro	□	14.3	10.5	62.6	291.9	0.0	16.8	4.6	36.5	4.75	109
Eaton Vance Stock	G&I	☆	14.1	35.6	133.7	317.5	3.2	12.1	11.8	84.1	4.75	98
Eaton Vance Total Return Trust	G&I	●	14.7	18.7	136.1	—	5.8	10.9	1.3	481.7	4.75	110
Eclipse Equity	SCG	—	15.2	—	—	—	3.6	N.A.	14.0	185.3	None	62
Enterprise Growth Portfolio	Gro	○	15.0	33.5	107.0	394.1	1.0	14.6	8.0	54.4	None†	133
Equitec Siebel Aggressive Growth	Max	—	14.0	19.7	—	—	0.5	17.0	11.8	39.0	None†	123
Equitec Siebel Total Return	G&I	—	11.6	20.2	—	—	2.4	12.8	18.5	135.0	None†	110
EuroPacific Growth	Intl	●	6.8	55.7	174.4	—	1.3	N.A.	17.0	245.7	5.75	126
Evergreen Fund	Gro	●	15.1	26.7	130.5	477.0	1.6	16.8	7.7	809.1	None	57
Evergreen Total Return	EqI	☆	13.4	26.0	124.9	435.7	5.7	15.7	8.3	1,373.4	None	56
Evergreen Value Timing	Max	—	15.4	—	—	—	1.5	14.8	10.6	29.6	None	85
Fairfield Fund	SCG	□	2.9	0.3	68.1	239.2	1.9	19.4	46.0	34.6	8.5	147
Fairmont Fund	Max	□	8.5	(0.7)	75.2	—	1.4	N.A.	2.5	55.4	None	69
FBL Series–Growth Common Stock	G&I	□	6.4	4.8	55.2	157.9	5.7	N.A.	43.3	37.3	None†	100
Fenimore International–Equity Series	Intl	—	8.7	28.2	—	—	0.9	N.A.	12.5	49.3	None†	159
Fidelity Balanced	Bal	—	11.5	—	—	—	5.9	18.7	2.6	134.2	2.0	90
Fidelity Blue Chip Growth	Gro	—	19.8	—	—	—	0.2	16.2	5.2	47.5	2.0†	114
Fidelity Capital Appreciation	Max	—	18.7	—	—	—	0.8	13.8	6.8	2,085.0	2.0†	105
Fidelity Contrafund	Gro	●	26.0	49.1	133.2	320.9	2.0	14.9	9.6	199.7	None	55
Fidelity Convertible	EqI	—	16.8	—	—	—	6.5	N.A.	11.0	45.6	None	87
Fidelity Destiny I	Gro	☆	19.6	49.5	161.3	557.3	1.8	11.8	4.2	1,701.0	9.0	33
Fidelity Destiny II	Gro	—	19.1	59.2	—	—	0.8	13.0	0.8	145.5	9.0	62
Fidelity Equity-Income	EqI	☆	15.6	43.0	137.1	524.2	5.3	14.4	4.1	4,768.7	2.0	54
Fidelity Europe	Intl	—	11.3	—	—	—	2.0	N.A.	7.2	70.7	2.0†	140
Fidelity Freedom**	Max	●	15.2	38.9	138.6	—	1.5	14.5	10.2	1,367.7	None	17

Key to rating symbols: ★ = Top 10%   ☆ = Next 20%   ● = Middle 40%   ○ = Next 20%   □ = Bottom 10%

† Fund may impose back-end exit fee.   **Open to retirement plans only   †† Figure reflects borrowing to boost investments.   N.A. Not available

FUND NAME	Type	MONEY risk-adjusted rating	% gain (or loss) to June 22, 1989				Portfolio analysis			Net assets (millions)	Expense analysis	
			1989	Three years	Five years	10 years	% yield	P/E ratio	% cash		% maximum initial sales charge	Five-year projection
Fidelity Fund	G&I	●	18.1	40.2	135.9	404.9	3.1	14.3	3.2	$988.6	None	$38
Fidelity Global Bond	Glo	—	(0.2)	—	—	—	8.5	N.A.	16.7	43.6	None	82
Fidelity Growth & Income	G&I	—	19.6	53.5	—	—	3.6	14.5	5.4	1,304.2	2.0	75
Fidelity Growth Company	Gro	●	25.4	30.3	144.1	—	0.6	23.1	10.0	259.1	3.0	85
Fidelity International Growth & Income	Intl	—	2.0	—	—	—	1.7	N.A.	3.9	26.2	1.0†	129
Fidelity Magellan	Gro	★	21.8	48.0	202.1	1251.3	1.7	13.5	5.0	10,808.4	3.0	91
Fidelity OTC	SCG	—	22.9	36.9	—	—	1.4	19.6	7.2	785.4	3.0	105
Fidelity Overseas	Intl	—	(0.9)	48.2	—	—	2.3	N.A.	1.6	967.3	3.0	103
Fidelity Pacific Basin	Intl	—	(1.9)	—	—	—	0.6	N.A.	4.4	118.2	2.0†	127
Fidelity Puritan	EqI	★	14.5	41.9	140.5	418.0	6.4	13.8	7.6	4,652.8	2.0	59
Fidelity Real Estate	Sec	—	10.3	—	—	—	6.2	25.0	4.2	57.0	2.0	90
Fidelity Select—American Gold	Gold	—	2.4	47.5	—	—	0.0	22.8	3.3	165.4	2.0†	153
Fidelity Select—Biotechnology	Sec	—	22.6	(7.4)	—	—	0.0	25.9	15.6	43.4	2.0†	162
Fidelity Select—Broadcast & Media	Sec	—	36.1	—	—	—	0.0	N.A.	8.9	41.5	2.0†	161
Fidelity Select—Chemicals	Sec	—	13.1	55.0	—	—	0.0	10.6	3.0	39.6	2.0†	134
Fidelity Select—Energy	Sec	●	18.3	52.4	68.9	—	2.2	20.2	21.4	74.2	2.0†	141
Fidelity Select—Energy Services	Sec	—	21.1	0.4	—	—	0.0	N.A.	17.4	37.1	2.0†	172
Fidelity Select—Financial Services	Sec	☆	22.8	4.4	132.4	—	2.5	11.7	0.4	40.9	2.0†	160
Fidelity Select—Health Care	Sec	☆	18.7	16.5	165.4	—	0.7	23.1	8.0	185.1	2.0†	119
Fidelity Select—Leisure	Sec	★	27.7	47.3	255.3	—	0.0	27.8	27.0	86.5	2.0†	135
Fidelity Select—Precious Metals	Gold	□	5.1	46.7	(7.2)	—	4.3	20.9	5.4	174.1	2.0†	138
Fidelity Select—Technology	Sec	○	14.6	(11.2)	(0.9)	—	0.0	17.7	9.9	122.5	2.0†	125
Fidelity Select—Telecommunications	Sec	—	31.9	97.0	—	—	0.5	27.3	5.2	90.3	2.0†	134
Fidelity Select—Utilities	Sec	★	18.8	31.7	150.5	—	2.3	14.5	16.5	150.8	2.0†	161
Fidelity Special Situations—Plymouth	Max	—	17.6	—	—	—	3.1	N.A.	0.4	189.6	4.0	134
Fidelity Trend	Gro	●	22.2	37.6	131.3	303.9	1.3	19.4	3.8	862.9	None	26
Fidelity Utilities Income	Sec	—	10.8	—	—	—	4.8	11.6	5.9	133.2	2.0	99
Fidelity Value	Max	●	20.5	37.8	117.2	370.0	1.6	19.1	1.4	129.0	None	61
Fiduciary Capital Growth	SCG	○	14.8	2.3	69.9	—	0.2	16.7	8.0	43.0	None	69
Financial Dynamics	Max	□	15.3	16.9	78.8	238.1	1.6	26.8	9.1	97.6	None	54
Financial Industrial	G&I	○	17.0	19.6	89.8	242.5	2.0	18.3	18.1	357.4	None	45
Financial Industrial Income	EqI	☆	16.9	38.2	141.8	400.0	3.9	13.9	7.2	408.4	None	43
Financial Strategic—Gold	Gold	□	(2.8)	26.8	(24.6)	—	1.3	24.5	15.5	28.4	None	87
Financial Strategic—Pacific Basin	Intl	●	2.6	75.1	210.1	—	0.0	32.0	7.7	23.7	None	89
First Investors Fund for Growth	Gro	□	16.7	2.5	2.6	109.4	1.8	15.4	7.2	35.6	8.5	139
First Investors International Securities	Glo	□	4.3	91.7	118.9	—	0.0	N.A.	2.4	84.4	8.5	171
Flex-funds Growth Portfolio	SCG	—	12.2	3.8	—	—	5.7	15.6	6.0	35.6	None	81
Founders Blue Chip	G&I	●	21.9	32.7	138.2	320.5	2.5	16.1	7.0	206.1	None	55
Founders Growth	Gro	●	30.1	43.5	140.8	466.5	1.6	22.8	8.0	71.3	None	75
Founders Special	Max	○	28.3	45.0	117.7	397.6	0.5	25.7	8.0	87.1	None	62
FPA Capital	Gro	●	25.2	58.2	151.5	316.3	1.4	11.6	1.2	76.9	6.5	111
FPA Paramount*	G&I	☆	15.8	71.9	137.9	451.9	2.6	21.0	29.8	204.2	6.5	117
FPA Perennial	G&I	●	15.7	39.8	107.1	—	3.4	12.6	15.0	52.9	6.5	125
Franklin DynaTech Series	Sec	●	20.1	27.0	58.4	294.4	0.5	19.0	4.5	34.6	4.0	86
Franklin Equity	Gro	☆	14.0	39.1	160.1	409.0	1.5	10.2	6.0	409.1	4.0	78
Franklin Gold	Gold	○	9.9	101.4	25.1	384.6	3.5	20.7	12.7	248.2	4.0	81
Franklin Growth Series	Gro	☆	12.6	50.8	133.7	327.3	2.0	14.6	4.8	117.1	4.0	81
Franklin Income Series	EqI	★	8.5	34.9	110.7	317.1	10.6	N.A.	15.0	988.3	4.0	73
Franklin Managed Rising Dividend	G&I	—	12.8	—	—	—	3.1	N.A.	25.0	36.1	4.0	133
Franklin Option	OpInc	●	12.1	33.6	91.5	312.8	2.8	14.4	13.4	45.8	4.0	85
Franklin Utilities Series	Sec	☆	9.8	26.1	118.0	297.1	7.4	12.0	2.8	601.9	4.0	74
Freedom Global	Glo	—	10.3	—	—	—	0.1	18.0	9.7	35.1	None†	156
Freedom Global Income Plus	Glo	—	0.6	—	—	—	6.9	N.A.	48.2	224.4	None†	121
Freedom Gold & Government	Gold	—	7.2	25.0	—	—	5.6	N.A.	3.2	63.0	None†	118

Key to rating symbols: ★ = Top 10%   ☆ = Next 20%   ● = Middle 40%   ○ = Next 20%   □ = Bottom 10%

†Fund may impose back-end load or exit fee.   *Currently closed to new investors   N.A. Not available

STOCK FUNDS

FUND NAME	Type	MONEY risk-adjusted rating	% gain (or loss) to June 22, 1989 1989	Three years	Five years	10 years	Portfolio analysis % yield	P/E ratio	% cash	Net assets (millions)	Expense analysis % maximum initial sales charge	Five-year projection
Freedom Regional Bank	Sec	—	15.4	37.6	—	—	1.3	11.6	4.6	$64.0	None†	$130
Fundamental Investors	G&I	☆	18.1	46.3	160.9	421.0	2.7	12.0	9.4	724.5	5.75	97
Fund of America	G&I	○	12.7	39.8	84.3	429.3	1.8	15.9	2.7	185.4	5.75	102
Fund Source International Equity	Intl	—	(0.8)	40.7	—	—	0.2	N.A.	5.1	39.2	None	118
FundTrust–Growth	Gro	—	13.7	31.1	—	—	0.9	N.A.	0.0	32.7	1.5	111
FundTrust–Growth & Income	G&I	—	12.1	30.6	—	—	2.1	N.A.	0.0	40.9	1.5	104
Gateway Option Index	OpInc	○	7.4	25.9	71.0	165.7	1.7	13.0	1.1	27.7	None	82
Gradison Established Growth	Gro	★	11.9	55.6	157.3	—	2.7	10.1	24.0	105.0	None	86
Growth Fund of America	Gro	●	23.2	52.9	143.1	506.2	1.4	23.2	18.9	1,466.4	5.75	102
Growth Fund of Washington	Gro	—	17.7	33.6	—	—	1.4	N.A.	11.0	57.3	5.0	139
Growth Industry Shares	Gro	○	16.2	24.9	88.6	329.5	1.3	17.6	2.3	64.6	None	51
G.T. Global–Bond	Glo	—	3.0	—	—	—	7.0	N.A.	19.1	31.6	4.75	155
G.T. Global–Government Income	Glo	—	2.5	—	—	—	11.2	N.A.	7.4	88.5	4.75	133
G.T. International Growth	Intl	—	10.4	65.3	—	—	0.0	N.A.	16.2	55.1	4.75	181
G.T. Pacific Growth	Intl	●	15.9	82.7	200.4	358.9	0.0	N.A.	17.1	90.0	4.75	182
Guardian Park Avenue	Gro	☆	17.3	37.2	165.4	513.5	2.3	13.2	10.0	157.0	4.5	82
Harbor Growth	Gro	—	18.0	—	—	—	0.9	N.A.	0.6	137.3	None	60
Harbor U.S. Equities	G&I	—	16.2	—	—	—	1.4	N.A.	0.5	55.9	None	56
Heartland Value	Max	—	12.7	22.5	—	—	0.8	N.A.	8.8	32.9	4.5	133
Heritage Capital Appreciation	Max	—	20.9	39.1	—	—	0.4	N.A.	28.1	54.3	4.0	149
Hidden Strength Growth	Gro	—	16.4	—	—	—	0.0	N.A.	0.0	33.7	4.75	156
Hidden Strength–Moderate	Bal	—	11.6	—	—	—	2.4	N.A.	10.1	41.3	4.75	152
IAI Apollo	Max	○	16.6	56.2	100.3	—	0.7	18.4	13.0	30.5	None	55
IAI Regional	Gro	★	16.8	40.8	172.9	—	1.3	17.3	23.0	112.2	None	55
IAI Stock	Max	●	16.9	43.5	126.7	370.9	1.3	15.1	11.0	76.1	None	55
IDEX Fund	Gro	—	30.2	69.9	—	—	2.0	N.A.	2.0	82.4	8.5	159
IDEX Fund II	Gro	—	30.6	73.0	—	—	1.9	N.A.	1.0	80.7	8.5	158
IDEX Fund 3	Gro	—	29.1	—	—	—	1.4	N.A.	6.0	75.5	8.5	160
IDS Discovery	SCG	□	18.6	9.8	60.3	—	1.4	21.5	5.0	171.9	5.0	83
IDS Equity Plus	G&I	●	14.2	31.5	120.4	297.3	3.5	13.8	3.0	383.7	5.0	87
IDS Growth	Gro	○	25.2	20.9	107.8	545.2	1.1	22.8	6.0	706.5	5.0	85
IDS International	Intl	—	0.1	35.1	—	—	0.8	N.A.	4.0	208.9	5.0	126
IDS Managed Retirement	G&I	—	21.3	40.0	—	—	2.8	18.5	3.0	699.4	5.0	101
IDS Mutual	Bal	★	12.1	44.5	136.6	322.9	6.0	9.4	6.0	1,593.9	5.0	87
IDS New Dimensions	Gro	☆	17.4	36.3	147.8	581.3	1.3	19.9	10.0	721.1	5.0	96
IDS Precious Metals	Gold	—	(0.3)	82.1	—	—	1.9	N.A.	23.0	88.8	5.0	123
IDS Progressive	Max	●	11.5	34.0	98.7	385.5	3.3	22.5	10.0	185.4	5.0	90
IDS Stock	G&I	●	15.1	38.2	118.9	295.2	3.1	13.8	13.0	1,314.5	5.0	83
IDS Strategy–Aggressive Equity	Max	●	24.4	17.9	138.1	—	0.0	18.1	7.0	284.7	None†	113
IDS Strategy–Equity Portfolio	G&I	☆	15.4	49.7	139.9	—	3.1	N.A.	19.0	263.4	None†	113
IDS Strategy–Pan Pacific Growth Port.	Glo	—	(1.3)	—	—	—	0.6	N.A.	2.0	52.6	None†	144
Income Fund of America	EqI	★	14.4	38.5	127.5	332.9	6.3	11.9	14.2	1,140.4	5.75	95
Integrated Capital Appreciation	Gro	—	16.6	34.2	—	—	1.1	N.A.	19.4	257.7	None†	139
Integrated Equity–Aggressive Growth	SCG	—	23.9	—	—	—	0.0	N.A.	16.9	49.4	4.75	159
Integrated Equity–Growth Portfolio	Gro	—	19.0	—	—	—	5.3	N.A.	7.5	40.0	4.75	144
Integrated Income–Convertible Sec.	EqI	—	11.2	—	—	—	5.5	N.A.	1.4	27.9	4.75	136
Integrated Multi-Asset–Total Return	G&I	—	13.3	—	—	—	2.7	N.A.	13.9	35.0	4.75	161
International Cash–Global	Glo	—	(2.4)	—	—	—	6.7	N.A.	100.0	87.3	1.25	119
International Investors	Gold	○	7.8	49.6	9.6	336.8	2.9	19.9	1.0	679.3	8.5	127
Investment Co. of America	G&I	★	17.4	44.0	154.6	422.2	3.7	12.9	20.4	4,810.8	5.75	88
Investment Portfolio–Equity	Gro	○	20.1	35.2	86.8	—	1.1	19.8	17.0	280.0	None†	128
Investment Portfolio–Total Return	Bal	—	12.9	—	—	—	4.0	15.2	3.7	516.0	None†	127
Investment Trust of Boston–Gro. Opp.	G&I	○	15.5	23.2	103.5	240.5	2.3	N.A.	0.9	60.8	4.25	132
Investors Research	Max	○	14.2	9.7	99.2	428.3	3.1	16.7	0.0	72.3	8.5	123

Key to rating symbols: ★ = Top 10%   ☆ = Next 20%   ● = Middle 40%   ○ = Next 20%   □ = Bottom 10%

†Fund may impose back-end load or exit fee.   N.A. Not available

FUND NAME	Type	MONEY risk-adjusted rating	% gain (or loss) to June 22, 1989				Portfolio analysis			Net assets (millions)	Expense analysis	
			1989	Three years	Five years	10 years	% yield	P/E ratio	% cash		% maximum initial sales charge	Five-year projection
ISI Trust	G&I	○	12.4	30.1	67.6	153.5	4.6	21.7	22.2	$103.5	6.0	$112
Ivy Growth	Gro	●	16.1	33.9	122.9	490.9	2.5	15.9	7.5	187.1	None	74
Ivy International	Intl	—	12.6	95.0	—	—	0.6	N.A.	3.5	37.5	None	103
Janus Fund	Max	☆	30.7	50.5	133.7	626.2	3.8	18.1	26.0	489.3	None	54
Janus Venture	SCG	—	26.0	46.3	—	—	4.4	23.2	19.0	48.0	None	77
Japan Fund	Intl	★	(6.8)	72.9	259.7	—	0.2	N.A.	9.0	374.7	None	56
John Hancock Global Trust	Glo	—	3.5	22.0	—	—	1.1	20.5	10.0	116.5	8.5	168
John Hancock Growth	Gro	●	20.6	28.5	120.7	365.4	1.4	20.7	6.0	115.5	8.5	139
Kemper Growth	Gro	○	20.1	42.9	107.1	386.9	2.6	17.8	19.0	314.0	8.5	127
Kemper International	Intl	●	1.2	49.2	178.2	—	2.3	N.A.	9.0	176.0	8.5	139
Kemper Summit	SCG	○	17.5	24.6	90.0	381.6	1.2	19.6	20.0	289.0	8.5	129
Kemper Technology	Sec	●	12.5	24.9	87.7	290.2	2.3	15.2	20.0	535.0	8.5	120
Kemper Total Return	Bal	○	14.4	22.3	99.4	348.4	5.0	16.0	17.0	957.0	8.5	125
Keystone America Omega	Max	●	17.6	39.5	144.5	232.8	0.7	12.8	6.9	37.7	2.0†	97
Keystone International	Intl	●	(6.7)	45.3	153.9	286.4	1.0	N.A.	3.8	115.7	None†	110
Keystone K-1	EqI	●	12.3	33.2	111.0	270.4	5.9	N.A.	4.1	721.2	None†	103
Keystone K-2	Gro	○	13.1	26.2	107.4	277.7	2.5	N.A.	10.0	347.1	None†	92
Keystone Precious Metals	Gold	○	3.0	72.3	8.9	218.2	0.8	19.9	3.0	190.3	None†	100
Keystone S-1	G&I	○	15.7	28.3	105.7	223.0	2.6	13.3	10.0	180.2	None†	96
Keystone S-3	Gro	○	17.0	30.6	97.5	294.6	1.4	16.3	8.6	256.6	None†	79
Keystone S-4	Gro	□	20.6	15.3	69.7	221.4	0.0	21.2	3.0	512.7	None†	64
Kidder Peabody Equity Income	EqI	—	17.9	25.4	—	—	3.3	N.A.	1.0	55.9	None†	129
Kidder Peabody MarketGuard	Sec	—	13.6	—	—	—	5.0	N.A.	54.4	26.4	4.0	101
Kleinworth Benson International Equity	Intl	●	4.4	60.4	221.7	357.7	0.0	27.2	3.6	62.0	None	141
Legg Mason Special Investment	SCG	—	30.0	26.5	—	—	0.1	14.2	12.3	56.0	None	133
Legg Mason Total Return Trust	Gro	—	14.3	20.7	—	—	1.7	11.7	7.2	29.5	None	123
Legg Mason Value Trust	Gro	●	16.6	28.5	130.0	—	1.6	12.7	12.7	778.0	None	106
Lehman Capital	Max	○	32.2	20.0	86.7	497.3	0.0	42.0	3.2	76.1	5.0	116
Lehman Investors	G&I	●	13.5	33.1	107.5	351.6	2.9	14.5	12.2	399.3	5.0	85
Lehman Opportunity	Max	☆	19.5	46.6	149.3	505.1	2.0	16.3	10.1	114.8	None	66
Lexington Global	Glo	—	6.4	—	—	—	0.3	N.A.	6.4	42.3	5.0	143
Lexington Goldfund	Gold	○	0.0	60.9	37.2	185.3	1.0	22.2	8.7	85.2	None	87
Lexington Growth	Gro	●	18.1	27.9	117.3	182.8	1.2	15.0	6.0	28.5	None	73
Lexington Research	G&I	●	18.6	31.9	115.4	328.3	2.9	21.8	7.4	126.6	None	61
Lindner Dividend	EqI	★	8.5	41.7	105.6	556.5	5.6	N.A.	25.0	113.6	None	54
Lindner Fund	Gro	☆	14.0	56.1	122.1	592.2	3.6	9.5	14.0	516.4	None	59
LMH Fund	G&I	●	15.4	30.3	95.1	—	3.8	10.9	20.2	38.4	None	79
Loomis-Sayles Capital Development*	Gro	●	13.4	30.4	160.0	732.0	3.5	14.5	0.9	201.9	None	51
Loomis-Sayles Mutual	Bal	☆	14.4	37.5	161.0	354.4	4.9	17.3	3.7	299.8	None	56
Lord Abbett Affiliated	G&I	☆	12.5	36.9	135.4	383.9	4.6	13.2	5.0	3549.0	7.25	96
Lord Abbett Developing Growth	SCG	□	8.0	(0.6)	26.4	165.8	0.4	17.9	9.0	157.0	7.25	128
Lord Abbett Value Appreciation	Gro	●	12.0	18.9	124.2	—	2.9	23.1	6.0	205.0	7.25	129
Mackay-Shields Capital Appreciation	Max	—	19.5	9.5	—	—	0.0	N.A.	0.7	26.0	None†	165
Mackay-Shields Convertible	EqI	—	5.0	6.0	—	—	6.9	N.A.	0.0	32.5	None†	170
MacKenzie American	Gro	—	13.4	57.4	—	—	1.7	N.A.	23.0	45.5	8.5	173
Mass. Capital Development	Gro	○	19.2	22.5	85.4	464.1	1.4	20.7	16.0	819.7	7.25	117
Mass. Financial Development	G&I	●	15.5	26.7	114.3	361.7	2.5	13.7	18.0	239.8	7.25	117
Mass. Financial Emerging Growth	SCG	○	19.5	9.0	81.3	—	0.0	29.0	9.0	243.1	7.25	148
Mass. Financial Intl. Trust—Bond	Glo	●	(1.1)	42.9	127.6	—	10.6	N.A.	38.5	126.3	7.25	130
Mass. Financial Lifetime—Capital Growth	Max	—	16.5	—	—	—	1.0	N.A.	15.0	172.9	None†	136
Mass. Financial Lifetime—Dividends Plus	G&I	—	10.7	—	—	—	5.9	N.A.	12.0	170.9	None†	133
Mass. Fin. Lifetime—Emerging Growth	SCG	—	17.1	—	—	—	0.0	N.A.	2.0	78.9	None†	143
Mass. Financial Lifetime—Global Equity	Glo	—	6.6	—	—	—	3.3	N.A.	17.0	42.3	None†	152
Mass. Fin. Lifetime—Managed Sectors	Sec	—	29.4	—	—	—	0.9	N.A.	10.0	164.4	None†	134

Key to rating symbols: ★ = Top 10%　☆ = Next 20%　● = Middle 40%　○ = Next 20%　□ = Bottom 10%

*Currently closed to new investors　†Fund may impose back-end load or exit fee.　N.A. Not available

STOCK FUNDS

FUND NAME	Type	MONEY risk-adjusted rating	% gain (or loss) to June 22, 1989				Portfolio analysis			Net assets (millions)	Expense analysis	
			1989	Three years	Five years	10 years	% yield	P/E ratio	% cash		% maximum initial sales charge	Five-year projection
Mass. Financial Managed Sectors Trust	Sec	—	29.8	25.4	—	—	1.3	22.4	10.0	$128.4	4.75	$124
Mass. Financial Special	Max	●	17.2	41.9	126.8	—	1.6	N.A.	20.0	133.2	7.25	140
Mass. Financial Total Return Trust	Bal	★	13.2	41.4	142.7	346.1	5.5	14.1	8.0	587.1	7.25	109
Mass. Investors Growth Stock	Gro	●	29.1	35.0	111.4	340.7	0.8	27.6	2.0	919.4	7.25	103
Mass. Investors Trust	G&I	●	18.5	41.0	129.1	318.0	2.8	15.1	5.0	1,296.7	7.25	101
Mathers Fund	Gro	☆	6.1	54.9	140.9	346.7	2.0	N.A.	78.9	217.1	None	56
Medical Technology Fund	Sec	●	15.1	4.2	91.7	—	0.0	22.0	16.0	34.0	None	121
Merrill Lynch Basic Value A	G&I	★	13.0	49.3	156.0	467.8	4.2	11.1	25.0	1,770.0	6.5	95
Merrill Lynch Capital A	G&I	★	12.4	41.7	149.3	428.5	3.9	12.7	15.0	803.0	6.5	96
Merrill Lynch Eurofund B	Intl	—	5.6	—	—	—	1.7	N.A.	7.0	209.4	None†	112
Merrill Lynch Fund for Tomorrow B	Gro	●	20.5	31.3	117.8	—	1.1	17.2	12.0	596.0	None†	101
Merrill Lynch Global Convertible B	Glo	—	2.5	—	—	—	5.8	N.A.	10.0	35.0	None†	132
Merrill Lynch International A	Glo	—	7.2	37.0	—	—	2.8	21.6	8.0	193.0	6.5	132
Merrill Lynch Natural Resources B	Sec	—	8.0	48.5	—	—	2.3	18.0	14.0	494.0	None†	100
Merrill Lynch Pacific A	Intl	☆	(9.9)	67.3	282.1	713.3	1.5	N.A.	7.0	286.8	6.5	118
Merrill Lynch Phoenix A*	G&I	★	11.1	51.9	149.8	—	3.4	22.4	36.0	280.8	6.5	125
Merrill Lynch Retirement Benefit B	Bal	—	9.4	23.2	—	—	5.0	N.A.	2.0	1,834.0	None†	99
Merrill Lynch Retirement Equity B	G&I	—	24.7	—	—	—	1.5	20.7	13.0	492.0	None†	104
Merrill Lynch Retirement Global Bond B	Glo	—	(3.8)	—	—	—	12.0	N.A.	4.0	268.0	None†	94
Merrill Lynch Science-Tech. Holdings A	Sec	●	3.6	22.6	73.1	—	1.4	N.A.	8.0	172.0	6.5	137
Merrill Lynch Special Value A	Gro	□	7.8	(13.3)	41.7	143.2	1.8	17.3	5.0	86.0	6.5	125
MetLife–State Street Capital App.	Max	—	23.5	—	—	—	0.1	19.6	0.5	35.5	4.5	123
MetLife–State Street Equity Income	EqI	—	13.1	—	—	—	5.3	12.4	12.0	40.4	4.5	123
MidAmerica Mutual	Gro	●	12.4	31.5	109.4	280.8	3.2	N.A.	28.8	36.5	5.75	110
Mutual of Omaha Growth	Gro	●	16.8	33.8	118.8	271.0	0.7	21.6	5.0	42.5	8.0	143
Mutual Qualified*	G&I	★	12.7	62.7	156.1	—	2.9	22.7	27.3	1,453.1	None	38
Mutual Shares*	G&I	★	12.9	60.5	153.6	528.6	2.2	22.3	27.7	3,305.8	None	40
National Aviation & Technology	Sec	●	30.2	43.7	119.2	265.4	1.0	20.4	10.0	86.0	4.75	118
National Growth	Gro	□	6.9	(4.4)	44.7	124.0	2.3	20.7	58.0	51.7	7.25	119
National Industries	G&I	□	12.8	21.2	67.3	153.4	1.0	N.A.	25.0	29.7	None	92
National Stock	G&I	●	19.3	37.4	134.3	323.3	3.4	N.A.	5.4	239.2	7.25	111
National Strategic Allocation	Max	—	6.9	—	—	—	2.4	N.A.	10.0	118.9	7.75	163
National Telecommun. & Technology	Sec	●	14.6	23.8	59.2	—	0.8	30.3	10.5	46.0	4.75	138
National Total Income	EqI	★	14.0	40.8	141.1	375.2	6.0	11.3	23.0	164.1	7.25	119
National Total Return	EqI	☆	17.3	31.3	116.5	364.9	4.5	N.A.	6.0	275.6	7.25	116
Nationwide Fund	G&I	☆	16.7	39.3	144.9	316.0	2.5	13.0	5.6	438.9	7.5	107
Nationwide Growth	Gro	☆	11.7	40.5	144.3	436.8	1.7	14.6	10.9	252.0	7.5	110
Neuberger & Berman Guardian	G&I	●	15.3	42.7	134.4	429.1	2.4	12.6	4.1	580.1	None	48
Neuberger & Berman Manhattan	Max	☆	19.8	40.6	156.3	528.0	1.5	17.6	1.9	410.6	None	66
Neuberger & Berman Partners	Gro	☆	14.7	37.8	136.8	487.7	3.4	20.1	3.1	750.5	None	55
Neuberger & Berman Sel. Sctrs. Plus	Sec	●	16.8	42.4	94.9	283.6	2.5	19.4	6.7	426.8	None	58
Neuwirth Fund	SCG	●	18.0	17.8	127.6	296.7	0.1	19.6	5.5	29.6	None	104
New Beginning Growth	SCG	●	22.2	29.2	128.7	—	1.2	33.3	10.0	55.0	None	66
New Economy	Gro	☆	21.6	43.8	161.1	—	1.9	23.3	16.7	799.6	5.75	96
New England Equity Income	G&I	●	10.2	21.2	108.1	310.4	3.1	14.1	16.9	58.1	6.5	145
New England Growth	Gro	●	13.5	33.5	132.6	642.9	2.8	10.6	1.6	523.3	6.5	130
New England Retirement Equity	G&I	●	13.2	23.8	126.3	385.3	3.1	13.8	7.5	144.8	6.5	129
New Perspective	Glo	●	10.3	54.8	153.0	431.5	2.9	13.1	16.4	1,097.6	5.75	99
Newton Growth	Gro	○	11.0	24.5	73.5	325.3	1.8	17.7	7.0	34.2	None	69
New York Venture	Gro	★	20.9	52.3	172.0	590.2	2.4	17.1	7.6	299.0	4.75	110
Nicholas Fund	Gro	☆	17.6	35.3	128.3	529.6	2.7	14.7	10.1	1,268.1	None	48
Nicholas Limited Edition	SCG	—	11.3	—	—	—	0.8	16.4	12.9	44.6	None	72
Nicholas II	SCG	☆	13.9	35.7	146.6	—	1.6	16.5	8.7	399.8	None	43
Nomura Pacific Basin	Intl	—	0.1	89.9	—	—	0.3	N.A.	4.4	67.7	None	70

Key to rating symbols: ★ = Top 10% ☆ = Next 20% ● = Middle 40% ○ = Next 20% □ = Bottom 10%

*Currently closed to new investors † Fund may impose back-end load or exit fee. N.A. Not available

FUND NAME	Type	MONEY risk-adjusted rating	% gain (or loss) to June 22, 1989 1989	Three years	Five years	10 years	Portfolio analysis % yield	P/E ratio	% cash	Net assets (millions)	Expense analysis % maximum initial sales charge	Five-year projection
Olympus Option Income Plus	OpInc	—	7.3	17.0	—	—	10.1	N.A.	6.0	$50.0	4.25	$165
Oppenheimer Asset Allocation	Bal	—	11.1	—	—	—	4.2	24.3	21.9	67.5	4.75	132
Oppenheimer Directors	Max	○	17.7	29.4	83.1	290.7	1.6	25.7	19.1	154.8	8.5	142
Oppenheimer Equity Income	EqI	★	12.1	42.7	137.7	442.7	5.1	15.6	17.0	1,021.3	8.5	127
Oppenheimer Fund	Gro	□	19.1	12.1	80.6	194.9	1.8	21.6	8.7	209.7	8.5	138
Oppenheimer Global	Glo	○	14.9	50.0	170.1	510.6	0.3	N.A.	0.7	442.1	8.5	178
Oppenheimer Gold & Special Minerals	Gold	●	10.8	180.9	115.3	—	1.4	N.A.	21.1	116.4	8.5	146
Oppenheimer OTC	SCG	—	26.1	—	—	—	0.6	29.5	21.6	48.4	4.75	126
Oppenheimer Premium Income	OpInc	●	4.0	61.2	91.5	251.8	6.8	23.4	10.2	294.0	8.5	139
Oppenheimer Regency**	Max	○	17.3	26.7	76.7	—	1.7	21.6	16.3	131.4	8.5	141
Oppenheimer Special	Gro	○	14.8	26.9	74.1	267.1	3.1	13.9	16.5	558.2	8.5	133
Oppenheimer Target	Max	□	13.7	5.3	68.8	—	1.4	14.4	26.6	75.5	4.75	108
Oppenheimer Time	Max	☆	21.2	41.1	149.6	471.5	2.4	23.6	17.9	323.2	8.5	134
Oppenheimer Total Return	G&I	☆	10.9	41.8	146.6	265.8	3.7	16.7	11.4	357.8	4.75	49
Over-the-Counter Securities	SCG	○	17.8	14.4	97.1	374.7	0.7	18.2	6.0	334.5	4.5	126
Pacific Horizon Aggressive Growth	Max	●	28.8	24.4	168.4	—	0.0	26.5	0.0	97.3	4.5	67
Paine Webber Asset Allocation	G&I	—	6.1	—	—	—	5.1	N.A.	56.4	640.6	None†	125
Paine Webber Classic Atlas	Glo	☆	3.2	41.9	209.0	—	2.9	N.A.	18.0	193.6	4.5	124
Paine Webber Classic Growth	Gro	—	22.2	35.7	—	—	0.7	26.4	6.1	68.3	4.5	118
Paine Webber Classic Growth & Income	G&I	—	17.5	31.4	109.1	—	3.3	20.9	4.1	59.0	4.5	120
Paine Webber Master Global	Glo	—	(3.6)	—	—	—	13.6	N.A.	34.2	1,091.4	None†	130
Paine Webber Master Growth	Gro	—	21.0	—	—	—	0.0	22.5	8.2	79.4	None†	138
Pax World	Bal	●	12.4	26.1	97.5	245.2	4.6	14.1	0.0	82.4	None	61
Penn Square Mutual	G&I	●	14.0	37.9	110.8	327.2	3.4	14.7	5.8	206.6	4.75	96
Pennsylvania Mutual	SCG	●	13.4	37.3	119.6	448.3	1.6	17.4	25.0	530.0	None	56
Permanent Portfolio	Bal	□	2.1	23.3	40.0	—	0.0	23.7	24.0	92.8	None	184
Philadelphia Fund	G&I	●	31.0	50.9	115.2	298.3	1.3	30.2	14.0	108.1	None	77
Phoenix Balanced Series	Bal	★	12.8	30.0	130.7	385.2	4.7	14.3	10.0	436.5	6.9	110
Phoenix Convertible	EqI	●	9.1	29.6	97.0	—	5.5	N.A.	16.0	156.7	6.9	112
Phoenix Growth Series	Gro	☆	12.1	36.1	137.2	640.7	2.3	15.3	15.0	649.3	6.9	113
Phoenix Stock Series	Max	●	12.4	29.0	120.8	621.1	2.8	17.3	14.0	129.2	6.9	112
Phoenix Total Return	G&I	○	10.3	25.3	82.7	—	3.2	15.8	9.0	33.8	4.75	127
Pilgrim MagnaCap	Gro	☆	15.9	30.6	144.6	408.3	1.5	14.8	2.0	211.6	4.75	127
Pine Street	G&I	●	14.0	23.8	112.1	280.1	3.6	11.8	1.8	52.3	None	65
Pioneer Fund	G&I	●	15.1	45.2	120.5	300.2	2.6	14.9	4.5	1,587.0	8.5	124
Pioneer II	G&I	●	16.0	42.9	125.8	408.1	2.8	16.1	8.4	4,236.0	8.5	126
Pioneer Three	G&I	○	17.3	32.8	107.5	—	1.8	16.2	5.2	733.0	8.5	124
T. Rowe Price Capital Appreciation	Max	—	13.8	—	—	—	2.3	N.A.	19.8	119.1	None	82
T. Rowe Price Equity Income	EqI	—	12.6	60.4	—	—	4.5	13.2	24.8	723.9	None	69
T. Rowe Price Growth & Income	G&I	○	15.7	38.1	96.4	—	3.6	13.1	10.9	517.5	None	57
T. Rowe Price Growth Stock	Gro	●	14.5	28.2	128.8	223.1	1.9	15.1	8.1	1,411.9	None	43
T. Rowe Price International Bond	Glo	—	(9.3)	—	—	—	9.1	N.A.	35.0	256.0	None	66
T. Rowe Price International Stock	Intl	☆	5.2	66.8	218.4	—	2.4	21.0	7.9	693.9	None	64
T. Rowe Price New America Growth	Gro	—	29.9	28.6	—	—	0.0	27.4	18.3	118.0	None	82
T. Rowe Price New Era	Sec	●	12.7	51.0	125.0	363.5	2.5	16.6	7.1	776.8	None	49
T. Rowe Price New Horizons	SCG	□	19.6	9.7	59.7	268.8	0.5	23.4	9.7	994.9	None	47
Primary Trend	G&I	—	12.0	—	—	—	4.7	N.A.	2.0	55.3	None	66
Princor Capital Accumulation	Max	●	14.3	35.4	140.1	401.9	2.6	15.2	4.4	117.3	5.0	113
Princor Growth	Gro	○	9.3	20.6	99.5	275.0	1.5	14.3	0.0	33.2	5.0	115
Provident Fund for Income	EqI	○	11.8	32.3	82.9	292.6	6.8	10.6	4.1	99.8	7.25	113
Pru-Bache Equity	Gro	●	16.9	31.7	127.9	—	1.7	N.A.	1.9	551.1	None†	98
Pru-Bache Equity Income	EqI	—	14.4	—	—	—	2.6	N.A.	9.4	70.1	None†	133
Pru-Bache Flexifund—Aggressive	G&I	—	10.8	—	—	—	3.2	N.A.	26.6	59.3	None†	138
Pru-Bache Flexifund—Conservative	G&I	—	8.1	—	—	—	4.0	N.A.	39.3	131.8	None†	122

Key to rating symbols: ★ = Top 10%   ☆ = Next 20%   ● = Middle 40%   ○ = Next 20%   □ = Bottom 10%

**Open to retirement plans only   †Fund may impose back-end load or exit fee.   N.A. Not available

STOCK FUNDS

FUND NAME	Type	MONEY risk-adjusted rating	% gain (or loss) to June 22, 1989				Portfolio analysis			Net assets (millions)	Expense analysis	
			1989	Three years	Five years	10 years	% yield	P/E ratio	% cash		% maximum initial sales charge	Five-year projection
Pru-Bache Global	Glo	○	(0.1)	27.2	159.2	—	3.2	N.A.	4.3	$422.0	None†	$111
Pru-Bache Global Natural Resources	Sec	—	6.8	—	—	—	0.2	N.A.	3.0	44.0	None†	112
Pru-Bache Growth Opportunity	SCG	○	13.2	19.3	86.9	—	0.9	17.1	1.1	145.2	None†	106
Pru-Bache IncomeVertible Plus	Sec	—	14.8	36.5	—	—	5.6	N.A.	8.2	498.0	None†	120
Pru-Bache Option Growth	OpInc	●	13.4	36.0	120.4	—	2.3	20.7	12.9	69.2	None†	102
Pru-Bache Research	Gro	●	16.3	32.5	124.8	—	2.6	N.A.	11.5	362.3	None†	108
Pru-Bache Utility	Sec	★	19.8	48.5	224.5	—	4.2	13.3	8.2	2,024.3	None†	94
Putnam Convertible Income & Growth	EqI	●	12.0	19.4	94.4	354.6	6.1	N.A.	5.8	887.1	8.5	134
Putnam Energy Resources	Sec	●	16.2	58.9	58.5	—	2.0	14.7	0.7	116.4	8.5	158
Putnam Fund for Growth & Income	G&I	☆	11.3	44.7	141.8	410.3	4.8	13.6	17.6	1,787.4	8.5	126
Putnam (George) Fund of Boston	Bal	☆	12.6	35.2	126.3	308.6	5.4	11.3	2.7	404.9	8.5	126
Putnam Global Government Income	Glo	—	(1.8)	—	—	—	12.6	N.A.	3.3	147.7	4.75	133
Putnam Health Sciences Trust	Sec	☆	17.6	24.6	140.3	—	1.4	20.5	3.9	253.7	8.5	139
Putnam Information Sciences	Sec	●	30.5	53.2	100.8	—	0.0	31.8	3.6	105.2	8.5	166
Putnam International Equities	Glo	☆	7.0	35.4	205.3	472.5	1.6	16.6	5.1	471.9	8.5	165
Putnam Investors	Gro	●	18.1	28.2	114.2	327.6	1.7	16.0	4.1	653.0	8.5	125
Putnam Option Income	OpInc	○	13.7	33.9	91.9	230.2	3.3	15.0	4.2	1,025.9	8.5	129
Putnam Option Income II	OpInc	—	13.4	28.1	—	—	3.7	18.0	4.2	1,234.8	8.5	126
Putnam OTC Emerging Growth	SCG	●	21.9	35.6	160.6	—	0.0	27.1	8.5	183.8	6.75	148
Putnam Vista Basic Value	Max	●	15.8	42.5	133.7	457.0	2.5	11.8	1.4	263.4	8.5	139
Putnam Voyager	Max	☆	24.4	46.2	173.2	484.8	0.4	26.6	8.2	679.5	8.5	138
Quest for Value	Max	●	11.2	23.9	102.4	—	1.1	14.4	9.3	78.3	4.5	140
Rea-Graham Fund	Bal	●	3.0	21.6	86.2	—	4.8	N.A.	80.0	49.9	6.75	139
Reich & Tang Equity	Gro	—	16.6	46.0	—	—	2.6	14.6	15.5	115.5	None	61
Rightime Blue Chip	G&I	—	6.3	—	—	—	6.3	14.2	6.0	75.3	4.75	177
Rightime Fund	G&I	—	5.4	15.2	—	—	0.4	N.A.	0.2	199.7	None†	137
RNC Convertible Securities	EqI	—	8.2	—	—	—	4.7	N.A.	0.2	29.8	4.75	135
Rodney Square Growth	G&I	—	21.2	—	—	—	0.7	N.A.	7.5	36.0	5.75	147
Rodney Square International Equity	Intl	—	1.9	—	—	—	0.5	N.A.	7.0	59.0	5.75	147
Royce Value	SCG	●	13.6	30.5	105.7	—	1.3	17.8	20.0	193.0	None	113
Safeco Equity	G&I	●	19.5	34.4	135.8	298.7	3.5	19.7	2.7	51.3	None	55
Safeco Growth	Gro	○	13.7	35.5	94.7	319.3	2.7	15.1	22.9	76.8	None	54
Safeco Income	EqI	☆	13.2	31.0	128.5	388.2	5.0	12.7	0.3	227.5	None	54
SBSF Growth	Gro	●	17.4	29.7	105.3	—	2.7	N.A.	18.0	87.9	None	64
Scudder Capital Growth	Gro	★	29.6	62.6	184.6	499.0	0.3	28.6	12.3	815.0	None	53
Scudder Development	SCG	□	12.8	10.4	60.6	257.0	0.0	24.0	1.1	325.4	None	71
Scudder Global	Glo	—	20.5	—	—	—	1.3	14.9	7.3	87.8	None	93
Scudder Growth & Income	G&I	☆	19.3	38.6	140.4	324.0	3.9	13.8	2.9	456.8	None	51
Scudder International	Intl	☆	8.5	56.7	197.1	433.8	0.0	N.A.	1.2	564.8	None	66
Security Action	Gro	○	16.8	19.3	94.0	—	1.2	17.2	1.1	204.3	8.5	47
Security Equity	Gro	●	22.1	48.2	140.1	386.3	2.0	15.2	2.8	262.5	8.5	140
Security Investment	G&I	○	13.9	25.9	73.5	211.4	5.9	11.5	1.2	85.3	8.5	147
Security Ultra	Max	□	10.9	0.5	63.3	280.6	0.3	17.4	0.0	70.1	8.5	178
Selected American Shares	G&I	★	19.7	45.5	159.9	389.7	1.4	15.8	22.8	341.8	None	61
Selected Special Shares	Gro	○	19.3	38.7	103.0	252.7	0.9	14.5	17.1	42.1	None	68
Seligman Capital	Max	○	18.4	11.1	92.9	411.3	0.0	18.0	2.3	125.0	4.75	100
Seligman Common Stock	G&I	●	13.8	26.4	132.7	372.2	3.2	13.2	0.5	517.0	4.75	84
Seligman Communications & Info.	Sec	☆	22.4	46.1	156.0	—	0.0	27.1	1.8	43.0	4.75	131
Seligman Growth	Gro	●	19.4	24.4	115.3	275.6	2.1	15.3	6.0	550.0	4.75	85
Sentinel Balanced	Bal	☆	10.9	27.0	119.2	306.4	5.6	12.3	11.6	68.3	8.5	136
Sentinel Common Stock	G&I	☆	15.4	33.5	140.2	425.1	3.7	12.6	3.8	542.8	8.5	128
Sentinel Growth	Gro	●	14.1	20.7	109.9	398.4	1.4	15.2	5.2	48.7	8.5	152
Sentry Fund	Gro	●	13.7	17.8	112.3	289.3	2.4	15.8	22.0	45.8	8.0	115
Sequoia Fund*	Gro	★	19.7	41.1	134.6	494.8	3.0	14.2	35.0	854.3	None	56

Key to rating symbols: ★ = Top 10% ☆ = Next 20% ● = Middle 40% ○ = Next 20% □ = Bottom 10%

*Currently closed to new investors   †Fund may impose back-end load or exit fee.   N.A. Not available

FUND NAME	Type	MONEY risk-adjusted rating	1989	Three years	Five years	10 years	% yield	P/E ratio	% cash	Net assets (millions)	% maximum initial sales charge	Five-year projection
Shearson Lehman Aggressive Growth	Max	●	30.4	42.9	146.3	—	0.0	42.8	0.9	$90.2	5.0	$108
Shearson Lehman Global Opportunities	Glo	—	5.5	12.5	—	—	1.2	12.5	6.8	97.5	5.0	118
Shearson Lehman Special Inc.–Utilities	Sec	—	9.7	—	—	—	6.6	N.A.	8.5	448.3	None†	N.A.
Sigma Capital Shares	Max	●	13.6	16.7	111.7	428.1	1.4	14.9	22.2	93.0	6.0	115
Sigma Investment Shares	G&I	☆	14.9	34.5	137.1	370.3	2.7	13.6	22.6	102.0	6.0	109
Sigma Trust Shares	Bal	☆	11.3	29.4	111.8	252.0	4.8	11.7	19.4	51.9	6.0	115
Sigma Venture Shares	SCG	□	11.2	(13.3)	47.4	221.1	0.1	18.9	18.5	49.1	6.0	122
SLH Appreciation	Gro	☆	16.8	41.6	149.6	496.1	2.2	16.7	8.5	705.4	5.0	96
SLH Equity–Growth & Opportunity	Gro	—	18.0	38.7	—	—	0.3	14.8	23.0	188.3	None†	129
SLH Equity–International Portfolio	Intl	—	4.3	19.0	—	—	0.0	N.A.	2.0	73.2	None†	155
SLH Equity–Sector Analysis	Max	—	14.2	—	—	—	3.6	N.A.	0.3	352.4	None†	124
SLH Equity–Strategic Investors	G&I	—	13.0	—	—	—	3.0	10.8	4.5	174.0	None†	133
SLH Fundamental Value	Gro	○	16.3	44.4	102.2	—	1.5	17.6	2.0	85.7	5.0	113
SLH Income–Convertible	EqI	—	9.4	—	—	—	6.4	N.A.	10.1	151.3	None†	105
SLH Income–Global Bond	Glo	—	0.2	—	—	—	4.1	N.A.	7.8	105.4	None†	118
SLH Income–Option Income	OpInc	—	11.7	31.5	—	—	7.6	11.3	7.8	590.4	None†	102
SLH Investment–Basic Value	Gro	—	15.8	26.9	—	—	2.4	N.A.	13.7	350.2	None†	105
SLH Investment–Growth	Gro	○	16.1	25.3	97.3	—	2.6	N.A.	30.1	972.5	None†	105
SLH Investment–Precious Metals	Gold	—	(0.2)	73.3	—	—	2.6	N.A.	3.0	82.4	None†	123
SLH Investment–Special Equities	SCG	□	12.4	2.4	66.0	—	3.9	N.A.	3.9	170.1	None†	118
SLH Precious Metals & Minerals	Gold	—	0.1	—	—	—	0.0	22.7	0.0	35.2	5.0	142
Smith Barney Equity	Gro	●	19.0	31.9	114.7	344.8	2.4	20.0	12.2	80.7	5.75	102
Smith Barney Income & Growth	G&I	☆	14.7	42.2	129.3	447.4	5.1	11.4	6.3	563.0	5.75	83
SoGen International	Gro	★	7.2	45.2	144.6	536.0	4.4	15.2	21.1	132.7	3.75	109
Southeastern Growth	Gro	—	16.9	13.3	—	—	0.1	14.8	5.1	106.1	None†	128
Sovereign Investors	G&I	☆	11.7	24.1	126.3	363.2	4.9	13.3	14.0	51.5	5.0	114
State Bond Common Stock	Gro	●	22.7	36.6	127.5	241.1	1.5	16.1	4.0	33.0	8.5	142
SteinRoe Capital Opportunities	Gro	○	28.0	24.9	87.6	323.2	0.4	20.8	16.6	203.4	None	56
SteinRoe Prime Equities	Gro	—	19.8	—	—	—	2.0	17.8	8.8	31.0	None	80
SteinRoe Special	Max	☆	24.9	51.5	159.4	549.2	1.1	23.2	8.1	275.4	None	55
SteinRoe Stock	Gro	○	20.3	24.0	99.9	296.3	1.9	18.2	3.4	188.3	None	42
SteinRoe Total Return	Bal	●	12.1	23.9	101.5	214.6	5.5	13.1	16.6	138.6	None	48
Strategic Investments	Gold	□	6.8	7.0	(57.5)	61.6	7.7	N.A.	5.0	40.7	8.5	162
Strategic Silver	Gold	—	(2.9)	(3.4)	—	—	0.0	N.A.	5.0	22.2	8.5	154
Stratton Monthly Dividend Shares	Sec	☆	13.1	15.6	112.8	—	8.2	11.5	11.0	33.1	None	66
Strong Investment	Bal	●	8.0	19.8	77.4	—	8.8	11.7	61.0	246.8	1.0	74
Strong Opportunity	Max	—	22.6	47.3	—	—	7.8	27.1	2.1	194.9	2.0	103
Strong Total Return	G&I	☆	13.8	39.3	127.7	—	10.9	29.4	10.3	1,204.4	1.0	75
Templeton Foreign	Intl	●	8.6	78.7	185.4	—	2.9	N.A.	14.0	380.5	8.5	126
Templeton Global	Glo	□	14.1	30.0	121.3	—	2.5	12.6	16.4	871.9	8.5	112
Templeton Growth	Glo	○	11.1	49.1	137.6	362.5	3.1	11.5	7.4	1,984.7	8.5	120
Templeton Income	Glo	—	2.8	—	—	—	7.6	N.A.	25.8	115.6	8.5	140
Templeton World	Glo	○	12.4	43.0	137.1	422.9	2.4	11.4	2.4	4,359.9	8.5	120
Thomson McKinnon–Global	Glo	—	13.1	—	—	—	0.0	N.A.	4.3	57.2	None†	148
Thomson McKinnon–Growth	Gro	☆	26.7	53.4	162.8	—	0.4	N.A.	5.3	359.3	None†	117
Thomson McKinnon–Opportunity	Max	●	23.2	30.6	118.7	—	0.0	N.A.	4.5	51.8	None†	128
Transamerica Growth & Income Shares	EqI	●	9.2	24.9	98.0	266.6	6.0	N.A.	48.0	66.7	4.75	115
Transamerica Sunbelt Growth	Gro	○	18.2	25.7	81.8	—	3.3	30.2	19.0	35.8	4.75	134
Transamerica Technology	Sec	—	12.1	74.5	—	—	0.6	N.A.	59.0	57.0	4.75	174
Tudor Fund	Max	●	19.0	29.4	117.8	545.7	0.3	18.8	2.0	194.8	None	63
Twentieth Century Growth	Max	●	30.4	43.9	150.9	576.0	2.0	20.3	3.5	1,427.0	None	55
Twentieth Century Heritage	Gro	—	20.4	—	—	—	0.9	15.6	2.8	80.5	None	55
Twentieth Century Select	Gro	●	20.8	29.9	137.0	639.7	2.2	17.3	1.5	2,489.0	None	55
Twentieth Century Ultra	Max	○	36.3	50.3	128.1	—	0.0	25.6	1.1	349.5	None	55

Key to rating symbols: ★ = Top 10%   ☆ = Next 20%   ● = Middle 40%   ○ = Next 20%   □ = Bottom 10%

†Fund may impose back-end load or exit fee.   N.A. Not available

STOCK FUNDS

FUND NAME	Type	MONEY risk-adjusted rating	% gain (or loss) to June 22, 1989				Portfolio analysis			Net assets (millions)	Expense analysis	
			1989	Three years	Five years	10 years	% yield	P/E ratio	% cash		% maximum initial sales charge	Five-year projection
Twentieth Century Vista	Max	○	31.8	27.7	122.6	—	0.1	27.8	0.9	$244.6	None	$55
United Accumulative	Gro	☆	17.0	41.8	140.2	448.8	3.9	15.1	16.7	823.9	8.5	117
United Continental Income	Bal	●	12.9	15.3	118.4	334.1	5.8	15.5	4.5	304.9	8.5	128
United Gold & Government	Gold	—	2.4	61.2	—	—	2.2	19.2	8.3	81.3	8.5	156
United Income	EqI	★	18.1	52.5	183.9	456.7	3.2	13.7	9.9	1,399.2	8.5	119
United International Growth	Intl	●	(0.8)	41.0	144.2	480.3	1.7	N.A.	9.4	263.8	8.5	141
United New Concepts	SCG	□	6.5	(3.5)	52.2	—	2.0	20.6	39.4	81.2	8.5	145
United Retirement Shares	G&I	●	14.5	26.5	97.7	305.1	4.5	13.4	12.1	123.9	8.5	131
United Science & Energy	Sec	●	16.3	44.5	114.1	333.1	1.8	18.1	10.7	230.4	8.5	130
United Services Gold Shares	Gold	□	12.9	36.2	(36.7)	169.7	6.4	N.A.	5.0	225.0	None	74
United Services New Prospector	Gold	—	(2.5)	42.3	—	—	0.0	30.4	15.0	87.5	None†	92
United Services Prospector*	Gold	○	5.9	56.1	3.4	—	0.0	21.5	15.0	37.9	None†	N.A.
United Vanguard	Gro	●	15.9	43.7	117.1	615.0	2.3	19.9	29.6	743.7	8.5	136
USAA Investors Trust–Cornerstone	Bal	—	9.4	55.4	—	—	3.7	21.6	0.0	501.0	None	67
USAA Investors Trust–Gold	Gold	—	(0.4)	43.1	—	—	1.7	23.6	14.9	153.9	None	78
USAA Mutual–Aggressive Growth	SCG	□	12.6	8.9	67.0	—	0.7	20.6	11.1	154.7	None	55
USAA Mutual–Growth	Gro	○	15.2	18.7	86.9	225.1	2.5	12.9	3.2	217.8	None	67
USAA Mutual–Income Stock	EqI	—	14.3	—	—	—	4.0	N.A.	2.9	45.4	None	55
U.S. Trend	Gro	●	18.2	40.3	110.1	287.6	2.6	13.4	4.0	87.0	4.75	101
Value Line Convertible	EqI	—	9.7	17.5	—	—	5.2	N.A.	7.3	61.3	None	59
Value Line Fund	G&I	●	17.1	26.5	115.3	328.2	2.1	15.2	4.4	196.6	None	40
Value Line Income	EqI	●	11.4	21.9	99.3	311.5	5.9	12.7	19.5	135.6	None	42
Value Line Leveraged Growth	Max	●	18.4	24.0	117.0	342.5	1.5	14.2	5.3	244.2	None	58
Value Line Special Situations	Gro	□	22.4	0.8	35.6	188.2	0.6	31.8	18.8	133.2	None	64
Van Eck Gold/Resources	Gold	—	(0.7)	56.1	—	—	0.2	27.5	3.3	208.5	6.75	138
Van Eck World Income	Glo	—	0.6	—	—	—	9.8	N.A.	26.7	36.2	5.75	144
Van Eck World Trends	Glo	—	(2.4)	28.1	—	—	1.1	N.A.	2.0	64.3	5.75	141
Vance Sanders Special	Gro	□	18.9	6.3	28.3	167.5	1.4	13.8	4.3	61.1	4.75	104
Vanguard Convertible	EqI	—	12.5	15.8	—	—	5.9	N.A.	3.4	69.9	None	47
Vanguard Equity Income	EqI	—	16.2	—	—	—	3.9	N.A.	5.1	150.2	None	35
Vanguard Explorer*	Sec	●	11.7	9.8	40.1	271.8	1.0	18.9	10.6	293.2	None	36
Vanguard Explorer II	SCG	—	13.9	11.7	—	—	0.4	20.2	9.4	85.2	None	41
Vanguard High Yield Stock*	EqI	★	9.1	43.0	166.6	562.4	6.9	9.3	4.3	168.1	None	30
Vanguard Index–Extended Market	SCG	—	18.7	—	—	—	1.4	18.7	1.4	79.8	1.0	73
Vanguard Index Trust–500 Portfolio	G&I	☆	18.0	44.6	146.4	369.9	2.9	14.2	3.8	1,405.4	None	12
Vanguard Naess & Thomas Special	SCG	□	14.3	10.4	50.9	252.0	0.4	N.A.	19.3	26.1	None	51
Vanguard Preferred Stock	EqI	☆	10.9	23.2	105.7	182.5	8.7	N.A.	7.0	71.5	None	37
Vanguard Quantitative Portfolio	G&I	—	18.0	—	—	—	1.8	13.4	4.2	157.1	None	36
Vanguard Specialized Portfolio–Energy	Sec	●	19.3	77.3	103.0	—	2.7	26.5	6.4	53.3	None†	22
Vanguard Specialized Port.–Gold & PM	Gold	○	2.5	69.1	20.2	—	3.2	N.A.	18.2	114.3	None†	27
Vanguard Specialized Port.–Health Care	Sec	★	15.5	44.3	182.1	—	1.7	22.1	8.5	61.4	None†	35
Vanguard STAR	Bal	—	13.1	41.4	—	—	4.0	N.A.	12.8	809.5	None	26
Vanguard Trustees' Commingled–Intl.	Intl	★	3.9	78.6	229.0	—	1.9	N.A.	7.4	493.6	None	29
Vanguard Trustees' Commingled–U.S.	G&I	●	16.6	52.7	122.6	—	2.6	12.4	2.9	140.4	None	32
Vanguard Wellington	Bal	☆	13.3	40.1	135.5	356.3	5.3	11.6	8.7	1,790.1	None	26
Vanguard Windsor*	G&I	★	15.4	56.1	180.0	558.8	4.3	8.4	8.8	7,670.9	None	26
Vanguard Windsor II	G&I	—	19.1	50.7	—	—	3.8	11.1	7.0	1,791.8	None	33
Vanguard W.L. Morgan Growth	Gro	●	13.3	37.2	116.1	347.9	2.0	13.6	7.4	699.3	None	26
Vanguard World–International Growth	Intl	☆	(0.6)	48.1	216.7	—	1.5	N.A.	4.1	456.4	None	37
Vanguard World–U.S. Growth	Gro	○	20.1	15.3	92.3	293.1	0.7	16.0	8.5	154.5	None	49
Van Kampen Merritt Growth & Income	G&I	—	12.4	—	—	—	2.7	N.A.	2.0	36.0	4.9	116
Washington Mutual Investors	G&I	☆	18.0	46.5	160.4	486.2	3.0	12.0	6.0	3,428.8	5.75	96
Winthrop Focus Growth	Gro	—	13.4	—	—	—	2.5	N.A.	3.8	53.3	None†	75
WPG Fund	Max	●	20.7	32.1	125.0	—	0.7	19.3	5.2	38.7	None	83

Key to rating symbols: ★ = Top 10% ☆ = Next 20% ● = Middle 40% ○ = Next 20% □ = Bottom 10%

*Currently closed to new investors †Fund may impose back-end load or exit fee. N.A. Not available

TAX-EXEMPT BOND FUNDS

FUND NAME	Type	Money risk-adjusted rating	1989	Three years	Five years	10 years	% yield	Average maturity (years)	% cash	Net assets (millions)	% maximum initial sales charge	Five-year projection
Alliance Muni Bond—Insured National	HGT	—	5.0	—	—	—	6.5	24.0	2.1	$106.8	4.0	$109
Alliance Muni Bond—National Portfolio	HGT	—	5.2	—	—	—	7.3	25.0	2.3	106.0	4.0	62
American Capital Muni Bond	HGT	○	5.5	18.3	78.8	93.7	7.3	26.0	7.5	230.1	4.75	84
American Capital Tax-Exempt—High Yield	HYT	—	5.4	16.1	—	—	8.4	22.0	3.7	230.7	4.75	92
American Capital Tax-Exempt Insured	HGT	—	4.3	13.9	—	—	6.8	24.0	3.6	36.4	4.75	92
AMEV Tax-Free—National	HGT	—	4.1	—	—	—	7.2	25.4	1.9	33.5	4.5	102
Benham National Tax-Free—Long-Term	HGT	—	5.3	20.1	—	—	6.9	12.5	5.9	33.4	None	28
Calvert Tax-Free Reserves—Limited-Term	ITT	□	3.0	19.0	42.3	—	5.9	0.9	3.0	133.5	2.0	61
Calvert Tax-Free Reserves—Long-Term	HGT	○	5.0	22.8	79.3	—	6.5	21.0	11.0	44.0	4.5	89
Cigna Municipal Bond	HGT	●	5.1	28.8	92.0	104.3	7.1	24.5	0.0	253.7	5.0	97
Colonial Tax-Exempt High Yield	HYT	○	3.9	24.8	60.3	183.3	7.7	12.6	5.8	1,484.0	4.75	105
Colonial Tax-Exempt insured	HGT	—	4.6	23.7	—	—	6.7	11.4	3.4	117.0	4.75	108
Composite Tax-Exempt Bond	HGT	●	4.1	25.3	86.4	83.1	7.1	8.3	1.3	99.3	4.0	83
DBL Tax-Free—Limited-Term	ITT	—	1.5	19.8	—	—	6.7	4.5	0.0	49.1	1.5	55
Dean Witter Tax-Exempt Securities	HGT	●	5.4	30.3	94.1	—	7.1	21.0	4.4	958.0	4.0	69
Delaware Group Tax-Free—USA	HGT	★	5.7	32.5	104.4	—	7.3	25.1	0.0	492.1	4.75	88
Delaware Group Tax-Free—USA Insured	HGT	—	4.9	27.4	—	—	6.8	23.7	0.9	51.4	4.75	91
Dreyfus Insured Tax Exempt	HGT	—	4.5	22.3	—	—	6.8	25.0	1.0	187.6	None	50
Dreyfus Intermediate Tax Exempt	ITT	○	3.9	24.4	65.9	—	7.2	8.6	3.1	1,056.0	None	41
Dreyfus Short-Intermed. Tax Exempt	ITT	—	2.3	—	—	—	6.1	1.8	9.1	60.7	None	41
Dreyfus Tax Exempt Bond	HGT	●	4.8	26.9	79.6	95.5	7.3	23.0	7.0	3,559.5	None	40
Eaton Vance High Yield Municipals	HYT	—	4.5	20.8	—	—	7.6	16.5	2.3	937.2	None†	124
Eaton Vance Muni Bond	HGT	★	5.5	31.0	98.1	113.2	7.2	15.4	8.2	70.8	4.75	101
Fidelity Aggressive Tax-Free	HYT	—	5.2	31.8	—	—	7.7	22.1	9.7	515.9	None†	43
Fidelity High Yield Municipals	HYT	☆	6.5	28.2	95.4	120.6	7.0	23.4	4.7	1,686.0	None	40
Fidelity Insured Tax-Free	HGT	—	5.2	25.4	—	—	6.4	23.3	11.6	159.9	None	48
Fidelity Limited Term Muni	ITT	○	3.4	23.3	70.3	105.0	6.6	10.8	7.0	427.5	None	41
Fidelity Municipal Bond	HGT	●	5.3	29.4	91.4	92.5	6.9	24.0	14.1	1,009.4	None	32
Fidelity Short-Term Tax-Free	ITT	—	1.8	—	—	—	5.8	2.8	3.4	65.6	None	33
Financial Tax-Free Income Shares	HGT	☆	6.5	31.8	105.1	—	6.8	26.4	10.0	141.0	None	43
First Investors Insured Tax Exempt	HGT	●	4.5	26.6	81.2	111.8	7.1	25.0	1.0	1,018.7	7.25	126
Fortress High Yield Municipal	HYT	—	5.8	—	—	—	7.0	15.4	6.6	51.4	1.0†	65
Franklin Federal Tax-Free Income	HGT	●	4.5	30.0	86.4	—	7.9	26.0	3.0	3,721.1	4.0	68
Franklin High Yield Tax-Free Income	HYT	—	5.2	32.9	—	—	8.8	26.0	3.0	1,041.5	4.0	75
Franklin Insured Tax-Free Income	HGT	—	5.5	27.5	—	—	7.4	25.0	1.0	616.7	4.0	73
Freedom Managed Tax-Exempt	HGT	—	5.1	—	—	—	6.8	20.0	11.0	83.4	None†	66
GIT Tax-Free High Yield	HYT	○	3.3	23.8	75.1	—	6.7	17.0	19.0	40.6	None	64
IDS High Yield Tax-Exempt	HYT	●	5.6	29.8	88.9	128.6	7.4	21.1	12.0	4,309.8	5.0	82
IDS Insured Tax-Exempt	HGT	—	4.9	—	—	—	6.4	22.6	12.0	74.3	5.0	92
IDS Tax-Exempt Bond	HGT	●	6.1	28.5	87.2	101.1	6.9	21.8	12.0	976.4	5.0	83
Integrated Insured Tax-Free—STRIPES	HGT	—	3.1	24.3	—	—	6.6	23.0	8.3	119.4	4.75	117
John Hancock Tax-Exempt Income Trust	HGT	☆	4.6	29.8	94.6	83.7	6.6	25.7	5.0	375.2	4.75	92
Kemper Municipal Bond	HGT	★	6.5	31.6	94.0	125.2	7.3	20.0	1.0	1,771.0	4.5	72
Keystone America Tax-Free Income	HGT	—	4.0	—	—	—	6.2	25.8	2.6	167.9	2.0†	114
Keystone Tax-Exempt Trust	HGT	—	4.8	27.2	—	—	6.8	20.9	5.9	580.5	None†	93
Keystone Tax-Free*	HGT	●	4.4	27.3	84.1	117.8	7.4	21.5	3.9	912.1	None†	97
Liberty Tax-Free Income	HGT	●	5.9	29.4	87.7	95.7	6.8	16.7	2.2	467.9	4.5	95
Limited Term Muni—National Portfolio	ITT	—	2.8	22.3	—	—	6.6	4.3	2.0	177.3	2.75	87
Lord Abbett Tax-Free Income—National	HGT	☆	4.9	32.6	97.0	—	6.9	23.5	2.1	301.0	4.75	83
Mackay-Shields Tax-Free Bond	HGT	—	3.9	23.6	—	—	5.9	25.0	3.0	104.0	None†	108
Mass. Financial Lifetime—Managed Muni	HGT	—	5.0	—	—	—	6.1	25.2	5.0	306.3	None†	132
Mass. Fin. Managed High Yield Muni*	HYT	●	5.5	24.3	72.6	—	8.3	20.0	5.5	457.4	4.75	82
Mass. Fin. Managed Muni Bond	HGT	☆	5.4	31.3	93.3	177.5	6.8	20.2	6.0	1,156.3	4.75	82
Merrill Lynch Muni—High Yield A	HYT	●	4.4	28.9	87.4	—	7.5	21.5	10.0	1,521.0	4.0	70
Merrill Lynch Muni—Insured A	HGT	●	4.8	28.4	85.6	—	7.3	20.4	10.0	2,136.0	4.0	68

Key to rating symbols: ★ = Top 10%   ☆ = Next 20%   ● = Middle 40%   ○ = Next 20%   □ = Bottom 10%

*Currently closed to new investors   †Fund may impose back-end load or exit fee.

TAX-EXEMPT BOND FUNDS

FUND NAME	Type	MONEY risk-adjusted rating	% gain (or loss) to June 1, 1989				% yield	Portfolio analysis			Net assets (millions)	Expense analysis	
			1989	Three years	Five years	10 years		Average maturity (years)	% cash		% maximum initial sales charge	Five-year projection
Merrill Lynch Muni—Limited Maturity	ITT	☐	2.7	16.0	34.8	—	5.9	0.9	12.0	$393.0	0.75	$30
Mutual of Omaha Tax-Free Income	HGT	☆	5.3	33.8	102.4	101.9	6.9	23.0	0.5	343.4	8.0	113
National Securities Tax-Exempt	HGT	●	4.9	30.2	94.3	98.2	7.2	21.0	6.3	93.8	4.5	88
Nationwide Tax Free	HGT	—	4.8	22.3	—	—	6.6	19.0	0.9	64.7	None†	58
New England Tax-Exempt Income	HGT	●	4.7	26.6	87.9	112.1	6.4	10.0	3.8	135.7	4.5	97
Nuveen Insured Tax-Free—National	HGT	—	6.0	—	—	—	6.6	24.0	10.4	79.3	4.0	86
Nuveen Municipal Bond	HGT	☆	6.1	31.8	91.4	112.8	6.7	22.0	2.4	1,088.7	4.0	75
Oppenheimer Tax-Free Bond	HGT	●	4.5	27.6	88.8	121.3	7.4	19.9	2.0	200.5	4.75	90
Paine Webber Muni—High Yield	HYT	—	4.7	—	—	—	7.3	22.7	10.4	59.4	4.25	67
Paine Webber Tax-Exempt Income—Natl.	HGT	—	4.1	28.4	—	—	7.3	24.2	6.2	321.7	4.25	82
T. Rowe Price Tax-Free High Yield	HYT	—	5.1	30.1	—	—	7.3	20.9	11.5	369.1	None	55
T. Rowe Price Tax-Free Income	HGT	○	4.4	19.8	62.1	109.4	6.8	20.2	3.1	1,086.3	None	38
T. Rowe Price Tax-Free Short-Intermed.	ITT	☐	2.4	15.9	38.5	—	5.6	1.3	29.7	213.1	None	43
Principal Preservation—Tax-Exempt	HGT	☐	4.1	15.5	22.0	—	6.7	16.9	1.8	79.3	4.5	100
Princor Tax-Exempt Bond	HGT	—	6.5	31.0	—	—	6.8	23.6	3.0	33.3	5.0	113
Pru-Bache Muni—High Yield Series	HYT	—	5.5	—	—	—	8.0	26.3	9.3	417.7	None	46
Pru-Bache Muni—Insured Series	HGT	—	5.4	—	—	—	7.0	25.1	12.0	350.9	None†	47
Pru-Bache Muni—Modified Term Series	ITT	—	4.2	—	—	—	6.8	11.0	17.3	41.5	None†	52
Pru-Bache National Muni	HGT	○	3.8	23.8	82.0	—	6.6	25.5	3.8	1,036.8	None†	65
Putnam Tax Exempt Income	HGT	●	5.9	31.6	92.4	175.6	6.9	26.6	5.8	1,217.8	4.75	75
Putnam Tax-Free High Yield	HYT	—	4.8	25.2	—	—	6.8	24.4	3.0	625.5	None†	126
Putnam Tax-Free Insured	HGT	—	5.3	26.5	—	—	5.8	27.4	1.4	289.2	None†	116
Safeco Municipal Bond	HGT	☆	5.1	33.5	99.4	—	7.0	21.7	3.8	250.8	None	34
Scudder High-Yield Tax Free	HYT	—	5.9	—	—	—	6.9	20.6	13.0	97.1	None	55
Scudder Managed Muni Bond	HGT	●	6.4	32.8	92.6	116.6	6.7	17.9	9.6	657.9	None	34
Scudder Tax-Free Target—1990	ITT	○	2.3	17.1	48.4	—	5.5	1.0	7.3	64.9	None	44
Scudder Tax-Free Target—1993	ITT	○	2.7	19.8	60.2	—	6.0	3.9	9.8	75.5	None	44
Scudder Tax-Free Target—1996	ITT	—	3.2	22.2	—	—	6.2	5.2	10.6	27.0	None	54
Seligman Tax-Exempt—National	HGT	★	5.2	31.1	104.3	—	6.8	23.5	0.0	140.0	4.75	91
Shearson Lehman Managed Municipals	HGT	☆	5.3	29.6	89.6	—	7.3	24.8	0.0	1,527.6	5.0	80
SLH Income—Tax-Exempt Income	HGT	—	5.0	27.0	—	—	6.7	23.3	0.0	538.6	None†	88
Smith Barney Muni Bond—National Port.	HGT	—	5.3	—	—	—	7.7	24.3	2.7	115.7	4.0	59
State Bond Tax-Exempt	HGT	—	5.8	30.1	—	—	6.9	24.6	3.1	47.9	4.5	90
SteinRoe High-Yield Municipal	HYT	★	5.4	31.9	99.8	—	7.4	17.1	2.4	270.8	None	42
SteinRoe Intermediate Municipal	ITT	—	3.1	20.2	—	—	5.9	4.7	2.7	89.3	None	44
SteinRoe Managed Municipal	HGT	☆	4.9	30.3	100.9	138.0	6.6	18.0	2.2	504.3	None	36
Tax-Exempt Bond of America	HGT	●	4.5	26.8	81.1	—	6.7	22.1	8.0	425.6	4.75	87
Thomson McKinnon Tax Exempt	HGT	—	5.4	26.2	—	—	5.8	17.9	14.1	65.9	None†	117
Transamerica Special—High Yld. Tax-Free	HYT	—	4.4	—	—	—	6.8	19.5	7.5	28.1	None†	131
United Municipal Bond	HGT	★	5.6	34.0	105.1	100.9	6.7	27.5	2.3	570.2	4.25	74
United Municipal High Income	HYT	—	5.1	27.0	—	—	8.4	23.6	1.1	155.9	4.25	85
USAA Tax Exempt—High Yield	HGT	●	5.6	30.1	92.4	—	8.5	23.6	4.2	1,055.8	None	29
USAA Tax Exempt—Intermediate-Term	ITT	○	4.6	25.1	69.3	—	8.1	9.2	4.7	422.7	None	31
USAA Tax Exempt—Short-Term	ITT	☐	2.9	18.3	42.4	—	7.2	2.3	0.0	251.1	None	31
UST Master Intermed.-Term Tax-Exempt	ITT	—	3.1	26.3	—	—	6.5	5.0	4.1	61.9	4.5	39
Value Line Tax Exempt—High Yield	HGT	●	4.2	26.3	82.5	—	7.7	24.0	0.7	275.6	None	36
Vanguard Muni Bond—High Yield	HYT	☆	6.1	31.9	100.1	113.1	7.2	17.9	18.1	830.3	None	16
Vanguard Muni Bond—Insured Long	HGT	—	5.8	31.0	—	—	7.1	15.8	9.3	898.0	None	16
Vanguard Muni Bond—Intermediate	ITT	●	4.8	28.2	79.0	90.0	6.8	9.5	12.7	939.2	None	16
Vanguard Muni Bond—Limited Term	ITT	—	3.0	—	—	—	6.1	2.8	34.9	165.5	None	16
Vanguard Muni Bond—Long Term	HGT	☆	6.0	30.4	95.7	92.2	7.1	16.9	17.1	604.7	None	16
Vanguard Muni Bond—Short Term	ITT	☐	2.6	16.9	35.6	86.8	5.6	1.2	49.0	711.4	None	16
Van Kampen Merritt Insured Tax Free	HGT	—	4.2	28.0	—	—	6.6	25.3	5.0	584.7	4.9	94
Van Kampen Merr. Tax Free High Income	HYT	—	3.6	31.1	—	—	8.1	24.8	1.0	564.8	4.9	93
Venture Muni Plus	HYT	☐	4.7	20.7	45.3	—	8.1	20.0	2.5	67.5	None†	131

Key to rating symbols:　★ = Top 10%　☆ = Next 20%　● = Middle 40%　○ = Next 20%　☐ = Bottom 10%

†Fund may impose back-end load or exit fee.

TAXABLE BOND FUNDS

FUND NAME	Type	MONEY risk-adjusted rating	1989	Three years	Five years	10 years	% yield	Average maturity (years)	% cash	Net assets (millions)	% maximum initial sales charge	Five-year projection
Advest Advantage Government Securities	USG	—	5.1	10.4	—	—	9.1	7.4	28.6	$123.2	None†	$80
Advest Advantage Income	Flx	—	10.4	26.2	—	—	5.7	12.1	1.1	56.4	None†	122
AIM High-Yield Securities	HYC	□	3.5	16.8	57.5	156.6	13.9	8.5	7.0	71.8	4.75	114
AIM Limited Maturity Trust	STT	—	4.1	—	—	—	8.3	1.4	2.3	72.3	1.75	105
Alliance Bond–High Yield Portfolio	HYC	—	3.7	13.7	—	—	13.2	8.0	9.3	273.9	5.5	118
Alliance Bond–Monthly Income Portfolio	HGC	☆	5.7	25.9	95.8	161.9	9.5	7.5	21.9	49.2	5.5	148
Alliance Bond–U.S. Government Portfolio	USG	—	5.4	24.4	—	—	10.7	7.0	1.6	520.3	5.5	114
Alliance Mortgage Securities	MBS	●	4.3	27.6	77.6	—	11.3	5.0	(19.1)**	597.7	5.5	113
AMA Income–U.S. Gov. Plus Portfolio	USG	○	3.8	16.3	62.2	123.2	8.7	9.1	32.0	40.3	None	93
American Capital Corporate Bond	HGC	★	4.2	29.2	96.4	165.3	10.5	12.0	6.8	233.1	4.75	87
American Capital Federal Mortgage	MBS	—	6.2	16.6	—	—	8.7	21.0	0.0	41.0	4.75	111
American Capital Government Securities	USG	—	8.0	21.0	—	—	10.1	10.0	2.2	4,853.4	4.75	92
American Capital High Yield	HYC	○	1.5	15.5	77.9	167.9	14.5	11.0	3.8	588.9	4.75	86
American High-Income Trust	HYC	—	6.0	—	—	—	11.2	9.7	10.9	112.2	4.75	101
AMEV U.S. Government Securities	USG	●	6.4	27.2	83.5	173.6	9.5	15.6	5.2	110.0	4.5	91
Axe-Houghton Income	HGC	☆	5.0	23.8	107.3	208.8	9.9	6.5	15.4	61.6	None	80
Babson Bond Trust–Long-Term Portfolio	HGC	●	6.8	25.8	81.2	168.5	9.5	11.5	3.0	70.0	None	39
Bartlett Fixed Income	HYC	—	6.3	26.1	—	—	8.9	7.0	15.0	161.0	None	55
Benham Government–GNMA Income	MBS	—	6.7	29.7	—	—	9.1	N.A.	0.8	257.5	None	42
Benham Government Treasury Note	USG	○	5.6	17.5	64.9	—	7.7	3.4	0.0	81.1	None	42
Benham Target–1995	USG	—	8.3	22.3	—	—	0.0	6.4	0.1	31.1	None	39
Benham Target–2015	USG	—	19.4	—	—	—	0.0	26.5	1.8	106.5	None	39
Bond Fund of America	HGC	☆	6.6	27.3	98.5	209.2	9.5	13.8	11.4	1,178.2	4.75	85
Boston Co. Managed Income	HGC	★	3.5	27.9	88.6	—	8.4	10.6	14.0	65.6	None	63
Bull & Bear High Yield	HYC	□	(1.9)	(5.8)	37.2	—	12.9	9.0	7.0	82.4	None	93
Bull & Bear U.S. Gov. Guaranteed Sec.	MBS	—	4.5	23.9	—	—	9.2	4.6	2.0	40.1	None	106
Cardinal Government Guaranteed	MBS	—	5.6	26.0	—	—	9.8	11.0	0.0	123.0	4.75	86
Carnegie Gov. Securities–High Yield	USG	○	6.0	22.4	74.9	—	7.6	14.0	11.0	56.5	4.5	112
Cigna Government Securities	USG	—	5.4	—	—	—	8.6	N.A.	28.0	51.3	5.0	102
Cigna High Yield	HYC	★	5.1	31.1	100.4	213.5	12.0	9.0	6.0	289.8	5.0	100
Cigna Income	HYC	●	6.9	25.6	92.6	182.3	9.2	16.6	12.0	216.2	5.0	101
Colonial Government Securities Plus	USG	●	6.3	25.0	83.6	—	8.4	19.4	0.3	2,740.0	6.75	126
Colonial High Yield Securities	HYC	★	3.2	28.4	90.3	192.0	12.4	9.1	4.6	457.0	4.75	111
Colonial Income	HYC	☆	4.8	25.4	86.0	164.4	10.3	17.8	1.7	159.0	4.75	109
Colonial U.S. Government Trust	MBS	—	5.0	—	—	—	9.7	7.4	3.1	56.0	4.75	113
Columbia Fixed Income Securities	HGC	●	7.1	27.9	81.2	—	8.3	9.6	3.4	100.3	None	43
Common Sense Government	USG	—	7.3	—	—	—	9.0	11.0	1.3	87.7	6.75	141
Composite Income	HYC	☆	3.5	25.1	83.0	143.3	10.7	3.8	0.6	138.4	4.0	94
Composite U.S. Government Securities	USG	—	6.3	25.4	—	—	9.2	17.1	0.3	77.8	4.0	87
Dean Witter Government Plus	USG	—	7.1	—	—	—	7.8	17.8	8.0	1,897.0	None†	102
Dean Witter High Yield Securities	HYC	○	0.4	16.8	72.2	—	16.5	10.7	1.3	2,006.0	5.5	81
Dean Witter U.S. Government Securities	MBS	—	4.9	24.1	—	—	9.9	15.6	2.4	9,987.0	None†	86
Delaware Group–Delchester I	HYC	★	4.6	33.3	106.7	203.4	12.5	10.8	3.8	677.7	6.75	112
Delaware Group–Delchester II	HYC	—	4.5	—	—	—	12.2	10.8	3.8	84.3	4.75	109
Delaware Group–Gov. Income Series	MBS	—	5.0	24.5	—	—	9.0	8.3	8.5	139.3	4.75	111
Delaware Grp. Treasury Reserves–I.S.	STT	—	2.9	20.3	—	—	8.3	3.3	2.8	112.0	None	50
Drexel Series–Government Securities	USG	—	7.3	18.4	—	—	7.0	25.0	12.0	151.0	None†	123
Dreyfus A Bond Plus	HGC	●	8.5	26.4	93.3	196.0	8.8	20.3	5.0	275.4	None	49
Dreyfus GNMA	MBS	—	5.2	23.7	—	—	9.0	17.9	0.0	1,608.0	None	56
Dreyfus Short-Intermediate Government	STT	—	5.0	—	—	—	8.8	2.2	8.0	30.8	None	0
Dreyfus Strategic Income	HYC	—	7.5	—	—	—	9.7	16.1	10.0	40.4	4.5	80
Dreyfus U.S. Government Intermediate	USG	—	6.0	—	—	—	9.1	5.2	1.0	58.2	None	26
Eaton Vance Government Obligations	USG	—	6.1	25.9	—	—	10.0	5.2	(8.6)**	301.6	4.75	143
Eaton Vance High Income Trust	HYC	—	3.9	—	—	—	12.3	9.9	5.1	280.6	None†	136

Key to rating symbols: ★ = Top 10%   ☆ = Next 20%   ● = Middle 40%   ○ = Next 20%   □ = Bottom 10%

†Fund may impose back-end load or exit fee.   N.A. Not available   **Figure reflects borrowing to boost investments.

TAXABLE BOND FUNDS

FUND NAME	Type	MONEY risk-adjusted rating	% gain (or loss) to June 22, 1989				Portfolio analysis			Net assets (millions)	Expense analysis	
			1989	Three years	Five years	10 years	% yield	Average maturity (years)	% cash		% maximum initial sales charge	Five-year projection
Eaton Vance Income of Boston	Flx	★	6.0	33.9	111.4	232.6	13.2	9.8	6.6	$88.5	4.75	$116
Equitec Siebel High Yield	HYC	—	4.7	20.5	—	—	11.1	7.0	12.8	28.0	None†	133
Equitec Siebel U.S. Government Sec.	USG	—	3.4	20.5	—	—	9.8	2.0	12.3	292.0	None†	113
Fidelity Flexible Bond	HGC	●	6.6	22.6	83.4	152.6	8.9	9.1	12.8	341.0	None	42
Fidelity Government Securities	USG	●	6.0	22.1	75.5	179.7	8.5	7.2	4.2	544.5	None	44
Fidelity High Income	HYC	☆	4.6	26.6	101.6	239.2	12.3	9.1	8.1	1,887.7	None	49
Fidelity Income—GNMA Portfolio	MBS	—	6.7	25.9	—	—	8.3	22.5	8.0	641.2	None	48
Fidelity Income—Mortgage Securities	MBS	—	6.6	26.0	—	—	8.2	23.3	1.9	394.0	None	50
Fidelity Intermediate Bond	HGC	●	5.6	22.6	84.1	209.6	8.9	5.9	27.8	540.9	None	48
Fidelity Short-Term Bond Portfolio	STT	—	4.5	—	—	—	8.8	1.9	5.1	229.5	None	51
Financial Bond Shares—High Yield	HYC	★	5.3	28.8	103.8	—	12.2	8.8	11.5	62.9	None	46
Financial Independence—Treas. Allocation	USG	—	7.1	—	—	—	6.6	0.2	7.0	69.8	4.0	105
Financial Independence—U.S. Gov. Sec.	MBS	○	4.5	24.7	71.5	—	8.2	25.4	40.0	31.0	4.0	112
Financial Select Income	HGC	●	4.8	22.4	86.1	169.0	9.9	4.7	61.5	30.2	None	55
First Investors Bond Appreciation	HYC	□	1.5	2.3	49.7	147.0	12.7	10.0	3.4	194.3	7.25	135
First Investors Fund for Income	HYC	○	2.3	19.4	65.3	130.0	13.2	8.3	6.3	1,680.0	8.5	135
First Investors Government	MBS	—	6.4	24.8	—	—	8.8	27.0	3.7	237.1	7.25	123
First Investors High Yield	HYC	—	2.1	—	—	—	12.7	9.1	5.7	715.8	7.25	139
First Trust U.S. Government	USG	—	6.4	29.0	—	—	8.8	24.5	7.0	240.4	2.5	77
Franklin AGE High Income	HYC	○	3.6	23.4	80.9	176.3	13.6	11.0	4.0	2,242.6	4.0	71
Franklin IS Trust—Adjustable Rate Mort.	MBS	—	4.0	—	—	—	8.4	29.0	4.0	41.8	4.0	67
Franklin IS Trust—Short-Intermediate	STT	—	4.8	—	—	—	7.4	1.7	3.0	28.4	1.5	58
Franklin Partners—Tax-Advan. U.S. Gov.	USG	—	6.0	—	—	—	9.7	27.0	6.0	52.4	4.0	54
Franklin U.S. Government Series	MBS	☆	6.7	29.1	85.5	136.8	10.1	28.0	3.0	11,244.2	4.0	68
Freedom Government Plus	USG	—	7.1	24.7	—	—	8.0	14.6	3.2	146.7	None†	97
Fund for U.S. Government Securities	MBS	●	7.2	28.9	77.8	150.7	9.2	23.0	2.2	1,050.1	4.5	96
Fund Source Gov. Securities Income	USG	□	6.4	18.3	48.2	—	7.5	6.6	0.0	41.9	1.75	101
FundTrust—Income	HYC	—	3.6	15.9	—	—	8.8	7.8	1.3	44.7	1.5	112
Government Income Securities	USG	—	7.3	29.1	—	—	8.9	21.0	1.0	1,417.2	1.0†	58
Hidden Strength U.S. Gov. Sec. High Yield	MBS	—	6.3	—	—	—	9.3	5.2	6.5	58.9	4.75	137
IAI—Bond	HGC	☆	9.0	24.8	88.6	182.5	7.3	16.0	15.0	61.9	None	50
IAI—Reserve	STT	—	4.2	21.2	—	—	7.3	0.4	15.0	70.8	None	47
IDEX Total Income	Flx	—	4.5	—	—	—	9.3	16.0	2.0	27.1	7.0	121
IDS Bond	HYC	●	6.7	26.4	93.3	200.8	9.2	13.9	16.0	1,737.1	5.0	91
IDS Extra Income	HYC	●	3.6	24.2	82.8	—	12.1	10.8	7.0	1,301.8	5.0	95
IDS Federal Income	USG	—	4.2	25.9	—	—	8.1	8.0	8.0	181.8	5.0	92
IDS Selective	HGC	●	6.1	27.5	92.0	194.5	8.8	13.9	16.0	1,075.0	5.0	91
IDS Strategy—Income Portfolio	HGC	●	5.5	25.7	91.9	—	7.4	9.9	7.0	183.0	None†	118
Integrated Home Investors Gov. Guar.	MBS	○	6.0	23.7	73.5	—	8.2	10.6	10.1	165.1	None†	112
Integrated Income—Government Plus	USG	—	3.5	—	—	—	10.6	8.6	2.8	53.7	4.75	173
Integrated Income—High Yield	HYC	—	3.8	—	—	—	12.	9.6	11.4	40.1	4.75	155
Integrated Income Plus	HYC	—	3.8	—	—	—	11.2	10.2	7.5	45.1	None†	155
Intermediate Bond Fund of America	HGC	—	4.5	—	—	—	8.8	7.2	43.4	89.8	4.75	95
Investment Portfolio—Diversified Income	HYC	—	8.2	11.5	—	—	14.2	10.8	53.0	385.0	None†	123
Investment Portfolio—Government Plus	USG	—	6.0	20.1	—	—	10.3	6.4	15.0	6,044.0	None†	117
Investment Portfolio—High Yield	HYC	★	4.0	33.7	94.8	—	12.	5.7	2.0	788.0	None†	123
John Hancock Bond	HGC	☆	6.3	26.9	95.0	159.3	9.5	14.9	3.0	1,112.4	8.5	127
John Hancock High Income—Fed. Sec. Plus	USG	—	5.1	—	—	—	9.9	9.1	4,0	83.7	4.75	111
John Hancock High Income—Fixed Income	HYC	—	3.4	—	—	—	12.5	9.2	2.0	95.4	4.75	112
John Hancock—U.S. Gov. Guar. Mortgage	MBS	—	6.6	25.7	—	—	9.1	10.7	2.0	362.7	8.5	130
John Hancock—U.S. Government Securities	STT	○	6.0	19.0	75.2	155.7	8.7	4.0	2.0	185.5	8.5	137
Kemper Diversified Income	HYC	□	10.3	19.0	49.8	180.6	14.8	10.7	43.0	333.0	8.5	134
Kemper Enhanced Government Income	USG	—	5.7	—	—	—	10.8	8.0	34.0	74.0	4.5	124
Kemper High Yield	HYC	★	4.7	39.6	110.2	252.7	13.0	5.6	8.0	1,499.0	4.5	83

Key to rating symbols: ★ = Top 10%   ☆ = Next 20%   ● = Middle 40%   ○ = Next 20%   □ = Bottom 10%

†Fund may impose back-end load or exit fee.

TAXABLE BOND FUNDS

FUND NAME	Type	MONEY risk-adjusted rating	1989	Three years	Five years	10 years	% yield	Average maturity (years)	% cash	Net assets (millions)	% maximum initial sales charge	Five-year projection
Kemper Income & Capital Preservation	HGC	☆	6.1	28.2	88.9	176.0	10.8	6.5	30.0	$358.0	4.5	$82
Kemper U.S. Government Securities	MBS	●	7.4	26.3	87.5	152.0	10.1	6.3	1.0	4,274.0	4.5	72
Keystone America Government Securities	USG	—	5.8	—	—	—	7.6	8.7	5.2	68.2	2.0†	122
Keystone America High Yield Bond	HYC	—	5.7	—	—	—	12.5	10.3	8.1	147.7	2.0†	117
Keystone America Investment Grade	HGC	—	2.0	—	—	—	8.5	9.1	2.1	30.5	2.0†	122
Keystone B-1	HGC	○	6.3	17.1	78.6	165.5	8.5	13.4	9.8	409.3	None†	89
Keystone B-2	HYC	●	4.1	19.6	80.3	190.3	10.2	15.8	9.4	948.8	None†	91
Keystone B-4	HYC	□	3.9	12.2	58.9	169.0	13.4	10.0	8.9	1,204.1	None†	99
Kidder Peabody Government Income	USG	—	5.9	26.0	—	—	8.1	27.3	2.0	113.7	None†	118
Lexington GNMA Income	MBS	●	8.3	28.8	80.1	127.5	8.6	19.3	17.9	93.8	None†	59
Liberty High Income Securities	HYC	●	6.0	26.1	88.2	194.0	12.8	11.1	5.6	378.5	4.5	100
Lord Abbett Bond Debenture	HYC	○	6.9	25.0	80.3	191.9	10.8	10.8	9.1	712.0	7.25	106
Lord Abbett U.S. Government Securities	USG	●	6.8	28.0	88.4	201.2	11.1	9.9	6.0	1,117.0	4.75	94
Mackay-Shields Government Plus	USG	—	6.8	25.0	—	—	9.3	8.0	5.3	461.7	None†	129
Mackay-Shields High Yield Bond	HYC	—	3.3	25.5	—	—	14.6	11.4	11.5	149.3	None†	139
Mass. Financial Bond	HGC	●	6.9	23.5	90.5	179.7	9.1	4.8	13.0	302.9	7.25	112
Mass. Fin. Government Guaranteed	MBS	—	6.2	21.9	—	—	9.3	3.4	14.0	348.9	4.75	109
Mass. Fin. Gov. Securities High Yield	USG	—	6.6	19.4	—	—	7.6	N.A.	1.0	1,309.8	4.75	119
Mass. Fin. High Income—Series I	HYC	○	5.5	22.6	76.7	233.6	12.9	9.6	5.0	813.3	7.25	117
Mass. Fin. High Income—Series II	HYC	—	5.5	—	—	—	11.5	9.6	5.0	41.4	4.75	124
Mass. Fin. Lifetime—Gov. Income Plus	USG	—	5.6	—	—	—	7.1	N.A.	3.3	3,310.1	None†	128
Mass. Fin. Lifetime—High Income	HYC	—	5.1	—	—	—	10.8	9.7	5.0	140.5	None†	136
Merrill Lynch Corporate—High Income A	HYC	☆	4.5	28.3	89.1	186.0	12.5	9.0	15.0	777.7	4.0	74
Merrill Lynch Corporate—High Quality A	HGC	☆	6.8	26.1	92.7	—	9.1	N.A.	13.0	316.6	4.0	72
Merrill Lynch Corporate—Intermed. Bond	HGC	●	5.9	23.5	83.5	—	9.0	5.2	5.0	86.4	2.0	54
Merrill Lynch Federal Securities	MBS	—	6.1	26.4	—	—	9.7	22.9	5.0	2,856.0	4.0	77
Merrill Lynch Retirement Income B	MBS	—	5.9	21.8	—	—	9.0	8.2	6.0	1,738.0	None†	75
MetLife—State Street Government Income	USG	—	5.7	—	—	—	9.7	N.A.	9.5	1,279.6	None	57
MetLife—State Street Gov. Securities	USG	—	5.6	—	—	—	8.6	12.0	15.6	27.8	4.5	111
MetLife—State Street High Income	HYC	—	5.1	—	—	—	11.9	10.0	4.5	99.1	4.5	111
Midwest Income—Intermed.-Term Gov.	STT	○	4.7	19.0	59.6	—	7.8	2.7	17.0	44.3	2.0	76
Mutual of Omaha America	USG	○	7.7	25.1	74.2	149.1	8.4	14.1	6.0	50.8	None	57
Mutual of Omaha Income	Flx	●	8.3	29.8	101.0	196.5	8.4	18.0	5.0	162.9	8.0	121
National Bond	HYC	□	2.2	6.3	56.1	117.6	13.6	9.0	6.0	682.6	7.25	123
National Federal Securities Trust	USG	—	6.0	11.1	—	—	10.3	11.0	6.0	587.3	6.75	111
Nationwide Bond	HGC	●	6.4	22.4	79.5	—	8.8	16.1	3.3	34.9	7.5	109
Neuberger & Berman Ltd. Maturity Bond	STT	—	5.1	21.5	—	—	7.9	1.7	17.7	107.2	None	36
Neuberger & Berman Money Market Plus	STT	—	3.9	—	—	—	8.1	0.7	47.2	80.4	None	36
New England Bond Income	HGC	●	6.6	24.6	79.0	140.1	7.6	3.0	1.0	70.4	6.5	127
New England Government Securities	USG	—	5.8	19.8	—	—	7.6	5.0	5.0	174.9	6.5	130
Nicholas Income	Flx	☆	4.0	25.8	83.3	155.7	10.2	6.4	17.9	79.0	None	46
Northeast Investors Trust	Flx	★	2.9	25.3	106.9	205.2	13.6	10.1	0.0	406.0	None	42
Olympus U.S. Government Plus	USG	—	5.2	20.4	—	—	8.8	13.0	2.0	80.9	4.25	135
Oppenheimer GNMA	MBS	—	5.6	—	—	—	9.0	N.A.	0.0	55.1	4.75	105
Oppenheimer High Yield	HYC	●	5.0	28.8	78.0	159.2	12.4	7.3	12.0	855.6	6.75	113
Oppenheimer U.S. Government Trust	USG	—	5.3	22.7	—	—	9.6	N.A.	2.5	217.7	6.75	126
Paine Webber Fixed Income—GNMA	MBS	—	5.8	24.0	—	—	8.8	9.2	7.5	1,038.8	4.25	78
Paine Webber High Yield	HYC	—	3.9	14.8	—	—	13.8	9.2	5.5	423.0	4.25	80
Paine Webber Investment Grade Bond	HGC	—	6.1	21.7	—	—	8.3	9.8	12.1	280.4	4.25	80
Paine Webber Master Income	Flx	—	6.0	20.7	—	—	7.5	8.6	10.8	229.9	None†	121
Phoenix High Yield Series	HYC	●	3.6	24.8	83.7	—	12.1	10.0	11.0	151.0	4.75	88
Pilgrim GNMA	MBS	—	7.5	24.5	—	—	9.5	23.0	0.0	145.0	4.75	99
Pilgrim High Yield	HYC	○	3.3	22.1	74.2	161.8	13.2	9.8	7.0	34.9	4.75	123
Pioneer Bond	HGC	●	6.6	24.4	75.6	157.8	9.0	8.0	8.4	62.0	4.5	92

Key to rating symbols: ★ = Top 10%   ☆ = Next 20%   ● = Middle 40%   ○ = Next 20%   □ = Bottom 10%

†Fund may impose back-end load or exit fee.   N.A. Not available.

TAXABLE BOND FUNDS

FUND NAME	Type	MONEY risk-adjusted rating	% gain (or loss) to June 22, 1989 1989	Three years	Five years	10 years	% yield	Average maturity (years)	% cash	Net assets (millions)	% maximum initial sales charge	Five-year projection
Piper Jaffray Government Income	USG	—	4.0	—	—	—	8.8	11.0	1.3	$58.9	4.0	$105
T. Rowe Price GNMA	MBS	—	6.5	23.9	—	—	9.6	9.5	10.8	347.1	None	54
T. Rowe Price High Yield Bond	HYC	—	3.4	30.1	—	—	12.7	9.2	5.7	1,203.4	None	57
T. Rowe Price New Income	HGC	O	5.5	23.6	70.2	167.4	9.5	7.6	6.0	924.2	None	48
T. Rowe Price Short-Term Bond	STT	O	4.0	21.2	55.4	—	8.5	2.8	63.3	213.2	None	53
Principal Preservation Gov. Portfolio	USG	—	5.1	22.2	—	—	8.4	24.7	0.6	31.5	4.5	108
Princor Government Securities Income	USG	—	7.9	31.4	—	—	8.3	25.5	2.0	54.7	5.0	106
Pru-Bache GNMA	MBS	O	6.4	22.2	66.4	—	7.8	7.0	6.0	222.0	None†	93
Pru-Bache Gov.–Intermediate Term	USG	●	5.3	23.0	72.9	—	10.2	3.8	18.9	427.1	None	46
Pru-Bache Government Plus	USG	—	5.7	21.2	—	—	7.6	19.1	3.1	3,751.4	None†	97
Pru-Bache Government Plus II	USG	—	8.5	—	—	—	7.0	20.8	8.1	147.2	None†	102
Pru-Bache High Yield	HYC	●	3.7	24.3	82.4	184.9	11.3	11.5	6.2	2,788.7	None†	81
Putnam Capital Preservation/Income	USG	—	4.9	—	—	—	8.6	4.2	13.0	54.0	4.75	79
Putnam GNMA Plus	MBS	—	7.4	18.3	—	—	8.5	8.4	3.1	1,074.8	4.75	98
Putnam High Income Government	USG	—	6.5	20.1	—	—	8.9	10.1	14.2	8,131.8	6.75	106
Putnam High Yield	HYC	☆	4.3	30.1	89.6	216.1	13.5	8.9	2.4	2,463.8	6.75	104
Putnam High Yield Trust II	HYC	—	5.1	31.0	—	—	13.0	8.6	3.9	439.3	6.75	128
Putnam Income	HGC	☆	7.0	28.1	91.7	186.2	9.9	15.7	9.0	368.3	6.75	107
Putnam U.S. Gov. Guaranteed Securities	MBS	☆	6.5	29.1	77.7	—	10.0	9.7	8.4	1,359.1	4.75	81
Rodney Square Benchmark–U.S. Treasury	USG	—	0.4	—	—	—	8.1	N.A.	28.0	39.0	4.50	103
Safeco U.S. Government	USG	—	5.8	—	—	—	9.3	16.6	27.3	25.7	None	58
Scudder GNMA	MBS	—	5.9	25.3	—	—	8.9	6.5	5.7	247.8	None	57
Scudder Income	Flx	●	6.7	26.2	89.7	168.4	8.5	8.7	1.1	253.1	None	52
Security Income–Corporate Bond	HGC	●	6.5	23.9	82.3	162.9	10.1	21.2	4.4	53.9	4.75	105
Seligman High Income–High Yield Bond	HYC	—	6.0	26.7	—	—	12.6	9.7	5.5	56.0	4.75	107
Seligman High Income–Sec. Mort. Income	MBS	—	3.9	24.0	—	—	9.6	N.A.	45.5	40.0	4.75	105
Seligman High Income–U.S. Gov. Guar.	USG	—	4.3	14.2	—	—	8.6	9.9	3.4	95.0	4.75	105
Seligman Income	Flx	●	9.9	23.1	102.9	243.9	7.8	N.A.	5.8	163.0	4.75	90
Sentinel Bond	HGC	●	7.1	26.0	84.4	165.7	9.0	7.2	6.7	26.7	8.5	131
Sentinel Government Securities	USG	—	6.4	—	—	—	8.6	4.9	16.4	32.0	8.5	129
Shearson Lehman High Yield	HYC	☆	4.1	25.4	84.0	—	13.0	9.9	5.6	508.9	5.0	89
Sigma Income Shares	HGC	●	5.8	20.0	91.3	157.2	7.9	26.0	8.5	600.9	None†	99
SLH Income–High Income	HYC	—	4.5	—	—	—	11.5	10.4	18.7	34.1	None†	98
SLH Income–Intermediate Term Gov.	USG	—	4.0	17.0	—	—	6.9	2.7	3.2	784.4	None†	92
SLH Income–Long-Term Government	USG	—	4.8	16.1	—	—	8.3	N.A.	0.0	65.4	None†	105
SLH Income–Mortgage	MBS	—	5.4	—	—	—	8.4	21.5	2.7	631.5	5.0	91
SLH Investment–Government Securities	USG	□	7.5	17.0	63.8	—	8.6	7.0	1.4	492.2	None†	99
SLH Investment–Investment Grade	HGC	●	8.6	22.6	102.6	—	8.6	25.8	0.9	2,394.7	None†	89
SLH Managed Governments	MBS	—	4.0	22.8	—	—	8.9	8.3	21.7	35.9	4.5	94
Smith Barney U.S. Government Securities	MBS	—	8.0	30.3	—	—	9.2	18.3	1.5	327.4	4.0	63
SteinRoe Government Plus	USG	—	6.0	22.1	—	—	8.1	19.5	20.8	30.9	None	55
SteinRoe High-Yield Bond	HGC	—	5.8	31.1	—	—	10.0	15.5	12.5	109.2	None	50
SteinRoe Managed Bond	HGC	●	5.9	22.2	87.7	165.1	8.7	12.7	25.6	159.5	None	41
Strong Government Securities	USG	—	7.4	—	—	—	7.7	1.2	32.4	32.1	None	24
Strong Income	Flx	—	6.5	30.6	—	—	10.3	5.2	34.4	243.1	None	67
Strong Short-Term Bond	STT	—	5.5	—	—	—	9.0	2.2	71.5	119.3	None	56
Thomson McKinnon–Income	HYC	—	6.3	21.4	—	—	9.1	N.A.	26.5	605.6	None†	107
Thomson McKinnon U.S. Government	USG	●	2.8	23.5	73.3	—	10.2	7.2	15.0	619.4	None†	112
Transamerica Gov. Securities Trust	USG	—	5.2	20.8	—	—	10.8	6.0	58.0	1,111.5	4.75	104
Transamerica Investment Quality Bond	HGC	●	6.4	21.3	92.2	—	9.7	8.1	71.0	108.4	4.75	107
Twentieth Century Long-Term Bond	HGC	—	7.4	—	—	—	9.0	7.8	5.6	36.9	None	55
Twentieth Century U.S. Governments	USG	O	4.5	21.0	60.0	—	9.3	1.4	2.2	418.8	None	55
United Bond	HGC	★	7.1	30.5	105.7	184.8	9.1	8.2	3.1	348.7	8.5	118
United Government Securities	USG	O	5.0	18.1	77.1	—	8.3	17.4	1.1	111.1	4.25	83

Key to rating symbols: ★ = Top 10% ☆ = Next 20% ● = Middle 40% O = Next 20% □ = Bottom 10%

†Fund may impose back-end load or exit fee. N.A. Not available

TAXABLE BOND FUNDS

FUND NAME	Type	MONEY risk-adjusted rating	% gain (or loss) to June 22, 1989				Portfolio analysis			Net assets (millions)	Expense analysis	
			1989	Three years	Five years	10 years	% yield	Average maturity (years)	% cash		% maximum initial sales charge	Five-year projection
United High Income*	HYC	●	3.8	21.7	85.8	—	13.1	12.8	8.6	$1,233.9	8.5	$124
United High Income II	HYC	—	3.7	—	—	—	12.1	10.3	25.4	312.7	8.5	131
USAA Mutual—Income	Flx	☆	8.4	34.2	92.6	201.3	9.3	13.3	1.0	309.2	None	34
U.S. Government Guaranteed Securities	USG	—	5.7	24.2	—	—	9.8	12.4	17.7	474.9	4.75	100
Value Line Aggressive Income	HYC	—	2.7	8.9	—	—	11.8	11.0	12.8	39.8	None	63
Value Line U.S. Government Securities	USG	☆	6.1	26.8	88.3	—	8.9	23.0	2.1	241.0	None	37
Vanguard Bond Market	HGC	—	7.0	—	—	—	8.8	9.2	9.9	81.2	None	20
Vanguard Fixed Income—GNMA	MBS	●	7.0	29.9	88.2	—	9.3	26.6	8.3	1,938.8	None	20
Vanguard Fixed Income—High Yield	HYC	☆	3.7	29.2	94.2	203.6	12.5	10.1	14.3	1,218.8	None	23
Vanguard Fixed Income—Invest. Grade	HGC	●	8.4	29.4	94.1	183.6	9.2	23.9	8.4	784.9	None	21
Vanguard Fixed Income—Short-Term Bond	STT	●	5.0	24.2	70.2	—	8.4	2.1	7.4	515.8	None	19
Vanguard Fixed Income—Short-Term Gov.	STT	—	5.1	—	—	—	8.6	2.3	3.2	177.5	None	18
Vanguard Fixed Income—U.S. Treasury	USG	—	9.8	24.9	—	—	8.3	22.4	6.7	254.3	None	20
Vanguard Wellesley Income	Flx	☆	11.5	33.4	121.4	283.7	6.3	14.7	5.8	650.1	None	29
Van Kampen Merritt High Yield	HYC	—	2.6	—	—	—	12.6	9.6	7.0	348.9	4.9	113
Van Kampen Merritt U.S. Government	MBS	—	6.6	26.6	—	—	9.1	9.5	(1.7)**	3,630.0	4.9	87
Venture Income Plus	HYC	□	4.4	11.5	60.5	—	13.9	7.3	11.9	52.9	4.75	107
Venture Ret. Planning of America—Bond	MBS	□	4.6	19.8	59.8	104.4	9.6	4.6	3.5	65.8	None†	132
WPG Government Securities	USG	—	6.6	28.0	—	—	8.3	19.0	2.4	89.4	None	46

Key to rating symbols: ★ = **Top 10%** ☆ = **Next 20%** ● = **Middle 40%** ○ = **Next 20%** □ = **Bottom 10%**

*Currently closed to new investors †Fund may impose back-end load or exit fee. **Figure reflects borrowing to boost investments.

Notes: To be ranked, a fund must be one year old, accept a minimum initial investment of $10,000 or less and have had assets of at least $25 million as of March 31, 1989. Gain or (loss) figures include reinvestment of dividends. The MONEY risk-adjusted rating appears for funds with at least five-year records and covers the 60-month period through May 31. The prospectuses of bond funds in the high-grade categories require them to invest primarily in issues rated BBB or better by Moody's or Standard & Poor's. Short-term taxables have average weighted maturities of up to five years. Intermediate-term tax-exempts have average weighted maturities of less than 10 years. Stock and bond fund yields are the latest 12 months' dividends divided by the most recent share prices adjusted for capital-gains distributions. **Source: Lipper Analytical Services**

Index